TOMORROW
WILL BE BETTER

Richky

TOMORROW
WILL BE BETTER

*A True Story of Love
and One Family's Triumph over
the Horrors of World War II*

ZDENA KAPRAL

HARBINGER HOUSE
Tucson • New York

HARBINGER HOUSE, INC.
Tucson, Arizona

∞ This book was printed on acid-free, archival-quality paper

Originally published in a slightly different version
as a privately printed, limited edition in 1989.

Diacritics over Czech names and words have been omitted.

Library of Congress Cataloging-in-Publication Data
Kapral, Zdena, 1913–
Tomorrow will be better : a true story of love and one family's
triumph over the horrors of World War II / Zdena Kapral.
p.   cm.
"Originally published in a slightly different version as a
privately printed, limited edition in 1989"—T.p. verso.
ISBN 0-943173-68-X (alk. paper)
1. Kapral, Zdena, 1913—Family.   2. Kapral family.   3. World War,
1939–1945—Personal narratives, Czech.   4. Czechoslovakia—
Biography.   5. Refugees—United States—Biography.   6. United
States—Biography.   I. Title.
CT948.K37A3   1990
929 ' .2 ' 0973—dc20   90-33083

And I said to the man who stood at *the gate of the year*: "Give me a light that I may tread safely into the unknown."

And he replied: "Go out *into the darkness* and put your hand into *the hand of God*. That shall be to you better than a light and safer than a known way."

So I went forth, and finding the hand of God, trod gladly into the night. And he led me *towards the hills* and *the breaking of day* in the lone East.

> M. L. Haskins, *quoted by*
> *King George VI in a radio*
> *broadcast to the Empire*
> *on December 25, 1939*

CONTENTS

Preface xi

BOOK ONE
THE GATE OF THE YEAR

1. Tranquility 3
2. Belgium 21
3. Opportunity 33
4. Richky Valley 51

BOOK TWO
INTO THE DARKNESS

5. Occupation 61
6. Wenzl Tragedy 85
7. Narrow Escape 103
8. Life Went On 117
9. Despair 131
10. Melancholy Christmas 151
11. Frau Thomas 161

BOOK THREE
THE HAND OF GOD

12. Dangerous Trip 187
13. High Court 193
14. Unexpected Development 209
15. Air Raid 231

BOOK FOUR
TOWARDS THE HILLS

16. The Russian Army 253
17. Liberation 267
18. Behind the Fireline 277
19. Doubtful Freedom 287
20. Bitter Decision 303
21. Farewell 313

BOOK FIVE
THE BREAKING OF DAY

22. West Again 325
23. On the High Sea 333
24. Lahore 347
25. India on Fire 371
26. Gandhi-Ji 385
27. Down Under 405
28. The New World 423

Epilogue 429

FOR CARRIE

CENTRAL EUROPE 1938
Scale: 242.7 miles to 1 inch

242.7 miles

404.4 kilometers

N O R W A Y

• Oslo

S W E D E N

Helsinki

Stockholm

F I N L A N D

B A L T I C   S E A

ESTONIA

LATVIA

LITHUANIA

EAST
PRUSSIA

• Minsk

U S S R

N O R T H
S E A

DENMARK

• Hamburg

• Berlin

G E R M A N Y

Warsaw

P O L A N D

E N G L A N D

• London

NETHERLANDS

• Brussels
BELGIUM

• Luxembourg

Breslau

Prague

Olomouc

• Brno

Vrbatky

Richky

CZECHOSLOVAKIA

• Kiev

• Paris

Munich •

Vienna •

Budapest

F R A N C E

Zurich
SWITZERLAND

Geneva

A U S T R I A

H U N G A R Y

R O M A N I A

• Milan

I T A L Y

A D R I A T I C   S E A

Y U G O S L A V I A

Belgrade •

Bucharest •

B L A C K   S E A

CORSICA

• Rome

Dubrovnik

• Sofia

BULGARIA

Istanbul •

SARDINIA

• Naples

ALBANIA

T U R K E Y

M E D I T E R R A N E A N   S E A

GREECE

Athens •

SICILY

PREFACE

Over the many years that have passed since the events in this book took place, I have from time to time recounted some portion or other of the story, often to hear: "You should write a book! This story should be told!"

I finally succumbed to the temptation. To my own surprise, what has emerged is a tale not only of hope and drama, danger and tragedy, but also one of happiness, one of incredible luck and fortune, and generous, unselfish help by a number of strangers—some of whom died by doing so.

I would like to thank my daughter Eve for her invaluable help in drafting the first version of the book. Further, and most sincerely, I thank my friendly literary mentor in Vermont, who in his modesty does not wish to take any credit. Yet for over a year he led me patiently and with great tact and impeccable taste through every page, always insisting that the writing, the thoughts and sentiments must be entirely my own. My unending gratitude goes to Dr. Cecil Robinson of the University of Arizona's Department of English for his warm words of encouragement. Above all I thank Alex for his unfailing support and great understanding.

BOOK ONE

THE GATE
OF THE YEAR

1

TRANQUILITY

The atmosphere on the SS *Mariposa* was friendly and festive as it sailed well past Australia, New Zealand, Fiji, and Samoa, silently and safely approaching the American soil. The flagship of the United States luxury liners of the mid-fifties carried a large group of mostly retired American medical doctors and their wives returning from a cruise around the world. Finally, after more than ten years of wandering and struggles, I was going to reach the land of my hopes.

As I looked on the crestless, innocent waves endlessly approaching our ship I saw my life in front of me with a precision of memory I had never achieved before. I witnessed again our many joys, going again with Alex through the rooms of the beautiful places we had lived, walking the streets of Paris in the days of youth, smelling the scent of pines at noon as our horses moved silently through our peaceful forests, reanimating the ecstasy in which my two daughters had been born.

Yet, more than the happiness, it was the danger that strengthened me. I experienced, once more, my personal war with the Gestapo and the battle between the Red Army and the Nazis fought in our backyard.

Times returned when despair and death had all but destroyed me. Again I sat leaning against my husband, holding our two little girls,

3

who drifted in and out of sleep while I wondered, as I had before on a different continent during a different war, if this was the end of our lives. I remembered how Alex had then hugged us to himself so that when death came it would take us together, all four of us, in one instant.

In this simple act of remembrance I found hope and comfort. By recalling the past, I made myself travel backwards out of India, across the oceans and Europe to our homeland. At first vaguely, then with great clarity, I brought to consciousness the recent history, not just of our family, but of our nation that had been betrayed by its French and English friends, plundered by the Germans, occupied by the Russians, and abandoned by the Americans.

The pain of this tragedy was not lessened by bringing it back into memory; but the act itself, the act of preserving the facts of our history if only in recollection, anchored me, fixing a point of purpose and hope for the future.

I traveled farther and farther back through my senses as a human being, as a woman, to meet myself, a pretty, blond girl singing to white clouds sailing in the powder-blue skies, and running through summer meadows toward the tall young man coming toward her.

I was fifteen years old when Alex strolled smiling into my life never to leave again. Going to some afternoon lessons, a good friend and I were running for a train, all flying scarves, flapping book satchels, and pink cheeks. Alex came walking toward us, a handsome, dark-haired, strong, and graceful young man of twenty-two years. He looked straight at me with a sophisticated, detached little smile. We ran by laughing, seeming not to notice.

And then, even more vividly, I remembered Alex as he was standing thin and deadly pale, dejected and sad in the Nazi factory of death, chained to fifteen other Czechs, all expecting to be executed by the guillotine for high treason. His sunken eyes looked at me with utter despair, the bones protruding in his ashen face, his hands handcuffed in front of him. It was a picture that haunted me for years.

In my reverie I discovered I had been given a great gift. I knew at last that evil had limits, that the hurt must end, that tomorrow will be better, and that fortitude and love can conquer many unconquerable things. I saw that the memory of all the martyrs, dear to my heart, of all the victims of this century's holocaust must be pre-served—even if in remembrance only.

———□———

The happy times of my early childhood were full of joy and laughter. My sister Liba and I used to spend our days in play, running around in the fields and meadows, lying in the tall grass, daydreaming and watching the fluffy white clouds go by. We imag-ined they were heavenly chariots of baby angels riding around the sky, one of them being our little sister Maria who died when she was just one year old.

We gathered wild poppies, cornflowers, primroses, wild irises and daisies and made flower chains to hang around our necks, or bou-quets and wreaths to place on the statue of the Virgin Mary that stood in the center of the village square symbolizing the heart of our community.

My parents and their forebears were well-to-do farmers in the black-soil province of Hana in central Moravia, a region of Czecho-slovakia. It was a rolling land, fertile and rich, with blue mountains reaching to the skies on the horizon. Our family had lived in the village of Vrbatky, the Place of the Willows, for several hundred years.

My ancestor, Pavel Sramek, had come there in 1525 from Gregov, a settlement about twenty miles away, a great distance in ancient times. He had his laborers build a large dwelling for his family. The house in which I was born had thick walls and a dark gray slate roof that protected the generations like the wings of a great mothering bird. Later, improvements were added—barns, stables, shops, and storage rooms—until the farm had become a grand square of build-ings around a cobbled courtyard.

By our time, the centuries had given the farm a quaint but palat-able aura of deep humanity. It was a kind place and much loved. Beyond the barn was the orchard and kitchen garden where my mother grew carrots, beans, peas, lettuce and tomatoes for the table as well as beautiful flowers. Dahlias and roses were her favorite. Their bright red, pink, and golden colors are among my first memo-ries. All summer long the freshly cut flowers beautifully arranged in crystal vases gave a cheerful and fragrant atmosphere to our living room.

I loved my parents, and I especially adored my mother. One of our duties was to help her in the kitchen when she cooked for the family and farm workers. I thought my mother worked so hard that I always felt I should help. I remember being about six years old, peeling one huge basket of potatoes after another, a memory that has returned to me during the darkest moments of my life.

The villages in my country had a social structure at once practical and humane. The big farms, with their massive, centuries-old homesteads, were usually grouped around the village square, with less affluent people living farther out in their cottages on small plots of land. It was remarkable how content everyone was. The province of Hana in my childhood was a prosperous land, with no hunger or poverty. Our people were united by a bond of loyalty based on mutual respect and compassion.

The larger landowners took care of their poorer neighbors who during the summer provided the manual labor that was vitally necessary in those unmechanized days. The farmers fed the workers and their families during their well-paid employment. In those days, many families were big. One woman who worked for us had ten children.

Every household "belonged" to one large farm or another, and the farmers took care of their workers' land. My father plowed his laborers' fields and harvested their crops and they came whenever he needed them. Everyone protected everyone else without fuss or sentimentality. If someone was short of money or ran into trouble, he turned to my father or to my grandfather for help without embarrassment and in full assurance of getting what he needed. It was like one large family, no less unified for its size; and the system worked.

Each season had its special delights. Fall was the time to harvest potatoes and sugar beets and to finish up the work in the fields, a time of excitement, comradeship, and mutual accomplishment.

When the barns were full, my father usually took us for a trip. Sometimes we went to Prague to see the sights, attend a play at the theater, or go to an opera. Other times we went to see a ruined castle. My father relished history, recounting tales about ancient Bohemian kings and queens in the times when our kingdom was great and powerful. The history of our land was an elemental part of my childhood, a living, breathing presence.

My father was a frustrated industrialist at heart. He was never so happy as when he was presiding at some committee or business meeting. He organized cooperatives, was the village mayor, was on the board of the local sugar mill, and was the chairman of the hydroelectric plant of which he was also the founder. Because my grandfather, although retired, oversaw the farm work, my father was able to fulfill all these functions with great success, mostly without any compensation.

Winter was the most wonderful time of the year. Everyone rested. In the evening we sat around the fire, telling stories. My grandfather on my father's side, who lived in the dower house across the square, was an especially renowned storyteller. He seemed very wise to me. Villagers sought his advice, and he never spared himself or betrayed a confidence. With his clear blue eyes and white hair, he strode about the village like a general, always smiling and chatting with people. He was most lovable to a little granddaughter.

With his large, dignified head bowed in concentration and eyes dancing with firelight, Grandfather often talked about his youth in the 1860s, when our country was involved in the Prussian wars. We shivered when he spoke about the terrors of the First World War. His youngest son was killed then, and until his dying day, Grandfather never recovered from the pain of that loss.

He told us about the many wars of earlier times, explaining that Bohemia has always been an unlucky country. Because of its position in the heart of the continent, it has been affected by nearly every European war. The Swedish and Russians fought there. Napoleon marched across Bohemia and Moravia as did the armies of the kings of Prussia. Soldiers killed men, raped women, and repeatedly plundered the country unmercifully.

Bitter experience taught the Czechs to dig tunnels under their houses. Whenever a foreign enemy threatened, the Czechs would hide underground and the marauding soldiers would find the village empty. Our house and many others in our village had mazes of subterranean tunnels dating back centuries and leading to neighboring houses and to hidden exits in the fields.

My grandfather's stories of the past misfortunes taught us to appreciate how blessed we were to be truly free, a fact that filled us with great pride. Grandfather and our teachers at school instructed us to treasure liberty, to live and work for it, so we children grew up in this patriotic atmosphere. We revered especially our President Masaryk, a wise old gentleman, for having obtained that freedom for us at the end of the First World War after three hundred years of oppression under the heel of Austro-Hungarian emperors, the Habsburgs.

All kinds of music, from folk music to modern opera, filled our lives. We lived in the Czechoslovakia that the world learned to love through the melodies of Dvorak and Smetana. My mother had a great respect for Czech opera. Her favorite was *Jenufa* by Janacek. We children loved *The Bartered Bride*. I was not quite six when I saw it for the first time.

In the parish church, which had both a choir and its own orchestra, the choirmaster was particularly fond of Mozart, Händel, and Bach. As the mass sometimes lasted two-and-a-half hours, and we had to kneel on the cold floor while the music played on and on, our love of classical music was almost destroyed. In my mind, Mozart remained for a long time associated with kneeling on those frigid, hard tiles.

Once every two years the archbishop came to the village. Special music was presented and the schoolchildren traditionally recited a poem to welcome our illustrious visitor. One year, because I was a good student who learned easily and was a pretty little girl, the pastor assigned a welcoming poem to me.

After dinner on the evening before the archbishop was due my mother said, "So, Zdena, come and recite your poem."

"I don't know it," I said. My parents exploded.

"You're supposed to recite it before the archbishop and the whole village tomorrow morning and you don't know it yet!"

Feeling I was about to dishonor the whole family, I cried and started memorizing the lines, cramming them into my head all evening, past midnight, until I could not remember another word. My parents sent me to bed, still angry with me, then woke me up at six o'clock in the morning, drumming the poem into me until it was time to go.

We arrived at the church, and although I do not know how it happened, I recited the entire poem without hesitation. To the gratification of my parents and the pastor, the archbishop declared, "This little girl was really excellent." He gave me a rosary and a beautiful holy picture.

Everyone worked hard in Vrbatky, but we never had to wait long for a holiday to break the routine, to fill life with festivity and refreshment. The most magical time for Czech children was Christmas. Our family put up a beautiful fir tree that we decorated with slim white candles, shimmering golden garlands, gingerbread hearts and gold- and silver-wrapped chocolate candies, and put our presents under it. There was carol singing and much visiting. The house was filled with the special smells of burning wax, warm fir, heated spiced wine and freshly baked cakes. The countryside was covered with sparkling snow which was crackling under our feet, and the night was full of silent angel voices in the moonlight.

Easter was the holiest time, but for my sister and me it was also made significant by the fact that each year we got new dresses. We wore them to church even if the weather was still cold and unsettled.

The most exciting holiday was May Day. Everyone from the youngest to the oldest participated in the festivities. To awaken on the first day of May in Vrbatky was to awaken to the sound of music. The village band gathered early in the morning and went from house to house playing Strauss and folk waltzes, polkas and marches, greeting May Day with the glory of trumpets and the booming of drums. The musicians played in front of each house for five or ten minutes and then the master of the house came out to give them some money. The music was heard until noon. It was altogether wonderful, a lovely beginning to the bright, warm days of high spring.

The Maypole was erected on the main village square. It had a small fir tree on top and floating down from it to the ground were ribbons of red, white, and blue, the colors of our country. The boys and girls, dressed for the occasion in gaily colored, embroidered national costumes, danced around it weaving the ribbons in and out, while the older villagers watched, remembering when they had been nimble enough for the young people's dance.

At noon the boys mounted their horses and began a traditional event, "Chasing King Barley," based on an old legend of an ancient evil king. One boy would be dressed as the king and the other boys would race after him. Sometimes they caught him, other times they did not. In the evening there was a dance in the Sokol-Hall that everybody attended and enjoyed.

Our parish church was dedicated to the Virgin Mary, and its solemnity was held on the ninth of September. Before the big day, everything throughout the village was cleaned until it shone like new. My mother had spent the previous week baking mountains of tarts, cakes, and cookies. My favorites were delicious little puffs filled with whipped cream, so light that they just melted in my mouth. Eating them was sheer delight.

Relatives came from all over, as this was truly the feast of our whole village family. My father's surviving brother, a doctor, came with his wife and two sons, Slava and Zdenek, both about my age. Then came my father's two cousins, one a surgeon in the nearby city of Olomouc and the other a professor of mathematics at Charles University in Prague. My father treated the two as though they were his brothers because their father died when they were very small and they practically grew up in my grandfather's home together with his three boys. They came with their wives and my third cousin, Vlada.

Our favorite uncle was my mother's brother, a judge in Moravska Ostrava. He never married and spoiled us as only a bachelor uncle could spoil his adoring nieces. He brought us presents, books, chocolates, games, and other good things.

My mother's mother was about the same age as my grandfather, but the effects of illness made her seem much older. She was very gentle and kind, her brown eyes always looking at us with loving tenderness. Her hair was gray and was worn combed back and tied in a chignon. A tall woman, she wore simple dark dresses with very long skirts. When we were small, she used to sit in her big, comfortable easy chair with us children sitting around her on the floor, and we all sang together the old national songs she loved so much and which we learned to love, too. With her came my mother's two sisters. The elder one was married with grown children; the younger one never married and lived with my grandmother.

This holiday marked the end of summer and thus a return to the village schoolhouse. I loved school, which for me was never a duty but fun, play, and sheer pleasure. I enjoyed learning new things;

I liked mathematics best, though my sister hated it and thought I was strange. I also loved history and languages. All schools in our country were public. The teachers, employed by the state, were well paid and greatly respected.

During the school year and also during summer vacations the children enjoyed the activities sponsored by Sokol, a gymnastics and cultural association for young people. It was founded in the nineteenth century by two Czech patriots and was popular throughout the country. A symbol of Czech patriotism, Sokol has survived as an institution in the United States.

Elementary-school years flew past without leaving me with strong memories. After grammar school, my sister and I attended high school in a nearby town. We had to take the train and were never quite on time. The train gave out a warning whistle when I was still somewhere near our barn, and I would run like mad to catch it. Even years later I dreamed that I was running to catch the train, but my legs would be rooted to the ground.

I enjoyed my high-school years and the social life they brought. We had dancing lessons with the boys from a neighboring school. The instructor was a dance teacher, a strict, elegant gentleman, who taught us how to behave correctly, how to bow to one's partner, and other points of etiquette. We did not take him quite seriously and had a lot of fun exaggerating some of his well-meant gestures, but we certainly learned how to dance well.

I was very popular and never sat out one single dance. Fully grown by that time, I weighed a slim one hundred pounds. I thought I was quite pretty with my big brown eyes, naturally blond hair and cheeks that were always pink. That was the era of Greta Garbo and Marlene Dietrich, and sometimes I wished my cheeks were not so pink and a little bit more hollow. Still, all in all I was happy as I was.

The day after my sister and I joined an amateur theater group, Alex happened to be at the rehearsal. He soon became involved in our productions. After rehearsals, we danced fox trots, tangos, waltzes, and all modern American dances to the music of a record player and occasionally we organized regular dances with live bands.

Alex was everywhere; wherever I went, there he was. As he was a good dancer, I liked dancing with him. Always sparkling with laughter, he was very amusing and fun to be with. I became fond of him. He often looked at me with a special expression in his blue eyes that was half humorous, half tender. I decided he was a very nice guy.

We both came from the same culture, the same soil. Alex's family was originally from my village. His father had been born in Vrbatky but left to become a high-school teacher elsewhere. It was the tradition for the oldest son to inherit the farm and the younger ones to be educated in some other profession, usually medicine, law, or holy orders. Alex's father, who chose education, obtained a job in another location after his graduation and did not return to our village, but three of his brothers still lived there.

Alex had just finished postgraduate work as an industrial chemist in Belgium and had taken a temporary job as an analyst in our local sugar mill. He had always wanted to be an actor. When he was fourteen years old and living in the city of Brno, his love of the dramatic urged him to go to the State Theater where he had the audacity to ask for a part in a play. The director was amused by the boy, sensed his flair for the stage, and gave him a job as an extra.

His first assignment was that of a soldier in *Aida*. Alex was ecstatic. His mother, a novelist, who loved music and theater, was pleased with his drive and encouraged her son's artistic ambitions.

His father, however, would never understand as he was conventional and wanted the boy to concentrate on his education. Alex and his mother knew that his father would never permit his son to appear on a stage if he had discovered what was going on. Fortunately, he was a member of a chess club involved in a lengthy state competition, returning home late most evenings by which time the young actor would already be safely in bed.

Alex loved playing in *Aida*. His mother came to see him perform. During one performance he became so lost in admiration for a young ballerina that he did not notice the departure of the troop of soldiers during Verdi's famous triumphal march. When trumpet blasts roused him from amorous contemplation, the tail of the procession was well across the center of the stage. Hoisting his banner, Alex galloped out after the marchers, an unexpected spectacle that brought the house down. It did not, however, endear him to the director or the rest of the cast.

The management decided to stage Wagner's *Lohengrin*, which was

Alex's downfall. Until that time, the opera star's father had remained in happy ignorance of his son's artistic career. *Lohengrin*, however, is exceptionally long and the production did not end until after midnight.

One night his father had arrived home at eleven o'clock, checked the boys' bedroom and found that someone was missing. Soon he knew the whole story. He was shocked by the impropriety and in a mounting rage paced the floor, working himself up to a fine pitch of fury with which to greet the former theater extra. Alex walked in to find his operatic career over. He never forgot the dressing down he received.

Years later, while on a skiing vacation in the mountains, Alex contracted meningitis. He was thought to be dying. His father, who loved him deeply and tenderly, was crushed with remorse that he had denied the boy his chances at acting. As Alex lay in a delirium, almost in a coma, the old man whispered to him, "If only you get better, Alex, you can do anything you like. If you want to be an actor, it will be all right." It is reported that the boy's eyelids flickered and from that moment Alex began to improve. When he recovered, he reminded his father of the promise and was told that after he obtained his technical-school diploma, he could enter the acting profession.

Surprisingly, his unquenchable curiosity and love of making things won out over art and he chose chemistry after all. His mother was astonished, his father vastly relieved. But his love of the theater and taste for the dramatic remained.

When Alex came to live in our village, he brought new plays that he directed with great success. He seemed to regard me as a child, which sometimes nettled me. When his younger brother arrived to spend his vacation I found him appealing. Zeno was about twenty, a nice-looking boy with blue eyes, easy to get to know. A gifted painter, he studied on a scholarship at the Paris Academy and later at the Brussels Academy of Art.

Alex spent the winter in my village and in March left for a job in Belgium. Before his departure he came to our house to say good-bye. I was sorry that he was going away because I liked his company and his sense of humor. Also, I found the way he always looked at me very flattering.

Schooling continued, and my interest in social life increased. Our first real ball was a rapturous experience that took place in the largest and nicest hotel in the nearby city of Olomouc. My sister Liba and I were excited about wearing our new long, beautiful dresses. Hers was a pale blue that went nicely with her lovely blue eyes, and mine was a flattering shade of lilac. Our hair was beautifully done, and each of us had a pair of long, white gloves, the height of sophistication. I thought we both looked gorgeous.

The ball was an elegant, very formal affair. Black dinner jackets, black tie, and white gloves were compulsory for men. There were two ballrooms: in the larger one the big band played fox-trots, tangos, and waltzes, and in the smaller one jazz and modern dances were on the program. I had a marvelous time, not missing a single dance. Many other parties followed, all of which I enjoyed immensely.

At that time my mother began to suffer with multiple sclerosis and could not accompany us. Being an unself-centered person, even when chronically ill, she wanted our lives to be radiant. It was as if her tortured body vicariously found a new health in our dancing and she insisted that we go to all parties. My chaperon father was most patient and never urged us to leave before the last waltz was over. He said he enjoyed the balls as much as we did, watching us. I hope he was not merely being kind.

As Mother's health deteriorated, she underwent an unsuccessful surgery. A family conference decided that I would stay home after finishing high school to take over Mother's duties of household management. I had always dreamed of going to the university to study mathematics, but I accepted the decision with as much good grace as I could. That night I cried myself to sleep.

My parents sent me to a finishing school in Olomouc, where I learned how to cook, sew, and keep house. Besides such domestic skills the students were taught languages, manners, and deportment. We often went to the opera and the theater. Parties were held at the school and occasionally we attended the social functions in the city. It was not unpleasant.

In mid-December I went home for the Christmas holidays. On the second day my father took me into his den, sat me down with a solemnity that made me fear an unknown worst, and handed me a white envelope. The postmark was from Belgium and I recognized the handwriting. My father told me to read it.

I took the letter out and was amazed to read Alex's proposal of marriage. He was asking for my hand! He wanted to marry me! I did not know what to say. All I had heard from him were a few letters and post cards. He was merely a good friend as far as I knew.

I was flattered but confused. It was nearly two years since I had last seen him. During that time I had met and gone to dances with many boys. I did not feel I knew Alex well enough to marry him and I told my father that. He agreed and told me he had already answered the letter, saying that I was still too young for marriage. Although in principle he had nothing against Alex, he thought I should wait until I was at least nineteen years old before thinking of it.

A few days after Christmas I received a charming letter from Alex, telling how fond of me he was, and he proposed marriage in a very poetic and flattering way. I replied, saying that although I liked him very much, I did not really know him well enough to marry him.

He answered by return mail that he was coming home in a few weeks. His brother Zeno, who was living with him in Brussels, was seriously ill. The doctor diagnosed the problem as pulmonary tuberculosis, at the time a grave illness. Alex was going to take his brother to a sanatorium in Switzerland and then come to see me.

I wrote him saying that Saturday afternoon was the only time we were allowed to go out on dates; the school was strict. I received a letter back saying that unfortunately he could not make it on a Saturday, but I was not to worry because he would arrange everything so we would go out on Wednesday afternoon. I was dubious. The headmistress was a formidable person.

But I did not know Alex well yet. He sent the headmistress a telegram from Brussels, asking her to allow me to go out with him on Wednesday afternoon. Suitably impressed, she called me in and informed me that I could tell him an exception would be made. I was stunned; such a thing had never happened in the history of the school, at least not to my knowledge or to that of my friends. When I told the other girls they could not believe it. They could hardly wait to see the man who could perform such a feat.

On the big day, Alex arrived at the school and was greeted by the headmistress, who served him coffee and cake. Who had heard of such a thing? When we went out I glanced up and saw heads craning out from every window of the school for a glimpse of the man of miracles.

Olomouc is a lovely city, centuries old. It has many parks with lakes covered with swans, ducks, and geese. Alex and I sat on a park bench and fed the birds while we talked about marriage.

I still felt I did not know him well enough. How could I leave my home and family and go to some foreign country with a man I hardly knew?

He was persistent, as always. He was coming back for a three-week vacation in the summer. He had everything worked out, and there was no doubt whatever that he would prevail.

He took me back to the school and came again to take me out on Thursday. The whole school was in a state of shock at this double breach of tradition. We walked and talked, and I grew more fond of Alex by the minute. He really was charming and understanding.

I did not see him again until the middle of July when he arrived to visit his uncle. We spent every moment we could together, going out for walks, to the theater, and to the cinema. Now I was in love. At the end of the month he left for Belgium. Parting was painful. We wrote to each other frequently and felt close.

The following autumn was a time of sadness for both of us. My grandmother died. The family had expected it for a long time, but still we missed her terribly.

Then I lost my beloved grandfather. One Sunday, walking to church he fainted, was carried home, and he died peacefully there of a stroke. I do not think he even knew what happened. His death was even more of a shock to us than Grandma's because he was so full of life, so active, and so much at the center of family and village life.

Alex wrote that he was returning. The doctors said there was no hope for Zeno, who was not improving and who wanted to die at home. Alex could not even begin to imagine life without his beloved brother and friend. He was very upset and deeply saddened, especially when he had to say good-bye to Zeno and go back to Brussels.

Zeno stayed with his parents. His mother took him to a health resort in the mountains near Brno, hoping for a last-minute miracle, but three months later I got a telegram from Alex saying that Zeno had died. He was twenty-two years old, a truly gifted artist who had showed great promise. Everyone who knew him grieved, mourning the untimely destruction of so much talent and creativity. His mother was inconsolable. Alex returned for the funeral, and in his sorrow he seemed to turn even more fully toward me. He wrote more and more often saying that in his loneliness he wanted to get married as soon as possible.

After the dark year of 1931, the next one turned out to be the happiest time of my life. Early in spring Alex returned from Belgium and gave me a beautiful diamond engagement ring. At that time my sister was studying at Masaryk University in Brno, the city where his parents lived. I went to stay with her in her small apartment and met his whole family. The days that followed were beautiful. I had not known how happy I could be.

Brno, the capital of Moravia, is another old city of many beautiful parks, situated in a valley with forests all around. The spring of 1932 was radiant, and Alex and I often spent whole days walking in the woods, making plans for our future. Other times we went to the park, where a band played popular music and one could buy refreshments and enjoy oneself. When it rained we went to a coffee house, or to the theater or the opera. I was deeply happy. Some days we played tennis with Ivan, Alex's surviving brother.

The days were endless, lasting forever, but time flew by and Alex was back in Belgium and I was alone. He promised to be back soon and that he would take three weeks of vacation in the summer. His father said jokingly that Alex was spending all his money on the train fare between Belgium and Czechoslovakia, a situation he hoped would be corrected soon.

I went back to Vrbatky and again took over the household. I was worried about leaving my mother, who now could not move around without help. She was aware of my hesitation and told me firmly not to think of her but only of my own life ahead of me. I should be concerned about myself, my husband, and our happiness. She reminded me that I could not stay with her forever in any event. If I was sure that I wanted to marry Alex, I should go ahead and do it right away and not wait. She liked Alex very much.

I always thought my mother was one of the most wonderful and strongest people I ever met. She accepted her terrible illness without complaint and continued with her life, giving support to her husband and unlimited love and understanding to her children. She never thought about herself, always finding pleasure in our happiness and contentment in our achievements. I loved her dearly. She understood me well and in spite of her illness always brought only pleasure and joy to my life.

In July Alex's family went to the mountains. They rented a room for me in a nearby house and asked me to come over for the three weeks that Alex was there with them so I could get to know them better and meet their relatives. Alex's and his mother's birthplace, Strmilov, was nearby. She had been born on an ancient farm, too, their house being even older than ours. I made the acquaintance of almost the whole family that summer.

We also made a trip to Lipnice, where one of Alex's aunts lived. In the town was a castle, also called Lipnice, whose ruins dominated the surrounding countryside. Author Jaroslav Hasek wrote the great Czech classic, *The Good Soldier Schweik*, in its shadow.

Alex always had a special feeling for this book because he almost had a hand in its creation. When young, he used to go to Lipnice Castle to watch Hasek write. In the ruins the author found the peace and solitude he needed, but he also drank quite a lot, and he used to send Alex to the village tavern for fresh beer.

Walking through the beautiful old forests surrounding the castle ruins, Alex told me stories of his own boyhood, using his flair for the dramatic to make them vivid for me. His father was a prisoner of war in Russia during the First World War. His mother and the children lived in a small town called Velka Bites, not far from Brno. It was a bitter time for the family, emotionally and physically. His mother had great difficulty getting even a little food from her small military pension, let alone feeding growing boys.

Her sister was a widow whose husband had been in government service. She had been able to obtain, by way of a pension, a permit to sell cigarettes and cigars. During the war this was better than having substantial amounts of money. She managed from time to time to save a few cigarettes and cigars for her sister, which made the difference between mere hunger and slow starvation. Alex's mother treasured those gifts, exchanging them for flour, sugar, and other necessities. She kept the tobacco in a special drawer in the house.

One day a circus came to town. There was no question about the boys going, as it cost money and there was none. They hung around the circus tent, enviously watching people going in, when the circus barker came out and said, "Well, maybe you have some cigarettes or something like that you could give me instead of money?"

Alex, Zeno, and Ivan ran home and raided the tobacco drawer. They said nothing to their mother. Three days later she needed the box of cigars. Alex said that it was the most rigorous beating the boys ever got. Alex's mother, for all her artistic talent and tastes, was a tough person. She had no time for what she called namby-pamby people. She believed in work, exercise, lots of walking, and washing in cold water.

Although he often used humor to cover the real suffering he had known when his father was away, Alex much preferred funny stories. Once he had to have a new pair of pants, but where was the material to be found in wartime? His mother finally came up with a solution. She had an old goat and a kid butchered, had the hides tanned, colored them with black shoe polish, and made the pants. For obvious reasons, one hide came out very soft and pliable, like chamois leather; the other was stiff and hard. When he told the story, Alex demonstrated how he was forced to hop around the town with one bendable leg and the other stiff as a board.

Alex was the family's goatherd, and part of his job was to chop silage for the goats. One day he was inattentive, and his hand slipped into the chopper, almost cutting off his right index finger. Bleeding and frightened, he ran to tell his mother. She took one look at the hand, cuffed him on the ear and said, "Now, that's for being stupid." Then she grabbed a bandage, stuck the finger on, and bandaged it tight. It grew back on, just a little crooked and with a big scar to prove the story.

Such were the tales of his childhood Alex told me during this wonderful summer. They helped me add understanding to my love. The problems, poverty, and need for self-control during the war years gave him the quality of courage and determination without in any way diminishing his natural optimism. He learned to be strong, and below his charm and light-hearted good spirits Alex developed a permanent strength of will and character that was to be severely tested in the grim years ahead.

The grand days of vacation in the mountains came to an end. Alex was off to Brussels and I to Vrbatky. Life was diminished when he was away as if everything was being seen through thin, gray smoke. I missed him and longed for November when we would be married. He would be twenty-five and I would be nineteen.

2

BELGIUM

My wedding day arrived at last.

Even years later I could not think about it without deep emotion. When I woke up it was raining—not a heavy rain but a soft, pleasant drizzle bringing me a feeling of peace and great happiness. Years before, when Alex asked for my hand, I could not imagine marrying him. This day the opposite was true. I could not imagine my life without Alex. He was everything to me; all my dreams and hopes were connected to him. And I was absolutely sure that his feelings toward me were the same.

My mother came into my bedroom with a smile, predicting that rain on a wedding day brings good luck and happiness. By the time we were ready to leave home, the only home I had known since I was born, the sun came out bringing even more gladness to this memorable day.

Our wedding was in Brno at St. Thomas, an old church full of history, situated in the center of the city. When our party arrived Alex and his family were already waiting for us. As I walked down the aisle on the arm of my father, I felt as though I was walking in heaven. I glanced at Alex. His blue eyes were looking at me with so much love and such tenderness that my heart was filled with immense joy. I smiled at him. I knew we would be very happy.

The wedding was officiated by Alex's Uncle Sylvester, and neither the solemnity of the occasion nor the mutual devotion of the priest and his nephew kept them from having an argument at the altar. Uncle Sylvester was accustomed to wedding rings being placed on the right hand, a tradition common in that part of the country. Alex took the ring from his best man, gave it to his uncle, and extended his left hand.

The priest whispered: "Alex, give me your right hand."

"No."

"Right hand."

"Why?"

"Because I said so."

"Emily Post says left."

"Emily Post I don't care about. I've been doing this since before you were thought of. Right hand."

"No."

It occurred to me I might never be married. Alex's parents began to look nervous.

There was a deafening pause, then Uncle Sylvester, glorious in gold brocade and crimson-faced, placed the ring on Alex's left hand and finally we were married. When Alex embraced me I felt such security. I knew that with him next to me I would always be safe.

After the ceremony and luncheon reception at a hotel, we all left Brno for my home in Vrbatky, where we had a sumptuous dinner. Then after many good-byes, Alex and I drove away to start our new life in a foreign land. In Prague we boarded the Orient Express, and the next day we arrived in Brussels.

Alex had already rented an apartment on the second floor of a small town house on Rue Dieudonné Lefèvre, a quiet residential street. Our landlady, Mme. Monpetit, who lived on the first floor, was a Parisian and extremely plump. As I weighed hardly a hundred pounds, she thought it her pleasant duty to fatten me up. Mme. Monpetit had rheumatism and could not walk well. Since there were no refrigerators and the marketing had to be done every day, I offered to do her shopping. Every day I stopped at her apartment to see what she needed; by ten o'clock each morning she was already drinking apéritifs. The first time I tasted one I found it so strong I could hardly swallow it.

Her cooking was extravagant. She cooked practically everything with wine, pouring it on meat, dousing the rice with wine, even adding a couple of spoonfuls into the soup. She drank two glasses of wine with her meal as well and was increasingly jolly and relaxed, dispensing valuable information which the new bride gratefully appreciated.

Even a greater help to me was Olga, advising me where to go shopping downtown, what to do and how to do it. She came from Nice on the Côte d'Azur and spoke with an accent she claimed was Marseillaise. As she talked rapidly and I saw her often, my French improved daily. We remained friends for life.

Olga was petite, slim, pretty, elegant, and marvelously witty and funny. Even when things did not go quite right, she always found something humorous to tell. Her dark hair was always beautifully coifed and her brown eyes looked at the world with unbelievable softness and friendliness. She was a great French patriot; when somebody dared to criticize her homeland, she became all excited and with an avalanche of her rapid French soon proved that France and the French were the greatest in the world.

Her husband, Paul Ondra, was a Czech, who at the age of eighteen moved to Paris to be a furrier. He was an excellent craftsman and did his own designing. When he was in his twenties he met Olga in Nice. They married, opened their own business in Paris, and stayed there for several years before moving to Brussels, where they met Alex. They were both good people, and we grew deeply attached to them.

Madeleine Collard, a charming, pretty girl, was another good friend. She had been engaged to marry Zeno and, even after his death, considered herself a member of the family. She taught herself to write and speak Czech, which was a Herculean achievement, considering how difficult the language is.

She had met Zeno in art school. When he came to the class for the first time, their professor held up his work and declared, "Here you can see how you should paint!" Madeleine never got over his death. She was a good artist herself and became a professor of art history. Throughout all the difficult years of my life we remained good friends, exchanging letters frequently.

Another member of our family was Barbie, an Irish setter. Alex had an old Ford, and once when he left the window open, he came back to find a dog sitting in the car. As no owner was found, Barbie remained with us. He was a charming, clever dog. With typical humor, Alex bought him a pipe and when we went for a walk he would put a lighted cigarette butt in it. As Barbie ran along, the cigarette started to smoke, invariably arousing a great deal of interest and smiles from passersby.

Alex and I were in love and happy together. We came to understand each other well. We went for long walks in the park, or to Laeken, where the summer royal palace was located. Sometimes we went to the cinema or to newsreels. We made excursions to Ardennes, Ostende, Antwerp, and all around Belgium.

Another one of Alex's good friends was Leopold Koutny, a chemical engineer who held a managerial position in a sugar and yeast factory in Chassart, a little town about thirty miles south of Brussels. His pretty wife was a kind, loving, and hospitable person, always in a good mood and completely absorbed in her family. They had three charming little boys who were full of mischief. We often visited the Koutnys and always enjoyed their company.

One evening in February 1933 Alex and I were listening to an opera on the radio when suddenly the program was interrupted by an announcement that the Reichstag, the German parliament building in Berlin, was on fire. It was a total loss. At first the Nazis maintained a Dutch Communist was responsible, then they accused the whole German Communist party. Some people believed the fire was set by the Nazis themselves, who wanted to get rid of the Communists.

Nobody knew what really happened, but afterward the Communist party was persecuted; many members were arrested and imprisoned. For us newlyweds, all this had no real meaning. We had no idea who those fanatic Germans with the strange-sounding names were, nor did we care. It was nothing more than an item on the front page of the newspaper that we read every morning. Little did we know what was coming.

I was becoming accustomed to my new life, and I enjoyed it. Brussels was a picturesque city, even more so in the spring when every corner was occupied by flower vendors. The roses, irises, tulips, carnations, and dahlias reminded me so much of home and my mother's colorful garden. But what I liked best in the pale sunshine of early spring was mimosa, which looked fragile, exotic, and immensely beautiful. I always bought some; it added brightness and charm to our living room. I love mimosa; it reminds me of that enjoyable and enchanting time in Brussels, the first year of my married life when I did not know anything but happiness.

I felt at home in this huge city. I enjoyed going downtown and browsing through the department stores and bookstores and dreaming about our future. Life was free of care and responsibility and filled with new impressions, new enjoyments, and new discoveries, a continuous pageant of surprises and glories.

Madeleine and I often went to one of the art galleries, where we spent hours walking through the vast halls, viewing the art, chatting about it, and observing art students as they copied the old masters. We admired Rembrandt, Van Dyck, and Frans Hals, as well as the impressionists and their successors, especially van Gogh.

In the fall before we married, Alex had started a small chemical company manufacturing dyes and preparations for the furrier trade in partnership with Olga's husband Paul. It was going quite well and he envisioned a great future. This was his first business venture but far from his last.

Toward the end of spring Olga wanted to go see her family in Nice and asked me to accompany her. I realized that if I went anywhere it should be to the old country to see my mother. Alex could not leave, so we decided that I should go alone.

I left in July, traveling with a woman secretary from the Czech embassy in Brussels, and the Germany we crossed was menacing. We saw multitudes of men wearing light brown uniforms with brown shirts, who, I was told, were Hitler's personal soldiers called Storm Troopers. More military personnel appeared in the railway stations, creating a much different atmosphere from when we crossed Germany as newlyweds.

In Cologne an elderly Jewish gentleman, sagging under a weight of years and fear, entered the compartment and sat in the corner. When the train started moving, he removed a bundle of money from his pocket, and put it in his shoes. We were wide-eyed with surprise. At Nuremberg we changed for the train to Prague, and he continued on to Vienna, and I believe, Hungary. Happy, fulfilled, and hopeful as I was at nineteen, I had no time to think about what it meant for someone to flee his country with only a bundle of reichsmarks tucked into his shoes. Only later did I realize the implications of this chance meeting for my life. I never found out if he got the money over the border, though I often thought about him and hoped he had succeeded.

It was nice to see my family again. I enjoyed the mixture of maternal solicitude and female admiration my mother showered on her well-wed daughter. Physically, she had not improved, and could not move easily, but she was no worse. Somehow the illness had been arrested, and I was happy about that. Mentally, she was as alert and aware as ever and interested in everything I told her about my life in Belgium. She made wise and useful comments in her own quiet, nonintrusive way. My father was, as usual, busy with his public life and with the affairs of his beloved farm.

I stayed two weeks, then went to visit Alex's parents in the mountains for a week. His father was worried about what was happening in Germany, as was everybody in Czechoslovakia it seemed to me. Our government had started fortifying the borders, an ominous sign.

Alex wrote nearly every day. He was lonely, and I missed him, too. I returned to my parents' home for another week before taking the train to Belgium with a mixture of relief and sadness.

Alex met me at the station with a dozen pink carnations. My heart was filled with immense joy when I saw him looking at me with the usual loving expression in his eyes. Smiling, I fell into his open arms. It was good to be back and exciting to rediscover our apartment and all the things which became dear to my heart in the silent, unassuming way they have of building themselves into one's life: the clock on the mantelpiece, my favorite arm chair, the Persian rug Alex and I bought together. Barbie, having missed his daily outings to the market, was all dog-happy to see me again. Alex and I settled down once more.

A month or two later he became worried; the depression in the United States had spread to Europe. Business was not good. The chemical company was doing moderately well, but Paul's furrier business was in trouble. Realizing that people do not buy new furs when times are bad, Paul decided to sell, take a vacation, and visit his mother in Czechoslovakia. She was getting old, and he had not seen her for several years. He also wanted to look at business opportunities there.

Olga had gone to Nice and planned to join him in Brno while Alex and I stayed on in Brussels, feeling a touch of homesickness. I tried to keep his spirits up but saw that he was becoming more worried about the effects of the economic slowdown on his prospects.

We made two new friends, Marie and Robert Uitenbrook, who lived in Waterloo where they had a perfumery. Their company manufactured essences for perfumes and bought some chemicals from Alex. We spent many happy weekends with them.

I was always sad when I passed the Waterloo Monument where Napoleon lost his battle to Wellington, thinking how terrible it must have been for him to come to such an end after so much glory.

Alex and I had a wonderful Christmas in 1933, with a warm fire in the fireplace and a big, beautifully decorated tree. I baked a lot of cookies, some tortes, special Czech Christmas cake and, what Alex liked most, lots of apple strudel, his favorite dessert. For a while we forgot our worries.

In February big newspaper headlines exploded across Brussels. Belgium's King Albert was dead. He had gone mountaineering in the Ardennes, fell from a rock and died instantly. The entire nation was crushed with sorrow. The king was no figurehead. The Belgians idealized him for his courage and patriotism during the First World War. The new royal couple was King Leopold and Queen Astrid.

Kings and queens and presidents from all over the world came to the funeral, and I made up my mind that I was going to see them. Alex, who had business appointments, thought my enthusiasm was crazy, but I was unmoved by his criticism, and set out at three in the morning. To my surprise, the streets were already full of people; I was unable to find a place at curbside with a view. I must have looked sad, for a couple, apparently husband and wife, standing on a ladder leaning against a wall invited me to join them.

Finally the funeral procession approached. First came representatives of each of the Allied armies that had fought with Belgium in the First World War, moving down the avenue with slow steps to the hollow sound of muffled drums, the sound of their boots very loud in the silence of the watching populace. Then came the coffin with the

Belgian flag draped over it. Great sadness overcame the crowd and many people started crying, realizing only then that their good and brave king was dead. It was a very touching moment.

Behind the coffin walked the new king, his ashen face set sternly; then came his brother, Prince Charles, and brother-in-law, Prince Umberto of Italy. They were followed by Ferdinand of Bulgaria, Carol of Romania, and the kings of Sweden, Norway, and Denmark. Edward, Prince of Wales, marched with them, and I, like every other woman in Europe, thought him quite handsome. We saw Monsieur Poincaré, former President of France, as well as that country's great Marshal Pétain and many others.

Though I did not realize it at that time, this funeral procession represented the closing of one act in the drama of European history. All the greats of the First World War were together for one last time. Soon they would disappear from the world stage to make room for new actors.

Life in Belgium settled down once again, but the economic depression deepened. Alex worked extremely hard; however, survival became ever more difficult. I had some money from my father, which we put, with every penny we could spare, into the business to keep it going, but we slid faster and faster.

The Uitenbrooks told us that they would buy us out, but Alex could not decide. It was a bitter choice for a young man with a good measure of pride and high expectations. The depression in Czechoslovakia was not as bad as it was in Belgium; at least there were still jobs.

The Ondras wrote to tell us that they had opened a successful salon in Brno. As I was expecting our first child, both sets of parents wanted us to return, so finally we gave in and decided to go. It was sad for me to leave the scene of so much happiness, but it was good to be going back home.

Alex and I said good-bye to everybody, from Madeleine to Barbie, and crossed Germany once more. There were many SA men, or Hitler's Brownshirt Militia, walking the streets and the railway terminals, making it obvious that Germany was rapidly changing into a military encampment. No Czech could see it without a tremor of fear. What was happening?

We arrived home and rented an apartment in Brno. Soon Alex was offered and accepted a managerial position in a small factory that manufactured chemical products for farmers and we settled again into our normal routine. I liked Brno; our life was pleasant and peaceful there. We had many friends and often saw Olga and Paul, who were doing well. We also visited my parents frequently as they were only two hours away by train.

When the owner of the company where Alex worked decided that they needed to expand, he bought an old factory building in Letovice, an hour and a half north of Brno. The manufacturing was moved there, and we had to move also. We decided that Alex would go alone, leaving my sister to stay with me and returning to Brno for weekends.

On the twenty-fourth of October my darling little Evie was born. She was adorable, the most beautiful baby I had ever seen, with her big blue eyes and blond curly hair. Everyone was excited over our daughter, a charming and happy baby, who smiled constantly. Alex's parents were especially pleased to have finally a little girl in their family.

Before Christmas we moved to Letovice, a pretty county town with an old castle dominating the landscape, where everyone knew everyone else. Soon we had many friends. The large public country club had a big swimming pool and tennis courts. Dances were held during the winter and we went to the theater often. It was a life similar to the one I had known in Vrbatky. When summer came, we played tennis nearly every morning and swam in the afternoons. I took little Evie with me. She was growing fast and was everyone's favorite.

Alex was busy with his job, which he enjoyed. As we had many house guests, I had to employ a maid, Mary, who was only seventeen years old and had a beautiful voice. When she took Evie for a walk or played with her, she either sang or talked to her continuously. Evie talked before she was one year old and started singing at the same time, surprisingly in tune for such a small baby.

She walked when she was only nine months old, but that is not entirely accurate—Evie never walked, she ran everywhere. When I saw her racing full-tilt into the dining room, I caught my breath because I was sure she would slam her head on the edge of the table, but she was so little that she would scoot right underneath.

The three of us were very content. Friends were abundant and our families came to visit us regularly. Even my handicapped mother was able to come when Alex fetched her in the car. My uncles and cousins also visited. Life was almost a continuation of my child-hood—warm, stimulating, and serene.

Though we tried to avoid thinking about it, darkness was falling over Europe. Mussolini was moving upward and made himself dicta-tor in Italy. My uncle Josef, the doctor, and my aunt vacationed in Italy with their son Vlada and returned amazed that Fascism had become so strong there. The people adored "Il Duce." Uncle said that while he was impressed by the new regime's beautiful highways, the *autostradas*, he was more powerfully struck by the way the spirit of the country had changed. He worried because of the increasing military emphasis in Italian life.

On November 18, 1935, his perceptions were proved accurate. Mussolini and his army attacked Ethiopia, then took over the capi-tal, Addis Ababa, the following May after a campaign that involved the use of airplanes and poison gas against tribesmen armed only with spears. Emperor Haile Selassie took refuge in Paris and ap-pealed passionately to the League of Nations but in vain.

As I read about all these events while sitting with Evie in the park, I wondered mildly why everybody was so excited. It was all happening so far away. *What could events in Africa mean to us in central Europe?* I did not understand what life would engrave deeply on my mind during the coming years. The world was so small that whatever happened in the farthest corner would eventually influence the lives of all peoples. Everything involved everything else.

Hitler was tightening his stranglehold on Germany. After Presi-dent Hindenburg had died in August 1934, Hitler made himself dictator, the head and chief representative of Germany. As this happened just next door, we were somewhat concerned but never really believed that the situation would get out of control or that we were in any substantial danger. Czechoslovakia had powerful allies in France, England, and Russia. We Czechs were sure, absolutely sure, they would help us if Hitler ever dared to attack.

Hitler, however, violated the Locarno Treaty in which the Ger-mans guaranteed not to militarize the Rhineland after the Allies evacuated it in 1930. On March 7, 1936, Hitler's troops went in but were prepared to withdraw if the French opposed the occupation. Though at that time the small German army was no match for the strong French armed forces, the French did nothing, and Hitler's army stayed in the Rhineland, gaining great military advantage as well as an important public relations victory.

For our country the situation was more complicated by the fact that Tomas Masaryk, our beloved president and founder of modern Czechoslovakia, retired as a result of old age. His close friend, Edvard Benes, was inaugurated. Benes had been foreign minister for many years and continued to direct foreign policy after he became president.

Alex became active in a new project that he enjoyed. As the foreign sugar market decreased drastically during the depression, the government had a surplus of sugar on hand, which it mixed with charcoal and sold to the farmers at a low price to be used as cattle feed. When people found out that it was easy to wash out the charcoal and use the sugar for themselves, sales of refined sugar fell, and illegal production of liqueurs, wines, and all kinds of bootleg liquor simply exploded.

The government announced a contest for the development of a chemical compound to be added to the sugar to make it palatable to animals but unpleasant to people. The company that produced such an additive would be allowed to establish a state-sponsored monopoly and would receive the entire government contract, promising considerable profits.

Alex took up the challenge and began concocting test batches. In his enthusiasm he even tried them out on members of the household. Once we both felt so sick afterwards that I refused to be a guinea pig any longer. Alex worked hard for more than a year and finally succeeded. His compound was accepted by the government.

The company patented the additive and put it into production. Business boomed, enhancing my husband's professional reputation considerably. As he also received royalties, our financial situation took a swift turn for the better.

We were never short of good company and plenty of laughter. Ivan and my brother Josef, accompanied by their friends, visited us often. Evie basked in our happiness. On her second Christmas, she was fourteen months old and already talking, singing, and running through the house. She was enraptured by festivities and her sparkling wonder flowed into Alex and me.

Without exaggeration, we were a supremely happy family. Alex and I understood each other well. We read each other's thoughts, and when in company, we only had to look at each other to know what the other was thinking. It seemed a miracle to me. We knew we could depend on each other in everything; we trusted each other completely and were profoundly in love. I often thought later that this complete trust was a great blessing. We were to need it in the grim years ahead.

3
OPPORTUNITY

When I first met Frantisek Wenzl, he was in his mid-forties. A man of great political power, he was a well-known personality in international agricultural circles who cut an imposing figure wherever he went. Tall, stocky, with a large head and kind eyes, he limped slightly as a result of shrapnel embedded in his leg during the First World War. He always walked with a heavy cane. Chairman Wenzl, a strong and competent corporate leader, was a professor of economics and chairman of a large association of farmers' cooperatives that owned several manufacturing companies, sold farming supplies, and bought the farmers' products. By selling to the association, the farmers received better prices and were also able to buy their supplies cheaper than on the open market. Frantisek Wenzl was also active in the Republican party, a moderately conservative democratic group interested in questions concerning Czechoslovak agriculture and its development. Alex met him through a good friend of ours, Mojmir Kolar, a lawyer, also an active Republican, at the time running for election to the Czechoslovak House of Representatives.

Chairman Wenzl had heard about the successful sugar compound. After explaining that his cooperatives were planning to start a chemical company, he offered Alex a position of chief executive officer of the new corporation and a participation in the profits. The factory was to be located in Modrice, a suburb of Brno, where cooperatives owned a large, idle sugar refinery that could be renovated for the new venture. Alex accepted the position and named the company Biochema.

We found a new and larger apartment near the center of the city in the shadows of Spielberg Castle. The castle gained notoriety during the First World War when Gavrilo Princip, who assassinated Archduke Franz Ferdinand in Sarajevo in 1914, was imprisoned there. The inside of the castle was sinister. It had extensive dungeons with dark, humid cells where in the olden times the unfortunate prisoners were shackled without food in total darkness while water dripped constantly on their heads. The place had become a museum, with a small garrison of soldiers stationed there. This grim fortress, however, had a lovely park where we spent many happy hours.

One of the pleasures of living in Brno was the State Theater. On one occasion we witnessed the world premiere of Sergei Prokofiev's ballet masterpiece, *Romeo and Juliet*. I do not know for sure why our city was chosen for this great event, but I believe it was because the main choreographer in the Brno Opera, Ivo Vana Psota, a Russian émigré, was a friend of the composer. As anyone who has heard those lovely melodies knows, the ballet is a triumph of twentieth-century music. It has remained my favorite; I have seen it many times since.

The Brno Theater and Opera was notable as the first theater in Europe to be lighted by electricity. It was installed by workers under the instructions of Thomas Alva Edison himself. It also staged the world premiere of *R.U.R.*, a play by the well-known Czech playwright Karel Capek, in which the word *robot* was first used. Few people realize that we owe this word to the Czech language and to this particular play.

Evie acquired a faithful companion when Alex's mother brought her a black-and-tan dachshund puppy called Nellie. She had long silky ears, an active pointed tail, and brown eyes that were almost human in their love and intelligence. Evie adored her; they soon became inseparable. Taking Nellie for her walks became a ritual, and Evie played with her for hours in her room.

One day Grandma, who could not resist a pet of any description, brought Evie a canary in a cage. Evie spent hours watching the bird, imitating its singing, and talking to it. One morning when she was playing with the canary, lying on the floor with Nellie beside her, she suddenly started screaming. I rushed to see what had happened.

Horror of horrors, somehow Nellie had gotten her paw inside the cage, killed the canary, then scooped him out and ate him up. Evie wept for the poor canary as if her heart would break, and the rest of us were equally divided between being furious with Nellie and afraid of what Grandma would say. Nobody had thought that Nellie could be such a cruel dog. Grandma came, and as the late canary and Nellie had both been her protégés, she understood, sympathized, and bought another canary with admonitions to watch it more carefully.

In March, Paul Ondra suddenly received an offer from some friends in London to join them in their large furrier company. Olga did not feel like leaving Brno because she had made friends there and had learned something of the language, besides being near us again. But Paul, who liked big cities, was very excited about going to London. They decided he would go first to see how he liked it, and if he found everything satisfactory, Olga would follow.

Alex was quite busy with his new company. He was elated that he was able to design the factory in every detail the way he thought it should be done. He started the Biochema plant in an already existing set of buildings in Modrice, enjoying immensely the challenge and the prestige of being, at the age of twenty-nine, a chief executive officer of a large, expanding company.

Behind the new factory, bordering the office block, was a huge, well-kept garden, complete with gardeners, a vegetable section, swimming pool, and tennis courts. There was a handsome and spacious apartment on the second floor over the offices for the president. We moved in.

After the move, the third in three years, I thought I had earned a real vacation, and as Olga was moving to London, I decided to accompany her to Paris. I took Evie and Mary to my mother's, and Alex took us to the railway station.

On the German border our passports were checked with even greater suspicion than when we passed through three years before. A uniformed guard, grim-faced and condescending, went along the train corridor arrogantly demanding that everyone give up foreign newspapers. Olga got herself into trouble because she would not give up her French magazine.

"No," she said, "we'll be crossing Germany for twelve hours, and I need something to read."

The guard was not impressed by her argument. "Buy something German!" he snapped.

She answered with a flash of Gallic temper, "I don't read German and I do not like it!"

When she continued arguing with him in her excitable French way, he started shouting back at her. I was afraid he would arrest her, but he finally fell silent and beat a grudging retreat.

This renewed contact with Nazism made us afraid. Fascism had spread beyond the German borders by this time, and some of our friends were worried that Hitler would invade Austria, but I did not think he would dare. His military occupation of the Rhineland in 1936, in plain contravention of the Locarno Treaty, was successful, but maybe, I thought to myself as we crossed the nightmare of Germany in darkness, that was because the French had just let it go.

I often wondered what would have happened if at that point the French had defended the Rhineland against German military occupation. Quite possibly the Second World War might have been averted and things would have turned out very different. In the morning we awoke in France and arrived soon after in Paris, the City of Light.

Beautiful Paris will always be for me the most beloved of cities. Olga had lived there for more than ten years and knew everything there was to be known about it. I saw Paris for the first time through her devoted French eyes, and I relished every moment we spent there together. It has been precious to me ever since.

We established a daily routine. After a continental breakfast of excellent croissants with butter from Normandy and café au lait we went sightseeing to Les Invalides, Montmartre, Sacre Coeur, Notre Dame and other attractions of which Paris has so many. Around noon we went to an excellent restaurant on the second floor of a building on the Boulevard des Italiennes that served meals of gourmet quality with five to seven courses. Following the tradition of the French, who ate their main meal at noon, we dined in great style enjoying not only the food but also the excitement of being in a fine restaurant among sophisticated clientele.

After dinner we usually went to the Exposition, located under the Eiffel Tower and well laid out. Every represented nation had its own pavilion to demonstrate its products and accomplishments.

Several ethnic restaurants were at the Exposition, some of them simple, some more sumptuous. In the evening we usually stopped in one and bought ourselves a snack. After those gourmet lunches we were not hungry for a large supper.

Late one evening, coming home from the Comédie Française, we passed a cinema showing a film we had wanted to see for a long time. We went in and eventually returned to our hotel about three o'clock in the morning to find a message for me that Alex had called. He would call again at seven in the morning. I was so worried I did not sleep the rest of the night, which admittedly was not long. "Maybe Evie is sick," I thought, "or something else awful has happened."

Alex called at seven o'clock sharp and immediately announced he was going to join us in Paris. I found out later that he had given a dinner party for a few of his friends, one of whom jokingly remarked, "Oh, I wonder what Zdena is doing in Paris right now?"

Without hesitation my husband replied, "What should she be doing? She's asleep."

A bet followed and Alex called me at two in the morning. When there was no answer, he was upset and decided to come to Paris as soon as possible. He asked us to come to the city's main airfield to meet him. Olga was not excited. She was enjoying herself, and although she liked Alex, she was afraid his presence would limit our freedom and spoil our stay.

The next day we got up early for a long trip by bus to Le Bourget. The plane was due at eleven; we were there at ten. Eleven o'clock came, but no plane appeared. Noon crept in, but still there was no sign of Alex's flight.

In the late 1930s airports were boring places as there were few people around. Aircraft landed at the rate of about one an hour. Olga and I sat and fidgeted, then finally went to the office to find out what happened. They could not tell us anything. After waiting until three o'clock with increasing nervousness, we went again to inquire. An official informed us then that the plane had crashed in Switzerland.

My world fell apart. Olga and I were frantic. I thought I would go insane with fear that Alex was dead. When we eventually returned to the hotel, dizzy with worry, there was a telegram at the desk. Alex was coming the day after next because he had to attend to some business in Amsterdam on the way. Olga and I were both ecstatic with relief.

The next day was spent in sightseeing, and on the following morning we set out again for Le Bourget. Alex arrived safely. It was marvelous to see him. Bubbling with enthusiasm, we eagerly described to him the excursions and outings we had planned for the three of us, but he demurred. He did not like walking any more. Olga and I walked everywhere and were now saddled with a third member of the party whose main desire was to sit down or, at most, take a cab. Olga became irritated with him.

One of our most memorable excursions was to the Palace of Versailles on July 14, the anniversary of the fall of the Bastille and the beginning of the French Revolution. I never again saw Versailles as radiant as it was that day. There was music playing, the fountains were spouting dazzling jets of water high up into the air above the golden statues, and the formal gardens were a carpet of colorful flowers. The palace must have looked as it did when the French kings lived there.

In the evening, after returning from the world of the Ancient Regime and the Sun King, we went to the Exposition again to hear the president of the republic give a speech from the top of the Eiffel Tower. At the conclusion of the ceremonies, there was not a cab to be had for love or money. Alex was upset. We could not squeeze into the subway either, so we were forced to walk all the way to the hotel to the women's silent delight, though it was not Alex's idea of fun.

We were rewarded for our efforts since our way home was through one continuous sea of good feelings. All Paris was celebrating that night. There was dancing in the streets, and people greeted us spontaneously. Everything was festive and gay, and the city itself was laughing. As we approached the hotel, we saw the young and handsome Maurice Chevalier dancing in the street with Mistinguette, who was the great love of his life. It was quite a thrill to see them. Has life ever again been quite as bright as it was in Europe before the war? It was excellent to be young, with other young people, and alive in Paris that night.

Our three weeks came to an end, and Olga had to leave to join Paul. As it turned out, Alex had some more business to attend to in England, so we went to London with her.

Alex decided we would fly. This seemed to be tempting fate, but he was not impressed with my objections and went to buy the plane tickets. As this was my first flight I did not know what to expect. Alex told me I would probably be airsick and that it would be advisable not to eat anything before the trip. For breakfast I had only coffee and one pitifully lonely croissant. Olga did not listen to Alex's advice, but I did not want to be airsick and boarded the plane hungry.

It was a big aircraft for those days, though small by modern standards. If I remember correctly, it was a Fokker biplane. Inside were tables with chairs on either side of a center aisle, much as they used to be arranged in the train dining cars. No food or refreshments were served.

The other passengers, a British party returning from the Paris Exposition, brought a picnic basket with them and set an ample table with chicken, salads, and wine. I could not help staring at them. I was so hungry and quite cross with Alex, who smiled knowingly and counseled patience.

Over the English Channel the plane was thrown about like a toy. I did not feel well. The turbulence became severe. We zoomed up, then suddenly dropped toward the waves. The British were all sick; the excellent food they had consumed went straight into bags thoughtfully provided by the airlines. Alex was proud of his foresight. He was right to have me fast, but I arrived in London with a thumping headache after three hours in the air. Paul Ondra was waiting for us. We had a great reunion, took a bus to Victoria Station, and continued by cab to the hotel.

I liked London. The weather was fine, each day better than the last, the air soft and warm under the blue sky. The four of us had a wonderful time doing nothing but talking. Alex and I went sightseeing and spent hours with Paul and Olga, who were enthusiastic about their future life in London. It was Olga's first time in England, but she immediately fell in love with the city, as I did.

One afternoon Alex and I were strolling down Oxford Street when we saw a crowd of people in front of a store window. We stopped to see what they were looking at. There was a small black box with pictures on it, something like a movie, only it was tiny. We asked the man next to us what it was and he said, "Oh, they call it television."

The pictures on the strange little box were minuscule, crisscrossed with lines and of miserable quality. Alex said with disgust, "I think it will be a flop." Decades later, as I watched television programs transmitted across the world via satellites, I occasionally remembered my husband's prediction and smiled.

The five days in London passed like a dream, and suddenly it was time to return to Paris and head home. This time we decided to go by train and boat. The train was luxurious and the channel crossing pleasant. We spent two days in Calais, lazing on the beach relaxing and enjoying ourselves. When we finally took the train to Paris, I felt as if I were returning home. The city had become a familiar territory.

With a substantial number of francs left, we stayed at the George V Hôtel, one of the best in Paris, situated on the Avenue George V, not far from the Louvre. We had a great time that week in Paris. It was like having a second honeymoon. Alex rediscovered the joy of walking as we went window-shopping, bought gifts, visited the Louvre, and did whatever our fancy dictated. I loved traveling with Alex because he was always full of high spirits, able to forget his worries and live for the moment.

Alex had told me that on his trip to join Olga and me he traveled from Brno to Prague in a small, open-cockpit aircraft that flew low enough for him to see people walking about in the towns. The flight was windy and there were only four passengers. Hearing him I realized that I had no desire to fly, so we left Paris for Prague by train. On the German border foreign magazines were again confiscated.

We arrived home, and when Evie saw me she flew into my arms. No matter how stimulating our adventures had been, in my heart I had missed her every moment. She had grown while I was gone, and although she adored my mother, she had missed me deeply. Our little family restored, the three of us returned to Modrice where I turned to the task of finishing up our new apartment.

Alex and I became more and more worried about Hitler, who made upsetting speeches declaring that Germany and Austria were one nation and that Austria belonged to Germany. A strong Nazi movement mushroomed in Austria, a threatening situation to the Czechs. If Hitler occupied that country, Czechoslovakia would be almost encompassed by Germany. Our southern border was unfortified. The scent of danger poisoned our air.

Nazism was sending up shoots in Czechoslovakia as well. We had about two and a half million German-speaking people in our country, some of them Jews, a significant number of whom considered themselves to be Czech. All German-speaking citizens were treated well in Czechoslovakia. There was neither prejudice nor persecution, though living in a heavily industrialized area, they suffered more than most from the depression owing to the diminished export of cut glass, textiles, and costume jewelry.

Our national aim was to develop a country similar to Switzerland, where all citizens had equal rights and equal respect. The German-speaking citizens of Czechoslovakia had their own German schools including two German universities, one in Prague, the other in Brno. As they were also represented in the Czech parliament, they were content with the arrangements.

However, the Czech citizens of German origin, especially those living close to the Bavarian and Saxon borders in the western part of Bohemia, were soon prodded from Berlin to start their own Nazi party. Their leader was an unknown German schoolteacher named Konrad Henlein. By 1937 it had become a frighteningly big movement.

Not all German-speaking Czechs were behind Henlein by any means. More than half of them were against him, at least at first. These wanted to stay in the Czechoslovak Republic and have nothing to do with Hitler.

In the spring of 1938 the impossible happened. Hitler's troops marched into Austria. It was an awesome shock to us. Czechoslovakia became almost completely encircled by Germany. Still, upset as we were, the general sense was one of embattled safety. We had an excellent modern army and air force. Our border with Germany was well defended, with fortresses similar to the Maginot Line. Remembering our mutual-aid treaties with France, England, and the Soviet Union we could not believe that Hitler would dare attack us. Nor did we think that the German army was as strong as it turned out to be.

When President Hindenburg died in 1934, it was well known that Germany had hardly any army at all because of severe restrictions placed on the size of its armaments by the Versailles Treaty. We had heard rumors that Hitler had been struggling to build up Germany's military strength ever since he had seized control of the country, but we did not believe that he could have succeeded to any significant degree. Perhaps we just did not want to believe it.

Jews began fleeing from Germany and Austria, with multitudes of them settling in Prague and Brno. They were quietly but warmly welcomed. We met many of them and heard their stories of brutal treatment by the Nazis, stories that wrung our hearts with sympathy. They felt safe in our country.

Alex continued to build up Biochema, which grew fast. By then it not only processed farmers' products, such as barley and all kinds of fruits, but had expanded into a number of different fields not directly related to agriculture. There was a soap factory, a factory manufacturing essences, a plant making malt extract, and yet another that dehydrated vegetables by freezing.

Biochema had two more branches, one in southern Moravia and the other in Bohemia near Prague. The former manufactured liqueurs as well as canned fruit, jams, and marmalades; the latter was a large chocolate and candy factory. Alex often brought samples home. Evie and I enjoyed our association with this particular department.

On top of all that, Alex built a new plant that manufactured glue and gelatin. The production of glue had been previously controlled by a tight cartel that realized high profits, but Alex broke the power of that coalition by obtaining the backing of the butchers' cooperatives, who agreed to supply all bones, hooves, and horns to Biochema. Biochema was then accepted into the cartel, a truly great achievement of which Alex was extremely proud.

At that time, Chairman Wenzl thought that the company was

growing far too fast, that a merger with some larger chemical concern would give Biochema the stability it needed to consolidate its meteoric rise. He and Alex were debating the issue when Alex, while in Prague, met Dr. Antonin Srba, the president of Aussiger Chemical and Metallurgical Corporation, one of the largest chemical combines in Europe and also a prominent member of the glue cartel. Dr. Srba became interested in Biochema, and a merger followed in due course. Thereafter the Farmers' Cooperative owned fifty percent and Aussiger Corporation had the other fifty percent. Biochema was at last an important company in central Europe, well on the way to becoming a giant in the chemical industry. Alex began planning branches in Romania, Yugoslavia, and Bulgaria.

Hitler's hate-filled attacks on Czechoslovakia became more frequent and wounding. Something unpleasant was in the air, but the consensus was that it would never become a true danger. It was hard for peaceful, moderate people to grasp the concrete implications of the thoughts and words of a man like Hitler, whose whole outlook was so different from their own.

As Nazism in Czechoslovakia reached epidemic proportions, Henlein's party became publicly abusive. They held a convention and agitated openly against the Czechoslovak government. Young Germans overtly attacked Czechs.

Once when Alex and I were driving through the suburbs of Modrice, a group of young German hoodlums about fifteen years old threw stones at us. Our car windows were open, but fortunately we were able to duck. A policeman was on the corner and Alex stopped the car immediately to ask him to arrest the boys.

The officer explained that it was impossible because Czech police were not permitted to arrest German-speaking citizens. That was disturbing. We were in our own country, and yet a minority siding with our professed enemy seemed to be gaining the upper hand. The incident upset us profoundly.

Throughout the first half of 1938, Henlein, instigated by Hitler, demanded with growing ferocity some concessions from the government in Prague. He wanted special privileges for German Czechs, delineation of special German areas carved out of Czechoslovakia, and much more.

When the summer of 1938 arrived Alex and I decided to take a vacation, and we wondered if it might not be our last one for a while. Remembering how we had enjoyed the beach at Calais, we chose a popular seaside resort in Yugoslavia so that we might spend the time on the beach, swimming in the Adriatic and relaxing. Evie came with us. We did not know it then, but that vacation would indeed be our last taste of real freedom for many years to come.

The three of us took the train south through Hungary and Yugoslavia to Trieste, where we boarded a ferry and steamed down the coast to a small seaside town called Baska. It was a friendly, clean little place nestled between the sea and the mountains along a wide strip of shining sand. Except for several small hotels, the town was a picturesque collection of quaint cottages with pretty little gardens filled with an abundance of red, yellow, and pink flowers. Most of the inhabitants were fishermen. Soon we made friends with several Czech families vacationing there, and because some had small children, Evie enjoyed a number of playmates.

The sea was azure blue, clear and warm. The weather was ideal, with blue skies from horizon to horizon every day. The sun, bright and hot, tanned the three of us quickly. Life was so cheerful that we soon forgot our worries about Hitler and the Henlein party while we enjoyed lazy hours lying on the sand or swimming in the crystal water.

Alex and I did much reading and caught up on some current novels. I remember a new book just published in Prague called *Gone with the Wind*. We were totally enthralled with it, could not close it, and actually fought over who would have it to read.

We took a side trip to Dubrovnik, a charming ancient city, built in the seventh century, with a famous cathedral, many quaint medieval houses, parks, and beaches. We also spent a couple of days in Fiume, an enchanting Italian resort on the Adriatic Sea. Our vacation ended too quickly.

It was a sad homecoming. The country was near panic. The crisis was deepening, and even France and England realized that the events in Czechoslovakia were tending toward war.

The British government sent an envoy, Lord Runciman, to Prague to open negotiations between the Henlein party and the government. He arrived in August. When the Czech government rightly rejected Henlein's demands, the interference of the British made it seem that the Czech government was responsible for the failure of the negotiations.

Hitler was hysterically violent. His speeches, reported in the newspapers, sounded as though he was trying to scare Czechoslovakia and its allies into passivity. His tactic worked all too well. Many of our close friends from Belgium rushed to visit us. Madeleine and the Koutnys came to say good-bye, believing our country would be attacked any day. Who knew if we would survive the war? An atmosphere of doom pervaded the whole country.

Hitler did not look funny to us anymore. What before had been a clownish figure with a silly little mustache and the lank hair that looked like a bad hairpiece slipping on his forehead was suddenly something thoroughly sinister. The third-rate actor had become a monster capable of destroying our happiness and prosperity.

While Madeleine was still with us, Hitler made another belligerent speech on September 12 from Nuremberg, demanding that the part of Czechoslovakia he called Sudetenland should be ceded to the German Reich. He ranted abusively about our president, calling him "Herr Benes" with such utter disdain and filling the word "Czechoslovakia" with such ugly hatred that every Czech was stung into speechlessness.

We were unable to grasp what was happening to us. We hardly understood what Hitler wanted. Czechoslovakia was one country with the same borders. Some German people lived in the border regions, but the land they inhabited had always been part of Czechoslovakia. There was no such place as "Sudetenland." The Sudeten Mountains are in the north of Bohemia, on the German frontier, true enough, but they were only a minor part of what the evil man called Sudetenland.

For him the Sudetenland was any and every piece of Czechoslovakia on which a single German lived, even though Czechs also lived there. And he wanted, indeed he demanded with insane egotism, that all that land be taken and swallowed up by Germany. Our government, of course, categorically refused to surrender Czech territory.

During the third week of September 1938 the British prime minister, Neville Chamberlain, went for the first time to negotiate with Hitler at the dictator's home in Berchtesgaden in the Bavarian Alps.

Chamberlain was a weak, ineffectual man, driven by his fear of war to make needless concessions, not on behalf of his own country, but on behalf of another country of which he was in no way the legal representative.

This sad, vague man was entranced by Adolf Hitler and hypnotized by his bluster. Trying to avoid violence, he created the conditions for an eruption of even greater violence. Hitler played on his weaknesses masterfully and compelled him to offer up Czechoslovakia to avoid war, though, of course, the German leader did not have the least intention of restraining his armies or abiding by his agreements.

Nevertheless, the British Parliament passed a cowardly decree stating that Czechoslovakia must cede that part of the country Hitler called Sudetenland to Germany in exchange for a worthless promise of peace in central Europe. The French delegation led by Prime Minister Daladier went to England for discussions and decided to support the British position.

France and England had joined the Nazis. It was a tragedy of the first magnitude. We had been betrayed by our allies. We were alone. Our entire nation, men and women alike, vowed as one person that no part of Czechoslovakia would be surrendered to Hitler. Walking through the streets one could feel the tangible force of the nation's determination. War seemed inevitable.

On September 22, Chamberlain flew to Germany again, this time to confer with Hitler at Bad Godesberg. To his great surprise the Führer demanded even more concessions than he had asked for at their first meeting. He also refused to give any guarantees whatsoever that, if given what he wanted, he would not attack the rest of Czechoslovakia. In the face of this wicked behavior, France reversed her position and reaffirmed her support for Czechoslovakia.

Our country prepared for war. The nation was ready to fight to the last man. In the evening of September 23 there was a general mobilization. Men left their homes, their parents, wives, and children and reported to their regiments.

Army divisions were quickly moving toward the German borders. Everything was done in the dark since the electricity was turned off. Trucks and tanks rumbled through the streets of Brno with great efficiency. Enormous strength was felt coming from those masses of soldicrs. One could feel that each of them realized that these were not just military exercises, this was for real. These soldiers were ready. They wanted to fight and were willing to sacrifice their lives for their republic. Railway stations were dark. Trains without lights wcre moving the army toward the border. Through the blackened night we could hear the noise of the engines and the rumbling of wheels. The country was ready to defend itself against the evil power of Nazism.

There was a general sigh of relief; people were glad that at last something definite was taking place. We had been living under an evil spell ever since the takeover of Austria, with nothing but uncertainty and suppositions, with threats of doom hanging over our heads and hatred toward us pouring out of Germany. Better to fight than to live in such ambiguity. We were proud and ready.

Everybody was prepared for a gas war. Masks had been bought some time before. I had taught Evie to wear one. I told her that it was like wearing a mouse mask; I was a big mouse and she was my little mouse. We expected bombers at the first moment of hostilities. We sat in complete darkness, waiting tensely for an air attack to start, as Brno was only about fifteen minutes by plane from the nearest Austrian airfield. All across the darkened city, familics, tense with fear, listened for the vibrations of distant propellers. It was a long and terrifying night. The time passed slowly. The stillness in the air was nerve-racking, but nothing happened.

The next morning our soldiers were on the borders and people were moving out of the frontier towns. Everyone with a car was leaving Brno. Alex, however, could not leave as it was his duty to remain with Biochema. He sent Evie and me to Velka Bites, a little town forty miles north of Brno where Alex lived as a boy and where we had some friends. I did not want to leave him but he thought it would be too dangerous for Evie and me to stay as he was afraid that fighting would start in Modrice if Germany attacked Czechoslovakia. The tension in the country was a concrete, living presence. No one knew what was going to happen.

Chamberlain appealed to Mussolini, and Il Duce suggested that they all meet in Munich, together with French Prime Minister Daladier, and talk out the situation in Czechoslovakia in order to prevent another world war. No representative of the sovereign nation of Czechoslovakia was present at the Munich conference called to decide its fate.

What happened there is the saddest of stories. Those frightened, weak men in Munich gave their consent to Hitler's demand that Czechoslovakia had to surrender to Germany, by October 10, all the fortified border territories of Bohemia and Moravia that had some German population, even though large numbers of Czechs were living there, too. The allies of the Czech nation simply sacrificed it in what they took to be their own interests.

The Czechs were allowed to move to other parts of Czechoslovakia if they wished, but had to leave their property and possessions behind. Our government saw that we had been abandoned; no one wanted to help us. We were completely alone. We were small; Germany was big. The situation was hopeless. The Prague government capitulated and agreed to the cession.

Some of our soldiers had begun fighting and some of them died. They did not want to put down their guns. They wanted desperately to defend their country, but they were ordered by the general staff to leave the border fortifications and retreat inland.

It was simply terrible for us all. Everyone was furious and frustrated. Everyone hated the Nazis so much that we wanted to fight even if we all died. We did not want to give up any part of our country to Germans. We had had only twenty short years of glorious freedom and independence after three hundred years of Austro-Hungarian oppression. Having been abandoned by England and France, we all felt totally desolate, heartbroken, and miserable. Our nation had been insulted and fatally wounded.

A commission was to demarcate the exact boundaries of the areas that would be ceded to Germany. It was an impossible situation to accept, but we had to. Evie and I returned to Modrice, and we all waited to see what would happen to us.

The division of the country was accomplished in three stages. I remember Alex and me sitting by the radio, listening to the names of the ceded towns and villages read off in the flat, dead voice of the announcer; every one was a wound cutting deeper and deeper into the country. Each name meant many tragedies. Behind each name of a village there were Czechs losing their property, their livelihood and their heritage. What would happen to us?

The first division was announced, and Modrice was not mentioned. Alex and I breathed a small sigh of temporary relief. On the following night (they always made the announcements in the evening), there was no mention of Modrice. On the third night, again Modrice was not mentioned. We were, after all, remaining a part of Czechoslovakia. We were relieved but at the same time extremely ill at ease. Modrice was a mixed community. To our great surprise Hitler ordered Germans living in Brno and Prague and other towns in Czechoslovakia to stay and not to move into the newly ceded areas, though most Czechs from the annexed territories moved to areas that they believed would be independent of Germans.

There were many Germans living in Modrice and most of them worshipped Hitler—and hated us. This was not the end of the matter. Something even worse was around the corner and coming fast. Behind our anger lurked the fear that we had not heard the last of Hitler.

After the loss of the so-called Sudetenland, Hungary sent an ultimatum, demanding annexation of southern Slovakia because a few Hungarians lived there. Then came our own Slav brothers, the Poles, with their ultimatum and they took Tesin, part of Silesia. The effect of this dismembering of the country was staggering. In two short months Czechoslovakia lost more than one fourth of its population including about 1,200,000 Czechs and Slovaks, sucked up by these devouring neighbors who had no rightful claims at all.

It was a nightmare. We regretted not having put up a fight to begin with, although, to be sure, Czechoslovakia would have been destroyed. It is such a long and narrow country that Hitler could have devastated it from the air in one day. Yet people said it would have been better that way.

Hitler's attacks on Czechoslovakia continued. Our president, Edvard Benes, resigned and, with his cabinet, left for London. We had a new president, Emil Hacha, a former chairman of the Supreme Court, an old, kindly gentleman who had a serious heart condition, hardly an inspiring leader for such an emergency situation.

Life continued with a superficial appearance of normality. Alex was busy at Biochema, but we both felt most uneasy in Modrice where the German youths were still throwing rocks at Czechs. It was a common occurrence for the Czech children to be attacked and beaten on the way to school. German boys in Brno were paid ten crowns each by the Nazi party to provoke the police, while foreign newspapers claimed the Czech police attacked the Germans, though the truth was the reverse.

Taking all these things into account and considering our family's need for some sort of security, Alex and I made up our minds to buy property in a village populated entirely by Czechs, where we would not be endangered by everyday contact with Nazis or their sympathizers.

4
RICHKY VALLEY

In the midst of so much agonizing ugliness, one of the most beautiful things of our lives happened. We found a little paradise. Hidden in a valley amid the fresh, green coniferous forests about six miles from Brno, we discovered an old flour mill with a big wooden wheel run by a rushing mountain stream.

I will never forget the moment I saw Richky for the first time. Alex and I were driving down the hill on a winding country road in the middle of a deep forest, when suddenly there was an opening. Alex stopped and we left the car to look down on the panorama in front of us. It was a picture of sheer pastoral beauty. The valley was not large and was bordered all around by a tall green forest. We could see a small rivulet coming from the east, dividing into two streams. The larger one was supplying water for a quaint, old flour mill, reminiscent of the times when life was full of poesy and charm. The other stream arched around the property, both branches joining into one brook at the beginning of a large, vividly green meadow. The stream was adorned by many tall birches. The air was filled with the delightful scent of pine trees. Everything was fresh and infinitely peaceful.

Looking at the beauty in front of us made us relax, forget all our worries, forget that there was Hitler getting ready to swallow us. We got back in the car and drove down into the valley. The mill was quite ancient with thick stone walls and a centuries-old slate roof. The inside looked even older, the thick oak beams and massive stairs leading to the next floor proving the good quality and charm of the building. I liked best the enormous wooden wheel, eternally turning around, run by a never-ending stream of crystal-clear water, which, as we found out later, never froze because a powerful underground spring kept it comparatively warm even in the coldest winter. We fell in love with the property and bought it immediately.

Next to the mill was a house and a small farm of about 150 acres of fields, meadows, and pastures. A huge chestnut tree, standing at the front door as a good guardian and protector, was at least a hundred years old. The house itself was in need of massive repairs, so we decided to rebuild it altogether.

The twin stream that fed the creaking mill wheel was full of fish, mainly trout, a great advantage during the meager war years. The place was called Richky, which means "Little Rivers." Located in a completely Czech area, the property was only a twenty-five minute walk to the nearest village. Our neighbors were welcoming and warm. Alex continued working at Biochema and we went on living in Modrice. The old mill with its need for rebuilding was not intended as a full-time home, but as a haven if something unpredictable happened.

The situation throughout the country, or rather what was left of it, was getting more tense with everyone becoming increasingly nervous. As an escape from the gnawing, debilitating stress, Alex and I decided to start horseback riding at the Sokol Riding Club. A frequent ride was a great relaxation, providing a few moments of sanity in an insane world. We planned eventually to have horses at Richky.

In Modrice the local members of the Nazi party became ever more provocative until the situation was almost unbearable. March 12 was a German holiday, called the Day of Heroes, and the Germans in Czechoslovakia decided they would celebrate it in 1939 as if they belonged to the Reich. In the town all the buildings belonging to the Nazis were covered with those hateful red flags with the black Hakenkreuz, the swastika with the arms turning clockwise that we had learned to detest. The Germans were going about smiling smugly. We sensed that something had been planned, something that would insult and further injure us.

On March 10, the Nazi party organized a march from across the border, now only about two and a half to three miles from our home in Modrice. As those fanatic people marched around the streets with torches in their hands, singing bellicose German songs, we knew something was afoot. Rumors spread that German tanks had been seen in the frontier Czech city of Moravska Ostrava, but nobody believed them. We hoped it was just alarmist gossip; nevertheless, it was unsettling.

On March 14, President Hacha and Foreign Minister Frantisek Chvalkovsky were summoned by Hitler to Berlin.

That night we went to bed worried beyond reason, not knowing what to expect. The next morning we woke up early and turned on the radio. The news we heard surpassed our worst fears. It was announced that at six o'clock the German army had entered the Czech territory and all Czech military units were ordered not to resist. If fighting broke out the Germans threatened to attack Czechoslovakia brutally by air with all their might and devastate the country completely.

There was total confusion. No one knew what to do. No one doubted that the Nazis would carry out their threat. Some soldiers did fight, and some were killed. An order was issued grounding all aircraft, but almost the entire Czech Air Force left, flying away into France and later to England where they fought with distinction in the Battle of Britain.

The announcements were repeated on the radio endlessly every five minutes as the German army was pouring into Czechoslovakia from all sides, crossing the borders in great hordes. Our tortured country was being strangled. To avoid the local Nazi fanatics in Modrice, we drove to my husband's parents in Brno.

Then Alex returned to Biochema to watch over the factory, as no one knew what was going to happen from one moment to the next. I became worried about my brother Josef, stationed with his military unit in the city. To find out if he was safe, I had to walk because there was no public or private transportation in operation.

Regiment after regiment of German troops were marching through the streets of Brno. They looked so strong and so well organized that it took my breath away. It was heartbreaking to see them goose-stepping through my city, through the streets of the town

Alex and I loved so much. There were many tanks and armored cars, an endless flood of helmets, uniforms, and bayonets. No words can express how I felt, what it meant to see those hateful uniforms, to hear the never-ending clamor of German boots marching the pavement of our streets. The sound was piercing my heart. My nation was betrayed, humiliated, crushed.

At the army barracks I learned that there had been no fighting. I returned to my in-laws' apartment, and Alex arrived soon after to report that Modrice and Biochema were full of German soldiers, but everything was quiet and calm.

We got in our car and drove home in silence, terribly sad. We could not imagine life under the occupation. To our generation all this was something totally repulsive, completely foreign and unacceptable. Our Czechoslovakia had always been independent. All our memories were of a life that was tranquil, dignified, happy and, above all, free. Now that was gone, and thousands of whey-faced German soldiers swarmed everywhere.

Later we learned that when our president arrived in Berlin, Hitler presented him with an already prepared capitulation document. He was ordered to sign or else face the obliteration of our country by the Luftwaffe's Junker and Stuka bombers. The president refused to do it; he actually fainted because of his heart condition. Hitler did not want him to die in Berlin and summoned doctors who gave him some injections to keep him going. After a long delay he was finally driven to sign early in the morning of March 15. By then German troops had already entered Czechoslovak territory.

Hitler's army had been carefully organized and rehearsed for the invasion. Every detail had been planned with typical German thoroughness. After they crossed the borders a printed directive was immediately issued ordering all automobiles to drive on the right side of the road. Customarily, Czechs drove on the left side in the manner of the British.

The Nazi soldiers brought with them signs bearing the names of the villages and towns written in German, and these were put up immediately. They also had street signs for every single thoroughfare in Brno as well as all other cities throughout the country. Names of many streets had been changed. Liberty Place, the main town square of Brno, bore a sign announcing that it had become Adolf Hitler

Place. The basic geography of our daily landscape was thus transformed suddenly and completely during that one tragic day by people who had no right to do it or even to be in our country.

The next day, March 16, Hitler himself appeared in Prague. He went straight to Hradcany Castle, the seat of our ancient Bohemian kings and an important symbol of Czech statehood. The newspapers printed photographs of him looking out of the window of the castle, gazing at Prague. The juxtaposition of that barbarian and a view of the beautiful, cultured city of Prague was grotesque. Hitler announced that the Czechoslovak Republic would be permanently partitioned. Slovakia would become a separate state, while Bohemia and Moravia were proclaimed a German Protectorate.

On March 17, Hitler arrived in Brno. We all stayed inside behind closed doors and windows. Not one Czech went out into the street, and the Führer was beside himself when only the German population turned out and congregated in front of the Town Hall, where he addressed them with one of his usual sardonic, rambling, rabble-rousing speeches.

An order was issued that all arms must be delivered to the authorities immediately. From then on, anybody found in possession of a gun would be arrested. Alex had a Belgian Browning and maintained that it was his own gun and no one could make him surrender it.

A few days later, friends came to visit. I was sitting with them, having afternoon tea, when Mary came in white-faced and looking scared and said, "Madam, there are some people here and they would like to talk to you."

There were seven German soldiers in the hall. I froze inside but tried to appear calm. They were tall, strong, and in their polished boots and helmets, with rifles hanging over their shoulders, they looked threatening. The hall was full of them. The officer in charge told me in a cold, arrogant voice that they were searching for weapons.

I remembered the gun Alex had hidden somewhere. I did not know where it was because he had refused to tell me. My heart started beating wildly as I tried desperately to compose myself and not show any sign of my anguish. I was terribly frightened.

The thirty minutes that followed were filled with suspense of a magnitude I never would have believed I could survive. My guests pretended nothing was happening and tried to keep up the conversation as one of the soldiers had been left with us, watching. The others searched one room after another. I heard them leaving the library, then I heard the closing of the bedroom door. How I wished Alex had told me where the gun was. Did they pass the danger point? Were they getting closer to it or farther away? The next instant could bring doom. I was frantic.

The intruders spent half an hour looking through the apartment. To me it seemed an eternity. Finally they searched the living room where we were sitting. They looked in all the drawers, in all the cabinets. I could not stand it; I thought I would go crazy.

They did not find the gun, and finally, after one last look around the room, they left. Afterwards Alex told me the gun was hidden in the library among some books. In the middle of the night he took it to the river and threw it in. The fact that we were betrayed, conquered people, without rights or hope was born in on us.

Soon after the incident with the gun I went to a textile store and was greatly surprised to see how many soldiers were jammed into the shop. The salesman who usually served me said the Germans were buying up everything and warned me to get anything I might need right away or it would be gone. He offered me cloth for men's and ladies' suits as well as some dress material, explaining, "Soon there won't be anything left to buy at all because they're snatching it all and sending it to Germany."

Wherever I went in what once had been my city I saw crowds of military men buying food and other goods to send back home. The new rate of exchange had been established by the conquerors at the ridiculous rate of one German mark to ten Czech crowns. The result was a sort of universal theft. The occupation forces found everything enormously cheap.

When Alex and I drove out of the city we frequently saw great convoys of fully loaded trucks carrying merchandise out of our country. The Germans were systematically plundering our homeland. Food, goods, raw materials, anything and everything was going to Germany as if being pulled into a gigantic vacuum. No one could stop them; nothing satisfied their ravenous greed. The restaurants and coffee houses were stuffed with boisterous German soldiers gobbling mountains of Czech cakes topped with quarts of whipped cream. Before the German occupation Czechoslovakia was the eleventh richest nation in the world, but the Nazis reduced it to pauperism almost overnight.

In the streets appeared a new kind of uniform, black with a silver skull-and-crossbones insignia. The SS and the feared secret police, the Gestapo, had come to Czechoslovakia. Large groups of people were suddenly arrested and imprisoned, and violence appeared and spread everywhere. The dungeons of Spielberg Castle, which had been for us only a curious reminder of an age of inhumanity long passed, were reopened. Before the Nazi invasion the castle had been a museum where families went on Sunday afternoons to be reminded of the cruelty of the olden times, but with the Gestapo it started to function as a prison again with new and refined tortures. The olden times had returned to our country, marching down from Germany.

Biochema was still growing rapidly, but now there were constant inspections and bureaucratic restrictions that made normal business far more complicated than before. One morning two German officers came to look over the factory. After their tour of the plant, they wanted to see the offices and then our apartment.

Barely containing his anger, Alex brought them upstairs. They asked for something to drink with a nonchalance I found maddening. We had no choice. After a few moments they began talking expansively and dangerously. Both were Austrians from Vienna and they bemoaned the fact that Austria and Czechoslovakia had not merged into one country before Hitler had attacked. If Hungary had joined this union, a strong state would have been created that Hitler would not have been able to swallow up.

Alex and I did not know what to say. Why were they chattering on like this? They concluded, after seven drinks, that Hitler was an idiot. I could see in Alex's eyes the same fear that was knotting my insides. Neither of us knew what to do. Perhaps they were honestly expressing their genuine opinions, but they could also have been agents provocateurs, of whom there were plenty and who were usually undercover Gestapo men. When their audience agreed with their traitorous statements, they were arrested and often never heard from again.

After the two supposedly Austrian officers left, we mulled over the situation. To denounce them, if they were sincere and they were on our side, would be cruel and stupid. On the other hand, if they were agents provocateurs and we did not report them, we would certainly be arrested by the Gestapo that very afternoon. Alex and I sat in our living room, completely confused. Finally we decided they were sincere and hated Hitler as much as we did; we gambled on silence and we were right. Nothing happened. We had staked our lives on those men. We had won this time.

BOOK TWO

INTO THE DARKNESS

5

OCCUPATION

A new man, Baron Konstantin von Neurath, a prominent Nazi, arrived in Prague on April 5, 1939, and took up residency in Hradcany Castle as the Protector of our country, now transformed by Hitler's decrees into a protectorate of the German Reich. At the same time, a new position was established in every Czech company and at every Czech factory: the *Treuhänder*, a German trustee appointed to a company by the Nazi government to make sure that the company was working for the good of the Reich. In this way Germany rapidly gained complete control of the economic structure of our country. Not all *Treuhänders* were capable. The one at Biochema, a former bank teller, had little knowledge of business and much less about chemistry.

Our armed forces were now formally dissolved, and the men were sent home. It was a grim return. Many did not stay long, preferring to cross the border into Poland, going from there to France and later to England in order to join the Allied forces.

Germany swallowed us completely without the smallest visible guilt or hesitation. Their army took our army's equipment, ammunition, tanks, motorized vehicles, guns, and the few planes left behind, then moved into the barracks and army buildings. The Czechs were desolate, their life rapidly plunging into despair. Our only remaining hope was that world war would come. And we believed it would because Hitler had started to move against Poland. That proved he was following his plan for world domination as stated in his book, *Mein Kampf.*

England and France, having learned from the betrayal of Czechoslovakia, announced loudly that they would come to Poland's aid if she were attacked, but Czechs were dubious. We asked ourselves why they would do it for Poland if they had not done it for us. We did not trust England any longer, though deep inside we hoped that eventually the major powers would wake up and stand together against Hitler.

Alex and I continued rebuilding Richky, our refuge in the country. In the summer of 1939 we stayed there for three weeks in just two rooms while the rest of the house was being reconstructed. It was quiet and soul nourishing.

A big surprise came on August 20 when Stalin made a pact with Hitler, which was astonishing because *Mein Kampf* indicated that the Führer planned to attack Russia. The alliance of two such violent enemies seemed unthinkable, and in spite of the agreement we believed that war between them was inevitable. Everything pointed to it. The Germans were feverishly fixing roads and railroad systems, readying themselves for a major movement. What could it be but a wider war?

Few of us were shocked on September 1 when Germany attacked Poland without any declaration of war. Alex and I were curious to see if England and France would honor their treaties this time. As Hitler's panzers smashed into the Poles, the Red Army attacked from the east, requiring the Polish army to fight on two fronts at once. Torn apart from both sides, the poor Polish people had no chance. The fighting was fierce and bloody. It was said that the river Vistula was full of bodies. England and France declared war on Germany and mobilized their armies, but surprisingly they did not attack the enemy and stayed behind the Maginot Line, which did not help Poland at all.

The beginning of hostilities presented the Nazis with a pretext to attack the Czech people as well. On October 9, a secret conference was held in the office of the German Protector of our country, Konstantin von Neurath. Of course neither Alex nor I nor any of our friends knew that this meeting had occurred at all until many years later. We did not know about it as a historical fact, but we all knew it intimately with our hearts. At this meeting a German policy decision was made that would destroy what was left of the Czech nation, and worse, that the Czech people were to be annihilated once and for all.

The German plan was to empty the land of all its rightful owners and then move in their own people to repopulate the vacant towns and cities, to restaff the deserted offices, and to man the idle industrial machinery. Hitler issued orders that the leadership class of the Czech people was to be arrested as quickly as possible and executed. The nation was to be stripped of its journalists, newspaper editors, prominent intellectuals, artists and industrial leaders. When that was accomplished, the remaining Czechs were to be exported to Germany proper to become industrial slaves in German factories. The Nazis planned to steal all we had, and then steal us ourselves. We were not going to be allowed to exist.

The Nazis were passing beyond the ideas of conquest and occupation to that of the greatest human horror, genocide. That October morning, as Alex worked at Biochema and Evie and I did the joyous little domestic things that mothers and daughters do together around the home, the German bureaucrats in Prague were deciding when and how to exterminate us like so much unwanted vermin.

Suddenly, without any knowledge at all, the meaning of our lives had completely changed. We were no longer fighting for freedom, for political self-determination, but for existence itself. To live was to triumph. From that time on, any act by any Czech, no matter how small and unimportant, any thought passing through a Czech brain, any tear rolling down a Czech cheek, any helpless little body conceived and borne by Czech parents was a victory, a great victory, for each of them in their own way extended the life of the people and the nation for one instant longer.

Alex and I were still going to our riding club. Those brief hours spent on horseback were the only bright moments in an existence lived under unrelenting, unrelieved stress. Not only did we find relaxation in riding in the country, but at the club we also could speak freely, knowing we were among friends. When war started, we all expected that the club would be soon dissolved and the horses confiscated by the Gestapo. We were upset as we did not want to give the Nazis anything at all.

We firmly believed that as the war had finally begun and the major powers had united against Hitler, it would not last long, two years at the most. Then it would be all over and we could start anew. Alex and I and our friends were convinced that Hitler would lose and that we would regain our freedom. If we had doubted, nothing of us would have been left.

The riding-club membership decided we should resist the Nazis if only in a small, hidden way. The plan was developed to save the horses. Whoever could afford to shelter some of them for the duration of the war would take them away before the Nazis arrived to steal them. After the war they would be returned. A few of the horses had to remain at the stables, otherwise the Gestapo would be suspicious. Of the club's fifty horses fifteen would stay.

Alex and I accepted three to keep at Richky. The transfer went smoothly. When the club was finally and officially closed and the Gestapo came to plunder the stables, they did not find as many horses as they expected, but we had carefully burned the documents thereby making it impossible for them to determine the truth. We got away with it and no one was arrested.

Consequently we had four horses on our farm, one heavy Kladrubian and three thoroughbreds. The house was nearly finished though only partly furnished. More and more frequently we were drawn to the peaceful green valley and soon the family was there most weekends. It was good to get away from Modrice where hatred between the Germans and the Czechs was growing more strained by the day. Richky restored us and gave us back our lives.

I discovered at the time that I was pregnant with my second child. The baby was expected in the spring and I was extremely happy about it. It was the one radiant goodness in the middle of an endless bleakness, a promise of life in the midst of death.

At the end of October the students at the universities rebelled. In Prague they organized a demonstration against Germany, an act of great heroism. The Gestapo arrived on the scene and arrested many students. Nine were shot.

Other acts of protest were more subtle if no less dangerous. A concert was announced in Brno to be conducted by Rafael Kubelik. I had bought two tickets but as Alex had to go to Prague, I asked Ivan to come with me. The program had been designed to make a moving statement about our present difficulties and the flame of freedom burning in us. The orchestra played compositions by our national composers, Smetana and Dvorak, a moving series of tone pictures that invoked the spirit of our landscape and history.

I was deeply moved thinking about the enchanting country we called our homeland, about my happy childhood, about the freedom and liberty we had just lost, hoping that my baby to be born in a few months would experience the happiness and peace I had enjoyed when I was growing up. The bewitching sounds of the Smetana symphonic poem brought tears to my eyes and a dreamlike yearning for the paradise we had lost, for the carefree times which would never return.

The magic of Smetana's music continued to fill the hall and the souls of the spellbound audience. Toward the end people were so stirred that a spontaneous demonstration for freedom, for our republic and against Germany broke out. It was started by students from Masaryk University in Brno. Soon many small Czechoslovak flags appeared. A deep emotion took hold of the audience and people started chanting patriotic slogans. It was very exciting and inspiring; we all felt we were one people sharing the same destiny.

Tumult and confusion in the hall were growing. The Gestapo arrived and started making massive, indiscriminate arrests. Fortunately, someone opened the side doors of the hall so that people could get away. Ivan and I were sitting close to the exit and slipped out into a side lane where no Gestapo men were posted.

The next day more students were arrested and the universities in Prague and Brno were closed, not to be reopened until after the war. The Law School building of Masaryk University in Brno was confiscated by the Gestapo and made into their headquarters, while Kounicovy and Susilovy Koleje, the dormitories of the university, were converted into a prison.

The court of the dormitories, where happy young people had played ball and studied in the sun, was transformed into an execution yard, in which multitudes of Czechs were shot or hanged. It was the saddest and most tragic place in the city, the site of so much suffering. The center of our culture had become a slaughterhouse.

The war in Poland ended quickly. By September 20, everything was over. Though the British and French armies were mobilized, they did not attack Germany at this time but stayed behind the underground fortifications of the Maginot Line. After its defeat, Poland was divided; the western half went to Germany, the eastern half went to the Soviet Union. As a result, Russia and Germany were face to face.

Hitler did not initiate hostilities on the western front either. The long gray days remained oddly calm, a stalemate before action. It was an uneasy winter in Europe, quiet with the stillness of a funeral parlor before the mourners arrive. Life went on, though everything was completely different.

I was elated at the approach of the addition to our family. Evie was growing up and I was looking forward to having a small baby in my arms again. Maybe, I thought, it would put our troubles back in perspective. I started preparing a layette and went shopping. The man who usually waited on me at the cloth shop apologetically informed me that the authorities required a letter from my obstetrician confirming that I was expecting before they would issue a necessary shopping permit. Only then could he sell me what I needed.

I got my document and returned to the store and my helpful salesman, who sold me not only what I needed for the baby but something for each of us. Yardage for a suit for Alex and a dress for me would be useful; also, Evie needed a new coat for the winter and a few dresses as well.

The clerk told me that the Germans continued to buy anything that they could find. He was genuinely pleased to be able to sell me whatever I needed before the store went out of business. I could see the shelves were almost empty, and I made a large purchase.

As he cut, folded, and wrapped the goods, I asked what had happened to the friendly Jewish family who had owned the store for many years. Pain stole over his face when he proceeded to tell me the story.

The family of four emigrated to England, but after they arrived, the daughter realized that she had left behind a valuable fur coat. She came back to pick it up, arriving in Czechoslovakia on March 14, the day before German troops occupied the country. She found herself trapped and was forced to remain in Brno. The rest was inevitable. She was arrested and later I heard that the poor girl died in a concentration camp, one of the many victims of Nazism.

Everything edible was becoming scarce. There was no butter, sugar was rationed, and milk was reserved only for children. Meat was unobtainable except on ration cards that were issued to the populace. One could not buy much even with these. A month's meat ration for a person was one and a half pounds and that included preserved meats such as sausages, ham, and bacon, as well as beef and pork. Even in restaurants one had to produce ration cards to order even the smallest portion of meat. Without them we could get only potatoes and spinach in summer or potatoes and sauerkraut in winter.

As Alex traveled to Prague every second week, he needed quite a few coupons every month and we had a problem getting by on the cards we were allotted. Menus had to be planned carefully. In summer it was not too bad because we had vegetables and fruits in the garden. We could create tasty meals making all possible variations of vegetable casseroles, potatoes cooked in twenty different ways, and meat served mostly as a tempting stew, naturally containing more vegetables or potatoes than meat. We also had strawberries and raspberries in summer and apples in winter, so we were able to make all kinds of crepes, cakes, puddings, and dumplings, which together with ersatz coffee or herb tea was for us a delicious meal. We learned to make hamburgers with vegetables instead of meat; in short, we became quite inventive. Very rarely did I buy meat on the black market.

After we acquired Richky and had our small farm established, we managed to have a chicken once in a while, which was a great help, especially when we had guests for dinner. Once a year we were allowed to kill a pig, but, of course, then for seven months we did not get any meat rations at all, except for Alex, who always needed them. But we got by. The food was not so important as staying alive and not getting arrested. We quickly learned our priorities.

Only potatoes and ersatz coffee were plentiful in the grocery stores. Potatoes were sold without coupons; ersatz coffee was on ration cards, but the rations were so enormous that no one used all the coupons. Ersatz coffee, a coffee substitute, was a horrible invention of the Third Reich. Made from roasted wheat and chicory, it was black and bitter tasting. Somehow we got used to not having real coffee as there was nothing else to drink except herb tea, which was not much better. Black-marketing was punishable by death or imprisonment in a concentration camp. Many items completely disappeared from stores. Things like coffee, chocolate, rice, and tea were fond memories. Fortunate were the people who had saved a stock for emergency purposes.

Alex and I decided to take the family to Richky for the Christmas of 1939. The holidays were going to be more peaceful and in keeping with the spirit of Christmas if we celebrated the birth of Christ in our snow-filled valley. Alex's parents and his brother were joining us. Ivan had grown accustomed to spending his vacations and all his free time with us. He had been studying law, but after the universities were closed, Alex offered him a job at Biochema for the duration of the war.

Mary had left us to get married. Our new girl, Lois, was an excellent cook and a great help to me. Life in the country during the holidays was not only pleasant but also more abundant. As we had two cows at Richky, we had milk, and our chickens provided eggs. We butchered one of the three pigs we raised and had a large quantity of roasts, chops, sausages, smoked hams, and bacon to keep our family through the winter.

As we had our own source of meat, according to German decrees we were supposed to turn in our meat ration cards. Because of Alex's biweekly business trips, we took a chance and kept ours.

In the middle of January 1940 we returned to Modrice with the meat and sausages from our hog and stored everything in the cold pantry. Now at least we had something substantial to eat and offer to our frequent guests without the frustrations and worries of juggling ration cards.

At the beginning of February Evie came down with a fever and a sore throat. Our pediatrician was out of town, so I called a doctor from Modrice, who spoke both languages fluently. During the republic no one knew, or cared for that matter, whether he was Czech or German, but with the arrival of Hitler, he was instantly transformed into a fervent Nazi and often sported a brown SA uniform. He came, looked Evie over carefully, and diagnosed a bad cold and sore throat.

As he was leaving, Evie brightened up and said with strong emphasis, "Doctor, I'll tell you a secret. You know, we have *so* much meat, you never *saw* so much meat in your life. We have a small piece like this, and a bigger piece like this," and she was showing him with her little hands, "and another piece like this. We have *such* a lot of it!" I was taken by surprise. Killing a pig and not turning in meat ration cards was a serious crime punishable by imprisonment or even by execution.

The doctor pretended not to hear. I said, "Evie, don't talk such nonsense and be quiet, please!" But Evie would not leave it alone.

She said accusingly, "You don't believe me, do you? Come on and I'll show you. I'll show you how much meat we have. It's ever so much!"

The doctor finally saw he had to acknowledge that he knew about the meat, so he said, "Yes, Evie, I believe you, but listen, sweetie, that's a secret and you shouldn't tell secrets to anybody. You should learn how to keep secrets. You know me, of course. I'm a doctor and a doctor is just like a priest or a lawyer. He always listens to people but he never tells what he heard, so you can be quite sure that I won't tell anybody your secret, but please don't tell this secret to anybody else!"

I knew that while seemingly talking to Evie, he was actually speaking to me. Soon afterwards he said good-bye, smiled at me, and left.

When Alex came home, I told him what happened, and again we waited, worrying. Whenever a car stopped in front of the house, whenever someone rang the doorbell, my heart would leap into my throat as I half expected it to be the Gestapo. This fear lasted for about two weeks, then I calmed down because I was sure that the doctor really meant what he said and that under that brown shirt of the SA beat a good heart after all.

I learned a stern lesson from this incident. We adults had to be cautious in front of Evie, careful about what she heard and saw. Poor child, she could not differentiate between people; she could not know who was friend and who was enemy. After that incident we never listened to Free Radio London in her presence. We knew that in many unfortunate cases Gestapo men would chat with little children with the result that whole families were shot, including the innocent child.

Alex and I listened to London avidly on the short-wave radio. It was our sole direct link with the free world and our only means of obtaining true and unbiased news reports on the international situation. The German newscasts, with their bombastic introduction "From the Führer's Main Headquarters," were collections of propagandistic lies. The British Broadcasting Corporation, whose programs began with the victory theme from Beethoven's Fifth Symphony, brought us news, hope and, most important of all, truth.

It also carried speeches by the members of our government in exile. Most popular was Jan Masaryk, the son of the late president, who was now our foreign minister in the exile government and who knew how to talk to suffering, oppressed Czech people to give them new strength, courage, and hope. It seemed to us that he understood us best. Sometimes President Edvard Benes talked to the nation, but I always thought his speeches were more formal. Jan Masaryk talked to our hearts and souls.

The Germans soon found out, no doubt through their network of spies, how widespread the BBC's audience was and immediately ordered the short-wave frequencies removed from all radio sets. However, an ingenious Czech invented a gadget that earned him undying gratitude of a nation starved for facts. It was known as a *churchillka*, a small attachment that could be snapped into any radio, giving it a short-wave capability.

When the Gestapo came for a house search and found one on a radio, the householders were immediately arrested and sometimes shot. Alex and I had to hide ours in the back of one of Alex's heavy chemical books where the Gestapo could not find it. It was very hard to conceal anything since the Gestapo looked everywhere.

We had some books by Karel Capek, Thomas Mann, Franz Kafka, and others, all of which were prohibited. To make them inconspicuous I covered them with dust jackets of perfectly innocent novels. The Gestapo never inspected inside of the books, at least in our house. They just looked at the titles on the covers, then tried the space behind the books which we always kept clear. Otherwise I tried not to have any illegal items in the house, especially after the incident with Evie and the doctor. The material I bought was folded between the blankets or between my blouses if it was a lightweight fabric.

The worst part was the food. At the beginning of the war I managed to buy a few pounds of coffee, some chocolate, and a few pounds of rice, which I considered treasures to be used only for medical emergencies. I stored them among the groceries we bought regularly, such as barley, flour, beans, and ersatz coffee. As the war progressed, all these luxuries slowly disappeared.

After the opening days of 1940, when I was in my seventh month of pregnancy, I started feeling dizzy and sick and even fainted a few times. My doctor said that I was not to worry; it was the result of the stress we were undergoing. It was not easy being pregnant in an occupied country during a war when there was not enough good nourishment available.

The next time I went for a checkup I did an errand on the way back, deciding to walk to a shop that was not far from the office of my obstetrician, when suddenly I felt faint. The idea that I might fall and hurt the baby filled me with panic. A kindly looking old lady came toward me, so I frantically rushed to her and fainted into her arms. The two of us were in front of the store where I was going. The shopkeepers saw what happened, carried me inside, and revived me with some water and ersatz coffee. I rested a while, then went to find my car.

Germany was already short of gasoline for its tanks and military vehicles. No one was allowed to use a car for private business of any kind. The question in this case, as in many others, was how to evade the Nazis.

Whenever I needed to go for a checkup, Alex's chauffeur Frank, from Biochema, would load a couple of crates of soap in the company van for the two of us to deliver in Brno. He would pull up in one of the quieter side streets near my doctor's office. I would slip out and walk the rest of the way. Afterward I would return to the lane, glance around for suspicious observers, slide into the seat next to him, and we would drive back home. Frank and I had been doing it this way for some time, until the day I fainted in the street. After that incident Alex always came along.

The arrival of my new baby was getting near. I wanted someone to stay with Evie while I was in the hospital, so my mother-in-law suggested her niece, Bolca, who arrived in March. During the first part of the month I had been feeling weak and ill. On March 14, I felt a little better and went for a walk around the garden with Evie and Bolca. People told me how depressing Modrice looked. The next day was the first anniversary of Hitler's occupation of our country, and to commemorate the event Modrice was smothered with the loathed red flags with the swastika, hanging from lamp posts and windows. While the Nazis were enthusiastically preparing to celebrate, the Czechs braced themselves to withstand the German scorn and their own bitterness.

Common opinion had held that in two years our republic would be free again. One full year had passed already and no light glowed on the horizon. The war had not even actually begun, and Hitler and Germany looked stronger than ever. How our lives had been transformed since the clamor of German boots had first been heard in our streets! How different were our hopes and how uncertain our future! A year before we had been a free people in a free country, and now we were threatened on every side, barely surviving, victims of constant brutalizing fear. Our night was long.

March 15, 1940, was the first anniversary of the beginning of our misery and the day my daughter Jana Marie was born. I started having labor pains early in the morning; Alex took me to the hospital, and my darling Janie arrived on the stroke of noon. She was a beautiful baby with black curly hair (which later turned blond) and big blue eyes. She was totally superb and I rejoiced that she was finally here. This grim anniversary was one of the finest, light-filled days of my life.

Alex came in the afternoon with a beautiful arrangement of delicate, aromatic violets. We sat quietly together in the knowledge that events would turn out for the best after all, for us and for the nation, and that life would triumph. The dear little child in my arms told us that tomorrow would be better.

Later in the afternoon an unexpected, heavy gale rose. The wind raced and roared through the streets, a grand cleansing act that tore red banners off the poles and deposed them, ripped and stained, in the gutter. Czechs found that to be symbolic and were pleased that God could not bear the sight of those flags either. The weather stayed so bad that it was nearly impossible for people to leave their houses, and most of the celebrations had to be canceled.

I felt physically well for a few days. Then one morning I woke up to find that my left leg was swollen and blue with thrombosis. Then a blood clot appeared in the other leg, and soon the swelling was up to my waist. My movements were restricted and I had to lie on my back with my legs elevated. The pain was continuous and grinding. Before long I had a high fever that made me delirious for long periods of time.

One morning, when the nurse rolled me onto my side to wash my back, a sharp, deep pain pierced my chest. Unable to draw my breath, I fell back onto the pillows and screamed. The nurse ran for the doctor, who found an embolism in my lung as well. He was angry with the nurse for changing my position and after that I was not allowed to move at all, not even a fraction of an inch for fear that another clot would tear loose.

I could not seem to get enough air into my lungs. Breathing was painful; it felt like having an ice pick plunged into my chest again and again. The doctors concluded I was fortunate to be alive at all because the blood clot apparently had passed through my heart on its way to the lungs. With all my suffering, I did not realize how lucky I had been.

The crisis worsened and I did not care. The pain was agonizing, as though many saws were constantly cutting my legs and my feet. The worst were the endless nights. I was always semiconscious, never fully asleep. The pain did not let me. Even during the day I was awake most of the time but pretended to be asleep because I did not want to talk to anyone.

Once when two nurses looked at my chart and were going out, I heard one of them say, "Poor lady, I don't think she'll live."

I was not even upset. I drifted in flames of pain; hope had died. All my desires had vanished except one: I wanted to see Evie. I missed her so much that I could not tolerate the separation any longer. Janie was with me continually, but she was a little baby. She was beautiful, growing fast, and I loved her dearly, but I was overcome by the desire to see Evie *one more time*. That was not possible since children under fourteen were not allowed into the hospital.

Alex came every day. On those mornings when he had to go to Prague on business, he would send me a telegram. He was sweet, supportive and loving, but, still, all I wanted was to see Evie.

The doctor urged courage. "You have to fight. You have to try to get better. You must make an effort."

All I could mumble from my heart of agony was, "How can I fight? What can I do? I just want to see my other baby, my other child."

As my condition deteriorated and death drew near, the situation became so serious that the doctor finally broke the rules and told Alex he had better bring Evie. She came the next day.

Sunshine burst into the room as if a shade had snapped up. I had not known she was coming and was completely surprised to see her run into the room all smiles, eyes sparkling, and talking like a mountain brook in springtime. She was all business. She had brought a little squeaky toy chicken for Janie, which she stuffed into the baby's little hand. Janie, of course, dropped it and Evie shook her head with frustration, exclaiming, "Look! She doesn't love me! I love her so much already and she doesn't love me at all!"

Weak as I was, I laughed, forcing words out of aching lungs, "But Evie, she's so tiny, so small. She'll love you very much when she's older."

The child's effect on me was a miracle. Strength and grace poured into me along with the determination to live. To my astonishment I discovered I did not wish to die. I wanted to resist being conquered by misery, cowardice, and death. I had to live for life's sake, for Evie.

When my left leg developed ugly bed sores that exuded plasma and broke open, causing new and agonizing worries, my doctor called a professor from the University Hospital who was an expert on skin disease. He examined the sores closely and said, "You'll have to put hot compresses on them, or she'll get gangrene."

"We can't," my doctor answered. "The treatment for thrombosis is ice packs!" This was the cure known at that time.

But the skin specialist insisted with authority, "I don't care about that. If you don't put on hot compresses, and fast, she'll get gangrene in that leg and you know what that could mean."

At that time there was no medication to dissolve blood clots. The only drug used was aspirin, which did not relieve the pain at all, and the application of cold compresses as opposed to the warm dry pads used twenty years later.

That afternoon my nurse brought a hot plate into my room and set a big pot with boiling water on it. She plunged a bed sheet into . . . it, and using a pair of tongs she wrung out some of the water and then threw the sheet on me. I did not feel a thing, not even the slightest sensation of warmth. This ritual was repeated for a number of days until finally the sores began to close up and heal. To everyone's surprise the swelling decreased and the leg looked much better. My doctor immediately ordered the nurse also to put hot compresses on the other leg in the morning and afternoon.

I will never forget the poor woman. The treatment was hard on her hands as she tried to apply the sheet as hot as possible. I still felt nothing, absolutely nothing. As she worked, she sometimes murmured in her discomfort, "I am looking forward to the day when you start yelling, 'It's too hot.'"

Evie came to see me every other day and I waited in vivid suspense for each visit. She arrived with a radiant smile and stayed for a full hour, singing and dancing for me and telling me her funny little stories. I lived on those minutes for the next forty-eight hours the way healthy people live on food. They nourished me; they nourished my spirit.

Alex came every day, and his mother and father came to see me often. I began to feel a miraculous, deeper health pushing out the sickness. I still had a fever, but my general strength increased and I became more aware of events around me as if I was slowly awakening. Though my legs were very swollen I could see for myself that my condition was improving daily while my heart was becoming lighter and brighter.

I had been in the hospital for two months, and Janie was growing fast. From the beginning she was everyone's pet. Alex brought a pram to the hospital and every day one of the aides took her for an outing. They all fussed for the privilege of taking her. Eventually she became the darling of the entire hospital because she was the oldest baby there.

By the end of May, I was able to take a renewed interest in the progress of the war. Hitler had invaded Norway and Denmark on April 9, 1940. On May 10, German troops entered Holland,

Luxembourg, and Belgium without warning. Because small countries were unprepared and defenseless, they were especially vulnerable to German attack.

A change occurred in the hospital as well. Its staff had been completely Czech, but suddenly a German doctor was appointed by the office of the Nazi Protector as a director, mainly to establish German dominance even in this Czech oasis of compassion. He was a military physician completely incompetent for his new position in a maternity hospital. Even simple surgery or a Caesarean section was beyond him. Young assistants, unable to tolerate his ineptitude, would often push him away from the operating table and finish the surgery themselves.

The nurses thought it was irresponsible to place the lives of women and babies in such feeble hands. No one could speak out frankly because this medical fraud was German. Resistance had to take a more subtle form, and the Czech staff did the next best thing. The doctors and nurses quietly warned the Czech women not to consult him, but to choose a Czech physician instead. The German-speaking patients, proud to have a German doctor in the hospital, gave him preference, in many cases with unhappy results.

One day this Nazi stomped into my room and announced tactlessly that he was taking over my case. I told him I was getting better, hoped to leave the hospital shortly, and did not see any point in changing doctors. As it happened, I was wrong and was in the hospital another full month because my health improved only slowly.

When June arrived, Belgium was completely in the hands of the German army. The Germans had occupied Brussels, Antwerp, and Ostende. As I was lying on my bed my mind kept drifting back to Madeleine, the Koutnys, and all our friends in Brussels. I spent hours worrying about how they were doing.

Another unthinkable tragedy happened on June 14: Paris became occupied by the German army. Alex and I never dreamed this was possible. The French government fled, and in the newsreels Hitler was seen marching with his armies down the Champs Elysées and driving victoriously beneath the Arc de Triomphe. It was so sad; I felt as if my homeland had been lost a second time.

There was, however, one glimmer of hope. The whole British

Expeditionary Force, encircled by Hitler's armies, was able to fight its way to Dunkirk on the English Channel. In an extraordinary feat of courage and determination the B.E.F. was transported to England in a flotilla of yachts, pleasure boats, and fishing boats, often manned by civilians.

Complete chaos reigned in western Europe. Panic-stricken people were evacuating their homes, escaping from Belgium, Holland, and northern France, fleeing southward toward Spain ahead of the Nazis. These were ugly, depressing days in the already conquered countries. No one could believe that Hitler had taken France so quickly.

Against that background of tumult, in spite of all logic, my health was improving. The long-awaited day came when the nurse threw the hot compresses on me and I started yelling, "Oh, it's too hot, I can't stand it." That pain was a great pleasure. Then, after many more compresses, I was able to get out of bed and take three steps, each one hurting so much that it felt as if nails were being driven up through the soles of my feet.

A few days later I managed to walk shakily from the bed to a chair by the window, where I sat for a long time looking out, enchanted by the green beauty of the world I had last seen in March. Across from the hospital was one of the parks Alex and I used to walk through before we were married. I thought back to the earlier, happy days of our courtship and to the sad days that had followed. I was indeed lucky to be alive, and getting well.

At the end of June, after three and a half months, Janie and I went home. Bolca had put flowers everywhere. The apartment looked beautiful, bright, and welcoming to the eyes dulled by hospital drabness and the veils of constant pain and fever.

The next morning, on an exalted day filled with blue skies and silver clouds of high summer, we went back to Richky. To my immense astonishment our farm had been transformed. In front of the house the garden was expertly landscaped. When I had last seen it, it was muddy and in disarray, full of building materials, heaps of excavated soil, and construction trash. Now it was neat and tended. The wide terrace in front of the house was bordered by a rock garden with an abundance of summer flowers descending into a sweep of mowed lawn which flowed toward a curving drive paved with flagstones. On the other side of the drive the creek gurgled away, shaded by apple trees and lush green bushes.

When we went inside I felt like Alice in Wonderland. The entire house was completely furnished in every detail, down to carpets and draperies. The colors were tasteful and harmonious, pale green being complemented by shades of deep rose, beige, and brown. The furniture was perfection in style and proportion, handmade in a comfortable country style that was simple, yet elegant, at once grace-ful and cozy. The whole effect was one of great simplicity, cheerful-ness, and good taste.

Marveling, I walked with slow deliberation from room to room, though I felt like running. Everything was impeccable and perfect. It was an overwhelming relief to realize that I could settle the family at Richky for the summer months without a single worry about furnishings.

Wide-eyed, I asked Alex how in the world he had managed to do it all while he was so busy in the plant and during wartime at that. He smiled, explaining that he had engaged a well-known Prague interior decorator who took care of everything. Alex was delighted that I liked the results so much. During all the time I was in the hospital, he never mentioned a word about what he had been doing. With his usual sense of the dramatic, he had waited patiently for the moment when I would walk through Richky's front door. He had his reward because I was immensely pleased.

Able to walk only with a cane and even then with difficulty, I still had much pain in both legs. However, being at home and sur-rounded by such obvious signs of love, seeing the flowers and grass from the windows, and having the children and our friends with me made a considerable difference and accelerated my recovery.

What had been at first a possible refuge, then an occasional retreat, now became our true home. Richky was set like a jewel in a quiet Moravian valley, surrounded by steep hills, deep forest, and gentle slopes covered with wild strawberries. In the midst of war, despair, shortages, and the ravishing of our beloved country, here was safety, sanity, and, above all, love.

Alex and I would wake each morning to the delicious aroma of pine needles bathed in the warm sunlight, and the ecstatic soprano of countless birds, singing over the cool, rippling bass of the crystal stream as it tumbled pure and clean. The sounds of nature around us formed a gentle chorus of constant reassurance that helped us to put aside the gnawing stress of fear. We lived as if raised into another world, onto a peaceful planet, where the intolerable could not happen. Richky healed and strengthened us.

The house was a large, graceful three-story villa built inside the walls of the original building with many verandas and balconies added. Out in front stood the huge horse chestnut tree, dappling the terrace with cool blue shadows while calmly welcoming tired travelers. In spring it was covered with large, fragrant, candelabra-like clusters of flowers and in fall with thousands of horse chestnuts with prickly green shells that, when opened, revealed nuts of the richest, shining-brown color imaginable. The ancient one was as much a friend as a tree.

The side of the property on the road was protected by a high, solid rock wall with secure wrought-iron gates. Across the drive from the house was a garage, with several old fruit trees scattered around the adjoining lawn, the remnants of the old mill-house garden. The drive then continued through another wooden gate to the barnyard, around which were grouped the horse stables, the cow barn, the pig sty, the carriage house, and the feed rooms.

From the barnyard a large archway led toward the mill, the mill office, and the apartment of our miller Peter and his wife Anna. A little farther along were chicken coops and root cellars where we stored potatoes, onions, and apples in the fall.

On the placid surface of the mill pond floated a flock of ducks and geese. Along the drive bordering the stream was another building with two apartments, one for the gardener and the other for Alex's parents, whom we expected to visit us often. The drive then continued on to the top gate. The main gate facing the house was called the lower gate.

On the far side of the house away from the road, a terraced rose garden led in a couple of steps up to a sprawling orchard with apple, plum, and pear trees, another inheritance from the old farm. Next to the orchard Alex built a large swimming pool with a latticed gazebo, beyond which were our meadows and fields and the forest itself.

Richky was altogether a lovely little estate, made all the more dear by the fact that we had planned and supervised its rebuilding ourselves. When we finished renovations, the only original building that remained intact was the three-hundred-year-old mill, still working away at its humble task.

Our house was the only one in the valley with the exception of a small holding of Mr. and Mrs. Müller, who lived a few hundred yards from our top gate. Several miles downstream stood two other mills on the same little river as ours. The old farm seemed to respond to our care and love. That summer, in spite of the war, was enormously pleasant. I was overcome time and time again with gratitude for being at home in ever-improving physical health with my two girls and husband. Many Czechs had much less.

At the beginning of September we had to return to Modrice. Evie was to begin school, which she was looking forward to. We enrolled her in the Czech school, but that created an unexpected problem. She had hardly been to her first class when two Brownshirt Nazis came to see Alex demanding that Evie should go to the German school.

Alex told them calmly that we were not going to do that because Evie was a Czech child and she did not speak German. They argued that the language barrier was a difficulty that could be solved easily. The family should engage a German maid to teach her.

Though by no means feeling it, Alex said placidly, "That's impossible. We like our Lois very much. She's a good cook and we wouldn't think of replacing her."

They left to think it over and returned in a few days to insist with even more fervor that Evie ought to go to a German school because, as they explained, we could employ two girls. Lois could stay on as the cook, and a German girl could be hired as a nursemaid and German-language teacher to prepare Evie for a German education. Alex told me later that while this nonsense was going on, it occurred to him that it would be nice, indeed, to have a Nazi spy in the house.

Wishing to finish the discussion and get the Brownshirts out of his office, he said, "Well, as it happens we have a German governess coming from Vienna to stay with us. She is arriving quite soon." Nonplussed, they left again.

When Alex came to tell me about this second interview I lost my temper.

"Now we are in a fine fix. We don't know anyone in Vienna and what's more, I don't want any German woman living in the house with us. I am absolutely against it." I was furious.

Taken aback, Alex replied, "Well, so what do you want to do? If we don't take in some German-speaking woman, if we don't do anything, they could send me to a concentration camp. You know what they're like!" After a pause, he added, "Listen, we'll try. Let's put an advertisement in the Vienna paper. After all, do you remember those Viennese officers who were here? Lots of people in Vienna are against Hitler just as we are. Maybe we'll be lucky and find somebody who's anti-Nazi, and that way perhaps we'll be protected against being arrested."

"I don't know."

"And what's more, if we have a woman from Vienna we can send her back at any time, but if we're forced to employ a German girl from Modrice, we can't get rid of her ever. Can you imagine? She'd be spying on us all day long. It would be an impossible situation."

I still felt an enormous dislike for the suggested addition to our household, but I did not know what else we could do.

We placed an ad in the Vienna paper and soon received many replies. One was written in German, but with capital letters written in the French manner. The applicant had been born in Vienna but had always lived in France and spoke German and French equally well. She had worked as a governess in Hungary and Romania, then for the last ten years had been employed by the nephew of French Marshal Pétain. Her letter looked reassuringly non-Nazi.

We answered with an invitation, and Mademoiselle Elizabeth Rosner, whom we called Madi, came into our lives. She was like someone from the last century, a true lady with perfect manners, petite, with blue eyes and blond hair that she pulled back into a severe bun. Firm with children, but loving at the same time, she fitted into our family well.

Madi loathed Hitler and with good reason. Marshal Pétain's nephew had been the French chargé d'affaires in Warsaw. In the summer of 1939 Madi took the children to France for a vacation, leaving her possessions in Warsaw, including all her money in the bank. When Warsaw fell she lost everything. Though she had a good position in France, that was taken away as well when the Nazis repatriated all German people, thus forcing Madi to return to Vienna, where she saw our advertisement.

She was a warm-hearted woman, quickly took our daughters to herself, and became like a member of the family. She delighted in the fact that Alex and I spoke French. Madi taught Evie French as well as German, and Evie was able to stay in the Czech school.

Next time when the Nazis came, Alex explained to them that the child had to learn the language first. He called Madi into his office, introduced her to the Brownshirts, who were suitably impressed by the high standard of her elegant German spoken with the soft, musical Viennese accent. They left satisfied, at least for the present.

In November 1940 a happy event took place in our family. Alex's brother Ivan unexpectedly got married. His bride was his cousin Jana, a lovely, clever girl. Everyone was glad she was not marrying a stranger who would take her away from us. It was a joyous happening in a tense situation.

At this time the Nazis intensified their effort to subdue Czech resistance by destroying large numbers of citizens. Many people, including some of our friends, were arrested. Among them was Mojmir Kolar, Alex's best friend, who had recently married the daughter of Chairman Wenzl. The newlyweds were much in love and she was heartbroken about Mojmir's arrest.

Alex struggled to find a way to get him released and in the course of his inquiries met Mr. Horky, the head of the Czech resistance in Brno, who became our good friend and whose help was to prove crucial to our survival.

Alex did whatever he could to get Mojmir freed. Mojmir remained imprisoned for nine months in Kounicovy Koleje, the dormitories at Masaryk University that were converted into a prison. He was finally released in 1941, just before von Neurath was replaced by the more brutal Heydrich. Mojmir was lucky. Another friend, a newspaperman named Jan Kulajta, was not so fortunate. He was arrested and sent to the Dachau concentration camp in Germany. We never saw him again.

Alex's work at Biochema was becoming more difficult and dangerous. Not only was the *Treuhänder* spying on him but so was a multitude of Germans sent by the authorities to supervise and to spy on Czech workers. To make matters worse, as Biochema was a large, important company, there was a constant stream of German bureaucrats arriving on trips of endless inspections. I remember one occasion in particular. Alex received an urgent message from the Czech Ministry of Commerce that another delegation was coming. Its chief was the German functionary in charge of allocating raw materials to the Czech factories, and it was imperative he should write a good report on Biochema so the company could continue to receive sufficient supplies. After the group arrived, one of the Czech members took Alex aside and advised him to invite the German for a game of cards after dinner. The Nazi enjoyed—even doted on—winning at cards. When he won he was always in a good mood and ready to sign any report or requisition they wanted him to sign. Alex told him to relax. He was, in his own estimation, one of the worst card players in the world. He was sure to lose.

Right after dinner the German, Alex, and the two Czechs from the party sat down to play. They chose a game that was pure and simple gambling, a game of luck involving no skill at all. Alex won, then won again and kept on winning repeatedly. Whatever he did, he won, and before long he had a heap of money in front of him.

The German was steaming, his little eyes bulging, but Alex, try as he might, could not lose. He was frantic, and still he won. Finally at three in the morning Alex excused himself, Ivan took his hand, played for him, and heroically managed to lose everything. The next day, his greediness satisfied, the German certified the requisition of whatever raw materials he was told Biochema needed. It was a disgusting way to run a business and Alex hated it, but there was nothing else to do.

The Nazi attack on the leadership of the nation continued. Sometime in February 1941 my cousin Zdenek went to Prague to visit Uncle Leopold, a professor at Charles University. When he arrived at the apartment door, he found it locked and with a Gestapo seal on it. Uncle Leopold and Aunt Anna had been arrested. They had both been taken to Mauthausen, a concentration camp in Austria, where they died two years later.

At the time we guessed they had been apprehended either because Aunt Anna had been a good friend of Alice Masaryk, the daughter of the late president, or because she was the vice president of the Czech Red Cross. Such innocent circumstances were sufficient pretext for the Nazis to send them both into a concentration camp and kill them in the gas chamber.

The family was shaken by these events. Life itself was becoming a ceaseless terror. One never knew what would happen the next day, and the constant uncertainty was emotionally debilitating. The only thing we had to look forward to were the evenings when we could listen to Radio London in the hope of hearing that the Germans had suffered a defeat. But that news did not come.

6

WENZL TRAGEDY

March 15, 1941, arrived and with it the second anniversary of Hitler's invasion and Janie's first birthday. The one-year-old was as happy as her world was sad. She smiled constantly, could stand alone, seldom cried, and shone with good spirits. We had a festive luncheon celebration. When Alex arrived Janie beamed and toddled on her plump legs in his direction, the first time she had walked by herself. Alex was delighted that her first steps were toward him.

In April, the Nazis intruded on our domestic life again, demanding that Evie be transferred to a German school. As the matter was getting out of hand, Alex and I decided to move the family to the safety of Richky, where Evie could go to the Czech school in the nearby town of Obce. Unpleasantness with the Nazis, which could create a dangerous situation for Alex, could be thus avoided. Our furniture was cloaked with dust sheets and the apartment was closed, but with one bedroom usable so Alex could stay over on those nights after work when he was too tired to travel to Richky.

Our cook's mother took ill, so Lois went home to nurse her. Alex put an ad in the paper to find a replacement. An interesting reply came from a Fanny Karas. I wrote her that as we were living in the country, I would interview her at her home. The address was on a stylish street of Brno, but when I arrived there I found a sad situation. The apartment was large, but the rooms had been divided into two or three small cubicles, each of which housed an entire family jammed in. The occupants were Jews. They had been thrown out of their own homes and stuffed into this miniature ghetto.

The Nazi persecution of the Jews began in our country on the day of the invasion. During the previous winter they had been forced to serve in the streets as the cleaning brigades. Most of them were highly educated professionals for whom the work was not only degrading but enormously tiring as well. They were compelled to sew a yellow Star of David on all their clothing, on the left side of their chest, to identify them wherever they went.

Fanny, a widow with a married son, was about fifty. For fourteen years she had been the cook for a Jewish couple who lived in Vienna. Just before Hitler occupied Austria the family escaped to Brno, where the husband died. Fanny stayed with the widow and her daughter, a fourteen-year-old girl. The lady had not believed that Hitler would attack Czechoslovakia, and by the time she found she was mistaken, it was too late. The borders closed and the family could not leave.

They were then evicted from their home and allocated a meager corner in this overcrowded apartment. With their usual cruelty, the Nazis had ordered Fanny to leave the little ghetto because she was not Jewish. Moreover, they issued an edict that henceforth Jews were not allowed to have servants. Fanny was heartbroken. This was her real family. She had brought up the girl since she was a baby and loved her as her own daughter. Fanny could not bear the anguish of being separated from the child, but she could not stay, and her employer urged her to leave lest she be swept up into their fate. Finally, she gave in, and when I described our arrangements, she was eager to come to work for us at Richky. Fanny was a good person whose friendship and loyalty were one of our main supports during the years ahead.

Her relationship to her former family continued. Every week on her day off she went to Brno to see her "lady" and the little girl. When summer came, I asked her to invite them to Richky so they could, at least temporarily, escape their depressing surroundings. They came from time to time to swim and relax with us. They were gentle, cultured people and the two families became friends.

Then one day when Fanny went to see them, she found the

apartment door closed and sealed. Some time later they sent us a postcard from Poland, giving us an address in some obscure little Polish town. Fanny and I sent food parcels, some of which they received, but most were lost.

Fanny wrote often, and they wrote back, but after several months they disappeared. Fanny was desperate, as was I, and depression settled like airborne soot on our daily routine. They had become dear to us in the months we had known them. Many similar tragedies were acted out around us. Everyday life was clotting with the pain.

Food was scarce. Fanny was a treasure, creating sumptuous meals from only potatoes and vegetables. Her skill was doubly appreciated because we frequently had friends as well as business acquaintances from Prague and Brno staying with us, and they had to be fed from our meager rations. Richky became a sanctuary for them, a place to relax, to get closer to nature, a place where sanity and simplicity prevailed.

It was soul healing to pick up wild strawberries in the clearings, or mushrooms in the deep forest. Trying to catch a few trout was an adventure in itself. When a fisherman was successful, he became the hero of the evening by providing us with a delicious dinner. And then there were the horses. Everyone agreed that to go horseback riding in our deep, majestic forest was an experience not to be forgotten.

I liked having friends staying with us as they always brought some news from the city. After dinner we would discuss the reports and speeches we heard from Radio London and thus make ourselves more secure in the belief that soon the war would be over and we would be free again.

One afternoon when I was resting in my bedroom, Fanny knocked, came in, and announced that there was a man downstairs who insisted on talking to me. "He has a business suit on," she said, "and he looks like a traveling salesman, except that nobody comes around selling things these days, so I just can't tell."

I was suffering from spasms of pain in my legs and was exhausted. I told Fanny to make excuses and to get rid of him. She insisted that he would not leave until I saw him. Reluctantly I got up and went down to the living room. The man was tall, powerfully built, and held himself militarily erect. He looked me straight in the eye as he showed me a small metal disc.

"What is it?" I asked.

"Gestapo," was the answer.

A chill came over me. I was sure he had come to pick up Alex or me or both of us. I did not know what to say or what to do. I felt like a small bird before a python. Then, bracing myself, I found my tongue and made myself say, "What is it you want?"

"We're looking for a man called Dufek. Does he work here?" he asked.

"Yes, he does, but I don't think he's here today—I don't know, I haven't seen him yet." I was thinking hard. I knew Dufek was on the grounds; there might be a slim chance he could be warned. The Gestapo man interrupted my scheming.

"Oh yes, he's here. My partner just arrested him, and I came to tell you that we're taking him to Brno, to Kounicovy Koleje." And then he left.

I was shocked by my first face-to-face encounter with the Gestapo. Alex and I thought they always wore those black uniforms with that terrifying silver skull-and-crossbones insignia on their caps and buckles. Apparently, when they were going to arrest people, they dressed in business suits.

Dufek was a stonemason who lived in a nearby village. He was finishing up a building job on our farm. I discovered later he had been drinking in a tavern and talked too freely, criticizing Hitler. He was heard by a German and denounced. Dufek remained imprisoned for about a year. He was fortunate that nothing worse happened to him.

The news from beyond Czechoslovakia remained bad. After the fall of France and the signing of the armistice, Hitler tore France in half. Germany took complete possession of the northern part, including Paris, while the southern part, called Free France, had a puppet government with Marshal Pétain as its figurehead. It was surprising that Pétain, the great patriot and hero of the First World War, accepted this position since he was the living symbol of the nation and the embodiment of its past glory. No doubt he believed, as did others before him, that one could deal with Hitler successfully.

The Luftwaffe threw its fighters and bombers against England in a crescendo of attacks, culminating in the Battle of Britain. Alex and I saw the newsreels of the catastrophic destruction of London, watching in pain the smoke and flames consuming the city that had given us such a fine time a few short years ago. We had had no news of Olga and Paul since the beginning of the war, and we wondered where they were when the bombs fell.

In November the city of Coventry was leveled by the Nazi fliers. In Brno and Vienna radio stations continually played a new German hit song, "Wir Fahren, Wir Fahren Gegen England." It was sung or hummed in the streets and all public places by the entire German population, nauseating Czechs who were deathly afraid that the Nazis might in fact invade England. The fall of Britain would spell the collapse of everything; it would be the end of our world.

In the spring of 1941, the Yugoslav government was invited to Berlin to make a friendship pact with Hitler. When they returned home they found a new anti-Nazi government in power that arrested and imprisoned their pro-Fascist predecessors. The new government then signed a treaty with Russia, giving us a new glimmer of hope. But soon afterward Belgrade was bombed and nearly destroyed by the Luftwaffe; then the Wehrmacht attacked Yugoslavia and Greece.

Neither country was a match for the German war machine. It was soon over, and endless convoys thundered across Czechoslovakia heading for Germany. We Czechs understood at once: new conquests meant new possibilities for provisions. The trucks were carrying merchandise and materials from Greece and Yugoslavia; the Germans had found new countries to plunder.

Then it happened. Hitler, bloated by egotism and driven to further violence by his successes, attacked Russia on June 22, 1941. Once more we saw many transports of German soldiers and supplies rolling through Brno, but going in the opposite direction, away from Germany, carrying soldiers and supplies east. Also countless trains rushed eastward.

One evening, while spending a couple of days in Modrice, Alex and I were sitting in the living room reading when the night guard at the gate called that two men wanted to talk to my husband. They did not give their names and said only that they were friends. Alex invited them to our apartment. Though we had never met them,

they said it would be better if we did not know their names. Mr.
Horky sent them, and Alex could verify it later. They wanted to talk
to Alex privately. He took them in the library and closed the door.

The men asked for permission to establish an illegal radio station
in Biochema for transmitting reports to England. Our exiled government had given an order to count the eastbound trains and railway
cars carrying tanks and ammunition to the Russian front. As the
railway tracks run along our main plant, it was suggested that it
would be best and safest to do the watching as well as the reporting
from the Biochema premises. It was up to Alex to determine where
to install the transmitter.

Alex agreed, and after a visit to Mr. Horky he decided that the
best place would be his brother's department. Ivan was in charge of
manufacturing essences and aromatic oils for the food and cosmetic
industry. The people who worked for him were all trustworthy and
the rooms were well positioned for watching the trains. Ivan was
willing to cooperate.

The radio station was established and transmitted a report to
London every night. Only a few people knew about the operation, an
extremely dangerous enterprise, but one that Alex, Ivan, and I knew
was worth the risk.

Food supplies dwindled rapidly until we had ration cards for
nearly everything. There was especially a desperate shortage of
meat. Shortening and cooking fats were impossible to find; there was
only an evil-smelling margarine, and even that was in short supply.
Children's milk rations became smaller, and eggs were a thing of the
past. Flour and bread were also rationed.

We were not as bad off as the city population, but the Nazis
would not allow any Czech to have anything even faintly resembling
an adequate diet. A regulation was issued by the Protector's office
that henceforth all country farms had to report how many cows,
pigs, chickens, geese, and ducks they had.

The Richky information was sent in, and in due course an official
order was received stating that so many liters of milk per year from
each cow had to be delivered in daily shipments of such-and-such
size, and so many eggs from each hen had to be surrendered to the
special office set up for that purpose in the nearby village. Alex
answered by return mail that it was impossible to deliver milk every

day because Richky was half an hour's walk from the village. We were instructed to deliver an equivalent amount of butter instead. It was a staggeringly large amount, demanding gallons of milk. I did not see how we could do it.

We were also directed to deliver forty eggs per year from each hen. The hens did not eat any better than the family did. There was not enough grain to make flour and bread, and little to spare for the chickens. As a consequence, their productivity declined. It was impossible to count on forty eggs per hen, even if we kept nothing for ourselves.

The directive affected the whole countryside. The farmers were furious and determined to retain something of what they produced for themselves. They registered only half their flock of hens, hoping to keep a few eggs for their own families. The Germans found out and several conspirators were caught, arrested, and imprisoned. At Richky we did not know what to do. Concentration camp was a high price to pay for a few dozen eggs.

The man in charge of the reporting office was willing to take risks for his neighbors, and he developed his own method of protecting them. When the Germans burst into the area to count the livestock and search for contraband, they had to go to the reporting office first to get the list of names from our friend, who in a comradely way shuttled them off to the local inn for a glass of beer. The innkeeper's wife would rush three or four boys around the village to tell everyone the Nazis were coming to count hens.

One messenger would run down to Richky, gasping for breath, to tell us that the egg stealers were on their way. Then the family, staff, and guests would feverishly gather up all the poor illegal hens, stuff them in sacks and tote them into the forest, where they would stay until the Germans had come and gone.

The people in the village discovered a good hiding place, too. A big cemetery was at the edge of town and the villagers put their hen sacks behind its high wall. Because it was dark in the sacks, the hens did not squawk and slept tranquilly through the uproar. They were hardly quiet, however, when they were finally released. This system was used throughout the war and the Nazis never realized that the area's hen population was twice the size of that recorded on their official chicken census.

The matter of the requisitioned butter was a constant vexation to me. I was always behind on the amount delivered. One day Peter, our miller, told me he had heard in the village our shortage had been noticed and we were risking arrest. The family stopped using milk altogether, saved every drop in spite of the girls' long faces, and finally made the butter quota. After it was churned, the precious golden lump was reverently carried to the pantry in a pan of water to keep it chilled during the summer heat.

Fanny closed the pantry door behind us and went to her room for her customary and well-earned afternoon rest. Some hours later she came running, ashen-faced, with a hand covering her heart as if to keep it from popping out. The pan was empty; the butter was gone. A telltale line of water led across the kitchen and the yard to the dog house.

Several months earlier Alex had bought a Great Dane puppy, and to amuse us, he taught her to open doors. My husband thought this was cute, but it was not so funny on this occasion. Gondola had opened the pantry door, discovered the butter, and gobbled up the whole ten pounds of it. I was furious at the dog and her trainer. I have never seen a sicker dog or been more pleased by the sight as she lay in her house in abject misery for days. She would not come out and, of course, would not—and probably could not—eat a thing.

But I felt sicker because I had to go to the village town hall and tell my sad story. Luckily, the person in charge to whom I had to make my confession was the same good, courageous man who had organized the chicken parade. He believed me, was sympathetic, and promised to make excuses to the Germans, though with a touch of urgency in his voice he advised me to get another ten pounds together as quickly as possible. Otherwise we were in real danger.

I went home in angry panic. Fanny and I started all over again, saving whatever we could and buying on the black market whatever other farmers could spare. They heard about my misfortune and were more than willing to help. The replacement took a couple of weeks, but what a relief it was when I saw that hated second glob of butter disappear into the storeroom of the office on its way to German stomachs. I had never thought I would be actually glad to give up food to the Nazis. The pantry door was kept locked from then on.

The summer of 1941 passed uneventfully. After a short discussion, Alex and I reaffirmed our decision to remain at Richky. In September Evie was to start school in Obce, as returning to Modrice was out of the question. Besides rekindling the affair of the German school, moving back into the apartment at Biochema would expose both our girls to a great danger if the existence of the underground radio transmitter in the factory was discovered.

That September, the position of the Czech people as a whole took an ominous turn for the worse. Our "protector," Baron von Neurath, was recalled to Germany, having been accused of being soft on the Czechs. In fact, he had never accepted the radical Nazi program to annihilate us both as a political entity and as an ethnic group. Hitler, who now listened to less moderate voices, appointed his chief expert in racial extermination to serve as protector and to implement the Führer's grand, insane plan for Czechoslovakia. He was Reinhard Heydrich, a thirty-seven-year-old SS general who was already in charge of solving the Jewish question once and for all.

The Holocaust was the work of this man. Heydrich, Adolf Eichmann's commanding officer and second only to Himmler in the SS hierarchy, was widely reputed to be one of the cruelest men in the Nazi regime. His long, narrow face with the fixed, blank, mean expression of a cobra and colorless blond hair spoke of a frozen heart. He was a pitiless man, a truly evil being without warmth, mercy, or humanity.

He immediately went to war against our people. Martial law was ordered in Bohemia and Moravia, and the very last of our legal rights were abolished. Heydrich issued a decree stating that anyone traveling to visit another town or village had to register on arrival at the nearest police station, even if the visit was only for a day. No Czech was allowed to go unaccounted for and, therefore, unsupervised.

Surprise searches were made every night in randomly selected areas. From then on no Czech was allowed to fall into simple sleep or peaceful rest. Anyone discovered without proper registration papers was instantly arrested. In Brno those unfortunate people were herded into the Gestapo offices in the Law School of Masaryk University, condemned to death without trial, then shot or hanged at Kounicovy Koleje the same day. If a person was apprehended in the streets after curfew, he or she was arrested. Hundreds were executed.

Wild terror ruled the country, overwhelming our mental balance.

Czechs knew with absolute certainty that the Nazi objective was to destroy our nation. In Hitler's and Heydrich's minds, Czechs and Jews were to suffer the same fate. Hundreds upon hundreds of citizens were murdered and thousands were seized and sent to concentration camps in Germany and Poland—which in many cases amounted to the same thing.

By that time the existence of the concentration camps was common knowledge, although we did not know fully what was happening there. Now and then a family would receive news that their father or husband died in one. Why or how, no one knew. The lack of hard knowledge served to increase the general fear and heighten the sense of horror. Everyone hated Heydrich—totally, unanimously, helplessly. There was no end to our national crucifixion. One had to hang on desperately to the few scraps of self-respect and goodness left to us.

Alex and I began horseback riding again and I found it was good for me as it strengthened my legs. More important, it sustained us spiritually. We rode out into the serenity of our green forests as often as we could. In sharp contrast to the rest of the world at war, everything here was peaceful and even miraculously joyful.

On Sundays we would start out at six o'clock in the dew-washed morning and ride through silent gothic groves where we met only deer. They were not afraid of us on horseback and came up close to gaze into our sad souls with their big, liquid eyes that were innocent, trusting, and somehow kind. We would ride on and on for hours, speaking only a few words, but saying much in the stillness.

The woods were tranquility itself. Tall pines and fir forests alternated with shimmering birch groves. We crossed high hillsides drenched in sunlight and covered with wild strawberries whose gleeful aroma on soft summer breezes held us safe as if in happy, loving hands. There we two, so dear to each other, were able to conquer the overwhelming horror looming over our homeland: the war, the Gestapo, the precariousness of existence, and all our worries. Heydrich could not reach us there. It was the only time we were at peace, when we let ourselves become lost and wander free, knowing the horses would pick their way back. Riding was our only brightness. As impossible as it may seem, the two of us were happy when out riding together.

Alex and his staff at Biochema encountered increasing troubles in Modrice. Innumerable inspections were held by German dignitaries close to Heydrich himself, and the Gestapo conducted many searches. One episode was especially terrifying. One morning, at about ten o'clock, several cars drove in front of the executive building and twenty Gestapo men jumped out. Without talking to anybody they started digging and remained busy at it up to five o'clock in the evening, though they did not find anything. Then they got into their cars and drove away, leaving behind an immense hole. Later, Alex learned that some Nazis from Modrice had denounced the company, claiming that Biochema kept a great quantity of arms buried in the factory yard.

Since some upsetting incident happened nearly every week, Alex was worried. What if some fanatic Nazi had put some munitions somewhere and then sent the Gestapo to Biochema? Finally it was decided to move the offices to Brno, where management would be less conspicuous. The company bought a five-story building in the center of the city and corporate headquarters were established there within a short period of time.

Brno, however, was by no means free of danger. At the headquarters of the farmers' cooperatives associated with Biochema, Chairman Wenzl was worried by the deepening of the persecution. As if in response to his fear, the Nazis began arresting people in his office. One of them was a friend of ours, Josef Svoboda, whom we had visited just days before. He was imprisoned in Kounicovy Koleje.

Dr. Wenzl confided to us that one of the reasons why Heydrich had been sent to Prague was to destroy the Czech resistance, whose existence and activities drove the Führer into hysterics. The resistance was gaining strength daily, had set up throughout the country many radio stations like the one in Biochema, and was in daily communication with London, transmitting essential information on German activities, especially important in that the war with Russia had started. It was rumored that members of the resistance were even working in Hradcany Castle, spying on Heydrich himself.

Furthermore, some Czech soldiers who had escaped to England in 1939 were now parachuted back into the country by the Allies, bringing with them much needed equipment such as radio transmitters, guns, and ammunition. They carried instructions from the government in exile to act in concert with the Czech resistance. The German informers soon found out about it, and Heydrich responded with demonic efficiency and will. The number of executions rose until it reached hundreds in a day. The lists of those murdered were posted in the cities and towns. Every morning, quiet, intense groups of white-faced people with red eyes could be seen searching for the names of friends and relatives.

Chairman Wenzl began spending weekends with us at Richky. Long a benevolent presence in our lives, he now became a close, cherished friend. His family lived far in the country on a farm, and he was lonely. He talked much about them and their future. His children were already grown.

His youngest was a son, a very handsome boy, tall and graceful with blond hair and clear, sparkling blue eyes. Jirka was eighteen years old and was to graduate from high school in June. He was the apple of his father's eye. Dr. Wenzl was looking forward to the moment when he would give Jirka his graduation gift, a gold watch.

His daughter Dana was married to Alex's best friend, Mojmir Kolar, and was expecting a baby in June. Our dear friend said several times that the coming June would be an important month in his life; he would become a grandfather at the same time that his son finished high school, entered adulthood, and chose a career. June in fact was an important month in his life, but in a different and tragic way.

———☐———

Living at Richky created a problem for Alex as far as getting to work was concerned. He could not use his car for commuting to the office because the "no private use" rule was strictly enforced by the Gestapo. The use of a car in the course of business was allowed only within city limits.

In a moment of inspiration he decided to ride on horseback every morning to the outskirts of the city where a forester agreed to stable the horse during the day. Alex's driver, Frank, then picked him up and drove him to the office in Brno or to the factory. This worked out well. In fact, the ninety-minute ride twice a day provided great exercise and relaxation, too.

Heydrich's reign of terror accelerated with more arrests, more bloodshed, and more victims vanishing into the concentration camps. By that time Jews had completely disappeared from Brno. News of the war went from bad to worse. Hitler had become the ruler of most of continental Europe. In North Africa, where Rommel fought the British Army, the Germans gained one victory after another, while the Wehrmacht was advancing in Russia. They had almost reached the Caucasus, with its great oil deposits that, once seized, could fuel the German war effort indefinitely. German soldiers had entered the suburbs of Leningrad and Moscow. Through the fall of 1941 there was no good news.

Alex and I persisted tenaciously in the belief that Hitler could not win and Czechoslovakia would be free again. This faith empowered us and was strengthened when in December 1941, the day after Japan's attack on Pearl Harbor, the United States joined the Allies in the fight against the Nazis. America became for us a symbol of light in darkness, of resurrection answering our frustration.

Because Hitler had so many men in the armed forces, Germany was short of factory workers. The Nazis therefore added a new crime to the growing list by conscripting Czechs to work in the German munition plants. University students were taken first, then all young people up to a certain age, the only exceptions being married people with children. Youngsters hardly out of high school stampeded into marriage with their parents' full blessings because nobody wanted his child working for Hitler. Other young people inflicted injuries on themselves to avoid being sent to Germany. Some who did go were killed when the British attacked the ammunition factories. The Royal Air Force had been expanding its operations. When we heard about air attacks on German cities we were elated and sickened simultaneously, knowing that our young people were being destroyed along with our enemies.

On May 27, 1942, Heydrich was driving in an open Mercedes-Benz from his summer residence to his Prague headquarters at Hradcany Castle when he was ambushed by two men. Two brave Czech soldiers, Josef Gabcik and Jan Kubis, who had joined the Free Czech Army in England, had been parachuted into Bohemia for the express purpose of killing Heydrich. The government in exile under the leadership of Edvard Benes had made the difficult decision that such an act would in the long run save more Czech lives than would be extinguished in the short run in reprisals.

Gabcik and Kubis had established contact with the Czech resistance, who hid them and aided them in scouting out the details of Heydrich's movements. They discovered that his car always slowed down on a sharp curve on the road to the castle, and they based their plan on this critical opportunity. Gabcik was to shoot Heydrich while Kubis snatched his briefcase and dropped a bomb in the car so that the resulting fire would destroy all evidence.

On the day of the attempt, things happened differently. The two men positioned themselves and waited in the agony of suspense. The long, sinister black car swung into the curve and slowed as anticipated. Gabcik ran up to the convertible, leveled his Sten gun and pulled the trigger. It did not fire. Heydrich and his driver pulled out their Lugers. Kubis had the presence of mind to throw his bomb. The explosion shattered the car and injured Heydrich.

The Czechs disappeared from the scene, in the confusion leaving behind a coat and a hat. Heydrich was rushed to a nearby hospital and operated on by Nazi doctors. The first reports were optimistic, predicting recovery, but suddenly, on June 4, his condition reversed as if by a quick act of an avenging angel and he died.

The Nazis went insane, the assassination releasing everything demonic in their natures. Sheer terror ruled the whole country as the Gestapo became absolutely ruthless, arresting people, searching houses, and furiously trying to uncover the hiding place of the two men who killed Heydrich. Martial law, which had been discontinued a short time before, was reestablished in a far harsher form. Whoever was found in the street after a certain hour was immediately executed.

It was announced that any person supplying information to the Germans about Heydrich's assassins would receive a reward of one million reichsmarks, a huge sum. The nation stood united; no one came forward. The reign of death continued, with a grisly routine established. Those swept up during the day were shot in the evening so their names could be announced on the radio in what is now called "prime time." In Brno, the executions took place in Kounicovy Koleje. Every day there were 80 to 120 names, and that was only in one city. Each evening hundreds of thousands of Czech families, including ours, sat and listened breathlessly to the roll of the dead, praying and hoping not to hear a name of anyone dear to their hearts. Those were tense moments. The following morning the names of the innocent victims were printed in the newspapers.

Over and over again the Gestapo struck viciously, quickly, and without warning. All the structures of ordinary reality were shattered by their terrorism as literally as Heydrich's car had been shattered by Kubis's bomb. The flow of time fell apart. One friend in Prague, home for lunch, told his wife he would be back for dinner at six o'clock. He did not arrive at that time, and while his wife was waiting, keeping the food warm, she turned on the radio and heard her husband's name in the execution report.

When Alex left in the morning, I never knew if I would ever see him again. Every parting was a final farewell. It was a heavy strain to live under. The times he had to spend away in Prague on business trips were hell for me. He always called me every evening to give me assurance that everything was all right and that he was still alive.

One night Alex and I heard on the radio execution list the name of Josef Svoboda. An associate of Dr. Wenzl and our good friend, he had been arrested months before. The official reason for the death sentence was that he had approved of Heydrich's assassination. As he had been in prison for the previous seven months, we did not think he even knew it had happened. We found out the chilling details of his death later.

Josef Svoboda was sentenced to be hanged. He was a tall, strong, well-built man, a member of the Czech team of the 1936 Olympics. Ironically, he was the perfect model of the German Aryan: tall, blue eyed, and blond. Even after having been imprisoned for months, he still had his strength. When the Nazi hangmen dragged him to the gallows he fought back, flailing about with his tied hands. He actually knocked a few Gestapo men down. The others rushed in with clubs and began bludgeoning him, but Josef fought on until they actually beat him to death. When he was dead, the barbarians, in their furor that a Czech would resist, propped up his bloody corpse, put the noose around his neck, and hanged him.

Kounicovy Koleje was situated in the middle of a suburban development. Because Brno is a hilly town, many of the surrounding houses were at a higher elevation than the former student dormitories.

Neighbors could see the executions from their windows, and ghastly stories were circulating throughout the city. One was a true report that the Gestapo were shooting little children. We heard about a young girl who was so paralyzed with fear that she could not walk. The Gestapo men carried her to the stake and tied her upright so that she could be shot. Onlookers in the surrounding apartments said that the sight was so horrifying that one soldier of the firing squad fainted.

The neighbors spent a good part of their time on their knees, praying for the dying and the departed. The Gestapo agents, on the other hand, brought their wives and mistresses to watch the executions, which they did avidly, with enthusiasm and applause. For them it was wonderful entertainment.

Then one of the brightest, warmest lights of our lives was snuffed out. One Friday in June, Dr. Wenzl came to spend the weekend with us. Terribly worried, depressed, and shocked by the events, he told Alex and me that he was going to leave Brno and stay at his farm for two or three weeks until things quieted down. After a visit to his Prague office Wednesday afternoon, he would leave for his vacation. On Wednesday morning, about ten o'clock, Alex went to see him to discuss a new project. He left about half past ten. Dr. Wenzl was taking the one o'clock train to the capital.

He never made it. That night we were stunned to hear his name on the radio. The Gestapo had arrived just after Alex left. Later we heard from the people living around Kounicovy Koleje that the execution had not actually taken place that night.

When the Gestapo brought the prisoners into the execution yard that evening, a fierce thunderstorm broke out. Dr. Wenzl and a few others were hurried in the rain back into the gray van, called the Gorilla by the Czechs, that was used for transportation of prisoners from the Gestapo offices to Kounicovy Koleje. The victims spent the night at the Gestapo headquarters in the old Law School. What a terrible night it must have been.

The next morning they were taken back to Kounicovy Koleje and their execution was completed while many weeping Czechs watched, murmuring prayers, pouring out their hearts for the poor dying people in the hope that in their suffering they might sense their support, that they might feel they were not alone in the last moment of consciousness, that in spirit their countrymen stood with them.

Chairman Wenzl's death tore our hearts apart; he had been like a father to us. Quite often he had talked about being arrested, but we had never thought that his life would take such a sharp and tragic turn. His wife and children were totally devastated. His son Jirka, who adored his father, became a member of the Czech underground. The boy left home and joined partisans hiding in the forests, sabotaging the German war effort and helping parachutists from England.

In March 1945, two months before the war ended, Mrs. Wenzl opened her door one morning and found her son's body lying on the doorstep. He had been shot by the Gestapo and brought home by his partisan friends for burial. Poor Jirka, he so much wanted vengeance for his father's death that he paid for it with his own life.

7

NARROW ESCAPE

Some months before Heydrich came to Prague, Alex visited his Aunt Slavi, who lived in southern Bohemia. Many years earlier her young husband was in government service in Bosnia-Herzegovina, at that time a part of the Austro-Hungarian Empire. There he acquired a beautiful set of antique weapons: a pistol, rifle, saber, and dagger. Over two hundred years old and of Turkish origin, they were made of fine steel and sterling silver, splendidly decorated and richly engraved. Clearly they had belonged to some important personality. Aunt Slavi had two daughters, neither of whom was interested in these antiques, and as Alex was her favorite nephew, she wanted him to have his uncle's treasure.

I was not pleased at all when the collection arrived with him at Richky. The Nazis had forbidden possession of any weapons and had shot many Czechs for keeping them. It was not a better part of wisdom to own such things.

Alex laughed at my objections. "Just try to shoot them!" he snickered. "You can't do it. They're antiques, that's all."

Against my will he hung them up in our game room for everyone to see. We argued bitterly about them. After Heydrich arrived and executions multiplied, I became even more determined that the weapons should be put away somewhere, but Alex maintained that hiding them would be more dangerous. At least, he observed with

103

maddening self-certainty, if they remained out in the open, even Nazis could see they were merely decorations. I remained unconvinced.

On Monday, following Chairman Wenzl's death, Alex had to go to Prague again. We said good-bye, both terrified and worried, since the sudden execution of our dear friend had made us realize more clearly how precarious was our existence. In the evening Alex called, saying he had arrived safely.

The next morning I woke up abnormally depressed. I could not get rid of an oppressive, unfocused feeling all morning. I felt a darkness coming toward me, a foreboding of another tragedy. After lunch I decided to go to the village. Evie needed some new clothes for school, so I picked apart some of my old dresses to take to the village dressmaker. I bundled up the material, said good-bye to the children, and left.

As I passed our neighbor's house, I saw Mrs. Müller working in the garden. When Alex and I bought Richky, we assumed that the Müllers were Czechs, but Müller was, in fact, a German-born man who spoke both languages fluently and had married a Czech girl. They brought up their four children as Czechs and sent them to Czech schools. The oldest girl married a Czech boy. When Hitler's soldiers occupied the country, Müller suddenly discovered he was really German and forced both his sons to join the German Army. He was even heard to say that he was prepared to sacrifice one of his sons for Hitler.

Mrs. Müller was unhappy about it, to say the least. She walked around like a woman without a soul. Though she was a patriotic Czech at heart, she was a timid person who did not dare to oppose her husband.

Karl, the younger boy, was in the Luftwaffe. He was stationed in Cologne, flying bombing missions over London. Mrs. Müller was worried sick about him because there were many casualties over the British capital. She lived for his letters. He was a handsome boy, her favorite child.

Sorrow for her wrenched my heart when I saw her, and I stopped to ask how she was and how Karl was faring. Brightening, she said she had just received a letter from him. She hoped the war would be over soon, for it made her very unhappy.

I continued on up the hill. The forest had always had a calming effect on me. The rustling of the wind in the trees, the aromatic smell of the pines, and the delightful singing of the birds were all soul soothing. Walking along slowly, I relaxed and put aside my anxiety. I noticed the individual trees along the trail, greeting them as old friends. Evie had named every single one of them. What a charming little girl she had become! My love for her and for my little Janie welled up in my heart, healing its pain.

Soon I was on top of the hill and crossing the field that was between the forest and the town. Wheat was undulating gracefully in the soft breeze, showing off scattered blue cornflowers that sparkled like sapphires in the bright sunshine. I arrived at the village feeling much better.

I realized at once that something was terribly wrong. The town was filled with German troops. There were many trucks, their grim, modern military bulks violating the rural village square. Soldiers were going in and out of the houses. Parked nearby was the Gestapo's dreaded Gorilla van.

Before I had gone a hundred steps past the first house, I was stopped by a brusque military request to show my identification card, which we were required to carry at all times. I was stopped twice more before I reached the dressmaker's house. Relieved to be free of German eyes following me, I walked in. She was in tears.

"What's happening?" I asked gently, touching her shoulder.

"Didn't you see the soldiers? It's awful! They are searching all the houses. They searched our house already," she sobbed. "They didn't find anything, thank God, but our neighbor . . ." She stopped, choking, and dissolved into weeping.

The oppressive feeling enveloped me again in full force. "Your neighbor?" I asked. "What's wrong with him?"

Between sobs she told me that the man's grandfather had fought in Prussian wars in the 1860s and had kept his handgun, an ancient, rusty weapon with some parts missing altogether. The soldiers had found the gun. When the neighbor objected that it was incomplete and rusty, impossible to shoot, they said with a laugh, "A gun is a gun." He was arrested and rushed into the Gestapo's Gorilla van. The officer in charge said he was going to be shot that evening at Kounicovy Koleje.

A chill came over me. If this man had been arrested and was to be shot for possession of one old, broken pistol, what would happen to us, with a whole arsenal hanging in our game room? I felt frantic, trapped, and momentarily confused, unable to think clearly. I forced myself to hold my voice level as I asked, "Do you know if they are going to search the cottages in the forest, too? Do you think they'll make it down to our mill?"

"Oh yes," she answered, "they have checked all the cottages on the east side already. They don't miss a single house. They're very systematic about it. Haven't they been to your place yet? I am sure they're on their way." And she started crying again, overwhelmed by fear, anger, and frustration.

For the first time in my life I experienced real panic. The world seemed to break apart and swirl around me in bits and pieces. I was terrified. What should I do? What was going to happen to us? The children! The children were in the house! Why did I ever let Alex hang those damn weapons? It was wrong, and I knew at the time that it was wrong! Why did I ever listen to him? I should have thrown them away. I should not have listened to his stubborn, never-ending arguments. I had to do something, but I had no idea what.

I was ruled by impulse, almost by instinct. Go home. Go now. Run. I knew I had to get home as fast as possible. There might be time. I still might get there before the soldiers came. I said good-bye to the dressmaker and left. I had to force myself to walk through the village unhurriedly, trying not to be conspicuous. I was stopped and questioned again three times. Each time I had to wait passively, eyes down, for the inspection to end.

Finally, after what seemed hours but was only minutes, I was out of the village and in the wheat field. I broke into a run, stumbling in the furrows and on the rough trail, trying to go as fast as I could, my heart pounding, my head hurting in the hot summer sunshine. The forest was getting nearer and nearer and seemed as far as ever.

Fear slashed at me, making it impossible for me to formulate any kind of reasonable course of action. Fragments of plans shoved each other around in my brain. "Maybe I'll get home before the soldiers come, maybe I'll be able to do...what? Hide the weapons somewhere? Run with them to the forest? They might see me. I wouldn't make it."

Gradually, in the midst of this confusion I started to feel a sense of conviction rise from within me. I began to be sure that while I did not know at that moment what to do, I would know when I got home. Once there, I would be able to do something, the right thing. I would find a good hiding place. I was sure it would be all right. "Oh, God," I prayed, "please just let me get home before the soldiers come," and I ran without pause, gasping for breath.

I reached the end of the field where the trail plunged into the woods and snaked down the steep hill into the valley. I froze. At the edge of the forest six soldiers in field-gray uniforms were sitting in the grass, leaning against the trees, smoking cigarettes. They were talking among themselves. Fortunately I had seen them before they spotted me. I started walking again slowly, as if without worry, as if merely out for a stroll in the country. I did not know what to do. Should I turn and go another way? Maybe they had already been to the house. Maybe they were waiting to arrest me. But then again, maybe they had not been there yet.

I almost turned around. Another trail led down into the valley, and I could have gone that way. But they had seen me. As they stood up and walked toward me, I knew I could not avoid the meeting.

I continued walking. There was nothing else to do. When I came up to them, the sergeant in charge asked for my identification card.

"Oh," he said, looking at it, "you are Frau Kapral from the mill that's in the valley?"

When I assented, he continued, "We are just going down there to search your house, but we are not sure which path to take."

The trail divided at that point. One branch went deeper into the forest and ended at a big mountain cave. The other one led to our house.

The sergeant added, "We thought we'd just take a little rest while we decided which way to go."

I was tempted to usher them onto the path to the cave, but I knew when they finally did find us I would be in bad trouble. I hesitated, but before I could speak the sergeant said, "Would you mind if we walk down with you?"

My heart was beating wildly at the base of my throat. I could not say no without looking suspicious, so I said, "Of course, I don't mind," trying hard to look unconcerned. I was terrified. I was leading my enemies toward my own destruction, toward annihilation of my whole family. My knees felt so weak I thought I would stumble at every step. I kept telling myself that I must not show fear, I must not show *any* fear. I concentrated on controlling the trembling of my knees and on moving my feet ahead, one by one, afraid that I would fall. My body was failing me. My legs felt as if they belonged to someone else. Every step required a conscious, precise effort of will. I was afraid my strength would be soon exhausted and I would collapse.

The soldiers were chatting and asking me questions. I was glad my German was good. I thanked God for my gift for languages because now I could carry on small talk and think about something else, think about those cursed weapons hanging on our wall.

Again, terrifying thoughts flew through my head. "Maybe they won't shoot us, maybe they won't arrest us." And then, "Maybe they'll just shoot Alex and me but not the children. Oh, please, God, don't let them shoot the children." My heart was pounding in my chest. I was sure the soldiers could hear it. I have to talk, I have to talk, I thought frantically, and I continued chatting with them, the words reaching me faintly as from a distance and sounding as if someone else was doing that inane chattering, for surely that was not my voice.

I asked, "Where are you from?"

One of them replied, "Oh, we are from Cologne in Germany, but after the murder of Heydrich we were sent to Brno to help in the searches for arms. Later on we are supposed to be going to the Russian front."

The word *Cologne* rang in my mind like a beautiful bell. Casually I remarked, "You come from a charming city. I was there a few years ago."

He replied with a softened voice, "Yes, it's lovely. We're all so homesick." We walked on. The soldiers had been grumbling about being thirsty and then one of them said longingly, "And the wine there is so good."

Suddenly an idea came to me. In the most offhand manner I could master, I said, "It's very hard to get good wine now, almost impossible, but we have a neighbor, Mrs. Müller, who makes her own wine from red currants. It's truly delicious. Her wine is so good. She has a real talent for it. It's absolutely marvelous."

Then I continued, very calmly, very smoothly, about the coincidence that her son Karl was in the Luftwaffe, stationed in Cologne, of all places, mentioning his flying over London and that Mrs. Müller, the winemaker, was worried sick about him.

"Are you going to stop there, too?"

"No, we're not searching German houses, only Czech houses."

"Oh, what a pity. Mrs. Müller would be so happy to see you since you're from the place where Karl is. She'd love to hear something about what it's like in Cologne. She'd very likely offer you some of her wine, too."

I fell silent and waited. After a moment the soldiers started talking among themselves and at last swallowed the bait.

"You know what, maybe we'd better stop at Mrs. Müller's place. We're not supposed to, but anything to comfort the mother of a comrade in arms."

We came close to the Müllers' and I prayed to God fervently that she had not gone out. I showed the soldiers the gate to her garden. They went in, their big boots clumping on the flagstones. I walked on, managing to keep to a saunter in case they looked back.

Once in our yard, I broke into a desperate run. I lunged through our front door, locked it behind me, and leaned against it, panting, face to face with those terrible weapons. I had no more than twenty minutes and maybe only ten. Feverishly I searched the hall and then the living room for a hiding place the soldiers would not think of looking into. I was desperate. I did not know what to do.

Then suddenly my eyes fell on the library. The wall at the far end of the living room was covered with a nearly ceiling-high bookcase. Because of the way the indirect lighting above it was installed, there was empty space between the bookcase and the wall. The arrangement frequently bothered me; I imagined the niches of dust growing back there, beyond the reach of brooms. In a flash the solution presented itself to me.

That empty space could save our lives. If I could manage to shove the guns and knives through the opening at the top, they would fall down between the wall and the back of the bookcase as if into a bottomless void. The bookcase was built in and could not be moved without first being dismantled.

I shoved a substantial chair up against the rows of books, rushed back into the game room, and grabbed the rifle from its hangers. It was big and heavy. I was sure it would not go through. I climbed up on the chair and with great difficulty hoisted the gun onto the top of the case and pushed. It fell down with a crash. The pistol went down easily. The saber and dagger followed, and finally everything was permanently stored behind the library. I wilted into the chair.

Fanny came bustling in. "What's all this noise?" she asked. Seeing me in a state of collapse, she added with real concern, "Why are you so pale? What happened? You look terrible!"

I told her the story. She was filled with admiration. From that moment on I had her total and lasting devotion. She brought me aspirin and tea, fussed over me, and eventually succeeded in making me relax.

The soldiers arrived half an hour later. Mrs. Müller had been happy to meet them and chat about Cologne. They searched the house, did not find anything, and left. It was a complete anticlimax. Fortunately Madi and the children had gone for a walk. I was glad they were not in the house when the soldiers came.

The dressmaker's neighbor, poor man, was shot that evening with many others. It was only by God's good grace that Alex and I were not executed with him. We had survived miraculously. If I had not needed to get out of the house and go to the dressmaker's, we all would have died.

———□———

The Gestapo could not find a trace of the two men who killed Heydrich, and they were furious. The reign of terror lengthened. Hitler was beside himself as Heydrich had been one of his favorites. He was furious at the murder and doubly furious at the Gestapo's inefficiency. He decided that he himself would teach the Czech nation a lesson. From the compounded rage of his diseased mind sprang the tragedy of Lidice.

Lidice was a small village a short distance from Prague. It had only a few farms. Most of the male inhabitants worked in the nearby coal mines of Kladno. No one knew why Lidice had been singled out. It was a humble, quiet little place. Rumors spread that perhaps the Germans suspected the villagers of harboring members of the resistance. More likely the choice fell on the innocent little town by chance, when some nameless bureaucrat stabbed a map of Czecho-slovakia with his pencil.

Before dawn on June 10, 1942, at about four o'clock in the morning while the hard-working residents slept, legions of Gestapo men surrounded Lidice in the dark. Then they stormed the town. Rifle butts and hobnailed boots broke through doors, and dazed victims woke to find black-uniformed demons at their bedsides.

Frightened and horrified, men, women, and children were dragged into the main square. Before leaving their houses, the villagers were ordered in loud voices to take everything of value with them—their money, bank books, savings-account books, and all jewelry. In the early morning darkness shattered by searchlights and fear, confusion was total, children screamed, dogs howled. No one knew for certain what to expect; most must have guessed. Driven by the muzzles of rifles, all obeyed without resistance.

Once assembled on the main square, the population was divided. The men and boys over sixteen were put at one end of the village square while the women and children faced them at the opposite side. No one was given even a moment to say good-bye before the women and children were loaded into buses and taken to Kladno.

The males were herded into the barnyard of a large farm. Then they were taken into the garden nearby, stood against a wall in groups of ten, and shot. Once the shooting began, those remaining realized what their fate was to be. The village priest led them in the prayers for the dying until he, too, went to his death with the last few. There were no survivors.

Trucks were brought in to pick the town clean. Animals, provisions, and anything of conceivable value were loaded on and driven away. Can after can of gasoline was then splashed in the houses and ignited. The next day the slave laborers from the nearby Theresienstadt concentration camp were transported to the ruins that had been Lidice to bury the executed men and boys left in piles in what had been a quiet farm garden.

Gigantic tractors then pushed still-burning building ruins onto the grave site. The village was leveled to the ground so that, as Hitler had promised when he gave the original order, not the slightest trace of Lidice was left. No one would know that it had ever existed or what had happened to it.

The women and children held in Kladno were sorted. The children were taken from their mothers and parceled out to various concentration camps, as were the women of Lidice. An exception was made for a number of very young, blue-eyed, blond children. They were shipped to Germany for adoption. Four pregnant women were taken to Prague, where their babies were killed as they were born. The mothers were then sent to the Ravensbrück concentration camp. Most of the women and children died in the camps, suffering a slow, miserable death unlike that which had been inflicted with merciful brevity on their men.

Only a tiny group survived. Until the moment of release after the end of the war they had no knowledge of what had happened to their town or to their husbands, fathers, brothers, or children. Women whose children had had fair hair wandered back and forth across postwar Germany in the hope of finding their missing babies. For all but three the hope was in vain.

The Czech infants had been absorbed into German families and had soon forgotten their parents and their mother tongue. Through the years they had remained imprisoned in ignorance, believing themselves true Germans and unaware of their real origins, their history, and their true nationality. Some of those mothers went on searching fruitlessly for their beautiful little babies for many years, the saddest, most miserable victims of all Lidice's tortured ones.

Hitler's promise was not realized. After the war the site of Lidice was made a national monument. A rose garden covers the mass grave with a memorial to the martyrs. Peaceful meadows are all around. The new village of Lidice was built nearby.

As the news of the massacre spread, the people of Czechoslovakia were stricken with horror. The Germans had reached an extreme of inhumanity. We had thought that we had experienced everything, but we were wrong. Yet, if the purpose of this viciousness was to intimidate some weaker member of the populace into revealing the whereabouts of Heydrich's assassins, the slaughter of Lidice was an utter failure. No one talked. No one said a word.

The Gestapo lost that one. They had no alternative but to raise the stakes. An official proclamation was published in the newspapers stating that unless the murderers of Heydrich were delivered to the

Gestapo within two weeks, every tenth man in every village and town would be immediately executed.

We could not believe that even the Nazis were capable of such wholesale slaughter; to murder every tenth man in each town and village meant killing hundreds of thousands of innocent people. The physical operation itself would have been huge; we did not know how expert the Germans had become in disposing of corpses. Still we prayed the Gestapo would never find those two brave men.

On June 18, Alex was in Prague. As he was walking to his office in Stepanska Street, rapid machine-gun fire erupted nearby. Hundreds of SS and Gestapo men were massed around the Karel Boromeus Greek Orthodox Church. No one knew why they were shooting at a church. Alex was told later that the two men who killed Heydrich were hiding there with five other agents who had been parachuted in from England with them.

After shooting Heydrich on May 27, Kubis and Gabcik had gotten away safely. They were hidden by several members of the Czech resistance, namely a Mrs. Moravec and a Mr. Zelenka, who contacted the clergy of the Greek Orthodox church in Prague, Bishop Gorazd, Father Petrek, and Father Cikl. They agreed to give sanctuary to the two fugitives and their companions.

The group was moved into a forgotten crypt that could be opened only by lifting a certain stone in front of the altar. The crypt was small, constructed to hold only a few coffins, and the men had to live there in great discomfort. As the space was dank and cold, the occupants needed heavy blankets, sweaters, and gloves day and night. They remained for more than three weeks in that stone tomb. Czech boys brought food and Mrs. Moravec did their washing.

The church was searched by the Gestapo several times without the men being discovered. Then the Nazis got hold of Karel Curda, one of the original group from England, and persuaded him to talk.

Though he did not know where the two comrades who killed Heydrich were, he did provide the Germans with the names of the Moravec and Zelenka families as members of the Czech resistance. The Gestapo burst in on Mrs. Moravec, who with great courage took poison and died rather than be forced to betray the brave men. Mr. Zelenka also had time to take poison.

This left the Nazis with young Ata Moravec, one of the boys who had transported food and water. He was taken to the Gestapo headquarters where he was brutally tortured, and when his resistance was at its lowest, he was stupefied with alcohol and presented with his mother's head floating in a fish tank. Broken by pain and shock, he finally gave his torturers a clue where to look for Heydrich's assassins.

The Gestapo surrounded the church. The shooting Alex heard had no effect. High-pressure hoses were brought in and water poured into the crypt through a small ventilation hole. The Czechs fired back, killing several Gestapo men and wounding many more. The battle lasted for hours, until the Czechs in the crypt ran out of ammunition. Those who had poison capsules swallowed them, and the rest used their last bullets to kill themselves. Thus, when the Gestapo entered the crypt, all they found were seven dead bodies.

They arrested Bishop Gorazd, Father Cikl, and Father Petrek, who were brought to trial and hanged. Jan Sonenvend, the leader of the congregation, and his wife and children were all shot. Young Ata Moravec was sentenced to death and executed. The entire families of the seven soldiers were executed, down to the last member.

Kubis came from a particularly large family, with seven or eight brothers and sisters who had spouses and children. All were shot, except one sister who was having a baby in a hospital and somehow escaped notice. We met her several years later and found her a most pathetic figure, unable to come to terms in any constructive way with the world that had crippled her life.

Another of the dead men (I believe it was Gabcik) had in his pocket a snapshot of a young woman to whom he had been engaged before the war and his escape to England. Though the girl had since married another man and had two babies, the Gestapo tracked her down by way of the photograph, arrested her and her husband, and executed both of them and also shot the two infants.

On June 24, as a punishment for the Czech nation and a deterrent to any future rebellion, the Germans destroyed the village of Lezaky. Following the pattern of the Lidice massacre they murdered the men and boys over sixteen, scattered the women and children into concentration camps, and sent the blond babies to Germany for adoption to swell the size of the pool of future soldiers.

The Gestapo was totally berserk. It was as though something strange, dark, and malicious had broken through into the contemporary world from a primitive layer of consciousness. The more blood the Germans shed, the more blood they desired to shed; the more of us they killed, the more they hated us. However, while the Nazis had let themselves become monstrous, on another level they remained calm, cool, and organized.

This combination of primordial brutality and modern efficiency was what terrified us most. Thousands of Czechs were executed and tens of thousands more were herded into camps, the names of which to this day cause shivers of dread across the civilized world: Buchenwald, Mauthausen, Dachau, Auschwitz, Treblinka. They were innocent victims of Nazism whose sufferings and deaths were not caused by their own actions but by the certainty of the Nazis of their own superiority and by their ruthlessness in their determination to rule the world.

There was no frame of reference or context that allowed Alex, me, our friends, and all other Czechs to understand what was happening around us. Nothing like this had ever happened in the modern world. None of us knew if we would be alive the next day, or who was going to be tortured, executed, or taken to a concentration camp.

8

LIFE WENT ON

June and July 1942 passed in this atmosphere of terror. By August the worst seemed to be over. People were still being arrested and executed, but executions were not held every day. It appeared that the Gestapo was easing off.

Life continued. We had to go on living, coping with shortages, loving each other, raising children, finding beauty and humor where we could. In the same way the Nazi occupiers of our country had created a new way of death, we Czechs, like the people in other conquered countries, were faced with creating in response a whole new way of life. This was our greatest achievement. Under the lash of hatred we learned to be survivors, true victors.

Living under such oppression was not easy, especially for a generation that had been raised in the sunny life of our democratic republic before the war and could not forget the horror of March 15, 1939, when thousands of German soldiers goose-stepped through our cities with rifles and bayonets. That March day our ordeal and our reeducation commenced.

The first benefit, if one can speak of benefits of evil, was in being thrown back upon ourselves. With the cacophony of the Germans' arrival ringing in our ears, the nation experienced a great upwelling of trust. Adversity united us as never before; helping each other became the most natural of acts. We found strength in our innocence, in the clear, certain knowledge that the Nazis were despicable aggressors who unquestionably would be defeated eventually. We knew we would be free again.

It was this feeling of national unity and national pride, together with a feeling of moral superiority, that carried the Czech people through the war and the horrors of occupation. It gave us the inner strength to survive. It was a positive, continuous experience in our hearts, generating the energy needed to continue resistance. Many times I found that it did not matter how great our suffering was; the knowledge of being right would not let us despair, not for a moment. We went on with life, trying to make the best of it, trying to be kind and gentle with each other.

What marked the social existence of the Czech people at this trying time was the fierce feeling of solidarity that arose from a collective belief in our ultimate triumph. The loss of freedom was painful and immensely difficult to adjust to. It was not only the loss of national independence that was hard to accept but also the loss of all personal liberties. As individual men and women, we had no rights whatsoever.

Even in our homes we were never safe. The Nazis arranged things so that even when not physically present, they somehow—call it spiritually—occupied all our spaces. Whenever a car stopped in front of our house, whenever someone unexpectedly knocked on the door, in the back of our minds was always one thought, "It may be the Gestapo." Day or night, we were never sure, never free of danger, never free of fear, never completely alone by ourselves. They could walk into our homes and arrest us whenever they pleased and we could do nothing to stop it. This new fact in our lives was hardest to accept.

Only slowly and painfully we adjusted to seeing the sinister black uniforms in our streets. Equally difficult was to adjust to the form of persecution that affected everyone most directly—and literally—at the gut level: imposed food shortages. It was especially hard for city people who seldom had enough milk for their children or enough food for themselves. Here the solidarity of the Czechs was critical. Urban dwellers ventured into the country to find a relative or a good farmer willing to sell them an extra dozen eggs or a few pounds of flour. That made all the difference. This was dangerous for the buyer as well as the seller, because if caught, both would be instantly transported to a concentration camp. But people were good to each other during the war. Everyone took risks for everyone else.

Everything changed after the Germans came. At the same time, everything seemed to be the same, at least superficially. People went to work every morning and children attended school, but the quality and meaning of these activities were different. The enjoyment of life had completely vanished. Existence was a burden to be borne, not a grace to be enjoyed. The nation was mourning the loss of its power, its freedom, mourning its temporary death.

Many comforts of everyday life that had been taken for granted were gone, and this kind of absence spoke silently of deep political privations. We were immobilized. Early in the occupation, the normal flood of automobile traffic disappeared from country lanes and city streets. In their place was mass transit—trains and buses for longer trips, and streetcars for getting around in the town. Though business people could use their cars in the city only for the purpose of conducting business affairs, soon even they started having difficulties with the gasoline shortage.

Alex had a large Studebaker and before long despaired of finding sufficient gas to satisfy its American-size appetite. He got together with his driver, Frank, and some men from the transportation department at Biochema who with much relish, good humor, and mutual enjoyment redesigned the car's propulsion system.

They installed in the trunk a large kettle with a little chimney that actually converted charcoal into a gas that powered the motor. It worked surprisingly well, though not perfectly, to be sure. The disadvantage was that the kettle needed to be refilled every thirty miles or so, and therefore an amazing heap of bags filled with charcoal was piled on the roof of the car.

Because it did not use gasoline, Alex was allowed to take it on his trips to Prague. Unfortunately, the charcoal-burning Studebaker could not make it up hills. To assist the new power source, passengers had to get out and push, creating a sort of human low gear that the driver could shift into when necessary.

We discovered this need to add person power to horsepower the first time Frank drove Alex home to Richky. The descent into the valley was easy, but getting up the long, steep hill the next morning was impossible. Everyone around the farm was called to push, but without success. Finally Standa, our stable boy, brought Fuksa and Nonyk, our strongest pair of horses, to supplement both the engine and the people. The picture of the Studebaker, all but flattened by its gigantic load of coal, being pushed by my husband in a business suit and by the farm workers, and being pulled majestically up the incline by two stoic horses, remained with me for a long time.

That was the first and the last time Frank brought the rebuilt Studebaker into the valley. Poor Frank. Sometimes his face got so black from charcoal that he looked more like a chimney sweep than a car driver. Still, it was a great advantage for Alex, as his frequent trips to Prague were less tiring. Anyway, Frank did not really mind.

The occupation of our country turned every act into a small battle against evil and every object into a symbol of either defeat or victory. Children's clothing was an example. Sometimes I went along on Alex's excursion to Prague to visit friends and relatives and check shops for warm clothing or shoes for the girls, although the stores there were usually as empty as those in Brno. It was a real fight to keep the children warmly dressed for winter.

Grown-ups fared better because they either possessed or bought quantities of clothing when the Germans invaded our country. But the children grew fast, and the occupation lasted more than six years. Even the coupons that were issued were frequently useless since the stores were usually empty. Mothers found a solution by picking apart their old outfits and making little dresses or coats from large ones. It was unbelievable what our marvelous dressmakers could accomplish.

Shoes were a far worse problem. It seemed that I had no sooner found a pair for Evie than she complained that they were too small even though I always bought them one size too large. Whenever a new supply of shoes arrived at a store, so many potential customers were waiting that the most characteristic social group, the line, would form. Only a few people at a time were allowed to enter the store. After they made their purchase, they were let out and a few more were let in. I often stood in line for hours, shivering in the cold wind, only to be told that the supply was gone. Defeated, I would have to swallow my anger and return home empty-handed.

Women were sold shoes with wooden soles, for which fewer coupons were needed. I had enough shoes from before the war, as did Fanny, but Madi announced that she desperately needed another pair. She came home with some sporty-looking lace boots with wooden soles that did not bend at all. Watching her trying bravely to walk in those inflexible shoes I felt sure she would fall and break her ankle.

Finally I could not bear the sight of her discomfort any longer. We sorted through my shoes to find a pair that would fit her. One did, with the help of inserts and heavy socks. Wearing them, she walked a little bit better but was still uncomfortable.

One day when Evie was in school and Janie was asleep, Madi invited me to her room to show me something. When she opened her wardrobe, I was amazed to see twelve pairs of beautiful, elegant shoes, each a different color, some low-heeled, some high-heeled. All were brand new and positively shone with unblemished splendor. With great pride she showed me each pair, one by one, explaining that she had bought them in Paris and naming the shop.

"Each month I spend one day cleaning them," she said with a tear of love in her voice as if they were her children. I could not believe my eyes and ears. I thought she must be crazy and all but said so.

"Madi, why aren't you wearing them? You suffer so much in those uncomfortable shoes. You'd feel much better walking in shoes that fit you well and have a leather sole. You won't be so tired."

But she insisted, more than a little scandalized, "Oh, I couldn't do that. These shoes are for the city, not the country. I paid so much for them and I want to preserve them until after the war."

"But you could buy new ones when the war is over. Please use them now."

But Madi had made up her mind. Madi, who was otherwise so practical and sensible, continued to wear my shoes, two sizes too large, or her wooden-soled boots and every month spent one day cleaning her treasures. Her Parisian shoes were a symbol of better and more enjoyable times, and subconsciously she believed that by preserving them untouched she was preserving the spirit of those years of freedom and thus speeding their return. Some essential part of Madi was at liberty as long as the Nazis did not get her shoes.

Stockings were another great worry; we could not get any at all, either for adults or for the children. Nylons did not exist at that time, only silk stockings. It was a calamity when I came home from shopping or visiting with friends and found a run in my hose.

But again, people were inventive. In Brno many small establishments started up that could repair those runs with the help of a small, cleverly designed machine. After the treatment the stockings looked like new. Mending was expensive but necessary in those times.

The stockings problem was even worse for children. Summer in Czechoslovakia, when children could go outside bare-legged, lasted only three or four months. The rest of the time little legs had to be kept warm. The girls used to wear a combination of stockings and panties, which garment in its nylon version started to be worn by women in the 1960s under the name of pantyhose. In no time at all the girls' cotton pantyhose had been so frequently repaired that there was none of the original material left on the knees. I spent days fixing their stockings.

Then Evie's pantyhose started to have torn seats as well. I could not understand the cause until one day I was in the village on business and picked up Evie from school so we could go home together. When we passed the wheat field and were on top of the steep hill, Evie said, "Mommy, would you like to get home faster? I'll show you how."

She stepped off the trail to where the slope was covered with dry pine needles. She sat down, pushed herself off, and with a whoosh was at the bottom. My eyes nearly popped out as in that instant the mystery of the torn pantyhose was solved. We had a serious talk, and her fast descents into the valley stopped, the result being a considerable improvement in the condition of her hose.

Other kinds of underwear and warm sweaters were in short supply as well. Before Heydrich arrived in Prague, when restrictions were less rigorously imposed, I managed to accompany Alex on business trips to Vienna. We stayed downtown in the beautiful Imperial Hotel, and nearby I discovered a small shop selling only children's wear. I was surprised to find that the stores in Vienna seemed to have a good supply of everything we so desperately needed. I had my coupons with me but was doubtful the Austrians would sell me anything since Vienna was now part of the German Reich, and our coupons in the protectorate were different.

I walked in and was met by a very kind, sweet old lady, who was certainly no Nazi. She accepted my coupons without hesitation and sold me anything I wanted: lovely warm sweaters, pantyhose, some socks, and underwear. Impressed by her friendliness, I worried aloud that she might have trouble presenting Czech coupons to the authorities in Vienna. She said that I was not to be concerned, that nobody would notice the difference. I felt as though I had won a fortune in a lottery.

Soon afterward, a friend from Letovice, an owner of a closed carpet factory, came to visit us and brought a substantial quantity of wool yarn as a house present. It was an unexpected and much-needed gift, another minute triumph. The yarn was pure wool and came in two colors, navy and wine. I learned to knit and I knitted all kinds of garments throughout the war. We were fortunate to receive such a treasure, even though the color of most of the girls' sweaters, gloves, and pantyhose was restricted to navy or wine from that time on.

When the weather was very cold the children wore slacks, and so did I. We had central heating, and our house was sufficiently warm all winter, as were most of the municipal buildings and schools. Enough coal was available, a great blessing, since the cold would have been doubly punishing for people suffering from malnutrition.

Above all, I loved to have a fire in our fireplace. Fanny used to start it early in the day, before breakfast. Fuel was not a problem as we had lots of wood. It was enormously cheering and encouraging to come into the living room every morning and hear the friendly crackling of the fire. Even during the worst moments of my life I always found a degree of peace and hope, sitting in my easy chair, watching bright flames dancing along the big logs.

From our childhood, both Alex and I had loved classical music and opera. We had collected many fine albums and records which we treasured. We spent many evenings in front of the fireplace with the lights off, listening together to the endless flow of beauty of the music of Chopin, Smetana, and Dvorak. The Czech composers reminded us again and again of who and what we were. In those difficult years, our favorite piece was Beethoven's Pastoral Symphony, which seems to be peace incarnate.

The radio furnished both entertainment and information. We had a choice of several stations including one from London on short waves. When the broadcast day of the BBC was over, we turned to Radio Brno or Prague, where musical programs were alternated with plays and educational programs. Czech stations carried many anti-Nazi and patriotic messages that were obvious to the careful listener.

Hidden meanings perfectly understandable to Czechs were everywhere, not only on the radio but also in the newspapers. A major part of our newly created art of surviving consisted of learning to be masters of double-talk and hiding information between ordinary phrases. Nazis did not understand it, nor did they seem to have the feel for it. I remember seeing a romantic poem printed in a daily paper. The first words of each line read in sequence formed a message to the nation not to lose hope, assuring us that our invaders would be defeated and that we would be free again.

One learned quickly to attend to those nooks and corners of everyday life where one could find encouragement and new strength. Those messages were normally missed by the global consciousness of the German world conquerors. The small and insignificant events that make up a daily routine rallied to our support and helped us communicate in special ways decipherable only by Czechs. We all became deeply and consciously appreciative of the flexibility and richness of the Czech language.

People developed extensive social lives during the occupation. I do not mean that they indulged in more entertainment or that a surge of frivolity and superficiality grasped us. Rather, our national life was suddenly saturated with the warmth of deep friendship based more often than not on a comradeship that arose between us as we shared rumors of new German defeats.

The country was transfigured by the spirit of hospitality. Richky became a favorite place for people to visit, not only to those who were formally invited but to all sorts of others who came. Many dropped by just to spend a day, to be refreshed, or simply to say hello.

I especially remember one business friend of Alex's, an older gentleman who was a widower and manager of a large distillery in Brno. One Sunday afternoon he stopped by and we invited him to stay for dinner. Wanting to repay our hospitality, he arrived two weeks later with a basket of mushrooms that he himself had gathered in the forest. We asked him again to share the evening meal

with us. Fanny and I carefully inspected each mushroom and prepared a triumphant mushroom omelet with fresh eggs. The event
itself was of no special importance. Yet the firelight, the smell of
cooking, soft laughter, gratitude that the old gentleman would not
have to be alone that night, the bubbling happiness of the girls, and
the chatter of the stream outside combined into a moment of calm
and companionship that symbolized concretely the goodness of life in
spite of tragedy. Such an evening could keep us going for a full week.
After that our mushroom collector came often, always bringing a
basketful of mushrooms with him.

There were many poisonous mushrooms in our forests and I was
afraid of them. My cousin Zdenek, who was also a frequent visitor,
told us a "mushroom story" that he swore really happened, an example of tales rendered around our dinner table during the war.

Before the universities were closed Zdenek had been studying
medicine, and many of his friends were doctors. One of them had a
summer cottage in the forest. Several of his colleagues decided to pay
him a surprise visit. He and his wife were enormously happy to have
company, as was everyone during the war, but they had nothing to
serve for dinner except a few eggs and some bread.

The group went into the forest and in a short time returned with
a basket of mushrooms. Some of them looked suspicious to the lady
of the house, but her husband, the doctor, assured her they were all
perfectly safe. To prove his point he gave a small piece of mushroom
omelet to their little dog who ate it with a great relish. After everyone was satisfied that the mushrooms were safe to eat, dinner was
served.

They hardly finished eating when the maid came into the room
carrying the dog in her arms and crying bitterly. The dog was dead.
Everyone was seized with panic, except the doctor-host.

He got out his black bag and expeditiously pumped out the contents of his guests' stomachs, ladies first, then gentlemen. An hour
and a half later, when he had done nearly all of his friends, it
suddenly occurred to him that he himself felt fine.

He called the maid and questioned her how the dog had died,
asking, "Did he have cramps? Did he suffer a lot?"

"Oh no, doctor," she replied, "the poor darling was dead after a
truck ran him over."

Alex and I were always happy to see Zdenek arrive. He had a cheerful, sunny disposition that made him a pleasure to be with. His story, however, did not make Fanny and me less careful with the mushrooms.

Another pair of dear friends who dropped in often were the Pernickas. The husband had been a colonel and veterinarian in the army and the manager of the state Lippizaner breeding farm in Slovakia. After Hitler partitioned our country and made Slovakia independent, the breeding farm was closed, and the colonel returned to Brno and found a job in private business. Animals had been his life and he missed horseback riding a great deal. We would saddle a horse for him and he would disappear into the hills, which was why he enjoyed visiting Richky so much.

His wife was full of wonderful energy and compassion. Whenever she arrived, before the front door was closed behind them, her rich alto voice would echo through the house asking, "Zdena, how many people have you invited for dinner today? How many trout do you need?" Then she spent all afternoon fishing, and without fail she always brought in more fish than I had asked for. She loved fishing as much as her husband loved horseback riding.

Sometimes she took Evie along on her fishing expeditions. She even bought the child a fishing rod and taught her how to use it. I have never forgotten how Evie was excited when she caught her first two fish. She did not allow them to be killed, proclaimed them her friends, and put them into the swimming pool.

I told her they would not be able to live there, that they needed to go back to the brook, but she insisted and promised she would take good care of them, would feed them, and visit them for a talk. I had hoped for a miracle, but one day, a week later, Evie came in crying with the news that both of her friends were dead. She was in mourning for several days. After that, whenever she caught a trout, she always let it go back into the brook.

Planning meals and cooking were a constant headache with many guests coming, but Fanny and I became used to it. Each winter we killed a pig, a process I dreaded and hated. It was necessary, however, for feeding so many people.

First a permit had to be obtained and a butcher engaged. Then, when the bloody deed was done, the pig was cleaned and cut into halves, the insides having been cut out. Both halves were hung in the barn until the German inspector came to weigh them in order to establish the number of meat coupons we were to lose.

Many people cheated. Most slaughtered two pigs, hid one, and left the other for the inspector. A farmer in a nearby village made the catastrophic mistake of doing this. He killed two pigs and hung up two halves. Each had a tail. The German inspector noticed the second tail immediately and the poor farmer was imprisoned.

I never became involved in any illegal dealings in meat after my first attempt, the one that Evie reported to the Nazi doctor when she was sick. That close call convinced me that the risk was not worth it. The killing of a pig usually meant the loss of meat coupons up to September. For a while we had plenty of meat, some of which would freeze naturally in the winter's cold. The butcher fixed us ham, sausages, and all kinds of salamis, so it was like the protein-rich old times. Come May, however, the meat would be all gone, and so would the coupons. The only protein available was on the black market. Two of the butchers in the village would let me have a piece of meat for a little more money, but that was about all. As small as these purchases were, I always worried that I might be caught. I did not do it often. The anguish was not worth it.

We built two hothouses in the gardens and had fresh vegetables even in winter, a blessing. In the summer we had chickens and ducklings, though not too many as we did not have much grain to feed them, but we managed.

Our guests' expectations were modest and easy to satisfy. Even when I returned their visit by going to elegant Prague, they frequently spoke of how much they had enjoyed our specialty: cold, fresh buttermilk in large glasses and potatoes cut in half and baked. The resulting golden puffed-up delicacy was served with butter into which garlic and salt were added. For city people who had not tasted any dairy products at all since the war started, this simple meal was a culinary masterpiece.

Fanny was expert at preparing many different stews, casseroles, and meat loaves from modest resources. Occasionally I let her roast a chicken. Her *kolacky*, little cakes with different fruit fillings, were delicious, and only for special celebrations could we afford to bake even a cake. Many times I blessed the day I had hired Fanny. She was invaluable as a help in planning our meager meals and arranging tempting and tasteful menus for ourselves and our guests.

Flour and sugar were also rationed. Peter, our miller, started running the mill at night as well as during the day. The producers were allowed to keep only a small quantity of wheat, so farmers came to Peter at night to grind the wheat they kept against regulations. They needed the flour for their relatives and friends in the city who otherwise would have gone hungry. Thus the mill with its dripping wheel clacked on in the starlight as well as the sunlight—during the day officially, and during the night, shall we say, less officially.

As the war progressed, shortages became more noticeable and frequent. From time to time there was even a shortage of beer. As people got a good supply of inexpensive ersatz coffee in their rations, beer lovers attempted to turn it into beer. I never tried the method, but Grandma did. She tasted it somewhere, thought it was quite good, acquired the recipe, and set about preparing her first batch, an adventurous undertaking.

Some of her beer turned out well, some badly, tasting like ersatz coffee at its worst, which is pretty wretched. The alcoholic content varied greatly, sometimes high, sometimes none. The bottles were unpredictable to open. Once Grandma opened one in the dining room and it came out like a geyser, spouting up to the ceiling. The next one she opened in the kitchen, and it turned out to be completely flat. But in spite of the ups and downs Grandma had made up her mind that she had to master this complicated procedure. She continued to manufacture her beer throughout the war.

Toilet soap was of much worse quality than before the war, but there was enough for everyone. Only poor-grade detergent was available for washing laundry. Both soap and detergent were rationed.

The history of the Czechoslovak people, even before the chaos of the German invasion, had been full of hardship and danger. We had to learn how to laugh at the barbaric and inhuman behavior of our conquerors. During the Nazi occupation many jokes were told to relieve tension and reassert our simple humanity. I remember two.

When the Germans invaded our country, a Protectorate was declared, which is a fancy name for a conquest. A wandering Gypsy came upon a farm where many chickens pecked and cackled around the yard. The Gypsy, no doubt hungry like the rest of us, caught one and quickly stuffed it under his jacket. The farmer was looking out the window and saw it. Furious, he shouted at the Gypsy, "Hey, you stole my chicken!" But the Gypsy innocently replied, "You are wrong, mister. I didn't steal it; I took it under my protectorate."

The second joke is from the period of the "Heydrichiad," the time of the executions. Every man and every woman in the country had been killed except the very last two Czechs. They were brought to the place of execution where they were tied to two posts side by side. The firing squad had checked their rifles and were just about to raise them when suddenly a German soldier on a motorcycle skidded up before the officer in charge and thrust an important-looking document into his hands.

The officer opened it, read it carefully, and after some great deliberation announced in a stern, Teutonic way to the prisoners, "I have just received an order from our Führer. Our great leader in his endless compassion, as a special grace, has changed your sentence from shooting to hanging. Therefore, by his authority, I hereby proclaim that both of you are sentenced to be hanged."

One Czech smiled and winked at the other and said, "See, what did I tell you? They're running out of ammunition."

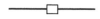

I found great comfort in the company of my girls. They were completely free of the evil that probed at us from all sides. I loved to read fairy tales to them, stories that I enjoyed as much as they did. I also taught them to sing the Czech national songs and told them stories of the old Czech kings and queens.

Usually they finished by Evie promoting Janie from playmate to queen, dressing her appropriately and having her seated in a high-chair throne, while she herself served as a lady-in-waiting. It was quite amusing to watch them, as the queen against all rules of tradition had to obey her lady-in-waiting unconditionally.

Alex and I had to be careful not to talk in front of Evie about our difficulties or listen to Radio London in front of her. We never knew what she might repeat, nor did I want to burden her young innocent heart with the problems of occupation. I wanted both girls to be as happy as possible.

It is hard to describe what it was like to live under circumstances where every detail, every act, and every word might suddenly cause one's death. Fear can destroy one's sense of proportion. We lived in a world that suffered from gross magnification; everything was too large, too heavy, too significant. We learned to preserve our spirit, otherwise we would die.

Sometimes, when I could not sleep at night, I remembered the beauty and charm of our life before the German invasion and occupation. It was hard to believe that in a little more than three years such a drastic change could have occurred. Four years before, we had been in Baska, Yugoslavia, swimming, sunbathing, and having a wonderful time, believing that nothing bad could happen to us. Those days seemed so very long ago.

9

DESPAIR

The weather in the spring and summer of 1942 was unusually beautiful. The friendly sun smiled nearly every day as if God wanted to make our suffering easier to bear, wanted to comfort our sorrowful hearts. Time passed slowly.

The execution of Chairman Wenzl affected both of us deeply. Alex lost some of his boyishness and lightheartedness. Living and working under the constant threat of arrest and execution for such a long period of time made him more serious and also more compassionate toward the suffering of others. We became closer than ever before. The possibility of losing each other made us appreciate every moment we spent together. We never talked about it, but it was constantly on our minds. His trips to Prague had become especially difficult to bear.

Since the death of our dear friend, Alex had to travel to Prague more frequently. On these trips he became better acquainted with Dr. Antonin Srba, chief executive of the corporation that owned half of Biochema. In August, we invited him, his wife Manka, and their two children, Jana and little Tony, to Richky for several weeks of vacation. The children were good playmates for my Janie as they all were about the same age.

My greatest pleasure was watching them, their happy faces, their

131

joy and laughter when they were playing in the orchard or swimming in the pool. After all that suffering of the past months it was so refreshing to hear young, happy voices, a promise of better times to come. Every morning we went riding, and soon Manka and Tony became as fond of our green forests as we were. They were charming, outgoing people who were full of optimism. Alex and I became very fond of them.

In the afternoons we swam, relaxing around the swimming pool and enjoying the peaceful beauty of our valley. Sometimes Manka, Madi, the children, and I went to a nearby clearing to pick wild strawberries. There were so many that year. It did not take long to fill our baskets. The children enjoyed these outings immensely. They always ate more of the delicious berries than they put in their baskets. And the aroma was unbelievable. Even many years later when I closed my eyes I could see that sunlit clearing in our woods and smell those aromatic berries.

And then we got a reward. After a simple dinner we had a delicious dessert: wild strawberries with whipped cream. That was a delicacy that I should not have allowed in the difficult war times since it caused a shortage in the butter for my biweekly delivery to the Germans. But we needed some brightness in our drab, sorrowful lives, even if it was only a dish of wild strawberries with a spoonful of whipped cream. We had a peaceful and restful time with our friends. It was good to be alive.

After the Srbas left, toward the end of August, Alex came home one evening gray with worry. Following a tense, silent dinner he took me upstairs to the library, a private and secluded room on the third floor. Carefully controlling his voice, Alex told me that sixteen employees at Biochema had been arrested that day.

Suddenly I felt dizzy and sank back in my chair. My first thought was the radio transmitter in Ivan's department. I asked in great alarm, "Is it the transmitter? Was Ivan arrested? Is he all right?" I was terrified. All the people at Biochema were our dear friends. What was going to happen?

"Ivan was not arrested," Alex answered. "Surprisingly, it wasn't the radio transmitter at all. The Gestapo didn't find it and we had already dismantled it this afternoon. It was the silliest thing you can imagine." And he told me the story. There was a messenger girl who carried the interoffice mail between the factory in Modrice and the Biochema branch near Prague. That morning when she arrived in Brno she ran into a Gestapo checkpoint at the railway station. In her briefcase the Nazis found subversive literature and a list of names of people sympathetic to the Czech cause. She was arrested immediately. The Gestapo arrived at Biochema within two hours, and the employees whose names were on the list were loaded into the Gestapo gray van and taken to Kounicovy Koleje. Alex was deeply afraid—almost certain—he would be arrested in the near future. He wanted to tell me what I should do if that happened.

He gave me two names. The first was Mr. Horky, the head of the Czech resistance in Brno. He was a very reliable friend who had access to information inside the Gestapo, which could be invaluable to me. Then I was to get to Prague and tell Tony Srba as well. Alex was businesslike, almost stern. He was sure that Tony and Mr. Horky would help. He ended by saying that he was sorry to frighten me and hoped that the arrangement would prove unnecessary. His voice faded and we sat in silence.

I did not sleep that night. The next day Alex went to work as usual. Nothing happened. Four days later five other people were arrested. Ten days later seven more were taken to prison, bringing the total to twenty-eight. Alex was still free. The strain was crippling. I could not get used to saying a final farewell to my husband every morning and then getting through the day trying not to wonder if he was dead yet.

September crawled by. In October there were no arrests at Biochema. Slowly we relaxed a little, barely beginning to believe that this was the end of the Biochema purge.

November was a special month for our family. That year it was my twenty-ninth birthday and our tenth wedding anniversary. Alex and I both felt we needed to get away for a while. We decided to take the children to my mother's and go to Radhost in the Beskydy Mountains, where we had spent many happy days skiing before the war. The timing was good for Fanny and Madi as well. They were due some time off.

Before vacation, Alex had to go to Prague twice more. When he returned from his first trip he gave me a letter from Leo Koutny. It was the first communication we had had from our friends in Belgium since the war started. He wrote of the agony of the German invasion of Belgium and the present suffering there.

When I expressed surprise that Leo had dared to send such a truthful and critical letter, Alex said the letter had not come by mail but had been carried by a young woman employed at the former Czechoslovak Embassy in Brussels. She had promised to take Alex's answer back to Leo with her.

Alex went straight to his desk. When he finished his letter and showed it to me, I was stunned. He had written openly about Heydrich, Chairman Wenzl's execution, Lidice, the cruelty of the Gestapo, and the persecution of the Czech people. He could not have been more graphic or frank about his opinions.

I told him that he was demented to write like that after all that had happened. "And besides that," I added, "it's totally irresponsible."

Alex accused me of exaggerating. He stubbornly argued that the girl was a friend of Leo's and had brought a similar letter safely here. She would put Alex's letter into the diplomatic pouch, and that would be that. His calm logic was infuriating.

I replied that the letter must go to Prague first. I reminded him of what had happened to the Biochema messenger at the railway station. Something like that could happen to him.

"How can you take the chance of sending a letter like this?" I pleaded. "It's too risky!"

He was adamant. On Monday, ready for his trip to Prague, he put the letter into his briefcase, which was strapped to his saddle for the horseback ride to the outskirts of Brno where Frank was waiting as usual with the company car.

Alex was to ride his favorite horse, Jura, an excellent animal, handsome, well trained, good tempered, cooperative, and willing. That day when Alex went out to mount, Jura shied violently. He then pivoted away again and again, backed up, reared, and fidgeted. He did not want Alex to mount him.

Finally the groom had to call Peter, the miller, and the gardener to help. Between them they managed to subdue the horse so that Alex was able to get in the saddle. Then Jura would not go out through the gate. Again he turned, reared, backed up, and did everything a difficult horse can do to avoid going forward. He acted like a wild bronco.

I saw this commotion from the balcony and shouted down, "Alex, something's wrong with him. Don't go today. Stay home. If he throws you in the forest, you could be lying there hurt for hours before we find you!"

It occurred to Alex to back Jura out. He turned him several times, backed him up, and finally managed to trick him through the gate. The moment Jura was on the road, he turned and walked on as if nothing had happened. The whole business of mounting him and getting him out the gate had taken three quarters of an hour.

My fear that something drastic was about to happen lingered long after Jura and his rider had disappeared into the woods. Alex phoned me from his Brno office. He could not understand what had happened to the horse. All the way through the forest Jura was obedient and quiet.

The weather was beautiful on that second day of November. The sunlight was golden, the sky without a single cloud. It was warm for that time of year, almost summery. One can hear Dvorak describe such transparent, gilded Czechoslovak days in his music.

We were in the middle of harvesting apples. It had been a bountiful year and everyone was helping, including Madi and Evie, who was on a school holiday. Janie was playing nearby. We worked hard and were grateful for the distraction. The morning flew by.

After lunch everyone went back to the orchard. I was in the root cellar lining up the apples on the shelves when Fanny came to say that Frank was on the phone and wanted to talk to me. I went to the living room and picked up the phone.

Frank did not sound his usual cheerful self. Hesitantly, stumbling over his words, he said, "Mrs. Kapral, something terrible happened. I don't know how to tell you . . ."

The sky went dark and the ground shook under my feet. The glory of the day was stilled like a sound of a bell muffled. Beginning to tremble I asked, "What happened? Did you have a car accident? Is my husband all right? What happened?"

"No," Frank said, "there's been no accident, but . . . but . . . Mr. Kapral was arrested by the Gestapo and taken to Kounicovy Koleje."

The wall before me was blank. I stared at it. I saw nothing.

Here it was at last. I knew; my mind told me what had happened, the thing I had been most dreading, the inevitable, inescapable destiny. But my heart could not take it in. My body turned to ice. A black shrieking nightmare was breaking into the waking world. Then my intellect failed me. My mind seemed to rear and then collapse in upon itself. I was totally devoid of feeling—conscious, but conscious of nothing.

I hung up the phone calmly, went back down to the cellar, and continued putting apples on the shelves. There were so many, baskets and baskets full of them. They reminded me comfortingly of the baskets of potatoes I used to peel when I was a little girl in my mother's kitchen. "We had a good harvest this year." I thought, "It will be good to have so many apples during the winter. Alex likes apples. Alex! The Gestapo! Alex in their hands!" Another part of my being scoffed gently, murmuring, "That couldn't have happened. The arrests have eased off. The purges seem to be over. I must have dreamt it. Yes, that was it. It was a horrible dream."

Fanny's voice said softly as if from a great distance, "Madam, Frank told me. Don't you think you should come in the house? I'll make you a nice cup of tea. Shouldn't you lie down? What do you want me to do? Don't you think we should do something?"

I wished the chattering would stop. I had work to do; it was my job to put the apples away, lining them up one by one. I continued placing them carefully on the shelves, one layer after another, nice and neat. It was important to get them in straight rows. Tidiness and order were important. Grandfather had impressed that on the children.

This merciful emotional deadness lasted for half an hour. Then the censor in my soul cut off the anesthetic. The fact asserted itself, dreaminess vanished, and I was confronted with the monstrous reality. I put the apple in my hand in its place in the last row and slowly walked back into the house.

"What should I do now?" I wondered dully as practicality began to reassert itself. "What did Alex tell me to do? He told me to call Tony, and he told me to call Horky. I cannot just pick up the telephone and call the head of the resistance in Brno, of course. Who knows who would be listening? I will have to see him personally. I will have to go to Brno tomorrow."

And then my head snapped back as if I had been slapped across the face.

The letter! What had happened to the letter?

It was death. Where was that letter? If the Gestapo found it, Alex was doomed. They would shoot him as fast as they could cock their rifles. Ideas flooded my mind. Maybe Alex did not have it with him. I had seen him put it in his briefcase. Perhaps he had left the briefcase in the car and the Gestapo did not have it.

It may be all right. How could I find out?

A plan began to form in my mind. I would go to Brno first thing in the morning and search for the letter at Biochema. I realized that I could not call Alex's secretary and ask about it. I remembered hearing, under Frank's voice, a flat, faint humming. Someone else had been on the line. If the letter was in his car or even in his desk, I had to find it and destroy it whatever the risk. If someone else found it, Alex would be dead, and so would the children and I.

I then called Tony Srba in Prague as Alex had told me to do. It took half an hour before he came on the line. I told him what had happened, though I did not mention the letter. Apparently his phone was bugged, too, because he asked me with a cautious tone in his voice to come to Prague. I told him that I had to go to Brno the next day, but I would come the day after. He said, "I'll be expecting you," and hung up.

I sat in the living room utterly drained, trying to collect my thoughts and marshal my energy for the next step.

Our neighbor, Mrs. Müller, rushed in.

"Mrs. Kapral, I just heard what happened. I can't tell you how sorry I am. You must be in shock right now. You probably haven't thought about this, but when somebody is arrested, the Gestapo search the house. They'll be coming here, if not today, then tomorrow for sure, but I think they might come even today, so you'd better be ready for it. If there's anything you don't want them to see, give it to me and I'll put it into our house."

I looked at her, stupefied. I had not considered the possibility that we would be searched. I was overwhelmed by a combination of fear and thankfulness for this truly kind and even valiant offer. She was willingly making herself a party to anti-Nazi conspiracy. Fanny, Madi, and I rushed through the house collecting various items to take next door. There was not much, but I was sure it would make things worse for Alex if they found the slightest illegal thing in our home.

In the evening Frank came.

The first question I asked him was, "Do you have Alex's brief-case?"

"No," he said, "Mr. Kapral took it with him to the office." My heart sank.

He told me the story of the arrest. After lunch Frank had driven Alex from the Brno office to the factory at Modrice. On the way he noticed a small car that appeared to be following them. It seemed to keep pace with them. When Frank sped up, it sped up. When he slowed down, it slowed down. Neither Alex nor Frank attached much importance to it. Alex took the briefcase containing the letter with him and went to his office. Frank did not know what happened to the briefcase after that. He could only say that Alex had it with him when he left the car. Try as he might, he could not remember anything more about the briefcase or the letter.

Bedtime came. Alex's name had not been mentioned on the evening news. There was at least a little hope that they had not executed him yet. I did not sleep.

In the morning I got up early because I wanted to catch the first bus to Brno. I was getting ready to leave when Alex's secretary, Miss Kepak, arrived and—handed me the briefcase! The letter was inside! My hands shook as I inspected it carefully. God be thanked; the envelope was intact as far as I could see. I opened it quickly and found Alex's letter. I was flooded with relief. I put a match to it and ground the ashes to a powder, then learned the rest of the story.

Alex had gotten out of the car in front of the administrative building and walked to his office. Earlier he had been coerced by Nazi officials into sharing the office with a German manager, a Herr Gerstner, introduced, no doubt, to spy on him. Their desks were placed together, facing each other. Alex had walked into the office and threw his briefcase on his desk. It landed with the larger part on Gerstner's. The two turned to a discussion of factory problems.

The door opened and two men in business suits walked in. They looked like salesmen, and when Alex asked them what they wanted, one of them said, "Herr Kapral?" and held out his hand as for a handshake. Alex said, "Yes," and put out his own hand. A handcuff snapped around his wrist, the other arm was jerked up, and there was another snap. Alex was a prisoner.

The agent flashed a metallic badge and said, "Gestapo."

The briefcase was still lying on the two desks. Gerstner unobtrusively drew it toward himself so that it was lying altogether on his desk. Neither of the Gestapo men noticed. They wrapped Alex's overcoat around his chained hands, took him outside, shoved him into a small Gestapo car, and left.

Gerstner took the briefcase and drove to the main office in Brno. He went straight to Alex's secretary, gave her the briefcase and said, "I think Frau Kapral should have this and I think you'd better take it to her yourself. Do it first thing tomorrow morning."

I did not know if he had read the letter or had even opened the briefcase. In any case, Herr Gerstner was a gallant man. He took a big risk. I was always immensely grateful to him. He saved Alex's life. He proved that not all Germans were inhuman Nazi criminals. He was one of those Germans who disagreed with Hitler and actively helped the Czechs, even at peril of death, as Alex and I were about to find out.

The return of the briefcase did not alter the fact that Alex had been arrested and was now at the dreaded Kounicovy Koleje. To be sure, the danger of instant execution was somewhat lessened. There was a hope that he could be saved. Miss Kepak and I left for Brno together.

I went to see Alex's parents first. They were traumatized and felt the situation was hopeless. I stayed for a while and tried as best as I could to comfort them a little, and then I went to see Mr. Horky. He promised he would do everything he could to find out the reason for Alex's unexpected arrest. He asked me to come back in a few days.

I called home. Fanny answered the phone.

"Madam, the gentlemen from the Gestapo are here," she said. They arrived soon after I left. There were four of them there, looking for the safe, but Fanny told them she did not know where it was. When they came Janie was asleep and they did not disturb her.

I understood what she meant. The safe was in the nursery. When we built the house we had planned to make that particular room into a sort of den, so we put the safe there, but when Janie was born we found it was more practical to make a nursery of it. However, the safe had already been built into the wall, so it remained.

Fanny continued, "They have Mr. Kapral's keys to the safe and they're saying they won't leave until they find it."

I sensed that somebody was listening on the extension, so I said,

"Well, Fanny, I guess you don't know it, but the safe is in Janie's bedroom. Why don't you show it to them? Take down the picture opposite her bed and you will see it. There's nothing much in it, just some of my jewelry and some documents."

She said she would tell them. I knew they would not leave without finding it and I thought it would be better to show it to them and get them out of the house as soon as possible.

I hung up and ran to catch the bus home. When I arrived I hurried to the safe to see what they had taken. Although it had obviously been ransacked very thoroughly, everything appeared to be there.

I blessed Mrs. Müller for her warning. Thinking about her and the Gestapo I remembered the horse Jura and his performance on the day of Alex's arrest. He plainly had not wanted to carry Alex to Brno that day. Had he known that he would be led back to the stable riderless?

Fortunately, our radio happened to be out of order. The Gestapo would often set a household's radio dial on the London frequency and execute the entire family for listening to London.

After a while Madi came and asked to talk to me. She said first how unhappy she was that Alex had been arrested. Then she went on desperately, "Don't you think the Gestapo made a mistake? Maybe they wanted to arrest his brother Ivan and got it mixed up. Shouldn't I go to them and tell them that they should have arrested Ivan, that it was not your husband but Ivan who had the radio transmitter in his department?"

I was shocked. Trying to keep my voice level I said, "Madi, you can't do that. Listen, if they arrested Ivan, they would arrest us all, probably shoot us all. It would be terribly dangerous! And just think about their parents with both sons in prison. The shock of it would kill them. Don't even think about doing anything like that!"

She looked only halfway convinced, so I added as forcefully as I could, "You wouldn't get my husband out of prison anyway, and it would make everything much more difficult and much more dangerous for us all, so please don't talk to the Gestapo at all. Keep quiet!" Suddenly a horrid thought struck me. I asked quickly, "Have you talked to them already? Have you said anything at all?"

"No, I was just thinking about it," she answered. "I thought it might help you, but then I thought maybe I'd better ask you first."

I felt weak with relief. I would never have dreamed she would think up such a crazy thing. I talked to her a little longer to reinforce my argument, and finally she promised to forget the whole idea.

The next morning I took the train for Prague. It was my birthday, the day we were supposed to be leaving on our vacation. I had been looking forward to that day for so long. I sat in the train, feeling completely exhausted. The clank of the wheels pounded in my brain until I thought I would go mad.

When I arrived in Prague I went first to Tony Srba. I told him the whole sequence of events. He thought it would be an excellent idea to find out the reason for the arrest and especially the name of the arresting officer. If he had his name, he might be able to do something.

As he was telling me all this I noticed several gaily wrapped packages on his desk. Tony saw me looking at them and said apologetically that they were for his wife, Manka, as it was her birthday and they were having a little family celebration that evening. I knew it was her birthday. We had always enjoyed the coincidence that she and I had been born on the same day, but with all that had happened I had forgotten it. The sight of those gifts only served to remind me of our current trouble. And, I thought dully, we had planned so much for that day and for our anniversary the following day.

I pulled myself together and told Tony I would try to do as he suggested, even though the idea of facing the Gestapo was frightening and repugnant. In the afternoon I went to a nearby cousin's to spend the night before returning to Brno. I could hardly bring myself to talk to anyone; everything seemed so bleak and hopeless. I felt depressed to the point of despair.

The next day was our tenth wedding anniversary, the day we had so looked forward to and which turned out to be such a gruesome day. There was Alex in Kounicovy Koleje, and here I was, sitting on the train. There was no future, no tomorrow.

I thought, "I have to do something. At least I have to try." And I forced myself by sheer willpower to begin planning my course of action.

I needed some pretext on which to approach the Gestapo. When I arrived back in Brno I called first on my in-laws. Immediately afterward I went to ask Alex's patent attorney if he could give me some document that I could tell the Gestapo required Alex's signature. I reasoned that in order to obtain permission for a visit, I first had to talk to the Gestapo man involved, get his name, and ask him the reason for the arrest.

The lawyer, a Czech and a friend, said that I should pick up the papers on Monday morning. I thanked him and asked him to make it sound highly complicated so that the Gestapo would be confused and would not easily understand it. Then I went home.

The house looked invitingly peaceful. Fanny had made a fire in the fireplace and everything was cozy and friendly. It was wounding. I missed Alex more than ever.

The children ran up to greet me as I arrived. They had missed us both. Janie, a small and cute little baby, laughed up at me and asked for Daddy, but she did not really understand that he would not be coming home.

Evie, sensing my mood, grew worried and began interrogating me. "Where's Daddy? We were supposed to go to Grandma's. Why didn't we go? Where is he?"

"Well, honey, something happened, and you wouldn't understand it, but Daddy is in a concentration camp."

"What's a concentration camp?" Evie asked.

I replied as lightly as I could, "Oh, it's a big place, you know, it's like a large hotel and the people all live there, only they mustn't go out."

"Do they eat there? Like in a hotel?"

"Yes, sort of . . ." I answered.

She said consolingly, "Then it's not so bad, is it?"

I hugged her close.

"No, darling, it's not so bad at all and Daddy will soon come back home."

"I'll be so glad when he comes," Evie said, "because I already miss him so much."

Friends later told me that whenever they met Evie and asked her how her Daddy was, she would say, "Oh, he's fine. He's living in a big hotel and he's having a great time."

Evie loved going to hotels and restaurants, and for her the word

hotel was synonymous with happiness. People found this very touching, and they always made a point of telling me.

Once a Gestapo man tried to ask her questions and Evie told him
the same story. She had no inkling of the truth, which was much
safer. I did not want to worry her. I wanted her childhood to be as
happy as possible under the circumstances.

We passed a gray weekend. On Monday morning I went to the
patent attorney. Fortunately, Alex had been working on some new
process at the time and the attorney had a lot of material. He had
concocted several official-looking documents and made them appear
extremely important and very scientific.

I went straight to the Gestapo building before my courage failed
me. When I arrived in front of it there was a long line of waiting
people. After more than one hour the woman ahead of me reached
the sentry window, behind which sat a grumpy, pompous-looking
Gestapo man. The woman pleaded to be let in. He refused her as he
had refused everyone else in the line. She started crying and begging
piteously. He shouted at her to go away and stop bothering him and
threatened to shove her inside as well. Sobbing, she turned away
from the window.

It was my turn. I was face-to-face with the Gestapo.

"What do you want!" he barked.

Calm took hold of me. My fear vanished.

I said steadily, "I have to speak to my husband who's being detained here. His patent attorney has some problems with these papers, and he needs something clarified. He gave me these documents
and he needs . . ."

I started reeling off some chemical words that apparently, to my
great relief, he did not understand at all. He stared at the paper for a
long time, puzzled and mystified, and finally said, "I'll tell you what;
you send it by mail."

All business, I replied matter-of-factly, "No, it would be too late
by mail. The patent attorney has to have it this week, and I have to
see my husband now."

He looked at me uneasily.

"That's complete nonsense. Here's the address, lady, and you just
put everything in writing and send it to this office. I can't do anything else for you."

I was unflinching.

"Well, at least you can let me talk to the agent who's handling my husband's case. I don't know his name, but you can surely find it in your papers there. I have to talk to him. It's very important."

The Gestapo man turned somewhat red in the face. Plainly he was not used to being argued with and in his confusion fell back on bluster. He stood up, leaned over the counter, and shoved his face so close to me that I could smell his bad breath.

"I said mail it in, and I meant mail it in!" he bellowed. "I can't argue all day long with you. Take the damn thing and shove off!"

Now I was furious, too. I was not going to see all the waiting and hoping come to nothing.

I bent forward and said as commandingly as I could, "Let me in and let me talk to the officer who arrested my husband! I can explain it to him and I'm sure he can do something about it."

"No!" he shouted, "I won't!"

"Very well," I said, in cool clipped words, with a total disregard for the consequences. "The process my husband is working on is extremely important to the army and to the Reich. You are blocking the whole German war effort. You'll be sorry all too soon that you didn't let me in. You'll regret it!"

I turned on my heel and stalked away, head high, but inwardly shattered. I had never even considered the possibility of failure. Now I had to accept defeat.

I walked toward the streetcar stop, with tears of rage and sorrow running down my face. I did not know what to do. I felt I had somehow let Alex down because I could not get past that fool at the door.

Suddenly somebody tapped me on the shoulder. I turned around and there stood the same Gestapo man.

"Look, lady," he said urgently, "I changed my mind. Seeing it's so important, I'll let you in and I'll give you the permit to go and see Mr. Levicek. That's the man who arrested your husband and who's handling his case. And I'll tell you where he is. You go straight down the corridor and then you turn right and then left and you take the elevator. He's on the third floor."

He was almost babbling in his haste to be helpful as he led me back to the Gestapo building. Quickly he gave me all the necessary papers, rushed me inside, and showed me the way.

I was never so surprised in my life. Apparently even the Gestapo supermen felt insecure, I thought. The fact that they too were afraid was quite a revelation to me. If the situation had not been so serious, I would have found his panicky reaction funny.

I walked along the corridor, took the elevator, and eventually found myself in Levicek's office. He was a man about thirty-five years old, short, and rather skinny. Another husky man was in the office with him. I introduced myself and told them that I had to see my husband because his patent attorney needed some information, and I presented the papers I had in my hand.

They looked at them. "What's it all about?" Levicek asked.

I repeated again that my husband was working on something of vital importance to the German war effort and that I must see him immediately.

They examined the papers, but I could see they could not understand any of it either. They both looked embarrassed by their indecision. They talked to each other in low voices. Then Levicek turned to me and said, "This is very irregular and we usually don't do this, but we'll give you a document allowing you to see your husband. But you have to go this week." And he wrote out a permit.

"Yes, of course," I said, and thinking that maybe I could try for a bit more, I added, "There's something else. My husband is quite sick. He has stomach ulcers and he's on a diet, so I would appreciate it if I could send him a parcel of food every week or so."

The two men looked with wide-eyed incredulity at this brazen woman. They started talking together again, and their amazement turned to amusement.

Levicek said, "You know, if he has stomach ulcers, I'm sure we'll cure him. We cure everybody who comes here with ulcers. We have a very special diet. There's no better place to get cured. But anyhow, here's a permit for a parcel twice a month," and he slid another piece of paper toward me.

"And can you tell me why he was arrested, why he's being kept in Kounicovy Koleje?" I asked.

Levicek glanced out of the corner of his eye at the other man.

"He was arrested for high treason. I can't tell you any more about it, but I will tell you this. We are going to chop his head off. And now, you can go." With this he turned away from me.

I stood still, unable to move. I was stunned. To be told that Alex was going to be executed was paralyzing. Levicek made a dismissing motion with his hand. Dizzily I stumbled out, with my hand leaning onto the wall for support. I could hardly find my way out of the building. I felt as if his words were blows by tight, hard fists hitting my body.

I groped my way to the streetcar stop, thoughts flying like storm clouds. "Maybe he was just joking," I said to myself. "Maybe he just wanted to scare me. They're so cruel, those Gestapo people. Maybe he just wanted the pleasure of seeing me suffer. They're queer, sadistic. Why would he have given me that permit if they were going to execute him? What kind of monsters are they?"

Standing in the street waiting for the tram with busy people swirling around me, I wept silently, my throat aching, hot tears stinging my face. Who could I turn to now? Was everything lost? Was it all over? What would happen to Alex, and what was to become of us all?

When I had composed myself somewhat, I went to Mr. Horky and told him what had happened.

"Oh, they're perverts," he said, trying to cheer me up. "Don't you believe them. Levicek's a nasty character. I know him. He arrested me, too, some time ago. He enjoys shocking people. Don't mind what he says." He went on, "I have a good contact within the Gestapo through my former salesman, and now that I know the details and that it's Levicek, I can find out more."

He told me that it was most unusual to get the two permits and that I had to use them the best way possible. He knew a Gestapo man, the mailman at Kounicovy Koleje, who was susceptible to bribes and who was working for the resistance.

"Seeing that you have a permit to send a parcel," he continued, "the best thing would be for you to come here and talk to him. He'll tell you what day he's on duty and when you should mail the parcel, and that way Alex will get it for sure. We pay him well, and we know he'll keep his promise. Otherwise somebody there is sure to steal it, and Alex wouldn't get anything at all."

I agreed to return on Wednesday evening with money and the parcel to make the arrangements final.

I was still trying to assimilate the flood of words when Mr. Horky added, "I can't speak plainly over the phone now, as you know, so when I call you I'll just say, 'Mrs. Kapral, your typewriter is ready.

You can pick it up Wednesday,' and you'll know that the meeting is on." Mr. Horky had a typewriter repair shop. He was sure that his telephone, the same as ours, was bugged. This message would seem completely innocent and in keeping with his normal business. "But if I say, 'Your typewriter isn't ready, and I'll call you when it's done,' you'll know that he's not in town and that the meeting will have to be later, say on Thursday or whenever I tell you."

He repeated a few of the points, more to reassure me than anything else. Feeling a little cheered, I went home to await his phone call.

Talking to Mr. Horky was encouraging. Perhaps Alex could be saved, maybe the agent Levicek was just amusing himself by trying to frighten me. Still, the terrible sentence, "We're going to chop his head off!" rang in my brain constantly.

We prepared Alex's first parcel, trying to decide which items would be most useful. Fanny baked some cookies with as much butter and eggs as we had, and we managed to buy some ham, which would be slow to spoil.

On Tuesday afternoon a car arrived and four men stepped out. One of them flashed the metallic Gestapo badge and said, "We've come to requisition your horses. We want to see them! Also, we must have some saddles and bridles."

Glad that it was nothing worse, I went with them to the stables. They wanted to look at each horse separately. We had three thoroughbreds and one draft horse that we used for working the fields.

When Stan, our groom, showed them the first two horses, Jura and Nonyk, they said they would take them both. Then Stan brought the third horse, a very flashy, good-looking animal.

"We'll take this one, too," said one Gestapo agent. "We'll take all three. You don't need them anyway. We also want three saddles and all the rest of the tack."

Suddenly Jura started to cough. He coughed and heaved and coughed. It was unusual for him as he was a very sound horse. The Gestapo man said, "What's this?"

"He's coughing, that's all," I said.

Frowning, he asked, "Does he cough often?"

"All the time," I said quickly, "but it doesn't seem to bother him any."

"What about the other two, do they cough, too?"

"Yes," I said, "they all cough now and then, but there's nothing to it, they just cough a bit and then they stop. It's not too bad. They're all right."

The spokesman said, "Well, we don't want any sick horses. We're not going to take them. Just give us three saddles and the tack!"

We gave them what they wanted and they loaded everything in their car and left. I looked at Jura standing there and thought, "So you saved yourself and two others! And you tried to save Alex, too!" It was probably pure luck that he started to cough just then, but all the same I patted his velvety nose in gratitude.

Mr. Horky called. "Mrs. Kapral, your typewriter is ready and you can pick it up tomorrow."

The next day I went to Brno, first to Alex's parents' apartment, where I left the food parcel, and then to Mr. Horky's office. I was a little early. The Gestapo man was not there yet, but at five o'clock sharp he came. He was a very tall, strong man and was in a business suit.

I told him I had a permit to send a parcel every second week and was anxious to make certain that Alex received it. I asked him if he could help me. He was straightforward and businesslike when he answered that he could for a consideration.

He counted the money, put it in his pocket and then said, "You can send a parcel today. Mail it at the railway station post office. From there we'll get it at seven o'clock tomorrow morning and your husband will have it by eight o'clock."

"I also have a permit to see my husband. I believe that an officer has to be present during the whole visit. Can you arrange it so that it's you?" I asked.

"Yes," he answered. "I can do it tomorrow, but be sure to be there at exactly ten o'clock."

The main door squeaked as somebody came into the outer hall. The Gestapo man, his back turned toward the glass door, jumped visibly. "Who is it?" he asked. "Tell me quickly!"

"It's just the cleaning lady."

I knew, as he did, that if we were caught he would be shot, but his greed overcame his fear. I would probably be executed, too, or, at the very least, imprisoned.

"Look," I said to him, "I have a permit to send a parcel twice a month. Can you help me with another one in two weeks?"

"I can, but see me first. Check with Horky, and then meet me here. And bring another envelope," and again he mentioned a sum. "I'll make sure he gets it. You can do it every week if you like."

"I have a permit for twice a month only," I said.

"That doesn't matter, I'll fix it. You can send him a parcel every week."

"Shall I see you next Wednesday then, at five o'clock?" I asked.

"If you don't hear from Horky, then be here. If I can't make it, he'll call you."

He left swiftly.

The next morning at ten o'clock sharp, I was in Kounicovy Koleje. It was a most depressing place—menacing buildings surrounded by a fence with SS men in field uniforms standing guard, many with machine guns. I got off the streetcar near the entrance to the complex which, not long before, had been full of happy young students but lately were the saddest and most desolate group of buildings in Brno.

I showed the guard at the gate my permit and my identification card and he let me in. Beyond the lawn in front of the building was another guard who rechecked all my papers and directed me toward the steps that led into the reception hall. Inside were some fifteen Gestapo agents.

My man strode up to me and asked, "What do you want?"

I said I had a permit to see my husband. He took it from me, asked for my ID, and beckoned me to follow.

He showed me into a small room and went out. As soon as I sat down, Alex came in. His face was drawn and he had lost weight. He looked downcast; his eyes were hopeless. It was heart-wrenching for me to look at him in that condition. I told him I was sure he would come home soon and that I was doing everything possible. Things looked as good as they could under the circumstances. Then I asked him if I could bring him anything in particular next time.

"Yes," he said, "I got a parcel this morning."

I told him that I could send him a parcel every week.

He nodded his appreciation and said emphatically, "Just remember you're sending it not to one but to five starving men! There are five of us in our cell. Some of the men have been there for two or three years, and they're very hungry. Also," he continued, "could you send me some warm underwear and maybe a warm overcoat? It's awfully cold here."

I looked at the Gestapo man questioningly.

"Yes," he said, "send it in the parcel. Don't bring it. Send it in the parcel and I'll make sure he gets it."

Alex asked for a Bible, but the Gestapo man interrupted saying that a Bible was not allowed under any circumstances.

"If you can't get a permit for the Bible," Alex said, "bring me a chemical book," and he told me which one.

Time was passing fast. I was trying to be cheerful but inside I was dying. That dreadful sentence of Levicek's "We're going to chop his head off!" still echoed in my head. Was I seeing Alex for the last time?

It was a tense and poignant meeting. I did my best to be optimistic, and keeping a smile fixed on my face, I repeated, "Everything will be fine, just see. I'll come to see you again. You have to be patient and you'll be home soon. You know I'll do all I can."

The visit was supposed to last only ten minutes, but the man let us talk for fifteen minutes. He let us kiss each other, against regulations.

"You'd better leave now," he said then.

As I walked in the hall I turned around and saw Alex returning to the cell with the Gestapo agent behind him. It was such a tragic picture.

I had to walk past the group of the Gestapo men in the reception room. Their eyes were pitiless, evil, cruel, bloodshot, and debauched looking, with baggy pouches underneath. In their somber, black uniforms with the death's-head insignia on the belt and cap, they presented a distressing and unnerving sight.

I looked through the window into the yard and thought of our dear friends, Chairman Wenzl and Josef Svoboda and all the other people who had died there, and I prayed that Alex would not be one of them. Panic clawed at my stomach.

10

MELANCHOLY CHRISTMAS

Several meaningless weeks drifted by. Every Wednesday I met the Gestapo man, gave him money, and mailed a parcel to Alex. The first Wednesday after my visit I sent him warm underwear, a sweater, a pair of heavy shoes, and also the topcoat he had asked for. The weather had turned much colder and I was very grateful for Mr. Horky's arrangement.

It was December and almost Christmas. I decided to try to visit Alex before the holidays and bring him the Bible he wanted, if that was at all possible. I had to get another permit, and as the patent story had worked so well last time, I thought I would try it again. The patent attorney very obligingly drew up some new papers for Alex's signature, and armed with these, I went to the Gestapo headquarters again.

The guard sitting at the entrance was the same agent I had bluffed four weeks before. To my amazement, he recognized me and let me in. I made my way to Levicek's office. When I entered he said, "I am not handling your husband's case any longer. He is going to be tried for high treason and everything concerning him is now in the hands of the High Court. Only the court can give you a permit to see him." This was totally unexpected.

"Can you tell me where to go?" I asked him.

He gave me directions. I went upstairs to the office where he had sent me. The man given charge of the case was a German lawyer who did not speak Czech. He was polite and correct and seemed to be of a different type from the Gestapo men I had met so far. He gave me a permit for a Christmas visit with Alex and another for food parcels. I remembered then about the Bible and asked, "May I bring him a present? I would like to bring him a Bible."

He looked at me and said, "No, Bibles aren't allowed in concentration camps."

"Would it be possible to bring him a chemical book then?" and I told him which one. He agreed and wrote me out a third permit.

As I was leaving, he suddenly stopped me.

"I don't know how to tell you this, Frau Kapral," he said, "but your husband is being sent to Breslau in Germany soon, probably in the middle of January. If you like, I can write you another permit and you can see him before he leaves, around January eighth. That will be the last time you'll see him. He's going to be tried by the German High Court in Breslau."

My heart sank and I almost gasped. I had been hoping against hope that somehow Mr. Horky or Tony Srba would get Alex released, but that hope collapsed. With a feeling of unreality I took the permit for the visit in January and left.

I became frantic as I suddenly remembered what I had heard, that many prisoners in the Breslau prison were put to death by the guillotine. Levicek's words "We're going to chop his head off!"— which I had managed to push to the back of my mind—leaped out at me again like some hound from hell.

Alex's Uncle Sylvester, the priest who had married us, once showed us a touching and sad letter from a friend of his, written before his execution in Breslau prison, and I could not get this out of my mind. I knew, of course, that not everyone who was sent to Breslau was executed there. Some were sent from there to Dachau, Mauthausen, or some other concentration camp, and some were sentenced to remain in the Breslau prison.

I had always hoped that somehow a miracle would bring Alex home. I had been quite sure about it until I became faced with this terrible prospect of Breslau. I decided that I would not mention it to Alex when I saw him at Christmas so as not to worry him. I thought that when I went to see him in January, just before he was due to leave, would be time enough to tell him. He could not do anything about it anyway, and it would only give him that much more time to worry.

When I arrived back home I did not tell anyone about Alex's transfer to Breslau, not even his parents. Christmas was going to be sad enough for all of us even without that.

I decided to bring the food parcel to Kounicovy Koleje and give it to Alex myself. The day before my visit I met my Gestapo contact and paid him, and he assured me that he would again arrange to be the supervising officer. This meant that I could bring a lot more food than would normally be allowed, so Fanny and I prepared as much as we could manage and packed it all into a small suitcase.

Christmas Eve dawned cold and clear. To my surprise this time several women were in the waiting room with their parcels and packages. I guessed that with Christmas coming, the Gestapo decided to show some leniency and allow more visits than normal.

I saw my Gestapo contact walking along the corridor toward me when another very tall agent suddenly moved in front of him and took my papers. I was close to panic because I had brought more food with me than was allowed. I was afraid this new man would appropriate it and Alex would get very little, if anything at all.

The guard took me to a large room full of people and noise. As I walked in I saw Alex standing at the far end of the room, facing the wall. He looked thin.

The Gestapo man directed me to a long table. I sat at one end, Alex at the other, and the agent sat in the middle, between us.

We began talking, and again I tried hard to be cheerful. The Nazi watched me constantly, listening to every word. While we were talking I was wondering how to give Alex all that food and what I should take out first. I doubted I would be able to give it all to him, permit or no permit, and I also knew I would not be able to stay for more than the regulation ten minutes.

After about five minutes I said to the Gestapo man, "I have another permit here. I was given permission to bring him some food."

"All right," he said, "what did you bring him?"

I started taking out of the suitcase one small packet after another, starting with a few pieces of baked chicken.

The Gestapo man said, "All right."

Then I brought out some bread, some Christmas cookies, a piece of salami, some ham, and a few other things. The Gestapo man at first appeared angry, but suddenly he started to look very amused.

"Is that all?" he asked.

"No," I said, "I have a few apples here, too," and I put them on the table, one by one.

The Nazi looked at me, then looked at the apples.

"I think he's got enough," he said. "I'll keep the apples for myself," and he put them in his pockets.

"I have another permit," I said. "I was allowed to bring him a book." The agent examined the chemical book, making sure that there was nothing inside, and then he let Alex have the book.

When it was over, I looked at my husband more closely. He was pale with violet shadows smudged under his pain-wracked eyes. In spite of the parcels he had lost much weight. I told him we all loved him, we were thinking of him, and I was sure he would soon be back home. His tortured face broke my heart when I said how much he would be missed at Christmas and I promised I would come to see him again in January.

At the end of the interview, I forced a smile on my face, saying, "Don't worry, darling, we'll see each other soon and I'm sure everything will be all right. Have a nice Christmas, a peaceful Christmas."

Then he was gone. I sat crying all by myself in the crowded room. After a while the Gestapo man came back with my empty suitcase and I left.

We spent a melancholy Christmas at Richky. How did the family survive it? Alex's mother and father came. I did not say anything about Breslau.

The winter of 1942 was bitterly cold. As the entire prison was unheated, I was glad that I had at least managed to get some warm underwear and the overcoat to Alex.

That was the year of Germany's first major defeats. The German army had penetrated Russia as far as Stalingrad, Moscow, and Leningrad, and while German troops were battling the bitter Russian winter, their losses on the eastern front and particularly at Stalingrad were enormous. They were also meeting with one defeat after another in Africa, especially after the United States entered the war and the big American war-production machine swung into action. Even so, we no longer believed the war would end soon.

New Year's Day 1943 was a very sad one for us. I was thinking about my next visit to see Alex and decided that it would be best to go on Wednesday, January 6. I did not want to wait until the last day in case the Breslau transport left earlier.

On Tuesday, January 5, I arranged a meeting with my Gestapo contact in Horky's office. He promised he would supervise my visit and also find out the name of the prison to which Alex was going to be transferred. I simply loathed having to tell Alex about Breslau. Anticipation of the sight of his face as my words sank in sickened me. Yet I had to do it so he could mentally prepare himself. I had no idea how he would accept the situation or how he would react.

On Wednesday morning I put on a heavy winter coat with big pockets, in one of which I stowed a package of prewar chocolate. It was our last piece and had been kept for an emergency. I arrived at Kounicovy Koleje on time and presented my permit and identity card. The guard swung open the gate and let me in. The second guard checked everything again and then allowed me into the main building.

As soon as I entered I sensed something was terribly wrong. Many people were milling around in the entrance corridor. I stopped at the door and looked toward the large hall and tried to discover the source of the confusion. Inside the hall were many Gestapo men, and among them, staggering from one to the other, was an old priest, the abbot of the nearby monastery. I saw with utter horror that they were beating him, using truncheons and clubs, raining blow after blow on his frail body.

I felt suddenly faint, unable to move, stunned by the unbelievable cruelty of these men. I did not know what to do. The abbot could barely stand. Swaying pitifully on his feet and with blood running down his face and shoulders, he was propelled around the hall, unable to fall and all but dead on his feet. One of his tormentors saw me and screamed, "Heraus, heraus, get out or you'll finish up here, too. I'll show you, you can be beaten, too. Heraus, get out!"

I wheeled and ran out past the guards, through the gate and down the street blind with anger and pity, not pausing to catch my breath until I reached the streetcar stop. I was beside myself. The poor priest was so frail and so old. He could hardly stand and those

Gestapo men with their frightful eyes were beating him like beings possessed. I had seen violence without any mask, and evil unchained. I was never able to purge my mind of that nauseating memory.

I rushed to Mr. Horky for advice and comfort. He was kindness itself and quickly calmed me. He then went on with the news. The transport for Breslau was scheduled to leave definitely the following Thursday, January 14, and Alex was to be on it. Mr. Horky would find out the best day for my last visit to Kounicovy Koleje.

The next day, Thursday, a week before the dreaded departure date, I received a call to come and pick up my typewriter on Friday morning. When I arrived, Horky told me that the best time for my visit would be that day at eleven o'clock. As our paid Gestapo man had been sent out of town, my last visit would be supervised by some unknown agent.

This was bad news. How would I pass the chocolate to Alex? I had heard that transports to Germany sometimes took up to three days and that the prisoners were not given any food in that whole time. The chocolate might help a little. I was determined to give it to Alex under any circumstances. I did not know how, but I knew I would.

On the appointed day, Alex looked even more emaciated. He was directed to a seat at the end of the long table opposite me and a grumpy Gestapo man seated himself between us.

In the middle of small talk, without changing my tone and enunciating the words carefully so they would not be missed, I said swiftly, "And I have another piece of news. Next Thursday you are going to Breslau to appear before the High Court."

The agent jumped and screamed furiously at me, "You mustn't talk to the prisoner like that!"

I thought he would arrest me or even strike me. I responded quietly and matter-of-factly that I had been given this information by the court lawyer, that it was hardly a state secret. This calmed him somewhat, but his face remained red and he watched me even more closely.

I chatted on about other things, scheming all the while as to how I was going to pass Alex the chocolate. I knew I could not simply hand it to him openly. The guard would certainly confiscate it if he saw it.

I continued talking with Alex until suddenly the agent said, "The ten minutes are up. You have to go." And he ordered Alex to stand.

As he did, I jumped up and ran as fast as I could around the table, my hand in my pocket, trying to turn in such a way that the Gestapo man could not see the transfer. The chocolate slipped into Alex's pocket as I embraced him with the other arm. "This is for the trip," I whispered. "Don't eat it now; it's for the trip."

I thought he understood because he muttered, "Sure."

The Gestapo man was taken off balance. His face turned red as he shouted at the top of his lungs. He was furious because I had dared to hug Alex, but he had not seen me put the chocolate in his pocket. He flew across to Alex and slapped his face, left and right and left, while screaming at me, "How dare you touch the prisoner! Don't you know it's against regulations?" Each slap, as it echoed through the room, seemed to go right through me like a bullet and hurt me as much as it hurt Alex. The officer eventually calmed down, shoved Alex aside, and turned on me.

"And now you go," he snarled.

I watched Alex walk down the long hall and disappear around the corner. I did not know if I would ever see him again. I was as spent as if all my blood had been drawn out of me. I did my long, single mourner's procession to the streetcar stop with tears dripping down my face.

Then it occurred to me that I should find out when Alex's transport was leaving, go to the station, and see him just once more before he left Brno. To do that much would be at least a small comfort.

However, Mr. Horky, with his usual wisdom, advised me against it. He was truly agitated.

"No, don't, under any circumstances. It would be the worst thing not just for you, but for Alex. The Gestapo usually ship the prisoners very early in the morning when there's nobody at the station and always load them into the freight cars at the end of the platform. You'd be conspicuous. It won't change the basic situation. It won't do any substantial good and it could do both of you a lot of harm if you were arrested. So forget about the idea." He sighed, shook his head, and went on, "But there are things we must do now to make his life easier in Breslau. We are in luck. My Breslau contact, a member of the Czech resistance, is coming here after lunch. He's a

railway man whose job is to accompany the mail from Brno to Breslau and so he's always on the Breslau train. As he keeps a room in
the city he has a mailing address there. This man has managed to
get around some guards in the main prison with petty bribes and has
been able to get food to a few Czech prisoners. I know several ladies
who send him parcels by mail and he smuggles them into the prison.
You can talk to him this afternoon and find out if he can do something similar for Alex. He'll be here at about three o'clock."

I spent the time before the meeting with Alex's parents. I had to
go there anyway to tell them about my last visit with Alex and about
his transfer to Breslau. It was not a pleasant task. They were
crushed. Such an eventuality had not crossed their minds, and I had
to talk to them for hours, trying to hearten them with courage that I
myself by no means felt.

At three o'clock in the afternoon I was back at Mr. Horky's office.
The railway man was exactly on time. He was impressive, clearly
trustworthy, and willing to help. I promised that as soon as I had
information about Alex's location I would forward it to his Breslau
address and then send a food parcel. He would take care of the
delivery to Alex.

Making these arrangements lifted my spirits. When I got back
from Brno I told Madi, Fanny, and my sister-in-law Jana that Alex
was being moved to Breslau. They were shocked and afraid for him.
Kounicovy Koleje was very bad, but at least it was in Brno, in
Czechoslovakia, and somehow familiar, while Breslau was in Germany and therefore more inaccessible and menacing.

I was particularly grateful for Jana's presence. When the arrests
began in Biochema, Ivan and Jana moved out to Richky. The apartment that had been built for my in-laws was empty because when
they came to see us they always stayed in our guest room in the
house.

Ivan had asked Alex if he and Jana could use the apartment. They
had a baby boy and could not find enough milk for him in the city.
Jana was a special blessing after Alex was arrested. Ivan was away
most of the time at Biochema, but Jana was always at Richky when I
needed her. I had liked her from the time I had first met her. We
became bosom friends.

Strong and steady, Fanny was in her quiet way a mainstay of our family life. She ran the house with efficiency, keeping a fire burning bright and true in the living-room fireplace so that whenever I came home from my sad, dangerous wandering in search of my husband's life and freedom, the old house was warm and homelike.

I was able to draw renewed energy from the mere fact of being physically at home. I was infused with strength by the presence of my two little girls. It was a healing delight to sit in front of the fire, let my worries dissolve away, and watch our daughters playing and hear their chattering.

We had a deep snowfall that winter. In the frigid, still morning the forest glittered. The branches of the evergreens were so laden that they drooped like rippling folds of shimmering silver-and-white satin. In the evening the whole valley was stilled in a great, majestic silence with close, pure stars singing their soundless songs. I survived.

A letter arrived from the Gestapo advising me officially that Alex had been transferred elsewhere, but not telling me where, and ordering me to come to the prison to collect his belongings. I took my last trip to Kounicovy Koleje. This time I had no permit. I showed the letter to the guards and they let me in.

An official gave me everything Alex had in his pockets when he was arrested. I received his keys, his billfold with photos, his gold watch, and his fountain pen. They had not let him take anything that could be said to be truly his, some substantial link with his past, something to remind him of who he really was. These articles I received were things that Alex never left the house without. They were so much a part of him that as I held them in my slightly tremulous hand, it seemed as if he did not exist anymore. They also returned the chemistry book I had brought him.

On my way home I stopped at Horky's office. He had already learned of Alex's location at Breslau and I could write to the railway man and send the first parcel. Jan Horky added that although the Breslau prison was generally outside his sphere of influence, if I ever needed any help of any kind, I was to come and see him and he would be happy to do whatever he could for me. He was a good man, a true Czech patriot, and a real friend.

11
FRAU THOMAS

One morning about ten o'clock Madi came in to my sitting room to tell me that there was a most peculiar-looking man downstairs who wanted to see me.

Alarmed, I asked her if he looked like the Gestapo. "No," she said, "I don't think so. He doesn't seem prosperous enough for that. He looks as if he should be fat but had lost a lot of weight. His appearance is queer, but he won't go away. I don't know. . . ."

I put aside my work and went downstairs. A short, stocky man with a heavy frame, though, as Madi had noted, far from fat, stood by the window. He had close-cropped, ginger-colored hair, a round, good-natured face, and strong, peasant features. He might have been a tradesman or a village shopkeeper. As I came in he turned to me and boomed, "It's really beautiful here, just like Alex said. And so you're his wife. We heard a lot about you and the little girls." He advanced upon me alarmingly, as if to gather me up in his arms and hug me.

"Good morning," I said, with an appropriate smile, backing away. "What can I do for you?"

"My name is Zouhar," he said expansively, "but you can call me Olda. Everyone does. I was in the same cell with Alex at Kounicovy Koleje. He asked me to come and see you if I was released. Here I am. I can tell you all about what it was like in there. My word, it's good to be out and able to speak frankly with people."

The loud, friendly voice, the big, warm gestures, the smiling, innocent face seemed completely false to me. I knew he was a Gestapo man, without the slightest doubt. The Gestapo often did things like that in an effort to get honest people to incriminate themselves. About three weeks before, another man had arrived at Richky claiming to be Alex's cellmate. I had not been at home at the time, so Jana talked to him. She immediately sensed what he was, remained polite but reserved and gave nothing away. The Gestapo agent had left disappointed.

Positive that Olda Zouhar was another spy I responded with chilling formality, saying nothing more than I was pleased that he had come. He started reminiscing about Alex. I listened with surface civility and inner skepticism, wondering how to get rid of him. He spoke good Czech without a foreign accent, but then most of the Gestapo agents did since the majority of them were former German-speaking citizens of Czechoslovakia.

Suddenly he broke off, looked me sharply in the eye, and said in a cool, edged tone, "You don't believe me, do you? You think I'm a Gestapo man, don't you?"

"Oh no," I replied calmly, "how could I think that? Of course, I believe you."

But I did not, and I remained cold toward him, wishing only that he would stop his silly talk and leave me alone. I did not want to be rude openly. If he was Gestapo he could make more difficulties for us, and God knew I had difficulties enough.

Olda appeared quite upset and answered desperately, "What can I tell you to make you believe that I was in a cell with Alex?"

I was a little disconcerted. "I do believe you, I assure you," I said, though I meant, "Will you never give up?"

He then told me what I had brought Alex for Christmas and what I had said when I had talked to him. The Gestapo knew all that, too, I thought cynically, and I kept my face fixed and uncommunicative.

"I know what I'll tell you," he said with glee. "Before Alex left for Breslau you came to see him. It was on Friday and you brought him a piece of chocolate, which you slipped into his pocket when you hugged him. Then the Gestapo man slapped him several times, but he didn't find the chocolate and Alex brought it to the cell. He didn't eat it, but kept it for the trip like you told him to."

I looked at him more closely. With growing confidence he continued and I began to listen more and more carefully to what he said.

Olda was a butcher from a village not far from Richky. He had spent more than three years in Kounicovy Koleje. The reason for his arrest was that he had a younger brother, an air force pilot, who escaped with a plane to England shortly after the Nazi invasion. Olda had been imprisoned for another man's actions. In the three and a half years he had spent in Kounicovy Koleje, he had never once been interrogated or accused of anything. He just sat there and waited. He was not told why he had been released.

Olda described the conditions in the prison in detail. The prisoners were given almost no food and were constantly and painfully hungry. Breakfast consisted of black water of no detectable origin called coffee and three ounces of dark bread. At noon they received a bowl of so-called soup. It was nothing but water in which floated a few small pieces of half-cooked beet. Dinner was black coffee without bread.

"You'll never know what good you did with your food parcels," Olda continued. "There were five of us in the cell. The cell was originally a dormitory room for two students and had only two narrow beds, so we put them together and four of us slept next to each other and the fifth one stretched across at our feet and this way we kept a little warm. It was terribly cold. They didn't heat the rooms, and being so hungry we felt it even more.

"When Alex started getting those parcels it was a godsend. He always divided each parcel into five equal parts and so everybody got the same amount of food. By the time he arrived we were terribly exhausted—you have no idea. You helped us so much, you'll never know. The other two especially. They were nearly dying of hunger, and were so weak they could hardly move. After those parcels began coming they felt a little better.

"The room was quite small. Each morning we were allowed to go out to the lavatory and had to be back in five minutes. In our cell was a window, which had been whitewashed so we could not see out, but in spite of that it was a little translucent, and if anyone stood in front of it for a few minutes, the guards outside started shooting with their machine guns. If somebody wanted to commit suicide, and many did, they would just stand in front of the window and be shot.

"Somehow we were able to communicate with other cells a little. Quite a few men in the prison were from the post office and knew Morse code, so they tapped on the walls and passed on the news from one cell to another. When somebody was arrested he brought news from the outside and in no time at all this telegraph code sent it all around the prison.

"Naturally the Gestapo heard it, too, but they could never find out where it originated, and it drove them crazy. Many people were interrogated and beaten up because of it, but they never caught anybody actually doing it, and so it went on. This way everybody knew about new arrivals, about who was executed, and who had been sent to Mauthausen, Dachau, Auschwitz, or Breslau. In short, everyone in the prison was well informed about what was happening inside and also outside."

He went on to tell me about the other men sharing the cell. One of them was Adolf Palkovsky, a weak, sickly teacher from Zlin in Moravia, who had come to Kounicovy Koleje about three years before and, like Olda, was never interrogated or told why he had been arrested. He was very musical and could whistle entire operas. Because the cellmates had nothing to read and nothing to do, this man entertained them and kept their spirits up by softly whistling operatic arias and even some compositions by Dvorak and Smetana. They all were grateful for his musical talents and his ability to touch their blighted lives with moments of brightness.

A week before Alex was transferred to Breslau, Palkovsky had been sent to Auschwitz. He knew he had been placed on the death camp transport and was more or less resigned to his fate, but his four cellmates were miserable about losing their friend. The poor man was extremely weak. He had been arrested in the summer, wearing light clothes, and in his depleted condition the cold racked his feeble frame.

Aware that what he would meet in the weeks ahead would be more severe than the Brno prison, Alex gave him his warm underwear and the heavy overcoat to take with him, but in vain. The teacher did not survive Auschwitz. He died in six months. The Gestapo, with their usual and ridiculous blend of meticulous efficiency and barbarism, sent the coat back to his wife. She then returned it to us accompanied by a sad letter.

Another of Alex's companions was an accountant from Moravska Ostrava named Janko Chmiel. He had an artificial leg in which he hid a small knife. The Gestapo never discovered its existence. With this knife and bits of precious paper the cellmates made themselves a chess set and so were able to distract themselves from time to time.

By the time Alex was thrown into Kounicovy Koleje, Janko had already been there for two years, having been arrested in 1940. He remained incarcerated until the end of the war, serving a total of five years. He was much weakened, but Alex's arrival and his food parcels gave him some new strength. He was never told why he had been arrested. He was never interrogated or informed of his crime. No one seemed to care about his case or even his existence. He believed that it was only a matter of chance he had not been executed.

The fifth man in the group, Josef Nimracek, had worked for the postal service and rode on the trains sorting the mail cn route. During the summer of 1942 Czech postal employees working for the railroads that had tracks running into the Soviet Union began systematically destroying all the German army dispatches on the way to the Eastern Front. This slowed and damaged the German war effort considerably and increased the general confusion. The Gestapo investigated the mystery of the vanishing mail and in October 1942 arrested over fifty of these postal employees, including Alex's cellmate.

All the mailmen suffered terribly. They were continually interrogated, repeatedly tortured, and brutally beaten. The Gestapo wanted to uncover the nature, structure, and membership of the organization behind the crime. Josef was taken out of the cell every other day and always returned covered with blood. Frequently he would be awakened in the middle of the night by the Gestapo, told that he was shortly going to be executed, and instructed to write a farewell to his wife. He would write a poignant letter that the Gestapo would rip out of his hands and read out loud, laughing and mocking its weeping author. Then they would beat him up again and throw him back in the cell.

Once they almost knocked out one of his eyes. Nearly all of his teeth were gone. He was so weak from loss of blood that at times his cellmates could hardly bring him back to consciousness. Night after night they cared for him, cleaning him up as best they could with their limited resources.

Josef never talked. Ten days before Alex was transported to Breslau, he was taken from the cell and executed in the yard of Kounicovy Koleje. All the other mailmen were executed with him.

Olda told me that Alex was interrogated by Levicek three times, each time for several hours. He was accused of supporting the Czech resistance and of donating money to further its work. His name had been found on a list of donors to the resistance, stupidly kept by an employee of Biochema named Novotny, whose job was to collect legitimate donations throughout the company for orphans, widows, the Red Cross, and other such charitable causes. He also secretly collected money for the resistance.

Alex denied it all, every word, unflinchingly and categorically. He maintained that he had never knowingly donated money to the resistance at any time, and that if they had found his name on such a list, he had no idea how it had gotten there. Alex pointed out that he had become so used to Novotny and his unending collections that whenever Novotny appeared at his office door, Alex would always reach into his pocket automatically and give him some money without even inquiring whom it was for.

On the day in question he assumed the collection was again for some sort of widows' or children's fund. He was at the time on the telephone, and seeing Novotny at the door he reached into his pocket and, without pausing in his phone conversation, gave him money. This was Alex's story and he stuck to it doggedly through several interrogations and beatings. My heart twisted painfully when I heard Alex had been tortured.

Finally, sensing they were getting nowhere, the Gestapo staged a confrontation with Novotny. Agents brought both of them into one room, sat them back to back so they could not look at each other, and asked Alex the same questions once more. Alex again repeated the exact same story with the same, strong, unshakable conviction.

When he was finished, Novotny piped up, "Mr. Kapral, you have to tell the truth. Tell them the truth; there is no other way. You can't save yourself. You just have to tell them what really happened."

"It is true, Novotny. I never gave you money for anything else but the Red Cross and the children's and widows' funds. That's all I ever gave you money for. And that's the whole truth."

Alex knew that if he varied his story, let alone broke down and admitted the full truth—that he had in fact contributed substantial sums to the resistance on this and other occasions—it would be the end of him. So he never argued, rephrased, or explained but maintained this line through all the interrogations, beatings, and threats. When the Gestapo saw that it was futile to try to thrash anything out of him, they decided to send him to Breslau for the High Court sentencing.

Olda, who by this time had vanquished every doubt in my mind of his true identity, told me that being a butcher he could perhaps help us. He promised to stop by now and then to bring me a little bit of meat, whatever he could spare for us. I was grateful to him. Food, especially meat, was getting more and more scarce, and our girls were growing. I thanked him warmly and invited him to stop by whenever he could.

As he was going out the front door, Olda paused and said, "By the way, did you find the note?"

"What note?"

"Before he was shipped to Breslau, Alex wrote a few words in the chemistry book you brought him. It was hard to do. He didn't write much because he was afraid the Gestapo might find it. We had only a very small piece of pencil, just a bit of lead kept for emergencies. He stuck it behind his nail, which was the only way he could hold it." With this Olda said good-bye and left.

I rushed to the chemistry book. I found the message, a few, pitiful, barely legible gray words. Alex said good-bye to me and to the whole family. He said he loved us. He told me he missed me and the children. He did not believe he would see us again.

He was saying a last farewell. Looking at the shaky, faint writing, I also saw my tears falling on the page.

Desolate as the future seemed, all course of action was not cut off. I still had to write to Karel, the railway man in Breslau, giving

Alex's exact whereabouts in the prison so that he could deliver the food parcel to him. I decided I would send not one parcel but two, one for Alex and one for our contact. Surely he did not have enough to eat either and I wanted to show him my gratitude. By now Fanny and I were expert in assembling the food packages. I wrote the letter, giving Karel Alex's block and the name of the prison. The existence of two food parcels was explained. Karel was to keep one for himself and deliver the other to Alex. As soon as the packing was done, I went straight to Brno and mailed the letter and both parcels in the main post office.

A few days later I received a telephone call from Jan Horky telling me that my typewriter was ready and that I could pick it up the next morning. His voice sounded urgent and I had the impression that something was very wrong. After a restless night, early the next morning I was in his office.

His first words were, "Did you mail the letter and the parcels?"

"Yes, a few days ago."

"That's terrible, just terrible. Karel has been arrested. The Gestapo arrested him as soon as he arrived in Breslau this last trip. As if that isn't bad enough, some of the ladies who were sending packages into the prison through him have been arrested, too. Most of them live in Brno, so I'm afraid you'll be next. If you are, be sure, be very sure, you don't mention me or my office under any circumstances. Too much work remains to be done. If the Gestapo ask you where you met Karel, tell them you met him at the railway station. You were waiting for your train and he started talking to you and that was how it all happened. Whatever you do, don't mention this office, because Brno's whole resistance movement would be jeopardized."

I went back home in a daze. I had to talk to someone. Thank God for Jana. I did not want Grandma and Grandpa to know. They were worried enough as it was.

Time did not flow, but oozed by. The waiting was unendurable. Whenever someone knocked on the door or there was a sudden noise outside, I felt for certain it was the Gestapo coming to pick me up. The spasms of erratic panic, following hours and hours of unbelievable tension, were torturous.

The first week went by. The second week crawled by more slowly, if that was possible. I was sure the Gestapo were playing with me as a cat plays with a little bird before it executes it with one quick bite to the neck. I did not dare go anywhere. If I was to be arrested, I wanted it to happen at home so I could say good-bye to my children.

At the end of the second week a letter arrived from Breslau without any return address. I opened it and inside was my letter to Karel, untouched; its condition was perfect. No one had tampered with it. I stood overwhelmed with wonder, turning the letter over and over in my hands.

Someone had intercepted it and sent it back to me before the Gestapo got it. That had to be what happened. Someone whose name I would never learn, whose face I would never see, had saved me.

Gratitude to the kind stranger overflowed my heart. The parcels never came back. I prayed that whoever returned my letter was able to keep the food for himself. At least in that little way I would have made a token repayment for my debt. Jan Horky was as relieved as I was.

February wandered in, gray and cold. I traveled to sad, oppressed Prague once more to talk to Tony Srba about the possibilities that remained after my contacts in Breslau had disappeared.

After I had brought him up to date, Tony was silent for a while. "You know, Zdena," he finally said, "the *Treuhänder* in our company is a lawyer from Berlin named Benecke. He is a powerful man in Germany. We pay him a rather large annual stipend and he comes here once a month or so. I'll talk to him about doing something for Alex."

When I saw Tony the next morning he had already conversed with Dr. Benecke. Tony had underlined the fact that Alex, as the chief executive officer of Biochema, was vitally needed at the plant and that his return was necessary for continuing high production and profits. Dr. Benecke said that maybe, just maybe, something could be done, but he had to know who the presiding judge at Alex's trial was going to be. That was crucial.

It was my job to find that all-important name, as Dr. Benecke did not want to start making inquiries that might draw attention to his involvement in the case. He could not do anything until he had that information. It was going to be difficult for me because I did not know anyone in Breslau. I had never been there and I had no idea how to go about finding out such restricted information. I said, of course, that I would do it.

Tony suggested that I see our mutual friend, Bozena, because her father, a former general in the Czech army, had been detained for several years in Breslau in the same prison as Alex. That afternoon I went to see Bozena, a charming young woman who was sympathetic and helpful. It turned out she did not know much about Breslau, but her mother, who lived in Brno, could give me more substantial information. Mrs. Voda, like her daughter, was a pleasant lady but unfortunately did not know anyone there either. She gave me a lot of information about the city, about the prison and the way to get there, and also recommended a hotel. She had been to Breslau herself the three times she had been able to get a permit to see her husband. Tony's suggestion had turned out to be a dead end.

I went to see Jan Horky again and told him what Tony Srba asked me to do. Jan Horky was pleased about the possibility of Dr. Benecke's intervention. He believed him to be one of the few people who could help us, as the charge against Alex was a truly serious one. To my great excitement, he informed me he could help.

The Czech resistance had a reliable friend in the office of the High Court in Breslau who would know the identity of the presiding judge. Her name was Frau Thomas. She was German but was giving the Czech resistance invaluable help at great risk to herself. Jan Horky told me to trust her implicitly.

I would, of course, have to go to Breslau myself to make contact; the matter certainly could not be trusted to the mail. The problem was that I needed a permit from the Gestapo to enter Germany because travel beyond certain limits, and especially across the borders, was strictly forbidden.

I went straight to Gestapo headquarters expecting to have to do battle for that tiny bit of paper, but, amazingly, I obtained a travel permit to Breslau without any difficulty. How mysterious are the ways of bureaucracy.

I was packing for the trip when to my great surprise and joy I received a most unexpected postcard from Alex himself. How in the world, I thought, had the card escaped the prison? He wrote, "I'm in Breslau now, and I want to tell you that when you come to Breslau, don't forget that we owe our Cousin George five hundred marks, so take the money with you and give it to him."

This was a thorough puzzle. We did not have any cousin in Breslau and no Cousin George anywhere. I was wildly happy to have heard from Alex, but I had no idea what he meant and was therefore completely confused. I took five hundred marks in an envelope along with me.

Jan Horky had told me that Frau Thomas was expecting me and he warned me to be careful what I said in her office. She might not be alone.

In Breslau I went to the hotel that Bozena's mother had recommended, only to be told there was no room available. German officers were on leave in the city and had filled all possible accommodations. The man at the desk added haughtily that hotels were not allowed to take in non-German guests anyway. At the next hotel I heard a similar tale. I went from one hotel to another as my feet became heavier and heavier. At each one the story was the same: no Czechs allowed. Finally after more than four hours of walking I arrived at the last hotel on my list. I had lost all hope, and sure enough, I was refused.

Back on the sidewalk I paused to think. It was five o'clock and almost completely dark. Antiaircraft blackouts were strictly enforced. The street lights were extinguished and every window was curtained with the black cloth required by regulations. Not even a glimmer of light escaped from some undiscovered chink. The sidewalks were full of weary-looking German soldiers, mostly officers, on short leave from the Russian front, where the fighting was becoming more fierce every day.

I was exhausted and afraid. The railway station was apparently the only place I could spend the night. There I could sit in the waiting room and doze a little on a wooden bench. I started walking toward the streetcar stop when I noticed the doorman who had come out of the hotel behind me. He looked like a kind man.

"Excuse me," I said to him calmly but with enough feeling to let him understand how serious my plight was. "I need some help. I'm Czech and I have to stay in Breslau overnight, but no one wants to give me a room. I expect to pay, of course, but they refuse me because of my nationality. Would you know anyone who would rent me a room? I don't mind how much I pay."

He looked at me and said quietly, "Let me think. I know an old lady who rents rooms. She doesn't live far from here. I'll go inside and give her a call."

After five minutes he came back and said with a smile, "Yes, she'll take you in for the night, but she doesn't heat her rooms."

I did not mind. It was enough that I would be able to lie down and sleep a little. I had risen at four o'clock that morning and was close to collapse.

I located the house easily and the old lady willingly rented me a room. I paid her in advance and forced myself to set out for the railway station to pick up my suitcase. On the way I stopped for a quick meal at a small restaurant. On my return to the boarding house I found that my room was indeed freezing. I went straight to bed with all my clothes on, including two heavy sweaters. Even so, I woke up shivering in the middle of the night and had to get up and put on my heavy overcoat.

In the morning I rose before dawn, driven from bed by the cold and my anxiety about Alex. I asked the landlady if I could stay another night. To my relief she agreed. She invited me into her kitchen, the only room she heated, and offered me some ersatz coffee and a piece of bread and told me to stay in the kitchen as long as I wanted.

It was still early. The offices of the courthouse did not open until nine o'clock. Winter in Breslau that year was exceptionally harsh. The cold was intense and the wind knifed ferociously through the streets, slicing through cloth, skin, and muscle to make bones ache. Even sitting in the heated kitchen I felt frozen.

The High Court building, an imposing presence in the center of the city, was easy to find. The doorman gave me directions to Frau Thomas's office. I climbed a long flight of stairs and at last arrived at the appropriate door.

Inside I found a woman I was not prepared to meet. She was beautiful, about thirty-four years old, and had masses of shining red hair that flowed in rippling cascades over her shoulders. Her eyes were large, deep blue, wise, and innocent. Her facial features were regular, handsome, and full of character. Her figure was elegant and graceful. My first impression was that she was a mature, clever, open, and trustworthy woman, the sort of person whose friendship was to be treasured. With her in the office was a man in a business suit.

I introduced myself with prearranged sentences. "I'm Frau Kapral from Brno. My husband is here in the prison and I would very much like to see him. Where can I get the necessary permit?" I said it exactly as Mr. Horky had instructed.

Her eyes turned sharp and cold as icicles and she looked me up and down as if I were some lesser, presumptuous being. Her voice was as cold as her eyes when she snapped out, "I can give you the permit," and added that visiting hours were from ten to twelve in the morning and from two to four in the afternoon. She scrawled something on a scrap of paper and slid it toward me. It was a permit.

Then she turned away as if I had ceased to exist, clearly expecting me to have left when she turned back. I was aghast at the savageness of her rebuke and could barely manage to ask her, "Could you tell me when my husband's case will come up before the court?"

She fixed me with a second cold, even more unfriendly, look.

"No, I don't know that, and there's nothing more I can tell you. I am busy."

The dismissal was final. She rose, went to the filing cabinet and started to do something with her files. The interview was over. Dejected, I walked out of the office. Mr. Horky had been very mistaken—as mistaken as my first impression was of this woman. The door to precious information had been slammed in my face. Mr. Horky's arrangement had failed, and there was nothing I could do but visit Alex and take the train home empty-handed.

I walked down the court building corridor when my sad meditation was interrupted by a sharp clicking of high heels. Glancing over my shoulder I saw Frau Thomas rushing toward me. As she passed she murmured in a low voice from the corner of her mouth, "Come to the powder room, please. Follow me."

She continued at a fast pace down the corridor without having laid eyes on me. Dazed by this new swing in my fortune, I moved slowly on, my eyes glued to her back. Several yards down the corridor, she disappeared behind a door. When I reached it, I saw it was the women's washroom. I looked around as casually as I could. No one was in sight. I went in.

As I closed the door behind me, she greeted me with a warm smile that transformed her face.

"Now we can talk," she said. "I checked, and there's nobody in here with us. I must apologize for having been so brusque with you. I'm afraid I was most cruel, but I had to do it because the man who's sharing my office is from the Gestapo. He watches everything I do. I'm beginning to sense they suspect me of helping the Czech underground. They wouldn't have placed one of their spies in my office if they didn't know something. Anyway, I have to be very, very cautious. Your husband's court hearing is on the fifteenth of March, and the presiding judge is the chief justice and president of this court."

She carefully spelled out his name and continued, "Actually, he's my immediate superior. I'm his secretary. I guess that's all you need to know. Oh, yes, there's something else. Don't talk to anyone. You can't trust anybody here but me and two men, the court translators. You can trust them completely. They, too, work for the underground and help the Czechs. They give the prisoners much assistance. Since you are allowed to hire a lawyer, the court translators can refer you to someone good." She gave me two names.

"Go and see them now. Just continue along this corridor and take the last door on the right. You'll find them there. They can give you more advice. Now is there anything else you'd like to know that I can tell you?"

I said gratefully, "Well, no, I don't think so. If I can come to the court hearing on the fifteenth, may I come to see you?"

"Of course," she answered, "but I'll have to be very formal with you again in the office. Afterward I'll meet you here. We can talk a little, but only here. As I said, I'm very afraid."

"May I ask you a personal question?" She nodded.

"Why are you doing this?" I asked. "You have a good job. You're German. You don't need to do this for us Czechs. You don't need to endanger yourself and you don't need to help us. Why are you doing it?"

She smiled. "I am a loyal German. I love my country. I'm most patriotic, but I deplore what is happening in my homeland. I hate

Hitler. He's evil and he's doing a great disservice to our Germany. He is damaging us as much as he is hurting other nations. He's cruel and inhuman. I'm so deeply ashamed of what is happening in Germany today that in my small way I'm trying to change it. I know it's not much, but I do what I can and try to make right at least some things which I know are wrong. It's dangerous, and I know I can be found out and could be executed for it, but I have to do it. I feel I couldn't look in the mirror if I didn't help you and the other innocent people who suffer so much here in prison." With this she patted my hand, kissed me on the cheek, and said, "I have to go!" Then she vanished through the door.

Exultant that I did indeed have the information I had come to Breslau to collect, I went to the court translators' office. They were in. I told them I was on my way to visit my husband after obtaining the permit from Frau Thomas, who advised me to see them so that they could add to my knowledge of the prison.

The two conversed with me freely and frankly. Since they were the official translators to the court, they were able to aid many Czech prisoners. Again I was sternly cautioned that of all the people in the building I could trust only them and Frau Thomas.

They instructed me to tell Alex first of all that when he made his statement in court he should talk only in Czech so that they would be able to translate his testimony in the best possible way. They were completely familiar with court procedures and terminology and were therefore more capable of presenting Alex's words in a style acceptable to the judge than Alex could himself even if he spoke good German.

Later I had the opportunity to hear for myself how the court translators operated. They did not merely present the testimony in the best possible light, but they actually shifted the prisoner's words so that a statement such as "I was there and I had the gun" often came out in German as "I wasn't there and I never saw the gun." Many of the prisoners came to trial following extensive brutal interrogations, half-starved and muddled in mind, and in their panic and confusion spoke the incriminating truth without realizing the consequences.

Alex managed to retain his native cleverness unshaken. He never told the Gestapo what really happened and was able to protect himself somewhat by repeating the same story in the same words over and over again, no doubt to the frustration of his interrogators. Many of the prisoners were incapable of protecting themselves as Alex did, and these two men saved the lives of many such victims.

Chatting in their office, I did not know the full extent of their courageous actions or the risks they were taking, but I did realize they were in a position to give the prisoners much help. I became convinced that one of them had to be Cousin George. I took the envelope out of my handbag and said, "I believe one of you is Cousin George? Alex asked me to give you this envelope."

One of them took it, looked inside it, and said with obvious embarrassment, "Oh, my God. It's lucky you gave this to us. If you handed it to anybody else you'd be shot for it. Be careful. Don't go around Breslau handing this envelope to whomever you meet." He gave me the envelope back.

I told them what Alex had written. One of the translators said, "I don't have the faintest idea what was in his mind, but we're doing this to help the Czech people, not for money. We want only one thing in return. When Hitler loses, and he's going to lose, we'll be put on trial with the rest. When that happens, we'll contact you to write a letter stating that we were helping the Czech people all along and that we didn't harm anyone."

I said with fervor, "Of course, you know I'd be glad to do it, but that's a long way off!"

"It may be sooner than you think!" the other man said with a spark of passion in his eyes. "We don't think he can possibly win, not possibly." I was surprised to hear this from a German. After the war I received a letter from each translator reminding me of this conversation and pleading for help. I wrote strong, appreciative letters recommending the dismissal of all charges. Both were freed and justice was done.

In the afternoon I went to visit Alex. The prison itself was an enormous, sinister, red-brick building with massive doors. When I rang the bell, a guard with a face as blank as the doors answered and let me in.

The Breslau prison was not a made-over building like Kounicovy Koleje. It was a real penitentiary constructed for the purpose. Alex's block had several stories of cells built around an open center court covered with a high dome. This was the first time I had been inside such an institution. The atmosphere was grim.

The guard led me to the visiting room. I waited for five minutes on pins and needles. Then Alex was ushered in by another man. Alex looked terrible, much worse than when I last saw him at Kounicovy Koleje. Painfully thin, with the skin of his face drawn back on the bone underneath, he looked ill. He was dressed in a badly fitting prison uniform with black-and-white stripes and wore wooden clogs that clopped hollowly on the tiled floor as he shuffled along.

The guard told him in Czech to sit at the far end of the table. I wanted to touch him, to hold his hand, to comfort him, to bring some hope and sparkle into his tired eyes, but I had to stay at the other end of the long table and all I was allowed were poor, empty words. I found myself repeating what I had said on the previous visits, that we missed him and that I was certain that everything would be all right. I had brought photos of the children. The guard snapped, "You can look at the pictures, but you can't keep them." Alex looked through the little collection as if eating them with his eyes. When he turned back to me, the guard grabbed them and slid them across the table to me.

"Do you know that I'm to be tried by the High Court?" Alex asked.

"Yes, on March fifteenth. I know about it."

"Find me a very good lawyer," he said urgently, "because we were told we can have legal representation."

"Yes, I already have one," I answered. "He's from Berlin. Tony Srba recommended him." When Alex heard Tony Srba's name, his face brightened considerably.

I paused to consider my words carefully, then said with heavy emphasis, "When you're in court, it would be much better for you to speak Czech only. You'll express yourself better that way!"

To my relief, Alex answered, "Oh yes, I wouldn't do anything else. I realize that's the best thing to do. I know that's much better."

The deliberateness of his words and the immobility of his normally animated features told me that he, too, knew more than he could say.

The guard announced the end of the visit. I promised I would be at the court hearing and that I would also come to see him on Friday, March 12, if I could get a pass. I was determined to do so.

We said good-bye across the long table, with our eyes meeting in love and pain. Not even a final embrace was permitted. Alex left, a pathetic figure in the striped outfit and wooden clogs.

Before returning to my frigid room I went in search of warmer accommodations for my next visit. Luck was with me this time. Near the railway station I found a small hotel, actually more of a boarding house, where no one seemed to care that I was a Czech. They showed me a minute room with only a bed and a wash basin, a solitary chair in the corner, and a few hangers on a nail in the wall. There was no wardrobe.

It was a shabby little place, but it had one wonderful feature. The building was centrally heated and, moreover, the central heating worked. The room was warm and cozy. As the first balmy air touched my cheek when the clerk opened the door, I blurted out, "I'll take it," and gave the clerk a deposit.

The journey back to Czechoslovakia was uneventful. It was good to be back home to see the children and to be warm again. The next day I called Tony Srba and told him I had all the necessary information. He invited me to come to Prague the following week. Early on Tuesday morning I was in his office.

"Fortune shines on us," Tony said as I came in. "Dr. Benecke is in Prague again. That'll make things a lot easier."

He picked up the phone and called him. Dr. Benecke asked us to come to see him immediately. His office all but shouted to us that this was an important man in the Reich. It was spacious, luxuriously carpeted, and appointed with antique furniture of obvious expense. Its big, spotlessly clean windows overlooked the city.

Dr. Benecke himself was a suave, elegant man in his forties, impeccably dressed. He rose courteously when we entered, bowed us into soft armchairs, and asked me the date of the trial and the name of the judge. When I told him the name of the president of the High Court in Breslau, he was visibly pleased.

"That's excellent, just excellent. He is an old friend and owes me a favor. Let me give him a call now."

Tony tactfully excused himself. Dr. Benecke insisted that I remain to hear his conversation with Breslau so that, as he put it, I could stop worrying.

It went something like this: "*Wie gehts*, Hans? How are you, old friend? And the family? Good, good. Say, do you remember . . . ?" He mentioned a past episode. "I helped you out with that. Well, now I need your help. You have one of our people, a man by the name of Kapral, in the Breslau prison. He's coming up before you on March fifteenth. Make a note of it, eh? Kapral, March fifteenth. I'd like him released. We need him here in the corporation. He's a superior chemist and we're having some problems we would like him to deal with, so the sooner the better. I would much appreciate that, my friend."

Dr. Benecke hung up.

"Well, that's that. You can be assured he won't let me down. We'll have to keep up appearances, of course. I won't go to the hearing, but I'll send my partner from the Berlin office, Dr. Weber. I'd like you to be there, too, to give him more information. He'll be there on, let's see, March twelfth, that's the Friday before the trial. Meet him in the lobby of the hotel. Be there at three in the afternoon. That will give him ample time to get his brief together." He gave me the name of the best hotel in Breslau.

He smiled at me confidently. With the air of a man unfamiliar with failure who has thoroughly disposed of a difficult problem he stood up and extended his handsome, well-manicured hand. His optimism was impressive. A still feeble hope stirred in me that Alex might return home after all.

I caught the afternoon train expecting to be at Richky in good time for dinner. The train was late getting into Brno. I ran as fast as I could to the bus terminal only to see the bus driver closing the door as I approached. He let me in. As the bus lumbered off I tumbled into a seat and tried to do something about my disarranged hair.

When the bus passed through the outskirts of town I noticed through a glaze of exhaustion that we were not taking the usual road to Mokra. I walked up the aisle, touched the driver's shoulder, and asked, "You are going to Mokra, aren't you?"

"Oh no, this is the bus to . . ." It was another town altogether.

"Oh, my God!" I said. "I live in the Richky valley, about half an hour's walk from Mokra."

"Yes, I know where that is," the driver answered, "but we're a pretty long way from Brno now, and I can't turn back. I think the best thing for you to do would be to get off at . . . ," naming some little hamlet I had never heard of. "It's about two hours from Mokra. You'll have to walk from there."

My spirit groaned within me and my body seemed to protest. I had been on the go for days and had not slept properly for several nights worrying about Alex and the future. The prospect of a two-hour walk in the cold was not appealing. It was getting dark. Who knows what I would run into? It would be best to phone Stan at home and ask him to fetch me with the horse and buggy.

At the designated stop I got off the bus along with some high-school students. It was half past eight and quite dark. I asked where I could find a telephone but to my dismay was told that the only phone was at the post office, but that was closed and the postmistress lived in another village. My heart sank.

The students graciously offered to walk part of the way with me. The sky was clear with a full moon, but still I did not relish the prospect of walking alone through the winter forest. One of the boys took my suitcase. After an hour we came to a crossroads. In a kind effort to comfort me, the students carefully explained that the way to Mokra was not hard to follow, that after a stretch of woods I would come into the clear and be close to the village. Luckily, not much snow was on the ground; the walking would be comparatively easy. We parted with an exchange of good wishes.

The path crossed a large clearing and then plunged into the darkness of the woods. Though alone, I was not worried out in the open, but when I got in the deep forest, fear buried itself in my heart. The bright moonlight, dimmed by the trees and filtered through interlaced branches, wrote ugly, twisted shadows on the narrow path. There were rustling noises among the trees.

"Deer," I said firmly to myself.

But perhaps it was someone. What kind of people hide out in forests on winter nights? A German patrol? Worry plucked at the hem of my consciousness. There was a sudden rustle nearby. I came to a full stop and peered around, trying to penetrate the black-and-silver camouflage projected around me by the moon. It sounded like twigs breaking. Was it someone following me? In the spectral twilight under the old trees, everything looked strange. I listened for a while, but there was no more noise.

The suitcase pulled at my aching shoulder as I set off again, pausing now and then to listen and ease my distress. The combination of fatigue, anxiety, and hunger was driving me almost to hallucinations. I dragged myself along the path, with every nerve taut with the expectation of sharp, sudden danger. Finally I came out into the open and Mokra came in sight.

The village streets were deserted at eleven o'clock. I entered the forest again. The path to Richky was all downhill. Black, cumulous clouds snuffed out the moon. I heard forest noises that would have merely amused me if I had noticed them on any other occasion. As I went on, ripples, snaps, and murmurs mumbled all around me in an unintelligible, sinister language. I became truly frightened.

It was now nearing midnight. My feet were heavy as stone, and my eyes ached from trying to see in the dark. After what seemed to be many hours of walking, I turned the last bend and saw our house, a welcoming, shadowy bulk resting among large trees. I quickened my pace, shifting the heavy suitcase from one blistered hand to the other for what seemed to be the hundredth time, climbed the patio stairs and entered. Fanny was still up, and as I came in she said, "My goodness, but I was getting worried. I thought you would be home on the last bus."

She fussed over me, eventually settled me down and served me a full dinner with a cup of hot tea. I relaxed slowly, but the memory of the walk haunted me for a long time.

The next day I caught up on war news. The Germans' situation in Russia was deteriorating daily. The Wehrmacht had suffered titanic defeat in the snow and cold at Stalingrad, and Field Marshal Paulus had been taken prisoner with the whole German Sixth Army. Hitler was hysterical. Rather than surrender, he preferred the entire army to be wiped out to the last man in an epic act of self-immolation.

In Africa, too, the Germans suffered one setback after another. Even Field Marshal Erwin Rommel, the supposedly invincible hero of the German army, met defeat. The Americans had entered the war in December 1941, but only in North Africa did their weight begin to be felt. The Germans were unable to hold the territory they had conquered in Morocco, Tunisia, and Libya. They retreated again and again. This news, received surreptitiously on a receiver illegally tuned in to Radio London, was heartening. But my mind took it in only superficially; my whole attention was fixed on my campaign to bring about Alex's freedom. Levicek's cruel words, "We're going to chop his head off," still clanged in my ears.

When I went to apply for another permit to allow me to go to Germany, the Gestapo man behind the counter asked with a sneer, "Why do you need another pass? You have just returned from Breslau."

"My husband's trial is on the fifteenth of March and I would like to be there."

"Why bother? What can you do? Absolutely nothing. You have no need to be present. No pass."

I was dismissed. I was more angry than frightened. I had to find a new way, for nothing was going to keep me out of Breslau in the middle of March.

Uncle Sylvester offered to go to Germany for me. I was grateful to him, but he was a Catholic priest, and knowing how the Nazis regarded religion and especially the Catholic clergy I could not let him take the chance. We did not need two members of the family in prison.

Then in a moment of inspiration I thought of an acquaintance of ours named Mr. Schmid from Modrice. He was German, a kind, reasonable, moral man, a midlevel government employee working at the Brno Courthouse. It occurred to me that he might be able to issue a travel permit of some kind to get me across the border. I went to see him.

He listened and said regretfully, "I'm terribly sorry, Frau Kapral, but I don't have that kind of authority at all. I'd like to help you, but only the Gestapo can issue travel permits across the border. There's nothing I can do." I thought of a mouse in a maze, rushing up an alley promising freedom but ending up in another dead end.

After a moment of thought, Herr Schmid went on, "Do you by chance still have the permit from the last trip?"

I was carrying the same handbag I had taken to Breslau. I found my pass. He looked at it carefully under the light.

"Do you realize that this is signed in pencil? It's in pencil," he repeated. "You can erase it. Think about it."

"But isn't that dangerous? The signature means it has been used and cannot be used again."

"Yes, it's very dangerous, but I don't see how you're going to make it through any other way. I'm sure the Gestapo won't give you a second pass. It's dangerous, but if you must get there, you'll have to risk it."

I knew he was right. What alternatives did I have? I had to go, so I had to use the illegal pass in spite of the realistic chance its use would lead to my death.

"Here," Schmid said, "Let's see. Maybe we can erase it so nobody will see it had been signed before."

"What do you think, will it do?" he asked when he finished and handed the pass back to me.

"You can see that something has been written there. It's not quite gone."

"It's up to you. Go at night. The late train gets to the border after midnight. It travels blacked out because of the recent British air attacks on trains. The Gestapo will be inspecting papers by flashlight, and probably a weak, shielded one at that. If you decide to go, take the night train. But I agree, it is very dangerous."

The conviction that I had to use this fraud grew in my mind. The facts were stark. Alex's attorney was going to be in Breslau and he needed to get as much information as possible, and only I could provide that. Without it Alex might die. Therefore, I had to gamble my life to save his. And that was that.

I went to Alex's parents and told them my plan. Grandpa became so upset he trembled.

"Are you crazy, Zdena?" he said. "You mustn't go. It's too dangerous. You have two small children. Think of them, and think of yourself. You have to protect yourself, too. Your life is just as important as Alex's. I'm not at all sure you'd save Alex, and if you are arrested, and maybe executed or God knows what, what's going to happen to the children? They'll be not just fatherless, but motherless as well. I'm absolutely against it."

He was adamant. Grandma remained quiet, with a pained, downcast expression on her face, and her eyes filled with the infinite sadness of a suffering mother.

I began to waver; I really did not know what to do. In Mr. Schmid's office I had been certain that this was the only way. Grandpa, who was right about many things, had dented my resolve.

I did have an obligation to the children and, I supposed, to myself, too. But Alex was Alex, my husband. I knew for certain that if I did not go and something went wrong because of my absence, I would never forgive myself. To do less than everything I could for him would be to betray our whole marriage and love and so ultimately be a complete treason to myself.

I decided to risk it. I decided to rely on the false pass and go.

BOOK THREE

THE HAND
OF GOD

12
DANGEROUS TRIP

On Thursday morning, March 11, I kissed my two little girls good-bye, wondering if I would ever see them again; embraced Jana, Fanny, and Madi, who in the presence of the children said few words but much with their eyes; and set out on my second trip to Breslau. The illegal pass was in the side pocket of my bag.

In Brno I first went to see Alex's parents. His father was warmly supportive, knowing that I had made up my mind. He explained that he had felt it his duty to warn me of the consequences, but once I had made the decision he was happy and proud of me. He loved Alex profoundly. I stayed in their apartment that afternoon and evening. The two of them then took me to the station.

The train, en route from Vienna, was on time. The only other occupant in my compartment was a Viennese woman about my age. She was going to Berlin to meet her husband who was on leave from the Russian front. She was excited about seeing him again and chattered away most of the time. I was glad that she kept the conversation going all by herself, aided only by an occasional "Oh" or "How nice" from me. Fear made me lethargic; I could not have said more if I had wanted to.

I rehearsed the details of the approaching check at the border crossing in my imagination until it all blurred together and I thought I would go insane. Again and again I saw the Gestapo man come toward me, take my pass with a thin, white hand, look at it ever so slowly, and give it yet another look, raising it toward his face, peering at it closely, and then lifting his blank, merciless eyes to mine. It was chilling to the core. Would he notice that something had been erased? Would those eyes detect the smudges of embedded graphite? If he did notice, what would happen to me? To Alex and Janie and Evie?

I could not begin to think of what would follow. My worry refused to function beyond that moment. Every clack of the wheels on the rails brought me closer to annihilation. But the train rushed on and I could not turn back even if I had wanted to. I prayed for courage.

At half past one the train slowed and creaked to a stop with a hiss of steam. Through the window I could see only the vague outlines of a platform. The banging of doors, the clamor of military boots, and the sound of muffled, harsh voices filled the car as the Gestapo started to move through the train. My pulse was so frantically loud that the other woman must have been able to hear that something was wrong. Even she was silenced by those heavy steps in the night.

The noise came closer. Voices spoke outside the next compartment. There was the sound of a door opening and then its closing, followed by more muted words. My Viennese companion and I sat still in the dark silence.

Our door opened and a black form stepped into our compartment. The Gestapo agent towered over us, a shielded flashlight in his hand. He checked the Viennese woman's pass and then he turned to me. He examined my ID card, and slowly unfolded the pass. It was my fantasy made alive. I tried to relax by taking a few deep, long breaths, my pulse beating erratically at the base of my throat. The lightheadedness increased. My attention took refuge in unimportant details, the threadbare train seats, a stain on the floor, his polished high boots, the shabby decor of the carriage.

I raised my eyes carefully. He was still inspecting the pass. He looked at it once, then looked at it again. Then he picked up his pen, signed it, and handed it to me. He left the compartment without a word, without a flicker of concern.

I collapsed back against my seat. My heart in one strong surge began to sing. Suddenly I felt optimistic. I just knew everything would work out well in Breslau. My thoughts were coming back to the first and basic miracle. How lucky, how blessed I had been that on my first trip the pass had been signed in pencil. Had it been signed in ink, I could have done nothing, and this trip to Breslau would have been impossible. How remarkable that death should be defeated by so small an incident.

With a creak the carriage gave a sudden jolt, the whistle blew, and the train moved and gathered speed. This was Germany. The Austrian girl started chattering and giggling again, but I simply fell asleep through sheer relief.

Suddenly I felt someone shaking me.

A voice shouted, "Wake up. Didn't you tell me you were going to Breslau? Wake up! We're here, you have to get off the train or you'll finish up in Berlin. The train stops here for only ten minutes." I grabbed my coat and suitcase, thanked the young woman for waking me, told her I enjoyed her company, wished her good luck in Berlin, and ran.

It was six o'clock in the morning and the city was still blacked out. I walked over to a small restaurant near the railway station for a piece of toast and a cup of ersatz coffee. I sat there until eight o'clock, pondering the future. When the nearby post office opened, I sent a telegram to reassure my in-laws and then went to my hotel. The room was even smaller than I remembered, but it seemed like heaven. The streets had been desolate and frigid, the icy wind cutting like a saw. Warmth was luxury indeed.

At ten o'clock I took the trolley to the High Court Building. Frau Thomas was at her desk and the same Gestapo man loomed nearby. I noticed he was only pretending to work while he examined me closely.

I asked Frau Thomas for a permit to see Alex. She wrote out the pass with the expected haughty indifference. As she walked around her desk to hand it to me, when her back was turned to the agent, she winked at me and silently mouthed the words "washroom." I kept my face expressionless and left. No one was in the corridor or the washroom. I waited there for about ten minutes, and then Frau Thomas arrived. She told me that the best time to visit Alex would be on Saturday afternoon because in the morning the lawyer from Berlin was going to see him. He had already arrived, talked to her, and made an appointment to see Alex.

"It would be a good idea for you to come here early Monday morning," she added, "because the court hearing begins at ten o'clock. Be here at eight o'clock and come straight to the washroom. I'll meet you here and show you where to go so you can see your husband before he goes into the courtroom." She wished me good luck, whispered, "I'll see you here Monday at eight o'clock," and disappeared.

In the afternoon I met Alex's lawyer. Dr. Weber was the opposite of the elegant Dr. Benecke. Slightly built, short, with large, horn-rimmed glasses, he was the exact image of Harold Lloyd, the silent-movie comedian. He looked more like an impractical academic than an accomplished, clever lawyer. However, when he began talking, I was pleasantly surprised.

He was a sympathetic person and assured me that everything would happen as planned and as desired. He would make sure it did. Dr. Weber told me that a deposition stating that my husband was urgently needed at the plant had been signed by the Chemical and Metallurgical Corporation *Treuhänder*'s representative. Then he asked me a few specific questions, which I answered to his satisfaction, and we discussed the whole case in detail from beginning to end. Before we parted he invited me to have dinner with him. I accepted, wanting to do anything I could to help. And it would be good not to be alone.

In the evening we met in the lobby of his hotel and went into the large, elegant, brightly lit dining room. The two of us had the most sumptuous dinner I had shared in a long time, but I was so tense that I could hardly eat.

The dining room was crowded mostly with German officers and their wives. The men were on leave from the Russian front. I wondered if that was why the hotel had such a variety and quantity of food. I had not seen so much food since the war had started. It was a disconcerting feeling to eat dinner in a room filled with one's enemies.

On Saturday afternoon I went to the prison again. When Alex came in I could see he was upset. He began talking as soon as he took his seat.

"Zdena, where on earth did you get that lawyer? He's a complete fool. Do you know what he asked me? He wanted to know why I was wearing this striped suit. He said I'm a political prisoner and entitled to civilian clothes! And then he wanted to know if I was getting my meals from a restaurant, as I should, being a political prisoner! The man's mad! He doesn't seem to know anything about present reality. You couldn't have got anybody worse, for heaven's sake! I don't think he's got the slightest idea of what's happening! If you'd engaged a second-year law student you could have done better. You said he came from Berlin?"

"Alex, calm down," I replied. "He's the best you can get. He's very clever. You have to trust me. You have to believe in me. You know Tony Srba found him for us. You can be sure he's the best."

But Alex would not be pacified. "You didn't talk to him. I did. I don't think he knows what he's doing at all. I don't trust him. I don't think he can handle the case. He's all wrong and there's not even time to find anyone else! Can you possibly try to find somebody in Breslau this afternoon? I don't want that character! Do you know who he reminds me of? He looks like Harold Lloyd. I'm surprised you chose him."

Despite his irritation he looked both sad and dejected, and animated and depressed at the same time.

I said soothingly, "Alex, you're wrong. He's a good attorney. You have to trust me. You know I've never done anything to harm you and I'm quite positive he's the best lawyer you could have."

We argued away the whole ten minutes without noticing it. Then we were shocked into silence when the guard stood up and announced, "Time's up," and I had to say good-bye. It was awful. We couldn't even shake hands.

For the hundredth time I said, "Don't worry, darling; I'm sure everything will be all right and I'm positive you're in the best possible hands."

I wished him good luck and said, "I'll be seeing you on Monday when you come to the court building. I'll be waiting there for you."

"I'll see you then," he said and gave me such a despairing stare that it wrenched my heart. He turned and left.

I was heartbroken. I had thought I would manage to convey to him that there was more to all these arrangements than I was able to tell him, but with the guard there I could not give him even the slightest hint. What a miserable weekend he was going to spend.

The lawyer would visit the prison on Sunday morning, when I hoped he would be able to cheer Alex up a little.

It was too early for my meeting with Dr. Weber so I went to my room and lay down, trying to relax and maybe attain some measure of inner peace.

Alex's desperation was understandable considering the conditions of his imprisonment. I was to find out later what a hell the Breslau prison really was.

13

HIGH COURT

My appointment with Albert Weber, the lawyer, was not at the same hotel we dined at the night before. Dr. Weber was already waiting for me in the lobby. After his customary courteous greeting he took me to the hotel's elegant coffee lounge.

It was a world so different from the Breslau prison that it seemed to be on another planet. We entered a large, brightly lit salon with small tables covered by stylish, starched white linen and set with fine china, crystal, and silver. Waiters in white jackets that seemed to shine scurried around with trays of coffee cups and a vast selection of Viennese pastries. A small orchestra played the waltz from *The Merry Widow* to accompany the murmur of intimate conversations and the endless cascade of glistening sound caused by the soft touch of silver cutlery on china plates.

The patrons were mostly German officers and their well-dressed, well-fed ladies. I was surprised that many of them were actually dancing. I had not seen people dance since 1939. As much as Czechs love dancing, no one among my friends would have considered taking a single step to music.

The restaurant with its air of happy prosperity was in such contrast to the prison and to my poor Alex in his striped outfit and wooden clogs that I found it hard to believe my eyes.

With zest, Dr. Weber, totally unaware of the dreamlike quality of the scene, ordered coffee and delicious cakes for both of us. While we waited he told me that Alex had remarked in passing that I spoke French fluently, adding, "Would you mind if we speak French from now on?"

I was pleasantly surprised. "Of course not, I'll be delighted," and from that moment all our conversations were in French. He told me that he had studied at the Sorbonne in Paris, the city he loved. After graduation he returned to Berlin and obtained a position in Dr. Benecke's office.

I described how despondent Alex had been earlier in the day and asked if he could try to cheer him the next morning. Reaching into his breast pocket, he said he had a note for me from Alex. The only thing written on it was a name, Frau Opel, and an address in Breslau.

"What is it?"

"Alex wants you to go and see this lady. Her husband, Dr. Opel, who is German, is in prison with him."

Then he asked me several things about Alex. After we had finished our discussion and coffee, he invited me to go to the cinema. Though I was not in a film-going mood, still less did I want to be alone. The evening stretched ahead, empty, dreary, and sleepless. It was a good picture, but I had a hard time following the plot. The thought of Monday morning kept intruding itself.

The next day was Sunday. Before we parted, Dr. Weber invited me to have lunch with him. We went to yet another large restaurant full of German officers and their wives. The food was delicious and plentiful. After dinner had been ordered and served impeccably by a host of expert waiters, Dr. Weber, to my complete surprise, launched into a violent diatribe against the Nazi regime. He became increasingly vehement as he got into the subject. Waving his hands for emphasis, and raising his voice, he described his hatred of Hitler and everything he stood for. In his opinion Hitler was destroying Germany and was the worst thing that could have happened to the German nation. There was much more to the same effect.

I was aghast. One could get arrested for making any statement even vaguely and indirectly hinting at criticism of Hitler and the

Nazi party. I personally had knowledge of several people who had had the bad judgment to utter far milder words in public places and were either executed or put into concentration camps.

"For goodness sake, Dr. Weber," I whispered pleadingly, plucking at his sleeve, the panic rising in my voice, "please don't say things like that here. What if somebody hears you? Instead of getting Alex out, you'll land us both in prison with him." I tried to smile for effect, but I am sure the resulting grimace was a poor approximation.

But Albert Weber would not be stopped.

"Don't worry," he said airily, "we're talking French; who'd understand us? And anyway even if they did, half of them feel the same way." He actually chuckled.

"I'm not so sure," I said urgently. "If they did, Germany wouldn't be what it is today; but anyway, I'd much prefer it if you didn't talk like that. I'm nervous about it."

He went right on. The dam had burst. He had found a sympathetic listener he knew he could trust. He railed against Hitler, the Gestapo, Himmler, Goebbels, Goering, calling them thugs. Meanwhile I was peering around us nervously, watching for a stern-faced man to start for us and thinking, "Oh, my God, after all this I will be imprisoned."

What had set him off? To be sure I was glad he was not a Nazi. I would have been even more glad if he had not chosen such a public place for his diatribe. I ate as fast as I could.

The lunch finally came to an end without anyone seeming to have overheard our conversation. I was never so happy to leave a restaurant in my life. We parted cordially and I set out to see Frau Opel.

She was much older than I. After greeting me warmly at the door, she asked me inside and introduced me to her mother-in-law, who lived with her, and her daughter, a handsome girl of about twenty. Her husband, who was in Alex's cell, had been in prison since 1939. He was a German with a doctorate in chemical engineering and was an expert in cracking naphtha. Dr. Opel and a friend had discussed Hitler and his book, *Mein Kampf,* in a streetcar one day and the opinion was expressed that not everything written in *Mein Kampf* was quite true. A woman sitting opposite overheard the conversation, jumped up, ran to the front, stopped the streetcar, and had the Gestapo called. Dr. Opel was arrested on the spot and was sentenced to ten years in prison.

As could be expected, Frau Opel was violently anti-Nazi and anti-Hitler. She sympathized with me when I recounted to her my story and told me how sorry she was that Alex had been imprisoned.

"I know how dreadful it must be for you!" she said, leaning forward and patting my hand. Then she paused for a minute with her brow knit in thought and continued, "You know that here you're among friends. But I must warn you. We have a son. He's almost fourteen now; his name is Hans. As a matter of fact, he might be coming home any minute now. When he comes in we'll have to stop talking about all such things because we can't trust him. He's in the Hitler Youth and believes Hitler is the greatest man that ever lived. I've talked myself blue in the face to him.

"I've told him, 'Hans, how can you believe that? Hitler is the man who imprisoned your father. You know your father is innocent. How can you admire the man who's making him suffer, making all of us suffer?' And do you know what he answered? 'Everybody's entitled to make one mistake, and my father is the one mistake the Führer has made. But everything else he's done is good. He's a great man for Germany.' My own son! Can you just imagine how sad that makes me? There's not a thing I can do about it. We can talk in front of my daughter because she shares my opinions. She hates the Nazis as much as you and I do, but we can't talk in front of Hans. We can't trust him; he could denounce us. Imagine, my only son. It's breaking my heart."

Her husband had found a way of sending her short notes from time to time, and over the years she had acquired some knowledge of the conditions of the prison. The Breslau penitentiary had been already notorious as a detention center for criminals before the war began and still had a fair number of nonpolitical inmates from the early years of the Nazi government.

The wardens were not Gestapo men but civilians, prison officials by profession. The only exceptions were the members of the execution squads and a number of so-called interrogation specialists, that is, torturers.

The cells had been originally intended for one person, but later the prison became badly overcrowded by the influx of political prisoners. Three men were jammed into a space meant for one. Each cell had three bunks. In the corner was a commode containing a slop bucket. These buckets were emptied daily, hosed out, and replaced. The revolting job of emptying and cleaning them was a coveted one. It involved visiting other cells and made possible a surreptitious exchange of news.

The most loathed work assignment was the job of guillotine attendant, which involved collecting the heads, carrying away the bodies, and hosing the blood off the floor and the mechanism. Though these prisoners received an increased food allowance, everyone tried to avoid the job.

The attendants brought back gruesome reports of the executions. Frau Opel told me about a condemned man who broke loose from the guards and ran toward the high wall that surrounded the guillotine and separated it from the rest of the room. In his terror the poor fellow, clad only in his paper shroud, clawed his way up this wall with his bare hands. The Gestapo men let him get halfway up, then, while deriding him, brutally dragged him down, wrestled him under the guillotine blade, and chopped off his head while laughing at the comedy.

According to his wife, Dr. Opel had been lucky enough to be assigned to the prison's print shop, and he asked the warden to get Alex posted there, too. The work was considerably easier there than the average normal labor. She told me the story of a man in solitary confinement who had become so mentally unbalanced by starvation and fear that in his hunger he ate the paper envelopes he was given to glue. He consumed so many that he died.

The prisoners were allowed to shower only once a month, though the elite, such as the trustees, could shower once a week. The so-called meals were of much the same quality as those served in Kounicovy Koleje. The prisoners' gnawing hunger was constant, and all weakened daily.

Frau Opel never managed to smuggle in any food. She was a very kind, good woman, and so were her mother-in-law and daughter. I spent as pleasant an afternoon as I could under the circumstances, feeling that I was not wholly alone and that there were others who could understand how I really felt. Though I stayed for several hours, I did not meet Hans. I was not at all sorry.

As I prepared to leave, I promised that I would let them know the outcome of the court hearing. They wished Alex and me the best of luck, and I left, thinking again that there were some good Germans. I returned to my room. I succeeded only in dozing fitfully, wandering from one nightmare to the next and waking frequently throughout the long and fear-filled night.

The next morning I was up early. After forcing down a skimpy breakfast, I hurried to the courthouse. Hoping that I might be near Alex or even speak to him during the day, I took three small packets of food along. Every time I had seen him he looked thinner and paler. At exactly eight o'clock I was in the courthouse washroom.

A few minutes later Frau Thomas arrived. She smiled good morning to me.

"We'll have to hurry," she said. "I'm going to show you where you can sit. There's a small bench outside the courtroom near the door where the prisoners are brought in, and you'll be able to see your husband. They'll bring them from the prison at about nine o'clock, and the court hearing will start at ten. Now," she raised her hand in order to give the words emphasis, "officially you are allowed in the courtroom for the hearing, but I wouldn't advise you to do it. The judges always ask the identity of the spectators, and I have noticed that those prisoners whose relatives are in the courtroom always get stiffer sentences, so I would stay out if I were you."

"But," she continued, "there's a peephole in the door and if there's no one in the corridor, you can look through it and see everything that's going on. But please remember, if you hear anyone coming, go back and sit on the bench and pretend you just happen to be there. The passage isn't used a great deal, and once the court hearings start I don't think anyone will come that way. You should be able to watch the whole thing."

I thanked her once more and said I hoped I would see her again.

"I don't know about that," she answered. "If you need any more help, come into my office, and then we'll meet again here, but if everything works out the way we hope it will, this will be good-bye." Saying this she gave me a quick, warm smile and a hug.

"I don't know what I should have done without your help," I said. "We'll always be grateful to you. I wish you the very best of luck from the bottom of my heart."

She waved away my thanks, opened the door, and went out. I

followed her at a distance. The building was deserted, and the hollow tapping of our heels on the hard floor, echoing and reechoing along the long, empty corridors, magnified the cruel, impersonal atmosphere of the courthouse.

We went down a flight of stairs and turned into a short passage with a small bench near a massive wooden door. Frau Thomas nodded at the bench and then went a few steps farther, toward the door. She pointed to the peephole to make sure I saw it, and when I acknowledged that I understood, she waved at me and disappeared down the corridor. That was the last time I saw her.

I shall never forget her. What a supremely good woman she was. My whole being was filled with love and great admiration for her. From that day onward whenever I heard anyone condemning the whole German nation down to the last man and woman for the Nazi atrocities, I recalled Frau Thomas. She was the bravest woman I ever met. She went on working for the resistance, but, tragically, her suspicion that the Gestapo was watching her proved correct. About eight months later this beautiful woman was caught, sentenced to death, and executed. I wept bitter tears for her the day Jan Horky told me, and I mourned for her in my heart for many years. She was an exceptional human being.

No one was in sight in the hallway, so I went to the big door and looked through the hole. As she had said, I could see almost the entire courtroom.

It was a depressing place, filled with echoes of past tragedies and endless suffering. On a podium at the far end of the room was a long table with five chairs positioned behind it, apparently intended for the judges. Two small desks were in front of the table, one for the court translators, the other for the stenographer. On the right side, behind the heavy railing, was a long bench for the prisoners. On the left side, opposite the prisoners' enclosure, several chairs were provided for the lawyers. The rest of the huge room was filled with heavy benches intended for the public. They remained unoccupied during the entire court session. At this early hour the courtroom was completely empty. It was a drab place, gloomy and menacing.

I went back to the bench and sat down. It was about half past eight. With typical German efficiency, the prisoners were always processed in groups, and Alex would be in a group of sixteen, all from Biochema. Frau Thomas had told me that this was the second group from Biochema to be tried. The first group had been before the court two or three weeks before.

I sat on the bench, my stomach churning, trying to think through the implications of all these pieces of news. As much as I wanted to believe Dr. Benecke and Dr. Weber, Levicek's words had seared themselves into my brain, and by now I also knew from Frau Opel that beheading was the standard method of execution in the Breslau prison.

I heard somebody coming down the corridor and looked up to see bearing down on me the most disgusting person I had ever laid eyes on. He was a man of medium height, dark complexion, and shabby appearance with small, shifty eyes, and several front teeth missing. He was unwashed, uncombed, and when he came closer I noticed a powerful, unpleasant smell emanating from him. I do not think he had had a bath in several months. His uncleanliness seemed to be something more than bodily in nature. He slid down on the bench next to me. I tried not to pay any attention that might start him talking—or delay his departure.

An ugly voice speaking ugly German said in my ear, "You Frau Kapral?" Amazed that he knew my name, I turned my face toward him, directly into the smell of his breath. I recoiled with nausea as the odor of intense putrefaction washed over me. His teeth must have been in the final stage of decay.

"Yes, I am Mrs. Kapral."

"Nice t'meetcha," he said, leaning toward me. "I'm Cousin George."

I was close to fainting. Where on earth had Alex met such a man? Even in prison, how could he bring himself to talk to someone like this? The man looked like a cutthroat, a loathsome outcast of society. It appeared obvious that this was not a political prisoner. His face was shifty and depraved, full of foxy cunning that gave him a peculiarly repulsive look. Later I found he had been imprisoned for armed robbery. I thought angrily, how could Alex have sent a man like this to see me when he knew I was all alone here in Breslau? The man was not merely repugnant, he was frightening. I edged away.

"What do you want?"

"Alex wrote you about me, and I think you have something for me," he said with a leer.

I handed him the envelope with the five hundred marks that I made sure I had with me whenever I went out in Breslau. I was glad to have the mystery of the money and its recipient solved, but, still, I wondered about the nature of this business transaction. What could a man like this have done for Alex to earn five hundred marks?

He took it, saying, "Thanks. Look, I want to talk to you. Can we meet tonight?"

Aghast, I looked at him. He was the last person in the world I wanted to meet anytime, day or night. Thinking fast, I gave him the address of the hotel where Albert Weber was staying. He did not seem to realize he was being tricked. Confident now to the point of cockiness, he added, "I'll be there at nine tonight and we talk some more. Also, I want to come see you in Brno."

God forbid, I thought. That would be all I needed. "We'll talk about it tonight," I temporized, knowing they would never let him through the doors of the hotel I had directed him to.

The sound of many footsteps rang in the corridor. A file of prisoners was coming, escorted by guards. When George saw them, he jumped up and said, "I don't want those guards to see me here. And I don't want to see them either. I've had enough of them." Turning to me with a leer I think he intended as a smile, he hissed, "I'll see you tonight." And with that, Cousin George disappeared. I was relieved to see the last of him.

I looked anxiously at the oncoming prisoners. There were sixteen in all, chained together, shuffling along behind the guard, dressed uniformly in the striped prison suits and shod in wooden clogs. They were thin as scarecrows. The sickly, pale faces made their eyes look huge and dark. All were our friends and colleagues from Biochema.

I stared at them. They moved with indescribable sadness. These were people I had talked with and laughed with, people I had seen in the gardens, on the tennis courts, at office parties, people whose company I had enjoyed in the past and whom I respected and liked. It was appalling to see them in these circumstances. They were glad to see me. Each of them managed to smile at me, and their eyes told me how pleased they were that someone from the world where they really belonged had managed to make it through to be with them in this terrible hour.

Alex was twelfth in line. His hands, like those of the others, were handcuffed in front of him. He, too, smiled at me, but I could see Albert Weber had not been successful in reassuring him.

The courtroom swallowed the procession. The corridor was as vacant and silent as before. I looked through the peephole. The defense lawyers had entered by another door and were taking their places. Dr. Weber was among them.

Another bedraggled prisoner under guard came shuffling down the passage. It was Novotny, the man whose testimony had caused Alex's arrest. Seeing him like this made me feel sorry for him. The guard shoved him into a small room opposite the courtroom, went in himself, and slammed the door behind them both.

I sat down on the bench to wait for ten o'clock. I felt completely consumed by anxiety. Moments flew by, but no time passed. I was here, but also seemed far away. Everything seemed drastically important and unimportant at once. There is a torture of the body, but there is also a torture of the spirit with a pain all its own. During the next half hour I underwent such an agony of the soul. In an almost biblical sense I was forsaken. Only one part of me was unshaken and remained a source of life in the middle of the inner chaos. It was my deep belief that Alex would be free. I thought about how my husband and all other prisoners must be feeling, what an agony they must be experiencing. What will happen to them? Had I seen some of them for the last time?

Novotny's guard came out to stretch his legs. He did not look unkindly. "Excuse me," I said, "can I give your prisoner something to eat? I have a few bits of food here and he's from my home town."

"Yes, all right," the guard answered. "Give it to me and I'll take it in to him." He was not Gestapo.

I took one of my food packets and handed it to him. "Has he already been tried?" I asked, making small talk.

"Yes, sentenced to death by guillotine. He's going to be executed soon. They've kept him alive so he can be a witness against one of the prisoners being tried today." And I realized with a shiver of dread that Novotny was here to testify against Alex. What might he say in some desperate attempt to save his life?

After the guard disappeared behind the closed door, a crescendo of voices drew my attention to the courtroom. I crossed back and peeked through the hole in the door. The five judges had arrived and were seated on the podium. The one in the center was, I supposed, the chief judge and president of the court, Dr. Benecke's friend. The prisoners were lined along the right wall of the courtroom and their lawyers were seated on the left side. My friends, the two interpreters, were sitting to the left of the judges, directly in front of me.

The clerk proclaimed the *Volksgericht*, the High Court, to be in session. The president of the court explained the procedure. The judges would hear and sentence each prisoner individually, according to the order in which their names were read out. Alex's name was fifteenth, next to the last.

The second man's sentence jarred me to attention. The word *death* rang out like a sledge on an anvil. He was to be executed by guillotine. I knew him so well. His name was Bohus Kolar, no relation to Alex's best friend Mojmir. He was a good person, a pleasant, friendly man who not only would never harm anyone else but always did what he could to help everyone. He did not deserve death, let alone such a barbarous death.

I could not stay another minute. I was suffocating. I had to get fresh air. I calculated another three hours would pass before Alex's case came up. I had to get out from under the shadow of this murderous regime, away from this grisly charade of justice. I left the building and wandered aimlessly along the cold, inhospitable streets of Breslau, forlorn, not caring or even noticing where I was going, scarcely conscious of my surroundings, one of the sad, lonely women drifting through the nightmare of that darkest of Europe's winters.

Suddenly the Catholic cathedral rose before me. The massive carved doors were open. I went in. There was no one inside but myself. In the great compassionate silence I sensed I was alone with God, who was ever so quietly, ever so tenderly beckoning me to come to Him. I tiptoed toward the altar, knelt down at an ancient wooden railing polished to the smoothness of flesh by centuries of anguished hands like mine. Too confused for formal prayer, too exhausted to demand reason, I simply asked Him, who loved us, to set Alex free, to take pity on us in this dark hour of our life. My heart opened and I prayed for all the poor condemned prisoners awaiting death, prayed for us all, our sad and forsaken Czech nation. I remained there on my knees for an hour. Then I rose, slowly walked back down the church aisle, and left the healing quiet. Something peaceful remained with me through the next several shattering hours.

When I reached the courtroom door I peered in to see what progress had been made. I heard a ten-year sentence, then one for fifteen years. I did not want to listen; it upset me too much. I knew these men and I liked them. I mourned for them and their families, but I could not bear to listen to the sentencing. It tore me apart. Number fourteen came up. The poor man was sentenced to fifteen years in prison.

Then the clerk of the court called out, "Kapral!"

The prosecutor read the charge and amplified it by adding that Alex was guilty of *Kommunistische Hochverrat*, that is, Communist-inspired high treason. Alex was accused of assisting both the Czech underground and the Communist party. Furthermore, he maintained, Alex had contributed large sums of money to both the underground and the Communist party. His name had been found on a list kept by a man who had been collecting money on behalf of the resistance and who had already been sentenced to death. The prosecutor ended his speech by demanding the death penalty for Alex.

I was shocked and terrified. Evidently the Nazis felt the need to buttress the accusation about the Czech resistance with some anti-Communist propaganda.

Dr. Weber took the floor asking Alex to explain to the court how it happened that his name was on Novotny's list.

Speaking in Czech in a firm and resolute voice, Alex repeated his story exactly as he had told it to the Gestapo through every interrogation session and many beatings.

"I was on the phone, talking to the Prague office, when Novotny came to the door. Because he was forever collecting money for various funds like the Red Cross and the Widows' and Orphan Children's Fund, I assumed he wanted money for something like that again. Without pausing in my conversation, I reached into my pocket . . ." Here Alex unconsciously copied the gestures of a man cradling the phone on his shoulder, reaching into his pocket, and taking out some money. ". . . and I gave it to him. I had no idea what it was for. I just assumed it was for some charity or other."

The gestures seemed unrehearsed and spontaneous. I noticed that the interpreter was not only translating each word with great accuracy but also copied Alex's gestures, looking up to see someone at the door, juggling the phone, reaching into his pocket, and absent-mindedly handing over some money, and thus doubling the effect and emphasizing Alex's ignorance of the situation.

The chief justice listened intensely. He interrupted at one point, nodding his head in agreement.

"*Ja, ja,*" he said, "that is quite possible . . . one is on the phone, an important call . . . somebody comes to the door . . . a man who always collects money for this and that . . . one holds the phone thus . . . ," and he, too, began acting out the movements as though reliving an experience of his own, "takes out the money, quite unaware of doing it . . . *ja, ja, das ist ganz möglich,* that's possible."

The sight of the three of them all acting out the same scene would have been comic in other, less-malignant circumstances.

As if on impulse, the chief judge picked up his gavel, banged it on the table, and almost shouted, "Case dismissed!" It was so unexpected that it took moments for anyone in the courtroom to respond. There was a minute of timelessness.

I myself could not grasp what had happened. Then my heart leapt, and I floated off the floor. The sensation was amazing. I was weightless. I had never been so happy, so very thankful to God, and so stunned and joyful all at once.

While I stood there in rapture, my palms pressed on the wood of the door to keep myself from falling, the sixteenth case began. The accused was a young man, scarcely twenty-two years old, and to my great relief there was another miracle and his case was dismissed, too. I was elated for him. Then the court adjourned. The door opened and the prisoners were herded into the small room across the corridor to wait for the police van.

Alex came out with Dr. Weber and the guard took them to a separate room. The lawyer saw me standing there and called out for me to come and join them. I embraced Alex with all my strength and both of us sincerely thanked Albert Weber.

When Alex and I calmed down a little, I asked Dr. Weber, "Can Alex come home with me immediately?"

Dr. Weber answered, "I honestly don't know. Let me find out," and he disappeared back into the courtroom.

I wanted to hold Alex tight and never never let him go. I wanted to shout, sing, dance, and thank God. But the guard was still there. We had been educated in the Gestapo's hard school never to do anything spontaneous, so I had to content myself with smiling at my husband and saying everything with my eyes. I offered him the sandwiches and cookies I had carried with me all day long. Alex was too nervous to eat. He nibbled at the cookies, but he had trouble swallowing even those.

I did not know what to do with the food so I asked the guard, "Could I give this to the other prisoners? I'm sure they'd like to have it." The guard said he would give it to them, so I took out a couple of cookies for Alex and gave the guard the rest of the food.

Dr. Weber came back and said it was as he had feared. Alex was not free to leave prison at that time. He would have to return to Brno with the next transport. He had been arrested by the Gestapo and so he had to be sent back to the Gestapo to be released officially by them. That would take at the most two to three weeks, and then Alex would be home again.

I was disappointed. If he was innocent, he should have been set free immediately. I consoled myself with the thought that this was the next best thing.

I remembered the poor men who had just been sentenced to death and I asked Dr. Weber if there was any chance he could do something for them. Could he and Dr. Benecke intervene and get their sentences changed? They both had wives and families. This would be terrible for them. Albert Weber promised to try. Maybe, he said, he would be lucky again.

Novotny's sentence was eventually changed to life imprisonment; but the other man was not so fortunate. Dr. Weber wrote me later saying that when, following Kolar's arrest, the Gestapo went to search his house they found guns and ammunition there. Anyone who was found in possession of a gun was automatically sentenced to death, so, Dr. Weber said, nothing could be done for him. Poor Kolar was executed. Novotny, as I was to find out later, returned home after the war, none the worse for his experiences.

Alex's guard returned, announced that the van was there and that it was time for Alex to return to his cell. This time Alex was not handcuffed—and we were allowed to kiss good-bye.

The ordeal was over.

I turned to Dr. Weber to thank him again. He asked me what I was going to do now. I replied that I had to go to the post office to send telegrams to Alex's and my parents, who must be worried sick waiting to hear the outcome of the trial. As his train was not leaving until later that evening and he had nothing to do, he offered to escort me. I accepted with pleasure as I did not want to face these bittersweet hours alone.

I sent both telegrams and we were about to leave the post office when I smelled a familiar stench and at the same time heard an oily hissing voice behind me, saying, "Well, Frau Kapral, what a nice surprise!" And when I turned around I again thought I would faint.

Of all the people in Breslau I had to meet this one again. It was Cousin George.

14
UNEXPECTED DEVELOPMENT

George apparently did not notice my reaction to his reappearance in my life.

"I was just mailing a letter, too. What a coincidence," he said chattily, evidently intending to make a social occasion of it in the hope, I assumed, of our spending the evening together.

Dr. Weber looked at George with growing amazement as if he could not believe his eyes. "Is this man bothering you?" he asked me under his breath. "Should I call the police?"

"No," I whispered, "it's all right." I then turned to George and said emphatically, "I'll see you tonight. Good-bye for now."

When he was gone Albert Weber asked, "Who is that man? How is it that you know him?"

"I just met him this morning in the courthouse. He evidently must have done something for Alex in the prison because Alex sent me a note some time back telling me to pay five hundred marks to someone called Cousin George, and it turned out to be this man. Isn't he awful? I'm quite afraid of him!"

"You should be. He looks like a criminal. I wouldn't have anything to do with him if I were you. Did you say you're meeting him tonight?"

"Oh no," I said. "He asked me where I was staying, and to get rid of him I gave him the address of your hotel. They won't let him in, so he won't know I stood him up, and I'm leaving at seven tomorrow morning." Dr. Weber showed his relief.

We went to a small coffee shop for a celebration cup of ersatz coffee. I thanked him again, with all the sincerity my grateful heart could generate, for everything he had done. He gave me his card and asked me to let him know the instant Alex came home. I felt I was parting with a friend.

It had been a long day and I was very tired. After a telephone call to Mrs. Opel to tell her the marvelous news, I made my way back to the hotel and packed for the trip home, all the while thinking about my little Janie, who had turned three that day. How happy both girls would be when they found out that Daddy was coming home again. This started me thinking about Alex, and I began to wonder about his connection with Cousin George. I found out the story later.

When Alex was delivered to the Breslau prison, he was thrown into solitary confinement, a tiny, cold, damp, dark cell. For weeks he was alone without books or without conversation to occupy his mind. He slowly sank deeper and deeper into morbid thoughts about the future. The only human being he saw was George, who three times a day brought him what passed for his food: moldy bread, ersatz coffee, and watery soup.

This ugly man was his sole contact with the world outside his cell, and Alex began to look forward to his visits. George became increasingly important to his psychic survival. The two exchanged a few more words at each mealtime, and after a while they became quite well acquainted, almost friends.

One day George said, "Alex, I was looking around in the locker rooms and I saw a nice pair of boots with your name on them. Listen," he went on, with a furtive glance toward the door, "let me have those boots and give me five hundred marks and I'll get you out of solitary into a cell with a couple of other guys. Maybe I can also get you a job in the printing shop. I'm being released next month after fifteen years in this hole and I need shoes and some money. What d'you say? Is it a deal?"

Some people tolerate solitary confinement better than others. Outgoing and gregarious, Alex was going insane without other human beings. He accepted George's offer. George told Dr. Opel about

Alex, and Opel, interested in having another chemist in the cell to talk to, asked the warden to transfer Alex into his cell and assign him into the printing shop. The warden agreed, and Alex was transferred. He believed he had made one of the better deals of his life: his mental health and perhaps even his life for five hundred marks and a pair of boots.

At half past six the next morning I was at the railway station. The train materialized out of the dawn mist on time and was soon chugging across the plains of what was then Germany but after the war became part of Poland. In a few hours it stopped at the Czech border.

When the Gestapo agent checked our passports he looked at my pass, read it carefully, and then put it in his pocket. My mind could not believe my eyes: "They don't return passes!" Only then did I fully realize how extremely fortunate I had been on my first trip. It was a fluke that the pass had been not only signed in pencil but also handed back to me. I saw as in a flash of bright light that only through the grace of an attentive God had I managed to get into Germany the second time.

Once the train was across the border and steaming through the rolling, snow-covered Czech countryside, I finally relaxed completely. I had not realized how drained I had been by the happenings in Breslau. Soon, I thought, I'd be at home and able to take things easy, have some quiet time with the children and wait for Alex's return. And then we could finally all return to a more normal life. My thoughts ran in a joyful fever.

Back home, however, I went straight to bed with a substantial case of influenza. Janie came back from her usual afternoon walk with Madi and, overjoyed to see me, flew into my arms. She was such a pretty little girl. Evie came home from school in the afternoon excited and happy that I was back. She was ecstatic to hear that her daddy was coming home soon. Evie adored Alex and had missed him as only a daughter can miss a father. The rest of the household—Fanny, Madi, Peter, and his wife Anna—were happy about the news, too. After so many pointless days when living had been an act of sheer will, our hope was renewed.

In the middle of the following week I went to see Jan Horky to tell him the details of the trial and Alex's release and to ask him if it would be appropriate for me to go to the Gestapo and find out when Alex was going to come home.

Jan Horky was delighted the case had been dismissed. Nevertheless, worry flickered in his eyes. He told me in no uncertain terms it would be a mistake to go to the Gestapo and thus draw attention to Alex's case. His contacts would investigate for me. In the middle of April, about three weeks later, Horky phoned and told me to collect my typewriter. Alex had been returned to Brno, not to Kounicovy Koleje this time but to Susilovy Koleje, another converted student dormitory building at Masaryk University.

"Well, what's going to happen now?" I asked him. "Have you been able to find out a definite date?"

"Not yet. Evidently there's been no decision made about your husband's release."

"But what's the problem?" I asked anxiously. "The court found him innocent and the case was dismissed. What right do they have to hold him? Why don't I go to the Gestapo myself and ask what it is all about? They surely can't keep him imprisoned after the *Volksgericht* found him innocent!"

But Jan Horky urged me to calm myself and go home. He would contact me as soon as he knew what the problem was.

The familiar pull of worry settled on my life once again. Horky called a week later. As soon as I entered the office and saw his face I knew he had bad news. His Gestapo contact had come to see him the night before. Alex was not going to be freed at all. Ever! He was to be sent to Auschwitz concentration camp on the transport leaving Brno on Thursday, May 6.

Auschwitz! The name hit my head like a hammer blow. I steadied myself against Mr. Horky's desk. Auschwitz? Surely I had not heard right. Alex was free. He had been found innocent. Why should the Gestapo want to send him to Auschwitz? It must be a mistake. But the look on my friend's face told me it was not. It was true. Auschwitz, my mind shrieked, that hell from which few returned. But how could they, and why, and who had made this murderous decision? I heard myself as from a long distance ask, "Why? Who decided this? He was freed. He should come home. Who said he is going to Auschwitz?"

"I asked the same question," Jan Horky said quietly with a look of infinite compassion on his face. "My contact said he had asked his commanding officer the same thing indirectly and was told that nobody suspected of high treason was ever set free, even if the high court, or any court, had found him not guilty. A defendant will always be under suspicion of working against the Reich. Alex could be held indefinitely under German law, and the Gestapo reserves the right to send him to any concentration camp they choose."

My legs would no longer support me. I sat down heavily in the chair Mr. Horky offered me. Only yesterday I had been happy because I believed Alex would soon be free and on his way home. Auschwitz was far, far worse than any prison in Breslau. It was the worst of the concentration camps. Dr. Benecke would have done much better if he had asked the judge to sentence Alex to five years in the Breslau prison instead of arranging a dismissal of charges. He would have been hungry and cold there, to be sure, but he would have had a better chance of survival than in Auschwitz. Auschwitz, the end of everything, the destruction of the world.

"Maybe if I go to the Gestapo," I said, half to myself and half to Jan Horky, "they might give me permission to visit Alex. At least I could say good-bye to him."

"No," Horky said sternly, "there's time enough for that later. I talked to Franz, my Gestapo contact. He's going to think the situation through over the weekend; he feels something might be done, but as of now he isn't sure what. He will meet you here on Monday. There's a chance we can get him out after all. If he can't do anything for Alex, then you go, ask for a permit to see him and say good-bye."

I was only half listening. There was nothing to be done. Jan Horky was just trying to ease my way through the suffering of the next hard days. Once more I went home in deep despair, all the deeper after the rebirth of hope and a few happy days. Before the trial in Breslau I would not admit the possibility of defeat. After hearing the sad news I felt trapped and braced myself for another parting; this one, the true, final farewell.

The weekend limped tediously by. Time, as it always seemed to do when irrational violence burst into our lives, had ceased. I could not settle down to my work and wandered around the house like a dismembered spirit, trying to stay out of other people's way to avoid talking to them, trying to keep my mind busy with other thoughts but never succeeding.

At five o'clock Monday afternoon I met Franz for the first time. Like most Gestapo men he was tall, strong, and dressed in a plain business suit. He had those wild, give-away eyes that were ringed with baggy circles. He looked unmistakably Gestapo.

"Pani Kapralova," he said, in clipped, proper Czech, "I want to tell you that your husband's position is very bad, really very bad indeed. His name is already on the list for the transport leaving for Auschwitz Thursday, the sixth of May, and there's no possibility of getting him off that transport using normal methods. There's only one way. I might be successful, though it's risky for both him and me. I haven't decided if it will work. You must understand that my head is much dearer to me than your husband's. Anyway, if I lose my head, he'll lose his, too, so I have to be extremely careful. I'll do it only if I'm absolutely sure it's safe."

Franz believed that the only way to get Alex off that transport list and to have him released was to get his boss, the top Gestapo officer in the whole of the Brno district, to sign his release papers. This he would never do willingly or knowingly, but Franz had a plan for getting the signature. The following Saturday he would throw a big party. His chief loved parties and heavy drinking. Franz planned to get him drunk. When he was only a little less than perfectly intoxicated, Franz would slip him Alex's release papers to sign, but only when he had reached the precise level of alcoholic bliss—too drunk to know what he was doing but in sufficient control to be able to sign the papers legibly.

I listened dubiously and then said, "Maybe he'll sign, but the next day he'll be sober and he'll know that he hadn't meant to sign any papers and he'll cancel everything and Alex will go to Auschwitz anyhow."

"No, you don't know him. He's a real egotist. He'd never admit he signed anything important while drunk. He'll know it's his signature. There's no mistaking it. If he signs your husband's release while he's drunk, your husband's a free man. The chief doesn't ever acknowledge being drunk, so you can be sure once he signs there's nothing to worry about for either of us. Believe me, I know him well, very well. Of course, to throw this party I'll need a lot of liquor and food. And then I'll have to have something for the risk I'm taking."

When I nodded, he continued, "I want two lengths of good English worsted for a man's suit and two lengths of the same stuff for a lady's suit, and then I want five hundred cigarettes and some coffee. I mean real coffee, not that ersatz rubbish. And some money." He mentioned a large sum.

"When do you want it by?"

"This coming Thursday. I have to be sure I have everything I need for the party before I invite my boss."

"I'll try."

"Fine, so will I. And I'll tell you something else. You bring it all to me on Thursday, I'll throw the party, and if I manage to get my boss to sign, your husband will be home on Monday, or Tuesday at the latest. If he's not home by Tuesday night, something went wrong and he's not coming at all. In that case he will be on the Auschwitz transport on Thursday. But I hope I'll make it."

He said good-bye and was gone. Where could I get all these scarce items in only three days? Jan Horky looked at me and patted my shoulder sympathetically.

"It's a good plan," he said. "I think it might work. Tell me if I can help you with anything."

"Thank you. You've done enough already. I'll try to collect it on my own first, and if I can't I'll let you know."

I went first to Mojmir Kolar, Alex's closest friend, who assured me he would have the cigarettes and some cloth at Horky's office on Thursday. At home I had two lengths of material for a lady's suit that I had bought at the beginning of the war before Janie was born, and I also had enough yardage to make a suit for Alex. So the cloth was taken care of. Franz wanted coffee. We still had a kilo of coffee at home and also enough alcohol and liquor saved from prewar times. We had chickens on the farm. The main problem was meat, ham, and sausages. Olda, Alex's butcher friend and ex-cellmate from Kounicovy Koleje, readily promised to bring these to Richky on Wednesday.

Item by item I gathered everything together. To my amazement it was rather easy to do. The difficulty was going to be in getting all these packages through the streets of Brno while avoiding sudden Gestapo searches. The railway stations and the bus and streetcar terminals were special danger points.

I decided to transport everything in a carriage. Stan and I started out at five o'clock on Thursday morning and arrived safely at Grandma's before seven, searches being less likely early in the day. In the afternoon I ferried everything to Mr. Horky's office.

Franz arrived promptly at five. He was obviously glad to see that I had been successful. I must have inspired confidence on our first meeting for he had taken a chance and arranged a party and had already invited his commanding officer, who accepted with relish.

After Franz left loaded down with the loot, I collapsed. The double realization that Alex's life was once again at stake and that there was nothing more I could do hit me fully and cruelly. I went to pieces. The plan seemed not just doubtful but positively ridiculous. How could one hope for a correct degree of drunkenness?

Jan Horky calmed me down. He was a wise and kind man. He himself had been arrested soon after the Nazis took over Czechoslovakia. He had been imprisoned in Kounicovy Koleje about eight months when he was taken for yet another interrogation. In the office he found a new agent, Franz. Horky was surprised because Franz had been a salesman for his business before the war and the two had been on friendly terms. Franz recognized him and said, "What in the devil are you doing here?"

With some asperity Jan Horky replied, "I was arrested, what else?"

Franz asked, "Would you like me to help you out of here? It'll cost you!"

Horky never found out how Franz had managed his liberation. Two months later he was a free man. It was Franz who introduced him to the Gestapo mailman who helped me get food into Kounicovy Koleje when Alex was there, and it was Franz who was instrumental in getting Mojmir Kolar released.

Jan Horky, doing everything he could to get some courage and hope back into me, concluded, "You know, you're not the first one he's helped. We've saved quite a few people. Of course, I must admit, he's not always successful, but in most cases it works out. He's a clever man."

The weekend was somber and gloomy, made even more so by the contrast between the bright spring days and our predicament. Saturday crept by. Sunday came. Had the party taken place? I waited. On Sunday afternoon a little boy puffed up on a bicycle. He had peddled over the hills from Brno with a note for me. It was from Alex, just a folded piece of paper with no envelope. I did not know how he managed to smuggle it out of Susilovy Koleje, but there it was, lying in my hand. I thanked the boy and gave him some money for his trouble.

How many times before this had Alex been forced through the excruciating ritual of bidding life good-bye? Here was another. Once again Alex had written a final farewell letter. He believed there was no hope. He was going to be sent to Auschwitz on the transport leaving Brno on Thursday. What made him saddest was the idea of never seeing me again. He begged me to come to the prison on Monday or Tuesday. It was an unbearably sad letter. I read it several times, weeping. I spent a sleepless night.

Finally Monday, May 3, dawned, a lovely day. The sun was shining with splendid warmth. Evie went to school in the morning and the household routine went on as usual. Wanting to avoid useless anticipation followed by crushing disappointment, I had not told anyone about the possibility of Alex's coming home. But this left me with no one to confide in about what was foremost in my mind. I felt as if I had fallen into a world of loneliness. I sat and waited by myself.

The family and staff had its normal, meager lunch. Evie came from school and she and Janie played together. Tension increased minute by minute. I wandered around the room, going nowhere, touching this or that for reassurance, and being reminded of Alex I would force myself to sit down, but the urge to get up would seize me and impel me back into motion. And so it went, through endless hours.

Toward evening I heard footsteps outside, coming up the terrace stairs and across to the entrance. I looked out of the window. In the twilight, there by the door, stood Alex! He did not move. It was a hallucination. I myself could not move. Then the apparition raised his hand to the doorknob and turned it. It was no phantom, no figment of my tortured imagination. It was Alex himself, really and truly Alex. He came back to us at last. Alex was home. He had come at the end of the day as if he had just finished a normal day at the office.

I shouted the news to everyone. Janie, Evie, Jana, and I ran outside and fell on him, making sure he was really there. It was Alex and no fantasy. Alex was really and truly home. He was so thin that his suit looked as if it had been borrowed from another man. He had someone else's shoes as his own boots were now Cousin George's, and he was very pale. But to me he was the handsomest of men and the most beautiful sight that had ever filled my now-weeping eyes.

The children swarmed over him. Three-year-old Janie remembered him, though she had been only two and a half when she last saw him. It seemed he had been away for years, whole centuries. So much had happened. Madi and Fanny rushed out, crying over Alex, weeping that he was so thin, so ashen. Then Peter and his wife Anna came running in from the mill, puffing with effort. Peter, a dour, unemotional man, for once lost his self-control and himself joined the weeping with a heart-rending, "Oh, thank you, Boss, for coming home, thank you so much. You're home, the Lord be praised, thank you, Boss, thank you for coming home." It was touching to see how much the old man loved him. How good life was!

The household had a radiant evening. Richky was a heavenlike place—all festivals, all birthdays and all Christmases, all good times and all good things pulled into a few shining hours. It was a feast of words with everyone trying to say everything at once. Alex recounted the saga of his imprisonment. We told him what had happened to us here on the outside.

Then the girls' bedtime came. After Madi had given them their bath and tucked them in, I went upstairs to kiss them good-night. Evie, smelling clean, with soft, damp curls around her face, held me close and whispered, "Do you know, Mommy, what I wish? I wish Daddy would be arrested again."

Jarred in my euphoria, I said, "What? For goodness' sake, child, what did you say?"

"I wish that Daddy would go to the concentration camp again."

"Why?"

"Because," she said, "when he came home today I was so, so very happy. I had never in my life been so happy, and I would like to do it all over again."

Marvelous is the logic of children. She still believed that a concentration camp was a large hotel where people had a most enjoyable time.

It had been a day of glory, this day that Alex came home.

Alex and I talked late into the night. He did not understand what had happened and knew nothing of Franz or the party. The Gestapo simply turned him loose without a word of explanation. Until the moment the gates slammed shut behind him he thought it was a joke, that he was going to be grabbed at the last second and sent back to camp amid the laughter of the guards. Then I told him about Mr. Horky and Franz and how I managed to circumvent the Gestapo. He was amazed at what we had accomplished.

Alex then described Susilovy Koleje, his prison on his return from Breslau. "You've no idea what goes on in there," he began. "I was lucky because they put me with two pharmacists in a small cottage in the garden to disinfect old clothing. I don't know where it came from. I guess some concentration camp. It was full of lice and fleas and God knows what else and we had to clean it and disinfect it. It was a revolting job. The good thing was that the Gestapo was too wary of it all to come close to us at our work, so they mostly left us alone, but except for that the work was awful. What made the job even worse was that right outside the cottage window was a large yard where the guards were always tormenting prisoners and beating them up.

"One afternoon, a Gestapo man formed a group of Jewish prisoners with their yellow stars into a circle. Then he ordered them to run. He began shouting, then screaming, "Faster, faster." Soon they were running as fast as they could. Many were stumbling, staggering, and bumping into each other. It was pitiful to see them. We felt so impotent.

"Then one fell. He did not get up. The Gestapo man pounced on him like a wild animal. He punched his head, beating him with his fists. Then he stood up and began kicking him. The other prisoners stopped running and stood still, staring in silence. The three of us watching from the window thought the guard had gone mad.

"I still think that the Gestapo man had broken down and was actually clinically insane. He foamed at the mouth, his spit dribbled down his chin, and his face was dripping with sweat. His eyes bulged in their sockets as he yelled and screamed without letting up until he was hoarse. But even then he did not stop. He continued beating the poor old man, who by this time was long dead. Finally, a second Gestapo man came over and quietly led away this maniac who in a trance of savage hatred would have gone on beating the corpse indefinitely.

"And that kind of thing went on every day. The Gestapo people were the worst sort of sadists. They reveled in their lust for blood. Being in Susilovy Koleje was like being abandoned in a hell where there was no reason, no humanity, no mercy. It's beyond the comprehension of a normal person."

I shuddered, remembering the scene with the monk I had witnessed a few months before. It was, I thought, as if the devil himself had taken possession of these evil people. As Alex said, there was nothing human about them.

To distract him, I told Alex about Frau Thomas, Tony Srba, Dr. Benecke, and Albert Weber and the months of worry and planning that had saved him. I explained how everything had been pre-arranged with the president of the court.

"You can't imagine," Alex said, "how disappointed I was after I had met Weber for the first time. He seemed to be completely in another world. Asking me if I had food brought from the restaurant! When the prosecutor made his speech and demanded the death penalty, I thought I was a dead man. I couldn't see how this stand-in for Harold Lloyd could do anything for me. I hardly even wanted to make my statement when he called on me. Then I thought, what's there to lose? I might just as well repeat it one more time.

"Then, when I saw how receptive the judge was and how he imitated my gestures, I thought I was seeing things. When he said, 'Case dismissed,' I thought I hadn't heard right. I was convinced my ears were not functioning correctly."

Alex had to talk out his experiences once and for all. It was all so sad. He told me many things I did not want to hear, but knowing he had to get it out of his system, I sat quietly and listened. He did not stop talking for hours, returning repeatedly to the prison in Breslau.

Every Thursday, week in and week out, fifty to a hundred people were beheaded there on the guillotine. The procedure was grisly. Early in the morning the men and women to be executed that evening were taken to Alex's block and herded into a large room on the floor directly below Alex's cell. There they were ordered to strip naked and dress in paper shrouds. Then the innocent victims were given their last meal, a piece of paper, and a stub of a pencil so they could write farewell letters. Each received a packet of cigarettes and they were allowed to smoke.

As the mere possession of cigarettes was strictly forbidden in the prison, the tobacco smoke wafting toward the central dome along the corridors, up the stairs, and permeating the whole block, came to be the concrete signal of the coming of bloody doom.

This added a new dimension to the horror of other prisoners' weekly expectations. They, with Alex among them, could neither forget nor escape this fragrance of death, the smell of the precariousness of their own existence. The condemned were left alone for most of the day and permitted to do whatever they pleased. Once an opera singer was there, a baritone, awaiting execution, and Alex said he and his cellmates could hear him singing sad Polish ballads and operatic arias all day long.

The executions began at five o'clock sharp. Alex and his fellow prisoners could hear the clomp of wooden clogs on the tiled floor below, then silence, and a crash of the guillotine blade. The living prayed for the dead and hoped not to be among those taking that sad walk one day.

"I can't begin to tell you, Zdena, what an unbearable effect that cigarette smoke had. And waiting, throughout the whole day, knowing what those poor people on the floor below us were going through. Then the sad, forsaken clop, clop, clop of the wooden clogs on the tiled floor followed by the awful, empty stillness, and a crash—and then another sad little clop, clop, deadly silence, and another crash. We sat there, immobile, staring at the floor, not able to look at each other. All of us were screaming inside. How can they do this to fellow human beings?"

One evening, when the executions were over and the prison was still hushed, two of the executioners walked past Alex's cell, and as they passed by, one said to the other with pride in his voice, "What an achievement today, eh? Seventy-five in just three hours. Fantastic!"

Alex's soul shivered.

"They can't be human, and so cruel and sadistic," he thought and a surge of disgust rushed over him, mixed with fears that at their hands he, too, might have met his doom.

Alex talked until dawn, until the need for sleep at last overcame him and he fell into a blessed, healing slumber. The next few days felt like a holiday. I called Jan Horky and told him that the typewriter was working fine and thanked him once more. Then I called Tony Srba and wrote to Dr. Benecke and Dr. Weber.

Alex had lost nearly sixty pounds and weighed now only about 110 pounds, though he was six feet tall. The doctor warned him not to eat too much all at once; many people returning home from imprisonment did and they died as a result. Therefore, he ate carefully and in a few weeks' time he began to look a little better. It took longer for the beauty of the Richky valley and the love of his family to ease his taut nerves and soothe his sorrowing spirit. Miraculously, his physical health had not been damaged.

Never one to enjoy inactivity, Alex wanted to return to work as soon as possible but found that as an ex-prisoner he was ineligible for his old position as chief executive of the company. Instead, he worked from home on the company's technical problems in a consulting capacity. We made a few alterations in the house and changed one of the downstairs rooms into a laboratory. We settled once again into a pleasant routine. It was pure happiness to have Alex around the house.

Every morning he would go in any kind of weather to the village on horseback for the mail, then he worked in the laboratory until lunch. On summer afternoons the two of us took an hour off for a swim. During the winter months this was replaced by short runs of invigorating cross-country skiing in our valley. Then Alex returned to the laboratory until evening.

Saturdays and Sundays we spent horseback riding in those quiet whispering forests. Though we had passed through experiences far more brutal than those at the beginning of the war, the woods retained their miraculous healing power. They let us forget, just as we had in the early days of the war.

Evie started riding with us and we enjoyed her company. She liked horses and riding, and when Alex bought her a pony called Regent she fell head over heels in love with him. In the summer the Srbas spent a couple of weeks with us, riding and sharing our love of the forests and meadows. The food shortages were even more severe, but living in the country made it a little easier. Olda was a great help; he had not forgotten the food parcels I had smuggled into Kounicovy Koleje and showed his appreciation in a generous way.

Many people were still being arrested, but the general situation seemed a littler calmer than it had been during the catastrophic year of 1942.

The German armies were in constant retreat. Their position in Russia was decaying, and the Nazi-controlled radio brought frequent jaunty announcements of "strategic withdrawals," each one of which the Czechs gleefully translated as a notification of yet another defeat.

In North Africa the American and British forces were pushing ahead steadily, and on May 11, 1943, a few days after Alex came home, Rommel's *Afrika Korps* capitulated, though the field marshal himself escaped back to Germany.

Soon after that the American army invaded Sicily, and the fighting leapt onto the Italian peninsula itself. In July, Italy's King Victor Emmanuel removed Mussolini from his position as dictator of Italy, Mussolini was arrested, and simultaneously Italy deserted to the Allies and declared war on Germany. The Germans lost Sicily but continued to fight fiercely on the mainland. The Allied advances were slow. In September the Germans freed Mussolini, and the war in Italy continued to drag on.

When the Americans invaded Italy, our hopes that the war would soon be over skyrocketed. In spite of the risk, Alex and I turned on Radio London every night. I remember hearing that General Eisenhower had been appointed supreme commander of all Allied forces in Europe. All our friends expected a major invasion of the mainland. Our government in London was more active now and President Benes and Foreign Minister Jan Masaryk frequently addressed the nation on the BBC radio. Alex and I hesitantly dared to begin looking forward to freedom.

Mrs. Müller, our neighbor, fell ill and was taken to the hospital.

The diagnosis stunned us: she had terminal leukemia. I went to see her just before she died. The actual end was sudden. She had been a good woman and died with a broken heart, torn between love for her country and love for her German husband.

A few weeks after her death, her fear for Karl, her son in the Luftwaffe, came true. The boy was shot down over London and perished.

There were frequent inspections in our mill by the occupation government. The inspector was a former Czech army officer, Bedrich Pokorny, who was forced by Germans to perform this duty. After checking the mill's books, he would often stop at the house for a cup of coffee and to chat a while. In time the three of us became friendly. Pokorny started visiting on weekends and often brought along a companion, a Dr. Zdenek Ripa. A well-educated lawyer in his thirties and the son of a well-known attorney, he was single, physically rather small, extremely musical, interesting, and a good conversationalist.

One Sunday afternoon they arrived with Pokorny looking ill. When I asked what the matter was, he replied weakly, sinking into a chair, "I had an awful experience on the way down here."

Ripa laughed, "I think the guy's going crazy. Nothing happened at all; it was just in his imagination. I think news of the war got on his nerves."

Pokorny said defensively, "That's not true. I was relaxed and happy walking along the trail. Suddenly I felt distinctly as if someone had thrown a noose around my neck and was strangling me. My heart started to pound. I was choking. It was real." Under questioning, Pokorny defended his strange experience, saying it had nothing to do with late nights or nerves. He told us he had never been so terrified in his life, that nothing like this had ever happened to him before. We served him some ersatz coffee and gave him something to eat, but he remained upset and distracted for the rest of the afternoon.

———☐———

Much later, when we had been living abroad for more than twenty years, while reading *The Masaryk Case* by Claire Sterling about the death of Jan Masaryk, I stumbled across a mention of Pokorny and Ripa. After the Communist takeover of Czechoslovakia, both men became fervent party members though they never showed any Communist inclinations at the time we knew them. They both scaled the political ladder with ruthless speed. Pokorny became the first secretary of the Ministry of the Interior and was himself somehow involved in Masaryk's death.

During the spring of 1968, the period of reform and liberalization in Czechoslovakia, Pokorny was found dead in the forest, strangled with a wire by an unknown hand. He was discovered hanging from a tree by his friend Dr. Ripa, who happened to be in the vicinity and who called the police. I rushed to Alex. After rereading the account, we both remembered that Sunday afternoon when Pokorny had a premonition of his violent death some twenty-five years before it happened, possibly on the very trail where he was later found strangled.

———□———

As the occupation continued and the fighting front drew closer to Brno, we learned that the forests around Richky were sheltering an increasing number of partisan fighters parachuted in from England. Most of these were Czechs who had escaped at the beginning of the war and had enlisted in the British forces.

One day a local forest ranger whom we knew well came to the farm to ask us for food for these guerrillas. We did not have much, but we shared with them what we had. The ranger collected what food we could spare every week, usually homemade bread and cookies and also pieces of sausages from Olda.

Our miller, Peter, noticed that a few shingles had been moved around on the roof of the mill. He was puzzled about it and reported the strange occurrence to Alex, who walked with him around the building for a look. Both house and mill were built on a slope. It would have been easy for a person to get on the house roof from the back of the mill, but no one could see any other sign that this had happened. The mystery remained.

A few weeks later at about seven o'clock one morning on my way into the kitchen I saw through the open door Fanny and Anna standing like pillars of salt, rigid with fright. In the middle of the kitchen stood a man dressed in a dark jacket and baggy pants tucked into high, black boots. He was holding a huge, black machine gun in his hands. It was pointed straight at the two women. When he saw me he jerked it around toward me. I, too, froze. I could see at a glance that he was not Gestapo.

He whispered with ferocious urgency, "I'm looking for my friends, the parachutists. I've just come from Russia and I am looking for my contact." He spoke a kind of unfamiliar Slavic language, not Czech and not Russian. It might have been Ukrainian. When he spoke slowly, I could understand him.

"There are no parachutists here," I answered. "There's only us, a Czech family, living here. We don't have any parachutists." I fervently wished he would put his machine gun down.

"Oh yes, you do. My partner and I saw them in the garden. We were hiding in the forest and we saw them early this morning."

"No," I said, raising my voice for emphasis, "there's no one here, only us, no one at all."

He glanced out the window and saw Alex walking across the orchard.

"See," he said, gesturing with his chin toward the window, "there's one of them right now!"

"Oh no. That's my husband."

"Look," he said earnestly, leaning forward, trying hard to convince me, "I'm a friend. My partner and I, as I've told you, we've just come from Russia, and we have to meet up with the others. Tell me where they are, please."

He was still pointing the machine gun at me, which was making me very uneasy. It was hard not to look at it.

"I'm sorry," I said, as persuasively as I could, "I'd love to help you, but I can't. I don't know of any parachutists here or elsewhere."

I saw that Alex had walked into the house, so I continued. "Look, talk to my husband. You'll see that he is the man you saw walking around the garden this morning."

Closely followed by the machine gun and the intruder, I entered the dining room where Alex sat waiting for breakfast and told him what was going on. When Alex got over the shock of seeing a strange man in dark clothes and high boots, pointing a machine gun at him in his dining room, he told him the same story I had just given. The man insisted that he had seen the partisans and flatly declared that he would wait for them to return. He asked for food; we gave him some breakfast. He ate without putting his weapon down. Another man with a gun was in the mill with Peter. We were held at gunpoint until two o'clock in the afternoon, and then as nobody had returned and nothing happened, the man and his friend decided to leave and look for the other partisans in the woods.

Before leaving, however, they impressed on us forcefully that we were not to go to the police. His exact words were, "If you report this, we'll find out about it. We'll be watching you from the forest, and if you do spill to the police, we'll shoot you. So keep quiet about us!" And then they were gone.

As soon as they had passed across the garden and vanished into the green dimness of the woods, Alex and I had a hurried consultation. Both of us were very suspicious. It struck us as unnatural that they were behind enemy lines and as totally unafraid as those two had been. We concluded, therefore, that the episode had been carefully staged. It was a Gestapo trap.

We were in a quandary. A strict regulation was in force stating that any strange person had to be reported immediately to the police. If these two were in fact Gestapo stooges and we failed to report them, we would be arrested. On the other hand, if we did report them and they were really agents of the Allies, their death warrant would be as good as signed. We decided to postpone any action until three o'clock; perhaps something would happen by then that would expose the truth. "Then," Alex said, "I'll go and tell the police. By that time, if they are really partisans, they will be long gone, and if not, we'll have done the right thing."

Toward three o'clock, Jura was saddled, and Alex rode to the police station in Obce, taking a roundabout trail. The policemen were patriotic Czechs who could be fully trusted. They had to report to the German authorities all unusual happenings, which they did in such a way that Czechs were always protected and Germans were never helped. When Alex finished his story, the policeman said, "Well, you can stop worrying about it. We already have them. About half an hour ago two men were found in the forest by a logging crew, both shot dead. Whoever they were, they won't be telling anyone anything. I agree with you. I think they were sent by the Gestapo."

————□————

Two years later, after the end of the war, Alex and I were invited to a reunion in Brno of wartime partisans and parachutists. The men at the meeting were mainly members of the partisan band who had been hiding in the forests around Brno near Richky and whom we had supplied with food for almost two years.

Toward the end of the meeting the leader rose and made a speech in which he thanked Alex and me for having helped them. He then awarded Alex an honorary membership in the group and gave us both an official testimonial expressing their gratitude for what we had done for the partisans during the war years. Following his speech Alex stood up and thanked them, saying that we had not done much, only supplied them with a limited quantity of food.

However, to our consternation, the leader answered with a smile, "You don't know it, Alex, but you did much more than that. Our group hid out in your house the whole time we were in your area. We stayed in your attic, above the mill."

And now we remembered those displaced shingles that had so often upset Peter.

"And," the leader continued, "I'll tell you something else. Do you remember those two men who came to your house looking for us at the beginning of 1944 and who were found shot in the forest? They were Nazi spies and we were the ones who shot them. We had to. It wasn't only that we were in danger, but they had seen us coming out of your house. If we hadn't taken care of them they would have reported it to the Gestapo and you would have all been arrested, so we were forced to kill them. We waited in ambush for them, and when we saw them come out of your house, we followed them into the forest and executed them."

A cold shiver ran down my back as I realized how close once more we had come to disaster and been saved without knowing it. If the Gestapo had found our unknown visitors under our roof we would have all been shot, not just Alex and I and the children but also our immediate household and everyone else as well—Ivan and Jana, their baby boy Zeno, Grandma and Grandpa, maybe even my parents and my sister and my brother, though we were all innocently unaware of the real situation. Many people of our acquaintance had been executed for far less. I thanked God that once again we had been rescued from destruction.

15
AIR RAID

At the beginning of June 1944 the American army took Rome and established air bases in Italy from which they conducted frequent, heavy air raids on Austria, Czechoslovakia, and Germany. The war itself had come to our poor, conquered country. Everyone constantly monitored the Vienna radio station that broadcast air-raid alerts whenever enemy airplanes flew toward the Austrian capital. True to the Viennese spirit the warning was not in the form of a siren but the birdcall straight from Strauss's *Tales from the Vienna Woods*, the cry of a cuckoo. Whenever the cuckoo sang his song everyone in Vienna, Brno, and points between ran for shelter. At first only an occasional bomb fell on Brno, causing insignificant damage, but in Vienna the attacks were heavy and the destruction was widespread. Vienna was less than eighty miles from us and when it was bombed our windows at Richky rattled. Faintly, far away on the edge of perception, one heard the distant thunder. Devastation had marched within the range of hearing.

In that year the Germans started recruiting civilians to work in the munitions plants. Madi was ordered to report to the Workers' Management Office, where she was told that she was in nonessential employment and was therefore being conscripted for factory work to aid the "fatherland." Alex and I also received a letter to that effect. Madi was furious. All her life she had worked as a children's governess and did not know anything about factories nor did she want to. Furthermore, because she absolutely loathed Hitler, the idea of doing anything to further his cause made her livid. Yet there was nothing she could do. She prepared to move into Brno since Richky was too far for daily commuting.

Alex's parents were by now spending most of their time at Richky, in a small cottage Alex had built for them in the orchard. Grandma offered a room in their Brno apartment to Madi, who gratefully accepted. It was surprising how well Grandma and Madi got along. Neither could speak the other's language, but using gestures they came to understand each other and became good friends.

Spring 1944 passed and on June 6 came the long-prayed-for invasion of Europe. The Nazis were driven back on all fronts. The situation at home became grave, as food was almost unobtainable.

A rumor circulated that German scientists had been conducting research on a superweapon that was going to destroy the Allies. We did not take it seriously and considered it to be just Goebbels's propaganda. Only after the war did we learn that scientists at Peenemünda on the Baltic had been feverishly working on a new destructive intercontinental rocket that could eventually reach the United States. They were very close to success.

In the process two new powerful weapons were developed. The first was a flying bomb, called V-1, which was launched by the hundreds at targets in England, mainly in and around London. At the beginning of 1944 the other one, an even more deadly rocket, was put into production. The V-2 flew high and undetected, cut its engine at high altitude, and fell on its target silently. The first two V-2 rockets hit two communities near London in September 1944.

After the invasion in 1944 Hitler made fewer and fewer public speeches. On July 20, we heard with disbelief that an attempt had actually been made on his life. Some of the Army officers had grown increasingly disgusted by the Nazi atrocities and Hitler's conduct of the war. At one of the Führer's staff conferences at his hideaway in the forests of East Prussia, a briefcase with a time bomb was placed under the large conference table by Count Klaus von Stauffenberg, a devout Christian German patriot. Unfortunately the table's heavy legs dampened the effect of the explosion. While some officers died and others were seriously hurt, a thoroughly shaken Hitler escaped with only slight wounds, mainly to his right arm.

Everyone connected—even tangentially—with the conspiracy was arrested, tortured, and executed, often in a most barbarous way. Field Marshal Rommel was forced to commit suicide. Because he was such a great German hero he was offered the opportunity to poison himself. His death was listed as a brain seizure. He was given a state funeral and his family was left undisturbed.

The war inched forward in its steady advance toward Richky. The American and British armies in Italy were getting closer to us by the day and both the western and Russian fronts were approaching the Czech borders. The Vienna cuckoo sang nearly every day. Still, nothing serious happened to Brno, except a few minor air attacks on Zbrojovka, the huge ammunition works with two large plants, both working at full capacity night and day. American planes often flew over our valley. We greeted them as friends even though they sometimes bombed Brno. This was the price that had to be paid for peace.

The region's first major air attack did not come until the end of August, and again it targeted the Zbrojovka factories. The Americans succeeded in leveling only a part of one plant, but also hit were numerous nearby houses and apartment buildings in which several people were killed. When the entire inner city of Moravska Ostrava was completely demolished, people in Brno began paying more attention to the air-raid warnings. One saw many worried faces on the streets.

On November 20, we turned on the radio early in the morning and were greeted by the Vienna cuckoo. On the local station the announcer interrupted the music; his voice, though quiet, was full of tension. American planes had been sighted approaching Brno from the four points of the compass. It looked as if a major air attack on the city was a possibility. He urged everyone to get into an air-raid shelter immediately.

The weather was unusual. All of Europe was flooded by bright sunshine; only Brno in its valley was buried in a heavy fog.

The first bombers passed over Richky at about eight o'clock. They flew so low that we could distinguish the markings on the bottoms of their fuselages. Our ears were deafened by their menacing, steady roar. The first squadrons disappeared beyond the treetops. Another followed closely behind, and then another. Soon they filled the entire sky from horizon to horizon with waves of noise until I thought there could not be one more airplane left anywhere else in the world. Still they came, in endless, perfect formations, flying steadily wing tip to wing tip and nose to tail in awesome precision. Our universe was shattered by their clamor. The noise was simply overwhelming.

Later it was reported from London that more than eight hundred aircraft were in the attack. The planes began circling overhead, their massive engines snarling at us with throttles wide open, waiting for the fog over Brno to lift. We did not know about the heavy fog obscuring the city, and therefore we could not understand why they did not bomb immediately instead of circling.

We wished that they would fly away, but the radio announcer reported in a tense voice that the air attack on Brno was expected to start any moment. He could not explain the unending circling of the bombers. Time had stopped. The tension was unbearable.

Slightly after ten the bombing began. The noise of the planes in the sky had been frightening enough, but what followed froze our blood and sent us running with our hands over our ears back into the house. Alex had been told that the safest place was under the arch of a door where the construction was strongest. We crowded into the doorway between the living room and the hall, knowing it would provide but scant protection in case of a direct hit.

The windows began to chatter in their frames. The building itself was built of stone and never moved in the most fierce of winter winds, but on this day the whole house seemed to rock with each successive wave of explosions. Some pictures fell off walls and ornaments toppled off shelves. The farm was engulfed by a crashing fury of sound. The world could not hold so much noise.

After each explosion I thought surely that that had been the climax and that would be the end. Each bomb just had to be the last. There could not be any more left, but many more followed. The attack continued for two hours, one explosion merging into the next, an enormous cacophony of destruction. Then the noise decreased. We ran out of the house and saw planes departing. Then they were gone. Behind them was a deathly vacuum of total silence. Perhaps it was a temporary deafness, or merely a matter of contrast.

In the direction of Brno oily, black smoke billowed into the sky. The sun was darkened. The horizon was blood red and the clouds above it were a fiery pink. We could smell acrid smoke. Then faintly, drifting gently on the breeze, came the distant wailing of many sirens. It was as if the city itself had just begun to scream.

Our first thoughts were of Alex's parents and Madi in Brno. We had to try to find out what had happened to them. Stan ran to hitch up the team to the phaeton and Alex and I climbed in and Stan started the horses. When the carriage came out of the forest onto the open area on top of the hill from which there was always a spectacular view of Brno, Stan pulled up.

Alex and I gasped. Below us boiled a sea of dark gray smoke spangled with scarlet explosions. A sharp, acrid stench saturated the air full of devastation. Flakes of soot and ashes sifted down around us. The demented shrieking of the sirens and clanging of bells were even louder up on the hill where we stood. Their screeching and ringing was sporadically erased by the crash of falling buildings. Stan started the horses and we sped down into the smoke.

In the outskirts an overturned streetcar partially blocked the road, looking like the corpse of some huge animal. Rubble had been flung across the streets by the explosive force of direct hits on the houses. People were beginning to dig down to those buried under it. Buildings were blazing on both sides of our route and the clanging of fire engines frantically trying to get through to the fires echoed around us. The road surface was buckled and cracked by the heat. Stan was having difficulty controlling the horses, which reared and refused to go ahead, their eyes bulging and their ears laid back in near panic. They were terrified by the fire, the insistent wail of ambulances, and the warning shouts of fire engines. Confusion was all around us.

Alex called out to a man who ran by. "Hey! Can you tell us what part of the city got hit worst?"

"It's everywhere. The worst was Udolni. Also one hospital was hit, some schools, but I can't tell you more." He turned and continued running down the street. We were even more concerned.

Stan whipped up the horses. They resisted, then plunged on, the phaeton rocking and swaying over the rough street surface. We turned a corner and saw a barricade with many vehicles halfway up the block. Helmeted men milled about. Stan reined the horses so hard that they reared and almost fell backward. The carriage skidded to a stop and Alex shouted to one of the air-raid wardens, "Do you know how Legionnaire Street is?" That was where his parents lived.

"Legionnaire? It got several direct hits! It's bad. You can't come through here. It's all blocked off. Half the street is down and there are unexploded bombs lying around! Go back! Nearly every street was hit! It's terrible, terrible." Alex caught my eye.

Stan swung the horses around, cracking his whip to keep them moving, and we galloped back the way we had come. The sights were extremely distressing. Among these huge piles of rubble, dust, and smoke we could hardly recognize the city we had loved so much. Trying to find another way to Legionnaire Street, we tried street after street, racing on past endless smoking remainders of what had only yesterday been shops, apartment buildings, and schools, all occupied by living people hoping for a better tomorrow. All around us were desolate ruins, leaning toward us as if waiting to topple on our defenseless carriage. Wherever we went the streets were clotted with fires and piles of partly collapsed walls. At last the way opened and we arrived at the far end of Legionnaire Street. It was barricaded off. A number of serious fires and several lesser ones were raging. A helmeted policeman, his face blackened by soot, emerged from the gloom. Alex asked about Number 31.

"Direct hit!" he said. "The house is half demolished and there are some unexploded bombs. There's no way you can go in. The other side of the street is all down, too. Very dangerous. Some houses are still standing, but only just. We can't allow anyone in."

"Survivors?"

"Don't know. You'll have to inquire at the district office. They're beginning to post the lists of the dead up there." He gave us directions.

Desperate, Alex and I hesitated, not wanting to leave and yet not knowing where to go. All through the years of our troubles, though our personal lives had leapt from one catastrophe to the next, the world itself and the familiar, physical setting of our existence had remained blessedly fixed and unchanged. Suffer as we did, the trees over the sidewalks, the railing on stairs, and the front doors, windows, stonework, and all the rest had gone on as they always had. But this evil of war we were witnessing had broken through the dam of normality and, escaping from the confines of human relations and experiences, exploded into physical reality. Our world itself had been changed. Alex, Stan, and I sat stunned with misery in the midst of this new and greater unrestrained total war, a Golgotha in our repeated crucifixions.

I remembered that our good friends, Dr. Pernicka and his wife, lived nearby on Nova Street. Amazingly, Nova, a broad street leading out of the city, had not received any direct hits. We left Stan at the entrance of Legionnaire and went on foot to the Pernickas' house. Mrs. Pernicka opened the door. "Come in, come in," she cried, her face radiant with delight and welcome. "You must have been so worried, but no need, no need at all. The poor dears are here, all safe and sound!" Grandpa and Madi were both sitting in the living room.

Alex and I rushed in. In a moment Alex and his father were in each other's arms, holding on in wordless happiness. I hugged Grandpa and Madi. Everyone was talking at once. The exaltation passed swiftly and the next question came to Alex and me at the same time: "Where is Grandma?"

"Well," said Grandpa, "you wouldn't believe it. Yesterday some friends of ours from the country came to visit and they brought us a goose. And you know mother. She said, 'What's a goose without sauerkraut?' and decided to go to Vrbatky to your parents' place," he nodded at me, "to try to get some sauerkraut. I'm sure she's safe there, don't you think? She left early this morning."

Alex chuckled. Then Grandpa told us his own story. For some unknown reason, after Grandma left on the sauerkraut quest, he felt more and more uneasy. At last he could not stand being cooped up in the apartment and went for a long walk, going as far as Spielberg Castle. As he reached the park the air-raid sirens started wailing. People ran to the shelters. Someone near him yelled, "Hurry, everyone. There are hundreds of planes flying toward Brno!"

He heard the far-off drone of many engines and knew he should get under cover fast. He found his way to a shelter in a nearby German girls' high school. After half an hour, before the attack began and while the planes were still circling above the fog, he decided he could not stand the deafening noise of the frenzied children any longer and left the school. He walked as fast as his legs would carry him to the nearby shelter at Spielberg, a cave excavated deep into the mountainside beneath the castle.

His restlessness saved his life. The school received a direct hit. All the children and teachers were killed. The hot-water pipes of the central heating burst in the explosion and the scalding water flooded the shelter. Those who had survived the blast were drowned in agony in boiling water. In terms of numbers killed in one place, this was one of the worst tragedies of the air raid.

When the all clear sounded, Grandpa slowly picked his way through the confusion of the bombed-out streets back to Legionnaire Street. The blazing fires kept him away, however, and he went to the Pernickas'.

Madi was at work when the air raid started. The ammunition factory turned out to be the safest place in Brno that morning; not one bomb fell on it. If by design or not, no one ever knew. After the all clear sounded she also tried to return home but was stopped, and she, too, went to the Pernickas'.

While we were talking, Grandma walked in. She, too, had tried to go home. Her first thought was of her beloved husband. The wardens refused her entrance to Legionnaire Street, but she waited until the men turned their backs, then slipped through the barricade and ran through the smoking rubble to the house. It was quite an adventure for a mature woman, but she was driven on by her concern for Grandpa.

Although one entire wall of their building had collapsed, the staircase was still standing. In an agony of suspense, fearing the worst, she climbed to the top floor and walked into the apartment. It was almost completely destroyed, with the exception of Madi's room and the living room. The possessions lovingly gathered through years and years of married life, objects that were tokens of many key moments of their existence, were simply erased.

In the living room she saw an unexploded bomb lying next to Grandpa's concert grand piano. She could not see Grandpa anywhere and hoped he was not under the collapsed masonry in the bedroom. However, as it was his custom to spend the morning in the living room, she concluded that he must have left the apartment before the bombing began. After coming across the unexploded bomb

Grandma was not inclined to dawdle and quickly left the building and decided to go to the Pernickas'.

As she came out of the main door of the apartment building she saw her goose, of all things, lying in the middle of the street unharmed, if a little dusty. Being a down-to-earth sort of person and relieved that she had not gone to Vrbatky for nothing, she picked it up, put it in her bag, and later presented it to Mrs. Pernicka, together with the sauerkraut she had brought from my parents' farm.

Next morning, when Grandma and Grandpa returned to Legionnaire Street they found the bomb had exploded and destroyed the piano. All they ever found was one leg. Grandpa was sad about the loss of his greatest pleasure. He was a dedicated and accomplished amateur pianist, having been a student of the great Czech composer, Leos Janacek. Alex's parents managed to salvage very little, but Madi's room remained undamaged. Everything had been spared, including her shoe collection. The three of them picked out what they could from the debris and after a few days came down to Richky.

Hundreds of people were killed that morning in Brno and thousands more were injured. One hospital had received several direct hits, substantially decreasing the amount of medical assistance available. It was therefore impossible to care adequately for all the wounded. Many died as a result, a horror added to horror.

A friend of the family had been visiting her little daughter in the hospital when the air raid began. There was a deafening detonation and in a fraction of a second the entire ward in front of her collapsed. She grabbed the little girl and ran. During the heaviest bombing she ran through the streets of Brno carrying the sick child. She said she never knew how she managed to get home. This picture of the mother holding her sick daughter while rushing blindly through suddenly unfamiliar streets remains with me as the perfect image of the new stage of suffering that our lives had entered.

Bombs were dropped even on the forest. When the planes began circling over a small nearby town where another friend taught, she decided to dismiss school. Some children had to cross the forest, but the teacher thought that they would be safer in the open than in the town. A bomber in difficulty jettisoned its load of high explosives. They fell on a group of her pupils and nine of them were killed. The teacher was horrified and blamed herself for the tragedy. The conviction was so deep that try as we might it proved useless to tell her it was no fault of hers. No one could have expected the forest, of all places, to be bombed.

The clean-up of Brno was slow. The hospital, schools, and other important municipal structures were repaired to the extent necessary to make them usable. Most of the remaining bombed-out buildings were left untouched and were rebuilt only after the war. There were not enough people, materials, or enthusiasm to undertake the job in 1944.

That was Brno's worst air raid of the war. Following it were several other air attacks but never anything to compare with that one in destructive force or extent of damage. It remained a bitter memory for its citizens for many, many years.

The air raid had one extremely important positive effect on our lives. Alex and I realized that living in the forest was scant protection against falling bombs and we decided to construct an air-raid shelter at Richky. The two fronts of the war were creeping closer every day. The Russians were already in Poland and had penetrated the mountains of eastern Czechoslovakia. The British, French, and Americans were advancing across Germany as well as northward up through Italy. The startling revelation of what real, total war was like galvanized us into action.

We surveyed the possibilities. The basement of the house was not strong enough to sustain prolonged battering, so Alex had a shelter excavated in the orchard two hundred feet from the house and designed to accommodate twenty members of our family and staff. It was actually a forty-foot-long, twelve-foot-wide, and nine-foot-high tunnel dug into the slope of a hill. The ceiling was reinforced with heavy wooden beams, and along both sides of the shelter two long benches were installed. At the far end was a small pantry lined with shelves. These I stocked with as much emergency canned and dried food as could be spared from our meager supply. I also added a few candles and matches. Though sufficient ventilation was provided, the air in the shelter was musty and unpleasant. We thought that eventually we might keep the heavy door open, as the entrance was hidden behind a dense growth of hazelnut bushes. With the shelter complete and stocked, we felt we could relax a little.

Early in the fall of 1944, Alex made a magnificent addition to our stables: two lively Lippizaner mares of the same breed as the world-famous dancing horses. They were beautiful, gentle animals. The mares, both sorrels with white blazes and white socks, had been trained for both riding and pulling carriages. They had been bred and were expected to foal early in the spring, probably in March.

Alex and I rode often with Evie that fall and her riding improved daily. She seemed to have a natural talent for the saddle and a deep, almost instinctive communication with animals. We were very proud of her. When the snow came, we combined riding with skiing. Alex often towed me behind him on skis, which was exhilarating for both of us.

The family spent a quiet, pleasant Christmas together, confident that that was the last Christmas we would be spending under the Nazi yoke. Next Christmas, we whispered to each other, we would be free again. As I sat quietly before the crackling fire in the living room hearth, I compared that Christmas with the one two years before. Here we were all together in health, full of hope and expectations. Two years before we had been divided, miserable, and distressed, with Alex in jail facing the ordeal of Breslau. I thought of and again blessed in my heart our good friends who made this possible: Jan Horky, Tony Srba, Frau Thomas, and Dr. Weber.

On New Year's Day Hitler gave his customary address on the radio. Far from ranting on with his usual slick eloquence, he sounded confused and defeated, constantly stopping to grope for a word. It was not the voice of the evil genius who in previous years had swayed the German nation with his bombastic speeches. We could not believe our ears. His time was running out; our time was rushing in.

Often Alex and I had the two Lippizaners hitched to a light sleigh. They enjoyed the outing as much as we did, trotting along briskly, nodding their heads to make their manes dance, their breath pluming in the frosty winter air. The snow whispered under the runners and sprayed back behind the sleigh in a glittering arc while we, enfolded in the warmth of a fur lap robe, rejoiced in the silent, white-blanketed forest that had become mysteriously transformed into a silver land of light and peace.

Once, while visiting our friends, the Lecians, who had a weekend cottage not far from us, we met one of their neighbors, a Dr. Hochman. He had recently returned from three years in a concentration camp. He was a lawyer, but his love was sculpture and painting, for which he had great talent. As it turned out, his pursuit of art saved his life during the war. When the Gestapo found out about his talent they ordered him to do portraits and busts of themselves and their families. As a result Hochman received better treatment than most. He was an ardent Communist. As we sat comfortably around the Lecians' fire, animated discussions sprang up about possibilities after the war. The majority of those present expected the republic to be restored, Edvard Benes to be president once again, and life in Czechoslovakia to begin again at the point it had been broken off.

Hochman was of a different opinion. He categorically proclaimed that after the war Czechoslovakia would become a Communist country. This caused general laughter, and Emil Lecian voiced the consensus of the group. "Are you crazy? There are hardly any Communists in Czechoslovakia. How could they get to be the ruling party? Such a small minority can't hope to rule a large majority! Absolutely not. It's impossible."

But Hochman insisted. Czechoslovakia, he stoutly maintained, was going Communist. He had a peculiar view of just what that would entail. He believed he would be able to commandeer a large house in one of the best suburbs of Brno, where he would have a large garden with a swimming pool for his children, and the drive from the street to the front door would be lined with his statues. All this would be because he was a son of a laborer and therefore a member of the new elite.

"Why, that's not Communism! You want to live like an aristocrat!" amused voices interjected into his fantasy. But Hochman was undaunted by the objections. The truth was clear to him: being the son of a laborer gave him the right to be a member of the ruling class when Communism came.

"And even if you are right and are entitled to all that," Alex said, pressing his point home with characteristic energy, "your children, being the children of a lawyer, won't be entitled to anything. According to your theory they'll have everything taken away and will have to revert back to being laborers. Isn't that right?"

"No," Hochman said indignantly, "the reorganization will happen only once. When the new social order is fully established, it will be permanent. The status quo will then remain."

People smiled at him indulgently, as adults do to a difficult child. We blamed his opinionatedness on his imprisonment. No one took him seriously.

In February the relative calm was snapped one snowy day. Jan Valek, the forest ranger who took the food from our house to the parachutists hiding in the forest, arrived as usual, but instead of taking the parcel and leaving, asked to talk to Alex, who took him into the living room.

"Alex," he said in a tense voice through blue lips, "I can't live with the strain of helping these men any longer. The Gestapo's going to catch us sooner or later. Then they'll shoot us. There's no escape. I've sent my wife and children away to stay with her mother in Bohemia, and I'm going to the Gestapo to give myself up. I can't take this pressure any longer. Death's inevitable anyway. Better to get it over with."

Alex was speechless. His apprehension was transformed into panic as Jan continued. "And I'd like you to come with me. Turn yourself in, too. It's the best way. You and Zdena are the ones supplying the food for them. You're as guilty as I. I can't take this fear any longer. I've suffered so much with this that I can't eat or sleep. All I want is to end it all."

Alex called me in and told me what had been said. I stared at Valek. The poor man was slumped in his chair. He was past caring about what happened to him. After the months of cooperation, I thought, Jan would have a good deal to tell the Gestapo. And if he did, a new purge would begin. We would be shot—all the adults, all the children. We had come too close to freedom to die. We had to help Jan hang on to the last strands of his shattered sanity.

Urgently, but gently, Alex and I started talking to our friend, attempting to convince him of his error, or at least to sow a seed of doubt in his paralyzed mind.

"Things aren't as bad as you say they are," Alex said. "The Ge- stapo doesn't know about the parachutists. They'll never know if we all keep quiet. The Americans and the British are almost at our borders. The Russians are approaching. The war is nearly over. Hold on, Jan. Everything will be all right if we stick together."

"If you tell them," I pleaded, trying to fill my voice with sympathy, "they'll shoot you and you'll never see your children and your wife again. You don't want that, do you? And think of how your wife would feel, and your children, when you give up and surrender."

Slowly Valek calmed down. By a fraction of an inch at a time, it took hours to return him to the neighborhood of his usual strong self. We fed him lunch and kept him close to us for the rest of the day. We let him go home but not before urging him—almost order- ing him—to come back the next morning. This he did, to our immeasurable relief.

A routine developed. Jan would come every morning and talk himself out. Nearly every afternoon Grandpa would go over to his house to keep him company and let him talk some more. The more of his distresses he got into words, the stronger he became until gradually his self-control increased. As time passed he was more easily able to fight back the temptation to surrender. Dr. Polacek, our physician and trusted friend, gave him some tranquilizing medi- cation and sleeping pills.

Alex and I nevertheless lived for some time in terror that he would crack, become psychotic, and rush into the arms of the Ge- stapo and confess and be executed. Until the end of the war and the ultimate removal of the Nazis, we were never completely sure of him. It was ironic that we had to be so deeply fearful of a fellow Czech we had worked so closely with and who had always been a personal friend.

Eventually, after listening to him hour after hour, I came to understand how, living alone in his isolated forest, with his wife and children gone and with no one to talk to from one end of the day to the other and bearing the full force of the psychological terrorism the Nazis directed against every single Czech, even a man as strong as Jan Valek could suffer such a serious nervous breakdown. So once again it was proven to me that one can resist evil easier with the loyal support of companions.

In the middle of February 1945, Fanny was ordered to report to the Zbrojovka munitions factory. Her job with us was classified as nonessential employment. The entire household was in turmoil over the news. Fanny was our dear friend and a central pillar of our family life. We could not imagine life without her. Alex and I went to the authorities and presented every excuse we could think of but to no avail. Fanny had to leave. Fortunately Peter's wife Anna came to my rescue. Her job had been the household laundry and the care of the farm animals, but she offered to add the cleaning of the house to her duties.

One especially cold, raw Sunday we were expecting the Lecians and Uncle Sylvester for lunch. I was busy in the kitchen cooking when the girls came to ask if they could go sledding outside. I gave them my permission, but not without trepidation. I warned them to stay in the orchard where there was a safe, little hill. They definitely must not go on the road, which was icy and therefore too dangerous.

I was setting the table when from outside I heard Janie screaming and Evie pleading, "Janie, please don't die, please be all right, please, Janie, please don't die."

The door banged open and wailing Janie rushed toward me, a Janie without a face. The entire front of her head was bloody. Fresh blood oozed from her eyes. Her nose, cheeks, and forehead were all bleeding in streams that ran down her chin and dripped onto her coat. Convulsive screams were coming from a dark hole in this scarlet mask. Evie appeared behind her, head hanging in an obvious agony of conscience, asking, "Oh, Mommy! She isn't going to die, is she?"

I remembered large abrasions are better cleaned with alcohol rather than iodine. I shouted for Alex and he came running from his laboratory carrying a bottle. Poor darling, how she screamed as I dabbed the stinging liquid into her wounds. Soon after we finished, Emil and Marie Lecian and their children arrived. Emil, who was a medical doctor, did not have his black bag with him, so Stan was sent on horseback to their cottage to get it. Emil told us we had done the right thing with the alcohol. He checked her eyes. Nothing was wrong with her sight. The bleeding came from badly torn eyelids.

After doing all we could for Janie, I turned on Evie. I was boiling mad and demanded an explanation. They had gone sledding on the rough, frozen road, not on the hill in the orchard. She should have known better and I told her so. When I finished and looked at her face, I did not have the heart to punish her further. She looked so frightened.

Janie's face took a month to heal. The accident occurred before penicillin was available, and we were lucky that no infection set in. I watched her constantly and was careful not to let her scratch the scab. It itched intolerably and she was miserable, but she healed without a single scar.

The fighting was crawling slowly toward Richky. Not a day passed without Allied aircraft roaring overhead. Usually they were Americans flying from Italy to Germany on bombing missions. Brno was also attacked frequently with bombing raids that were mostly directed at the Zbrojovka munitions factories.

No large-scale attacks were made on the city and no serious damage was added to the already general devastation. Our beautiful capital, Prague, was bombed but fortunately not heavily. Buildings on only a few streets were damaged. Prague, in fact, received only one air attack during the entire war. What a tragedy it would have been if this grand, graceful baroque city had been destroyed as Brno had been. Vienna was pounded daily and our windows rattled incessantly. Sometimes the planes did not stop at Vienna but continued on to Brno or to Breslau or Berlin.

Berlin was under a constant assault in 1945, often by a force of more than a thousand American aircraft blanketing the city with explosives. Destruction was total. On February 13, Dresden was firebombed. The attack was a complete surprise to everyone. This beautiful, historic city, much like Prague, was not a manufacturing center and therefore not crucial to the German war effort. We were sure it would be spared. It was bombed so intensely that a firestorm was ignited and the entire city center was annihilated and thousands of its inhabitants were either incinerated or suffocated when bombs burned up the oxygen in the air.

The Russians were making rapid advances toward us daily and disturbing rumors had begun to circulate about the Red Army. Soviet infantry was said to be undisciplined and ruthless in their treatment of the civilian population. The Russians were already fighting in the eastern part of our country, while closer to us the battle for Vienna began with the Germans under attack by an army under Marshal Malinovsky.

Radio London reported that in Poland the Red Army had liberated the concentration camp at Auschwitz. Unfortunately, before its fall the Nazis had loaded many prisoners onto trains and transported them to other concentration camps deeper inside Germany. Many of these trains passed through Czechoslovakia. We were told by eye witnesses that when people died of hunger and exhaustion their bodies were thrown off the moving trains and left lying by the railroad track. In spite of such massive evacuations many thousands of nearly dead prisoners were found in Auschwitz by the Russian army.

The Americans and the British liberated other concentration camps in western Germany and the news of the existence of these dreadful places spread throughout the world. No one had realized the immensity of that empire of death or the character and extent of the atrocities committed there. The descriptions we heard froze in our hearts. Alex and I had known many Czechs who were sent to Auschwitz and we silently remembered that Alex was only three days away from transport to Auschwitz when he was released.

In Poland the Russians launched their assault on Warsaw. When the Poles saw the Red Army approaching they rebelled and with limited resources and vast courage attacked the Germans. They believed that the Russians, seeing the signs of their uprising, would make a double effort to help them. The Red Army, although surrounding Warsaw on all sides, did just the reverse. They stopped and watched from the outskirts, enjoying, no doubt, the sight of two of their enemies killing each other.

The fighting in the city between the Polish resistance and the Germans, mainly the SS troops, was fierce. Tens of thousands of Polish lives were lost. Many people who had nothing to do with the uprising were executed and Warsaw was almost completely destroyed. Only then did the Soviets enter the Polish capital.

The Russians continued westward and after crossing the River Oder entered Germany proper and were only a hundred miles east of Berlin.

Meanwhile, the American Third Army under General George Patton and the British under Field Marshal Bernard Montgomery forged across the Rhine and raced toward Berlin and the borders of Bohemia. Patton advanced so fast against the crumbling resistance of the German army that Alex and I allowed ourselves to entertain the hope it would be the Americans and not the Russians who would free Czechoslovakia. We had good reasons to fear the Russians because of the wild stories that were added daily to the earlier rumors. Marshal Malinovsky's army from Siberia was mentioned frequently and always with dread. His men, we were told, were primitive and uncivilized, many being criminals who had been paroled to fight in the front lines.

One day we received a phone call from Dr. Martinek, a friend in Prague who had spent many pleasant days with us riding and vacationing at Richky. He anxiously advised us to flee the Russians and come to Prague right away before it was too late. We could stay with them in their country house near Prague. Dr. Martinek called twice more and each time begged us to leave everything and come to the capital. Alex and I were tempted to go, but Grandpa dissuaded us, telling us that we were worrying ourselves needlessly. The Russians were good people, he insisted, and, furthermore, we lived in a forest far from industrial centers. More than likely the front line would pass us by altogether. He was convincing. We stayed.

Radio London reported that Roosevelt, Churchill, and Stalin had signed an agreement about the political future of Europe at Yalta, a resort in the Soviet Union. The people of Czechoslovakia had no idea that once again their future had been determined by foreign powers.

In April a new Polish government was established. The new regime seemed to be entirely Communist. We should have heeded the hint, but we were only puzzled as we knew there were not many Communists in Poland, and neither Alex nor I believed for a moment that the Polish people wanted Communism as their form of government.

Radio London announced that Berlin had come under such heavy and constant bombardment that even the Chancellery had been hit. Hitler had to retire to an underground bunker.

Then came the long-awaited day when our President Benes stepped on Czechoslovak soil for the first time in six years and from Kosice addressed the Czech nation in an emotional speech. The whole country rejoiced. Dawn was breaking on Czechoslovakia, though it was still quite dark where we were.

Brno continued to be bombed frequently. For the first time we saw a few Russian planes, which were unimpressive compared to the snarling armadas the Americans threw into our skies. There were sounds of heavy artillery in the direction of Vienna, a constant menace mumbling in the distance like a remote summer storm, oppressive, ever present and pregnant with catastrophe.

Malinovsky's army had surrounded Vienna. The city was bombed repeatedly and methodically by the Americans, British, and Soviets until it capitulated to the Soviet Union.

Russian columns were streaming into Moravia toward Brno from both Slovakia in the east and Austria in the south. Alex and I were growing very uneasy. We had no idea what to expect, and after all the years of upset, our resistance to worry was impaired. Because we were hidden away in the vastness of the forests, we clung to the reassuring hope that the fighting would not come anywhere near Richky.

Many friends and acquaintances from Brno thought the same and the property gradually filled up with frightened people. Every day a dozen or more came. Before long three hundred men, women, and children were at Richky. The house was large, the garage spacious, and various farm buildings available. People brought mattresses, bedding, and some provisions, and soon a whole refugee camp was organized.

I cooked for the family and close friends staying in our house; Anna cooked for the rest. The fare was of extreme simplicity and sparseness, consisting mainly of potatoes, beans, and lentils. People were cooperative and subdued. The occupation had taught everyone the virtue of patience and civility under strain.

The underground bunker was ready and another shelter was offered in our large root cellar. Mr. Müller also made his own deep cellar available, so everyone had somewhere to go if events turned nasty. Arranging all this was a monumental task. Three hundred people was a vast multitude for a property which normally housed only twenty.

Madi was a cause for worry. The Russians were not likely to draw a fine distinction between Germans and Austrians. Reports drifted in from liberated areas that many Germans were being shipped off to Russian concentration camps, a forbidding prospect. Madi could not go to Vienna, her real home, which was already in Russian hands. The three of us talked the matter over and reached the conclusion that she should make her way into Bohemia and from there cross the border to Linz in Austria.

Madi agreed but only reluctantly. She packed a small suitcase with bare necessities, leaving everything else in our safekeeping. The family hugged and kissed her, all of us weeping. Alex and I asked her to come back after the war. She agreed, promised to write, and left, a small but somehow redoubtable figure moving down the driveway and through the iron gate.

After the war, to our delighted relief she sent us a card from Austria. She had crossed the border into territory freed by the Americans and had been lucky enough to obtain a good job as interpreter to the French army. She was happy she had made the move and thanked us for our advice.

By the first of April the snow was gone and the spring mud was slowly drying out. The population at Richky waited for the Red Army with impatience mixed with apprehension. Alex and I staunchly held to Grandpa's belief, reassured each other with references to our "Slav brethren," and usually ended the discussion by agreeing that nothing could be worse than the Gestapo.

The Red Army was trying to surround Brno before making an assault on the central city. Artillery pulsed over the horizon and low-flying fighter planes replaced long-range bombers overhead. At night the sky burned.

The atmosphere grew tense, as before the approach of a hurricane. People fell silent more frequently. Nothing at Richky seemed any longer personal or even familiar, and the hordes of refugees added a note of unreality to our valley. Everything was suspended in a kind of limbo, encapsulated in tiny segments of time like people isolated in a series of movie frames snipped apart.

Most conversations and thoughts ended with the words "After the front line goes through . . ."

There was a suffocating feeling of irrevocability. It was too late to escape; we were assigned to the unknown. Fate had us in its grip, and we went on waiting for what it would force on us.

BOOK FOUR

TOWARDS THE HILLS

16

THE RUSSIAN ARMY

The sun had just risen when a cloud of dust was spotted drifting above the road from Mokra. Out of it emerged a column of German soldiers. This was not a stray platoon but dozens of rusty tanks and dented military vehicles, followed by hundreds of war-weary men. Many of them were fifteen or sixteen years old, with sunken, stunned eyes, sad youths lost in flapping uniforms made for full-grown men. Moving in good order, they crossed our creek and plodded up the hill toward Obce, paying no attention to the landscape through which they were marching.

For an army that had suffered so many defeats the column was surprisingly well organized and well equipped. Alex and I stood outside of our house and watched our persecutors drain away. How very good indeed it was to see the last of those hated uniforms.

A somewhat older soldier at the end of the column broke ranks and walked over to Alex and me. He had a cigarette in his hand and asked us for a match. Alex gave him a box and the man searched his pockets for change to pay him.

"No, that's not necessary," Alex said in German. "Forget it."

The soldier nodded his thanks.

"Listen," he said, looking Alex in the eye with a calm, sad resignation, "the Russians will be here around four o'clock this afternoon. We're withdrawing, and I don't think we can stop on top of those hills. I think we'll go a lot farther. We were defeated back there and we need to regroup before making another stand. You shouldn't have any fighting here as I am sure the Russians will press behind us hard. They'll take this valley and then go right up the hill. We've been ordered to move at least fifteen kilometers farther along. You'll be safe. Thanks again and good luck."

He turned and walked off to join his column.

"Thank goodness there won't be any fighting here," I said to Alex. "I do hope he's right."

The German soldiers remained orderly. They did not touch anything, did not bother anyone, and did not talk much among themselves. They just shuffled along in their slow, defeated, dejected fashion until the last of the rear guard disappeared in the woods on the road to Obce.

Alex and I stood silently. I knew what he was thinking. We both hated them and we also pitied them. Listening to the quiet scuffing sounds of their worn boots I remembered the arrogant, boisterous soldiers who had marched into Brno in 1939. They had believed the world was theirs and showed it. I wondered how many of the original invaders were alive on this day some six years later to witness this dejected, sad ending to Hitler's imperial fantasy.

Most German civilians had by this time fled Czechoslovakia. A few old people and children were left, but anyone who had held any position of importance had disappeared. All the Gestapo and every government official had vanished, escaping to Austria or Germany, fleeing before the vengeance of the Russian army, the wrath of the Czechs, and their own despair.

The last rustle of German steps faded. It was two o'clock in the afternoon, a beautiful spring day, quiet and serene in pale cool sunshine. The blue, cloudless sky seemed to portend happy times to come. Alex and I had a single, common thought: this was freedom. At last, we were free. After so many years of German oppression, we were free again in our own republic; free to live, hope, plan, and rejoice; free of the endless, gnawing, and torturing fear; free of violence that had held us suspended and stagnant for six years.

We stood in front of the house, eagerly waiting for our first glimpse of the Russian army. They would come along the same road as the Germans had. We ardently anticipated their arrival.

At quarter to four a troika of horses hitched to a gun carriage careened around the bend on the Mokra road. Crowds of soldiers were barely clinging to the lurching vehicle, yelling and wildly waving their free arms. We could not make out what they were shouting so emphatically. Many wagons, and still more wagons, all horse-drawn, followed the first gun. The scene was straight out of the nineteenth century. The group of Czech refugees that was gathered around us could not believe their eyes.

So this was the exalted, victorious Red Army that had conquered the Germans! They were fighting this modern war, this war of panzers, rockets, and radar, with—horses? Alex and I had not seen a single horse in the German army during the six years of the war, let alone a horse-drawn artillery carriage. Horses had been used by the Gestapo only for recreation or ceremonial occasions and crowd control. Here was the famous Red Army looking like the troops from Napoleonic wars some 140 years earlier.

In a sustained explosion of dust and sweating horses they wheeled into our drive and crashed to a stop. The soldiers dropped off the wagons and spread out to check the premises for Germans. The shouting continued. The scene was conducted with a sort of crude spontaneity.

An officer came up to us and introduced himself. Russian and Czech are both Slavic languages, and when spoken slowly a speaker of one can understand the other. We had little problem with communication. We told him how happy we were to see the Russians and that we welcomed them as liberators and brothers. Alex added that the Germans were retreating, that they had been ordered to move fifteen kilometers farther on before trying to regroup, and that the road up the hill was clear.

But the Soviets had no intention of following the Germans up the hill. The officer paid no attention to Alex's information and announced ponderously that they would remain in this valley overnight. The men unhitched the horses, unloaded feed, and started to set up a camp of sorts. Alex decided that the moment should be immortalized. He went into the house and returned with his camera, an expensive Contax, with fine optical lenses, and arranging our group around the Russian officer he took several snapshots.

The Russian's face became more animated. He looked at the Contax with interest, and putting out his large hand he said to Alex, "*Davai!*", which means, "Give it to me."

Alex smiled, thinking he had found another photographic enthusiast, and handed him the camera. To our surprise the Russian, after looking it over carefully, dropped it into his tunic pocket. Alex hesitated and then asked politely, "Excuse me, that camera's mine. May I have it back?"

The Russian shook his head, pursed his lips, and shoved the camera deeper into his pocket. Then he smiled. "Now it's mine!" he said simply.

Alex and I caught each other's eye. A nice beginning, I thought. Maybe all those horror stories were true after all. But we were in for more surprises. The Russian started chatting with us amiably. He had a strange mannerism of continuously and ostentatiously pushing up his cuffs as he talked. I glimpsed the glint of much gold. I blinked and realized my eyes had not deceived me. There was not just one watch on his hairy wrists, but dozens of gold, obviously expensive watches encircled both his arms and ascended under his uniform sleeves toward the region of his elbows. His hands looked as if they were the heads of exotic serpents escaped from a fairy tale. Gazing at them admiringly he said to himself, "Da, da, many watches is much better than one watch."

When he turned away to shout a command at one of the men, Alex leaned toward me and whispered, "Now aren't you glad we put that jewelry in the chemicals?" I had wanted to leave my jewelry in the safe. Alex was sure any searchers would find it there. Instead he had cached it in several big glass jars of chemical salts in his laboratory.

The first onslaught of soldiers was followed by an avalanche, and in no time Richky was stuffed with Russians. They were everywhere and took over the house completely. Then the Russian army women arrived. I had thought the men were noisy, but their female counterparts made our tranquil valley burst with their unrestrained activity. Their strident voices drowned out the male hubbub.

The military efficiency was nonexistent. When asked why they did not pursue the Germans, the Russians replied laconically that they wanted to relax. And relax they did. Soon they were singing and playing their balalaikas as if the war was the last thing on their minds. Richky's lawns were transformed into the site of a grand party.

One glance around and it was clear to us Czechs that we would be safer in the shelter. The Germans might return and this festive mob was no defense.

The three hundred refugees had been divided into three groups. Our shelter, originally built for our family and staff only, housed sixty people, squeezed in as tightly as possible, elbow to elbow. The root cellar was packed with another two hundred, and Mr. Müller's cellar held the balance. Anna had decided to stay in her own apartment with her sister who was pregnant and close to her confinement. She had come to stay with Anna because she felt sure that our valley was safer than Brno.

Also, Fanny had come back. She quit her job in the munitions factory and returned to Richky to spend these difficult times with us. We all were happy to see her as she had become a dear friend during the trying years of occupation.

Because Mr. Müller had become a widower, it was decided that Fanny would help him prepare food for those in his cellar. I was assisted by a girl named Annie. She had arrived with her employer, Mr. Mader, who had recently been in the hospital following a thrombosis and had not recovered full use of his legs. Like the rest of us, he thought he would be safer at Richky than in Brno.

More Russians with their troikas and cannons continued to pour onto the property and found themselves a spot in the orchard to unpack and rest. The whole place was full of soldiers: the garden, the orchard, and the meadows surrounding the house. Wherever one looked one saw the Red Army. This was a primitive army indeed. The cannons were old-fashioned and had none of the deadly stream-lining of German guns. We could not believe such antiques were being used in this century. There was not a single tank. The Soviets must have had tanks; they probably used them in other sectors of the front, but the troops in our valley certainly had none.

Having set up their camp they turned to serious celebration. The festivities warmed up quickly. The troops had raided an inn down on the river and brought with them the stock of wine and liquor that the innkeeper had illegally secreted in his cellars. The liberated liquor did its job. The soldiers sang and danced and drank with complete abandon.

Standing in the door of the bunker, Alex and I were wide-eyed. We wondered how they could fight a battle in their condition. This was like some big peacetime celebration. Their obvious indifference to the fact that the war was still on was unsettling. The Germans who had come through earlier had spoken of "regrouping," and although they were in retreat, it was highly possible they would return once they found out they were no longer being pursued.

And this is exactly what happened. Shortly after midnight the night exploded. The Germans decided they would keep the Russians bottled up in the valley where they made an excellent target for heavy guns on the surrounding hilltops. When well dug in and secure, they laid down a heavy barrage from dozens of guns, all pointed at our valley.

The Russians were not at all fazed or inconvenienced. They did not bother to lessen their celebrations, let alone stop. Eventually they did install several machine guns and some light artillery in the orchard just outside our shelter. To the horror of its sixty inhabitants, they also placed a gun on the roof of the shelter directly over our heads.

Alex rushed out to see the officer in charge. After a search among the growing number of drunken Russians he finally found him and asked, "Is there any way you could move that gun off the top of our shelter? The bunker's full of civilians and little children. You're risking all their lives."

The Russian drew himself up to his full height and made a speech. Russians were very fond of making eloquent speeches.

"Russia is full of people, too. Russia is full of children. The Russian people are dying, the Russian children are dying. Czech people are dying, Czech children are dying. . . ."

He went on and on. In the middle of the cannonade he talked for half an hour while shells were crashing down only slightly less emphatically than his sentences. In the end Alex returned to the bunker disgusted. The gun remained on top of the shelter. Every time it was fired everything and everyone in the shelter jumped. The timbers supporting the roof shook and dust sifted down to a chorus of coughs and sneezes. The shattering roar of the gun's concussion saturated our overcrowded darkness, adding to the agony.

Minutes took hours to pass, stretched out by our fear. Some of our companions slept while the majority merely slipped into lethargy. Sometime in early morning the door opened and an officer barged in. "Who's the *gospodin* here?" he inquired. *Gospodin* means the head of the household, the master. Alex stood up and the Russian shouted, "Come with me."

Alex followed him to Grandma's cottage. A boisterous officers' party was in full swing. As soldiers danced folk dances, a young, broad-faced officer strummed a balalaika fiercely, trying to drown out the snarl of falling shells. Another was accompanying him on Grandpa's precious new piano, a birthday gift from Alex. The two were playing a cossack tune, the piano player slamming the keys as hard as he could and wildly waving his elbows in time to the music. The balalaika player flailed his instrument, laughing all the while at several drunk lieutenants who were trying to do a strenuous cossack dance but who were failing badly, bumping into each other and falling over.

Their hilarity was in no way hampered by the bullets zipping through the thin walls and riddling the cottage. The officers appeared to be totally unaware of their situation. They acted as if they were at someone's house in a Moscow suburb on Saturday night. Alex did not enjoy it one bit.

One of the soldiers yelled, "You, *gospodin*, you play the piano."

Alex was extremely aware of danger and did not find the party at all attractive. He politely demurred, "No, I can't, I don't know how to."

An officer pulled out his revolver and gesturing with it, said peremptorily, "Play!"

Alex played. His repertoire of classical music was not well received. He was shoved aside and a new pianist swung into a popular Russian tune. A happy shout went up and the party shifted to a higher gear. The company became extremely rowdy, but things were not merry enough for the participants and more vodka was brought in.

Alex was offered a stiff drink. He tried to refuse, but out came the revolvers again: "You drink!"

He drank. The vodka was raw and strong, not liquor at all, but pure alcohol. It seared Alex's mouth and throat so that he choked, coughing and sputtering. The Russians were delighted and laughed uproariously as if their victim had said something clever and very funny.

"You don't know how to drink vodka, *gospodin*! You drink it with one hand, like this, and with the other you pour water down your throat, real quick, like this."

This was demonstrated by the speaker, who downed what appeared to Alex to be a full pint of liquid fire.

Poor Alex was forced to stay for almost an hour. He was sure he would never make it out alive. The bullets continued whizzing through the room with regularity, leaving the marks of their entrance on one wall and marks of their exit in the other. Several of the partygoers were hit and slightly wounded. Under the influence of all the alcohol they had consumed, they seemed hardly aware of their injuries.

Between the drinks, in an endless series of long-winded toasts, Alex had time to look around the cottage. Grandpa had been so stubborn in his insistence on the good qualities of the Russian people that Grandma announced she would put his beliefs to the test and establish their truthfulness once and for all. During one of her periodic trips from the shelter to the cottage to get this or that, before the shooting had begun, she placed several cigarettes in the sterling silver cigarette box on the table in the living room, making a careful note of how many there were. On her return she told us what she had done and added, "When I get back there, I'll just count how many cigarettes are left in the box, and then we'll know if they're honest."

Grandpa snorted that there was no need for such moral gymnastics. She would find that the box had exactly the same number of cigarettes. He would hear no further arguments.

Grandpa was sadly wrong. When Alex surveyed the room he saw that not only were the cigarettes gone, but the box itself had disappeared as well as everything of the least value in the cottage.

The battle was heating up. The Russians had at last allowed themselves to take notice of their opponents and attempted to return the German fire. They were so drunk that most of their misdirected shells fell short. Several hit our own house. Returning from Grandma's cottage, Alex noticed that the garage was also badly damaged and there were gaping holes made by the Russian guns in the stone wall surrounding the property.

A German dive bomber swooped down across our farm, spattering stick bombs. One scored a direct hit on the house, destroying the chimney. Another smashed the top story of the mill building. Anxiety was rising in the shelter and everyone was becoming more frightened by the minute. This was no passing skirmish. Every minute the sounds of the battle outside intensified. The staccato bursts from the machine guns were punctuated by sharp explosions from the cannons, and all around us were the deep, rumbling explosions of the falling bombs like the bass drum in a demon orchestra.

Voices in the shelter's dimness offered the consolation that the next day the Russian troops would pull themselves together and storm the hills. The ordeal would be over. I was not so sure. I doubted that they could take the hills easily since the Germans had obviously regrouped and dug in. I was right. The Russians were paralyzed by their frenzy.

The next day they were still celebrating. They had settled down in our house, eating their rations and drinking vodka out of my beautiful Rosenthal china, which they flung into the fireplace when finished. As the day passed, the pile of dirty and shattered china grew higher and higher.

The soldiers discovered the pantry where we had stored canned food. There was not much, mostly fruit and vegetables we had canned ourselves, together with a few precious prewar cans saved for times of real need. As they could not read our alphabet, the Russians simply opened can after can until they found what they liked. The rest was thrown on the floor, which was soon carpeted with a slippery mess of ruined and spoiling food.

The children were hungry. We had only some bread and sausage. I decided to go across the garden into the kitchen and check on the milk, hoping that Anna had been able to milk the cows when the shooting stopped.

I ran as fast as I could, jumping over the discarded equipment, bottles, and shell casings that littered the lawn. There was a peculiar sucking in of air behind me, an instant of suspended silence, and then I was propelled through the door into the house by the loudest noise I had ever heard. An enormous hole appeared on the garden path at the spot I had just vacated.

I found the milk and, taking as much as I could with me in a large pitcher, went to look for Alex who had been summoned by the Russians again.

"Zdena, what are you doing here?" he yelled over the noise of the gunfire when I found him. "Are you out of your mind? You might be killed!"

"I know," I gasped. "Alex, I just missed being blown up. I think we should go back. I'm afraid!"

He answered me, but I did not hear a word. The valley was filled with continuous detonations, one explosion enfolding after another, punctuated by rifle and automatic weapon fire. I could see Alex's mouth opening and closing. It was as if he was mouthing the words without producing a sound. I strained to catch what he was shouting when suddenly there was a lull in the cannonade and at last I got the drift of his words, "I don't think we should go back together! You run first. When I see you have made it, I'll run across. The children will have at least one parent if one of us gets killed."

As much as I did not want to leave Alex, I knew he was right. Clutching the container of milk, I raced out across the garden into the orchard, running as fast as I could until I fell through the doorway into the shelter, my heart pounding and my breath wheezing. Afraid of what I might see, I had to force myself to look back. Alex, still in one piece, was just arriving at the bunker door. He had covered his head with his arms and hands to shield it from the flying shrapnel.

Four Czech civilians who had come to Richky for safety had already been killed. As I crossed the garden, I saw several dead Russians lying among the early spring flowers.

Waiting for Alex at the entrance to the shelter, I had time to watch the Red Army's method of conducting a battle. They did not stop drinking, not for a minute. The field gun placed nearest to the bunker was manned by a soldier who was operating the gun with one hand while clutching a bottle of vodka in the other. He would shoot and drink, shoot and drink. As I watched he staggered and toppled over dead, still holding the vodka bottle. Another soldier trotted up, shoved his comrade's still-bleeding body aside, plucked the bottle from the dead hand, took a long swig, and commenced shooting. Several dead bodies, all of them previous possessors of the vodka bottle, were lying around the gun.

None of the Russians made even the slightest attempt to shield themselves from injury or even death. They spurned helmets as a sign of weakness. Under fire, officers and men alike moved in a straight line instead of zigzagging or dodging from tree to tree as even common sense would seem to dictate.

When asked why they did not protect themselves, the answer invariably was, "*Nichevo . . . nas mnogo!*" "It doesn't matter. There're lots more of us." They did not seem to care about dying at all. They had a fatalistic, almost oriental approach to life and death.

One explosion merged with the next. We huddled together, our senses numbed by the noise and our spirit convulsed by anguish. The shelter had become a closed world, a small, claustrophobic, damp cosmos populated by shivering people and wailing children. We were submerged in a black pool that shook and groaned constantly with each explosion, an emptiness filled with nothing but fear, noise, and the dank smell of tortured earth.

About two o'clock in the morning a hush fell, followed by a silence more ominous than the barrage of gunfire preceding it. We grew frightened. Surprisingly, the gunfire had become a contact with the outside. Now we were cut off. There was something ugly about this unnatural quiet. In the stillness one could clearly hear, for the first time in hours, voices of friends mumbling their anguish in the dark. A woman wailed. There was a murmur of what sounded like a prayer.

The door creaked, and a figure slipped in. Someone lit a candle. It was a Russian officer. A babble of voices clamored for information about the stillness.

"Shhh!" he said, "be quiet! The Germans are coming back. We've had to retreat."

A hissing broke out.

"What?"

"What did you say?"

"The Germans. My God, he said the Germans are coming back." Each person passed the information on to his neighbor. The news was a wave of horror flowing down toward the back of the shelter.

"Aren't you going, too?" someone asked the Russian.

"No. I have to stay here and report back." He began fiddling with some radio-telephone equipment.

"That's bad," Alex murmured to me. "If the Germans find him here they'll shoot us all for collaboration!"

I squeezed his hand. I could not say anything; there were no more words left. How much more, I thought, dear God, how much more of this will there be? We sat and prayed the Nazis would not find us. There was some comfort in the fact that the entrance to the shelter was not obvious. Hazelnut bushes masked the door and the darkness afforded further protection. No one inside moved. We could almost hear one another's heartbeats.

Then a German voice barked orders outside. Heavily booted feet stamped by, running. A voice shouted a command nearby. They were coming in. All was lost.

But, no, the voices faded as the men went past.

A little boy cried out. His frightened screaming was instantly muffled by his mother who frantically clamped a hand across his mouth. A woman sobbed once in the darkness. Time passed. We sat frozen, each one of us isolated in his own prison cell of fear.

After sixty minutes of unbearable tension the silence ended as suddenly as it had started. Shooting erupted, and the battle resumed with the Russian reinforcements.

Poor Janie had been sitting on my lap throughout the ordeal. I whispered little stories to her to distract her. Being a placid little person, she had been content with my presence. The gunfire, accompanied by the barbaric yelling of the fighting men and the neighing of many horses, had become so violent, however, that she had become afraid.

"Mommy," she asked, holding me tight, "what's that noise?"

"Sweetheart, it's nothing. It's just the war. It came and it will go away again."

"What is it . . . 'war'?"

"Well, you know how sometimes you fight with Evie and I'm always telling you you shouldn't do it? Well, it's the same with big nations. When they fight with each other, it's called war; then their men shoot and kill each other, and this is what it's like."

"Is it something like a storm? It sounds like a storm. . . ."

"No, darling, it's not a storm. It's big guns, the artillery. They're big cannons and machine guns and they make all that noise."

Janie was quiet for a moment and then she asked, "But will it be over soon?"

"Soon, sweetheart," I said, hoping I was right. "It'll be all right."

She quieted down, drank a little of the milk, ate a piece of a sandwich, held me tight, and, to my amazement, fell asleep. How meaningless the whole malignant world of human violence is to the heart of a child.

Evie was also traumatized by the fighting. She sat on Alex's lap holding her beloved Nellie, the dachshund, tightly in her arms, taking comfort in being able to give some consolation to the quivering little animal. The girl's face was pale and her big green eyes were full of terror. Evie knew far better than her baby sister what war meant. Poor child, I thought, how can God allow something so dreadful as war to happen to little children?

Toward five o'clock in the morning the fighting quieted down some. The Red Army observer who had hidden with us left the bunker. Russian voices were heard giving orders.

We thanked God for their return.

17
LIBERATION

The door of the shelter was pulled open. Two Russian soldiers stalked in. They left the door behind them slightly ajar and surveyed us slowly in the dim light. One of them pulled out his pistol and waving it over our heads shouted, "Give us your watches, and make it fast."

A friend of mine sitting opposite to me had a beautiful antique watch which she had inherited from her grandmother.

"No," she said to the Russian, "I won't give it to you. I've had this from my grandmother. I won't give it up!" Defiantly she placed her right hand over it. Without wasting words, the Russian cocked his gun and would have shot her if her husband, sitting next to her, had not intervened.

"Are you crazy? You want to die for a watch?" he hissed. He pushed her hand away, pulled the watch off her arm, and gave it to the Russian.

Soon not a single watch, ring, or bracelet was left in the whole shelter. The Russians disappeared, slamming the door behind them.

"My God," someone in the darkness exclaimed bitterly, "if these are friends, we don't need any enemies." The cliché had proved to be truer than we had ever thought possible.

The lull in the battle continued. Alex and I decided to risk going to the house for milk and water. The water supply had been limited from the beginning, and this was our third day underground. There was no water left.

As we emerged from the shelter, the daylight world outside our cave was a jarring experience. Dead bodies of men and horses carpeted the orchard and the garden.

When we entered the house, my breath caught in my throat even though I was panting from the effects of the run. The living room was the image of complete, incredible destruction. Overturned and torn furniture was flung about, my Rosenthal china lay splintered in the fireplace, the windows were all broken, and lying on the floor were unattended wounded and dying Russian soldiers, soaking the carpets with their blood.

In front of the radio on which we had often heard London broadcast its prophecy of freedom lay a very white, young, dead Russian boy. The radio cabinet, the whole wall behind it, and the ceiling above it were covered with his blood. It had gushed out of the huge wound in his neck.

The furniture had not been torn by gunfire. The damage had been done by the Russian bayonets. Chair backs were slit open as were seats and sofa cushions. The stuffing was strewed all over the floor. Legs and armrests jutted out crazily at all angles. Had the Russian soldiers been searching for valuables, or were they just malicious, or merely drunk? When I passed the laboratory I noticed through the open door that the bottles with the chemicals were untouched. Obviously Alex had been right. The lab had been a safe place.

The Russians were burying their dead. Two soldiers came downstairs, arms overflowing with blankets, sheets, and coverlets stripped from the beds.

"We need them," they told me with great solemnity, "because in this foreign soil our brothers need something soft to lie on so they are comfortable in their long sleep."

It was sad and so touching. These strange men were such a singular mixture of sentimentality and brutality, of childlike behavior and uninhibited violence, that they were utterly beyond my comprehension.

I found Anna in the kitchen. She had brought some milk for the children. As I prepared to leave she suddenly put out her hand and gripped my elbow.

"Oh, madam," she said with a peculiar, stunned expression on her face, "we've spent such a terrible, terrible night."

Just as the Germans had attacked, her sister had gone into labor. The Russians would not let them stay in the apartment. Anna and her sister had to go to the mill and hide underneath the stairs where the expectant mother had to lie on the dirty floor. She had such agonizing pain that Anna herself became deeply upset that she could do nothing for her. Water could not be heated. The women could not even wash. Anna herself was childless and had never seen a child born.

Both women lost control and began to cry. The soldiers in the mill ordered them to be quiet, threatening to shoot them both if the sister screamed in pain. They did not want to attract the Germans' attention. Just as the Nazis returned, a baby girl was born.

As Anna told the story, she appeared to be reliving the whole experience. Her kindly, lined face crumpled under the burden of remembered terror, and tears streaked her cheeks. She could hardly speak.

"Oh, my God," I said, "how's your sister?"

"She's fine. The Russians promised they'll let Peter and me take her to Mokra. There's a field hospital there. They said we can go when the fighting lets up a little. You know, I've never seen a baby born before," she repeated, "and then to have it happen in the middle of that terrifying battle, on a dirty floor like that. Oh, the poor darling."

"And how is the baby?"

"She looks all right, I guess, but I think my sister needs some attention. It was all so dirty there. I'm afraid she might get some kind of infection. You know, we couldn't even make a light. It was scary, so scary. That was the longest night of my life." She shuddered.

"Anna, how are you going to get her to Mokra?"

"We're going to put her and the baby in the wheelbarrow and Peter and I will push her," she said. "I have to get her some medical attention. She might die otherwise, so don't look for us tomorrow. We won't be here."

I took the milk and returned to the shelter. Alex had to remain in the house because the Russian commanding officer wanted to talk to him.

He informed Alex that they were going to take our horses. Our horses! Our good friends and dear companions during the happy hours spent wandering in the forests.

Alex agreed reluctantly, although he asked, "Could you leave the Lippizaner mares?"

To our intense excitement, both the Lippizaners had given birth before the front had reached Richky. One foaled a colt and the other a filly, both as pretty as a picture. "They foaled only a week ago and the foals would not survive without their mothers, so please leave the mares!"

The officer stood up and made a long, poetic speech.

"Russia is great. The Russian people are a loving people. The Russian soldiers would never take a mother away from her children, nor the children away from their mother," and he promised the mares would remain.

Of course, by afternoon the mares were gone, and the two poor little foals were left abandoned. They did not know how to eat solid food and whimpered for their mothers most pitifully. Alex found an old baby bottle with a rubber nipple, put some milk into it and tried to feed them, but then the Germans launched another attack. He had to abandon the foals and run back to the shelter for safety.

This time all hell broke loose. What had gone before was child's play compared to this.

The Germans must have realized that the Russian position was weak and surmised that most of the Russians were drunk. Being determined to win the valley back a second time, they launched what could only be called an all-out offensive. Every conceivable kind of gun fired simultaneously. The heavy German artillery joined in for the first time. Every minute, with the regularity of a heartbeat, an enormous shell hit the farm with a detonation that submerged all other sounds. We were wrapped in a blanket of death.

Janie started to cry. "Mommy," she wailed, "is it still war, or is it a storm now?"

And I answered, holding her tight, "Darling, it's still war."

How I longed for a drink of cool water. But all I took was a tiny sip from our dwindling supply and passed the glass onto Evie.

"Only a mouthful, darling," I whispered, "we don't have enough."

"Oh, Mommy, I'm so thirsty," Evie wailed. "My mouth's so dry, I can hardly swallow. . . ."

"I know, my love, but only a swallow. Think of the other people."

We all suffered from thirst, fear, cramps, and lack of air. A large Russian officer came in and announced in a bass voice, "This bunker no good! No good! One direct hit, and phhhhtttt! All fall down."

He found the idea amusing. Laughing boisterously he stamped out again, leaving behind him another dreadful thought: we might all be buried alive.

Dirt sifted between the solid beams holding up the roof. A baby was wailing loudly and monotonously. Its mother tried in vain to quiet it. The noise, the little voice sobbing, the fury outside, and the fetid atmosphere inside nauseated me. The shelling got worse by the minute.

I was still holding Janie on my lap, and Alex held Evie, with Nellie, the dog. "Sit close to me," he whispered. "Stay very close. If we're to be killed, I want us all to be killed together. Keep close so that we all go at once."

Tears filled my eyes.

Alex went on, "Try to be calm. Look, we had such a beautiful life. I've been very happy with you, darling. I am glad we met. Even in all our troubles it's been a great fulfillment living with you. I hope you feel the same. Not everybody is so lucky in this world. We've had the best of it. Let's be grateful for what we've had and accept death if it's meant to come. Let's die peacefully all together, all four at once."

He held Evie with one hand, and me with Janie with the other, and we waited. It went on and on, one endless explosion, finality itself, the full fury of the war unleashed. No one who has not experienced being a target of such total war can imagine the absolute terror it inflicts.

Hours later, at about two o'clock in the morning of our third night in the bunker, the gunfire diminished a little, then a little more. Then it was quiet. As we sat in the blessed, unbelievable silence, hardly daring to relax our grim attention, thanking God that the shelter had held up and we were still alive, another huge Russian stalked in.

"I want to talk to the *gospozha*," he bawled. *Gospozha* means the lady of the house.

I started to get up, but when I tried to put Janie on the bench she began to scream with fear, holding me tight.

Annie said, "Why don't you let me go? I know where the keys are. I can tell them anything they want to know."

She was gone for a long time. The shooting started again. I grew worried. When she appeared, Annie was a fearful sight. Her dress was torn, her hair tangled, her face puffy. She was hysterical.

"Don't ask what happened to me," she moaned. "It was terrible. They're not human. They're not even animals. They're devils. Don't ask me. Don't ask me. We can't stay here. Let's run away. We have to leave. We can't stay here. Don't ask me what happened, don't even ask . . . ," and she broke down completely.

The story was patched together from spurts of information that came out between sobs. Annie had been raped. She was raped many times. She did not know by how many soldiers. She had been a virgin. She had gone in my place. I felt terrible.

The shooting intensified. The situation seemed to be hopeless. The people in the bunker decided that when the next lull in the fighting came we would leave and attempt to reach Mokra, which was already behind Russian lines. By then we had been in the shelter for three days and three nights.

All of us were ready to go except one woman who had come to our farm with two little boys. Her husband, a policeman, had to stay in Brno. Before parting he told her to wait for him at Richky, which she was determined to do. We tried to dissuade her.

"Your husband didn't know how the situation would develop. He didn't know how the Russians behave. Please, come with us. We'll help you to find your husband in Brno."

But she was adamant. She would do as he had told her. She would stay. "After all, I have these two little boys here. I am sure the Russians wouldn't harm a woman with two little babies."

We could not force her. She remained, was raped many times, over and over, and beaten and abused. When she returned to Brno she was insane. After several suicide attempts her husband had to put her in a mental institution. How bitterly he regretted having told her to wait for him.

Finally the expected pause in the fighting came. We readied ourselves to leave. Evie prepared to take Nellie with her.

"Evie," I said, "you can't take Nellie. She's too old and fat. Leave her here, she'll be better off. You can come to get her after the war."

"No," Evie said positively, "I can't. She's coming with me."

She had a piece of string and this she tied to Nellie's collar in order to lead her. I had a couple of small suitcases, one with underwear and a few sweaters and dresses for the girls, and the other with some food. Alex took the food and I took Janie and the suitcase with the clothing.

Before we left, Alex gave last minute instructions.

"When they start to shoot again, lie down. Don't try to run then. Throw yourself on the ground so you make as small a target as possible. Don't forget."

He impressed this on both Evie and me. We had to cross the orchard, then the swimming-pool area, and finally a large meadow. The meadow, which was open and exposed to the German guns, would present the greatest danger.

We were at the back of the shelter and among the last to emerge from the stifling blackness into the silver-gray half light of early dawn. A line of fifty people ahead of us was already running across the orchard toward the swimming pool and meadow. Evie, dragging Nellie behind her, wasted no time, and breaking into a run she disappeared in their wake.

Alex wanted to wait for me and Janie, but I told him, "Go after Evie. I don't want her to go all by herself." He went after her, clutching the case with the food.

I grabbed my suitcase in one hand and Janie's hand in the other and set off after him. The five-year-old followed willingly, trotting along on her plump legs. When we came around the hazelnut bushes she saw the multitude of corpses of men and horses lying between the orchard trees. She stopped in her tracks. I yanked at her hand. She started ahead again, but her little face blanched and her eyes had a terrible, strained expression in them as if they had been visually abused, as if the child had been forced to look at more than such a young mind could ever accept. She did not speak and plodded along a pace or two behind me, trying to keep up. We threaded our way between the bodies across the orchard and reached the swimming-pool enclosure.

Barring the way lay one of our horses. It was Fuksa, our heavy draft horse. She had been a familiar and beautiful sight at Richky, patiently pulling our wagons, happily galloping in massive playfulness in the pasture, or contentedly munching her feed in her stall. Fuksa was dead. She lay at the gate, her belly ripped wide open with her intestines spilling out, blood puddling under her, her head twisted back and to the side. Her brown eyes were open and seemed to be staring up at something unexpected in the sky. The corpse was surrounded by other dead horses and soldiers thrown down in grotesque positions with smashed heads and torn bodies. Blood was everywhere.

Janie's legs locked. Then she fell to her knees and screamed hysterically.

"Mommy, please, don't go anywhere, please, Mommy, let's go back home, I'll always be a good girl, I'll never fight with Evie again, please, please let's go home." Her full weight hung on my arm. She could not get up.

My heart was breaking. In spite of my fear and need for haste, I knelt down by her and took her in my arms.

"Janie, sweetheart, you're the best little girl in the world. You didn't do anything wrong. You're always my best little girl, but we have to go now, Janie, darling. We can't stay here and we can't return. We have to go on. Please get up. Please come on. Let's go. I love you, sweetheart, but we have to go now."

While pleading with her, trying to overcome her hysteria, I looked back at the house and somehow realized that part of the building was gone. In its place there was only a bombed-out hulk. The windows were all smashed in, the roof had vanished, and some of the walls had partly collapsed. The middle part of the complex, where Jana's apartment was, was completely destroyed.

The ruins of what only three days before had been our home, the visible sign of our family's love, stood stark and forlorn against the gray skies, surrounded by all those poor soldiers who had come to die here, so far away from their homeland.

This is what it had all come down to: ruins that had been a home, dissolving in acid gray light; lifeless, torn bodies of soldiers and animals lying in pools of their own blood; and my little Janie kneeling here in the mud by our dead horse with her mother trying to protect her from a depth of despair no child should ever be forced to know.

"Janie, sweetheart, come, we have to go now."

I put down the suitcase, patted Fuksa's matted, bloodied mane for the last time, and picked Janie up. She was still screaming.

"Hang on tight, darling," I told her. "You know nothing bad can happen to you with Mommy holding you."

I stepped carefully over Fuksa's body, crossed the swimming-pool area where we had spent so many happy moments, and began to run across the meadow as fast as I could with Janie in my arms.

Just as we began to cross it, the firing started up again. Remembering Alex's instructions, I threw myself on the ground with Janie's body protected by mine. The shooting lasted about five minutes and stopped.

I picked her up and started running, and again the guns erupted. Once more we fell to the ground. I held the still-screaming child against my body hoping that the enemy soldiers would not see the forlorn pair and kill us.

The pattern recurred repeatedly: the shooting would stop; we would go forward only to be halted by sporadic bouts of gunfire. It seemed to take us forever to cross the meadow.

Finally we arrived at the stream, one of the twin creeks for which our place was named. It was running briskly from bank to bank with cold water from the melting mountain snows. Someone had thrown a rough log across. To cross on such a narrow log would be difficult at any time, but I was holding a squirming, screaming child. Slowly I inched across the primitive bridge, teetering at every step, the water gurgling and bubbling beneath me as it rushed by.

With a sigh of relief I stepped onto the far bank. I felt a twinge of hope that we might survive. Janie and I had reached the road to Mokra, an old friend. We were still within reach of German fire coming from the far side of the valley, and I ran as fast as my aching legs and abused lungs would let me. Ahead was the bend in the road that would take us out of the reach of death and into safety.

Once around the bend I put Janie down. She seemed to be a little better. She had become quiet, as if in a trance. Her eyes still held the tormented, shocked look, but she did consent to walk with me. We made better time.

Around another bend in the road, sitting on the grass under a tree, were Alex and Evie, with Nellie. Poor Evie was hot and sweaty. She had to carry fat Nellie.

Alex was soaking wet and shivering. He was wearing his pair of riding boots, and with their slippery leather soles, and burdened with the food suitcase, he had lost his balance and fallen in the creek. He had been able to keep the suitcase out of the water. Our food had been saved.

After a few moments of rest the reunited family continued on to Mokra. A comparative peace enfolded us. The shooting came from the other side of the mountain and seemed far removed from us.

Suddenly, we heard the fast-approaching roar of engines. Between the gaps of the trees we could glimpse a number of British and German fighters engaging in a large-scale dogfight. Stray bullets and shells fell around us. We were in the middle of the war again.

Janie started shrieking and I picked her up again. The four of us hid underneath a clump of pine trees, where we waited out the battle. It lasted for thirty tense minutes. One never knew from which side the bullets were going to come. They whizzed around us, hitting the ground, spraying up little fountains of dirt and ricocheting off rocks and boulders. The screaming of the engines punctuated by heavy explosions was a hellishly appropriate accompaniment for the sight of a wounded aircraft as it plummeted to the earth, streaming flames and dense, black smoke.

When it was over, we slowly made our way to Mokra, grateful to have survived once more.

18
BEHIND THE
FIRELINE

Mokra was a hive of activity. A first-aid station, a field hospital, and supply companies had been set up. The wounded were coming back from the front line and replacement troops were moving out to take their place. The area teemed with Russians.

Alex's company chauffeur, Frank, lived in one of the small villages near Mokra. We decided to go and see how he had fared during the fighting. Frank's mother made us welcome with bread and ersatz coffee. It was the first hot food we had had in three days.

When we entered her kitchen we found, to our surprise, many Russian women bunched up around the stove concocting something with sugar. Several of them had been doing the same thing on the roadside on open fires.

"What are they doing with that sugar?" I asked my hostess. "Surely they're not making candies?"

"Oh no!" she exclaimed. "They melt sugar and pour it into these little cones. When it is cooled, just before it hardens, they take the watches and bracelets collected from the Czechs, pack them in soft tissue paper, and drop them into the cooling sugar. Then when the sugar is hardened they send it off to their families back in Russia. Quite a system, isn't it?" she added, seeing my astonishment.

"Yes, they're very well organized."

I wondered idly if our watches had found their way here. Maybe they were being dropped into a cone of sugar syrup right here in this house. Then I shrugged. What did a watch or two matter compared to being alive, breathing fresh air and seeing sunshine.

A friend, Robert Hochwald, arrived. He had been the very last person to flee Richky. He was carrying my suitcase.

"I found this in the orchard by the pool," he said. I was glad to have a change of clothing and some warm things for the children.

Brno was still behind the German line so the Hochwalds invited us to go to Lisen and stay with them. After a short rest our party continued our journey. It was most pleasant to be out in the open without the sight of uniforms or armies.

On the outskirts of Lisen we stopped to see a forest ranger with whom we had become acquainted while horseback riding. In those peaceful days, we often used to drop in for a chat and a glass of water.

We found him alone in his nearly empty house. Having heard many stories about the Russians and their ways, he and his wife had wisely decided to store all their furniture in the cellar, which they locked up, leaving only the most necessary items, such as the bed, a table, and a few chairs. His wife and children then left to stay with her sister in Bohemia.

While we were talking, Alex, still in his wet clothes, suddenly shivered and said, "Maybe I should take my shirt off and hang it out to dry in the sun. I feel quite cold."

The forest ranger offered to lend him a shirt while his was drying on the clothesline in the backyard. We were sitting in the forester's kitchen sipping hot tea when Alex glanced out of the window. Two Russian soldiers were approaching the house. Seeing his shirt and undershirt drying on the line, the two men stepped across the low fence dividing the yard from the forest and quite openly began removing the garments.

Alex jumped up and ran out of the house.

"Hey, comrades!" he called, "that's mine. I need it. Please give it back to me!"

The Russians gave him a cold stare and then, still clutching the garments, one of them took out his gun, having apparently no intention of surrendering his prize.

"*Nichevo!*—No!" he said belligerently.

Alex decided that a shirt was not worth being shot for and,

muttering, came back into the house. Several weeks later, when we returned to Richky and he found all of his clothes gone, he could truthfully say that he finished the war without a shirt to his back.

In Lisen everyone was still in air-raid shelters as a protection against Russian lust and greed. The shelter in the Hochwalds' building was large and equipped with bunks almost wall to wall, with men sleeping at one end and the women at the other. They had all brought down their mattresses and blankets and were quite comfortable. Without hesitation they made room for us.

We went to bed shortly after we arrived. In my sleep, tired as I was, I heard Janie crying and I sat bolt upright. Evie had vomited all over her sister and even as I was staring at her, she retched again. Alarmed, I reached out and touched her. Heat was blazing out of her. Grateful that Robert had found our suitcase, I cleaned up both girls and changed their clothing. Janie fell asleep again instantly.

It was clear that Evie was very sick. Then she began to cough. A woman in the next bunk gave me some aspirins. After swallowing them Evie dozed off. In the morning I went over to the men's side of the shelter and asked Alex to get a doctor. Fortunately, Lisen was the home town of our own physician, Dr. Polacek. Alex went to find him and brought him back to the shelter. He examined Evie, diagnosed pleurisy, and asked Alex to come with him to his office for some medication. Before leaving he told us about his experiences with the Russian soldiers.

He had opened up his office in order to help anyone injured in the fighting, but he was totally unable to understand the Russian mentality. Once a Russian officer came to his office bleeding heavily from the chest and asked for a couple of adhesive bandages. He had been shot through the lungs. The bullet had entered through his back and went out the front, and he was bleeding profusely.

"I ordered him to lie down or he would die from loss of blood. The officer replied that all he needed was the bandages, one in the front, and one in the back. Then he'd go back to fighting. I tried to stop him, but he insisted and left. He could not have lasted for more than three hours."

Dr. Polacek also recounted to us his experience with two privates looking for alcohol. They immediately drank whatever they found, including a poisonous chemical.

"I was unable to stop them. They drank it up, and I know both of them must have died a couple of hours later at the most. But there's no reasoning with these people. They're just not normal, not normal at all. All they seem to live for is liquor!"

Poor Evie lay almost lifeless on the narrow bunk with her head aching and her body burning, with Nellie snuggled up against her. I stayed with her throughout the day. Mrs. Hochwald went up to their apartment during the day and made some herbal tea, which was the only liquid Evie was allowed to drink.

The second night came. I was afraid to go to sleep in case Evie got worse, but apparently the medication had begun to work because by morning she was feeling much better. Relieved, I began to take some interest in the communal life of the shelter.

In the evening one of the young women bunking nearby felt cold. She left to get a sweater upstairs, but she soon reappeared, dripping wet. On her way to her apartment she had met a Russian major in the corridor. When he saw that she was alone he made a grab at her. She managed to evade him and raced out of the building, the major hard on her heels. She was nimbler than he was, and her fear gave her additional speed. A big tank of rain water for washing clothes was around the corner of the building. The major was pounding along behind her, getting closer by the second. She jumped into the tank and submerged herself, stayed underwater as long as she could and then peeked out. As the major was nowhere in sight, she got out and hurried back to the shelter. The women dried her off and found her some warm clothing. After a cup of hot tea she warmed up and began to feel better. The incident proved to us again that it was unsafe to venture out of the shelter at night.

Evie felt better the next day, but we decided to wait the full five days recommended by Dr. Polacek before undertaking the last leg of our journey. We heard that Brno had finally been taken by the Russians and that all German resistance had been wiped out.

After a week in Lisen we thanked the Hochwalds for their kindness, and with our friends, the Krobots, we set out for Brno.

The city was a depressing sight. The streets were full of rubble. The shop fronts were boarded up and the windows of the apartment houses were all broken. The few people out in the street had to pick their way slowly through the devastation.

As neither of us had a watch, we asked a passerby for the time. The man looked at us and shook his head.

"You, too?" he said. "Nobody in the whole city has a watch. We've had to learn to tell the time by the sun. I think it's about ten o'clock now, or pretty close. But watches? They're a thing of the past. There's not a watch left in Brno!"

Early in the afternoon we finally reached the Krobots' apartment building. It was still standing, but much like the other buildings it was a mess. All its windows were broken, shattered bottles and garbage were strewn around the front entrance, and the main door had been repaired with rough planks and rusty iron strapping.

Marie Krobot began to cry. We went up to their apartment on the fourth floor. It was dirty and full of dust and soot, but nothing had been stolen.

There was no electricity or water, but to our surprise the gas was on and we were able to make ourselves a cup of tea and some hot soup with the little water we had carried with us. Marie had left some potatoes and flour in the pantry and to our delight they were still there, undisturbed.

In the evening, being without windows, the apartment began to chill rapidly. Marie did not have many blankets and we had only the clothes on our backs. We spent a cold night but were otherwise warmed by the knowledge that the worst was behind us.

Alex and I worried about the rest of the family. At first they had been in our shelter. On that first day of the Russian occupation when everything seemed quiet, Jana, who was in her sixth month of pregnancy, began to feel ill. As she could not lie down in the over-crowded bunker, she and Ivan decided to return to their apartment. Grandma and Grandpa went with them to increase their safety by adding to their number. They were expected to come back to the shelter when the fighting and shelling intensified, but they had not returned. I had had no news from my parents either. Vrbatky was some sixty miles away. There was no mail, and telephone lines were all torn up.

Even though they had pulled out, the Germans continued bombing and shelling Brno. Still, it was nothing compared to what we had experienced in our valley. We sensed that the end of the war was near and that we did not have long to wait for peace.

Not much food was left. We had some bread, a chunk of salami, and a few potatoes. This was divided among the six of us and a strict rationing system was instituted. I gave most of my food to the children, who were hungry all the time.

Evie coughed constantly.

Although her pleurisy was getting better, she was thin and pale and had dark shadows under her eyes. She was not her usual self at all, suffering from traumatic memories of the front. Whenever a few people met, they would always recount their experiences with the Russians, talk about the shooting, and discuss the casualties. But Evie just could not bear to hear any of that. She would leave the room, or if that was not possible, she would stuff her fingers in her ears.

"Mommy, why do people have to talk about it all the time?" she asked me plaintively one day. "Wouldn't it be better if they forgot about it? I wish I could forget it."

Janie had changed, too. She became withdrawn and never once complained of being hungry. She grew pale, as if life was draining away. Her enormous dark eyes, ringed with purplish shadows, were full of sadness. Both girls needed time to get over the shock of those last days.

Alex and Bohus Krobot found some people living about ten blocks away who had an old-fashioned well in their garden, a relic of the old days. Every morning they set out to get our water, each carrying two buckets. They had to wait for their turn at the pump as there was always a long line of people. The water was heavy and had to be carried a long way back, but it was fresh water and we were grateful for it.

The second night, sometime in the early hours of the morning, a sudden commotion arose near the entrance to the building. From the window we saw Russian soldiers trying to break down the door to get in. We knew only too well what was likely to happen if they succeeded. There was no way to call for help. We were completely isolated since there was no telephone service. They made a great deal of noise, but the door was solid and well barricaded.

Next morning we all talked it over. By then we were as afraid of the Russians as we had been of the Nazis. We had no idea what to do. Alex and Bohus returned with good news, however, from their water expedition. They had bumped into their friend, Spurny, who had been sheltered at Richky with us. It was his wife who had almost gotten herself shot over her heirloom watch. When he heard of our problem, Spurny said, "Why don't you come and stay in our apartment? You sheltered us, now it's our turn to shelter you. We have a large apartment and there are about fifty people sleeping there. Bring your mattresses and blankets. There's room enough. You'll be safer there. You can spend the nights with us and return to your place during the day."

Down the street from Spurny's building were the police headquarters. A kind of security system had been set up with the other buildings. Each building posted a guard, and at the first sign of trouble, if the Russians started breaking in somewhere, the man on watch yelled out as loudly as he could, "PATRO-O-L!" The fellow in the next building took up the cry, "PATRO-O-O-L!" Then the next and the next, until the message reached police headquarters. The police marched out accompanied by a Russian officer and arrested the troublemakers.

That afternoon we moved our mattresses to Spurny's apartment, which was only about four blocks away from the Krobots. We found their place set up much like the shelter in Lisen: men and women slept in separate rooms, and the whole apartment was filled with wall-to-wall mattresses.

About three o'clock in the morning we were awakened by "PA-TRO-O-O-L!!! PATRO-O-O-L!!! PATRO-O-O-L!!!" repeated over and over, each one fainter than the one before, in an endless chain of calls stretching down to the police headquarters. Before long we heard a car race up the street, then a little later we heard it returning, and soon all was quiet again.

Our food situation was becoming desperate. We had eaten everything, and after being hungry for so long, churning stomachs and constant lightheadedness were taken for granted. The children, growing thinner and more drawn daily, looked sickly and weak. The only thing left to us was to go out to Lisen to get some bread and potatoes, leaving the girls with the Krobots.

Early in the morning I dressed in a pair of Marie Krobot's slacks and a raincoat and her husband's hat, and Alex and I set out. I hoped to pass for a boy, at least from a distance, since I had lost so much weight and was thin. The masquerade seemed a necessary precaution with all the Russian troops around.

We had to walk all the way, a journey of four hours. As long as we were in the city I felt safe, but when we came out into the country we kept a constant lookout for Russian soldiers. Whenever we saw any coming we would leave the road and hide in the fields until they passed.

At eleven o'clock we arrived at the Fosters' farm in Lisen. The first people we saw there were Grandma, Grandpa, Ivan, Jana, and Zeno, their little son. It was wonderful. When the shelling began to get heavy, they had gone to the Müllers' cellar. Then, as the fighting grew worse, the people there decided that they would be safer in the forest caves.

The caverns they went to were very well known, the site of many archeological discoveries. Neither the fighting nor the Russian army came anywhere near them.

We had a good lunch, our first warm, completely cooked meal in three weeks. Alex and I were so hungry that it tasted like a gourmet meal in a five-star restaurant.

We had to be back in Brno before dark. On our return we saw an army convoy and wondered if the soldiers were perhaps reinforcements for the troops in our valley, which was still under siege. To avoid the Russians we walked in the fields for most of the way, though it made walking difficult, especially with our bundles of potatoes and bread.

Alex and I were very tired when we got to town. Near our building we ran into a young man who had worked at Biochema. He was happy to see us and offered to help us get some food. His wife used to run a small grocery, and when we visited him the next day he gave us several jars of Biochema jam, canned vegetables, ersatz coffee, herb tea, and sugar—a great treasure. We carried it home, feeling rich. We still had to be careful and ration everything strictly, but at least we had something to eat.

Alex and I looked around for another place to live. Richky was still a battlefield, and the house was in ruins. We talked to the superintendent of the Krobots' building and were told that he had an empty apartment on the second floor.

"There were some Germans living there," the superintendent said, "but they ran away when the front approached. All the furniture's there."

We went up to see the apartment. It was identical to the Krobots' but two floors lower. The next day we moved in. We stayed there during the day and continued going to the Spurnys' at night.

The fighting flared up around us. The Russians had installed heavy artillery in Brno and were shelling the Germans, who in turn were doing what they could to recapture the city.

Suddenly at the beginning of May the Germans weakened, the front line moved forward, and the heavy artillery pulled out of Brno. The city became almost uncommonly still.

Clearing of the streets began. Workers undertook repairs on water mains and pipes that had been broken in more than 250 places. The authorities were anxious to get the water system back in order so as to prevent further spread of cholera and typhoid that had broken out in the city.

The people of Prague, still under German occupation, staged an uprising by erecting barricades in the city and fighting the Germans. They took over the radio station and made pleas to the American army for help, saying, "Our American friends, we beg you to come and aid the people of Prague," a message that was repeated many times on Radio Prague. General Patton had taken Pilsen, conquered western Bohemia, and was only fifty miles from the capital. We heard that a few units of American soldiers had been sighted not only in the Prague suburbs but even on Wenceslaus Square in the city center.

But the Americans were ordered back. At the Yalta Conference it had been decided that Prague was to be taken by the Russians—which proved to be a catastrophe. Even then we knew that we would have much preferred the Americans. The overwhelming desire of the Russians to occupy Prague seemed to us to imply a sinister intention. The people of Prague fought on valiantly but vainly. The Americans did not respond.

On May 7, a delegation of the Czechoslovak government headed by President Benes arrived in Brno. He addressed the people on the radio, announcing that our national crucifixion had ended and that freedom was at hand.

Early the next morning, May 8, we were still at the Spurnys' when wild shooting erupted outside, accompanied by yelling and commotion.

"My God," someone exclaimed, "surely the Germans haven't taken Brno back again. The Lord save us!"

We all rushed to the windows to look. Hundreds of Russian soldiers were milling around shooting in the air, laughing, slapping each other on the back, waving their guns above their heads and firing them again and again. They were yelling that the war was over and that they could go home to Mother Russia. The air blossomed in peal upon peal of church bells. The glorious news spread through the city.

We hurried down into the street. It was suddenly full of cheering, laughing people, all hugging each other, dancing around in the street, slapping the Russian soldiers on their backs, all fear and enmity forgotten. They would be going home soon. Why not fraternize with them?

We were ecstatic. Finally, after so many years our republic would be reborn and we were going to be free again. It was six and a half years since Munich and six years and two months since Hitler's army had goose-stepped into Czechoslovakia. It seemed longer, much longer. The German occupation had been endless; suddenly it was miraculously over.

For many Czechs it was a literal forever. Many had been left behind in concentration-camp gas chambers, prison execution rooms, and on battlefields. They would never taste this freedom, this exhilaration. They would never return.

With great sadness, in the midst of the celebration I was thinking about martyrs dearest to our hearts: my uncle Leopold, Aunt Anna, Chairman Wenzl, Jan Kulajta, Josef Svoboda, Frantisek Pilc, Bohumil Kolar, Jakub Konopac, Jan Heres, most of them from Biochema, and all of them executed by the Nazis.

But here, people embraced and kissed each other. The day brimmed with gaiety and optimism. In spite of hunger, in spite of being dirty, in spite of the loss of electricity and other conveniences, in spite of the destruction of our home, we were overjoyed. We were alive. We were free at last. It was marvelous, glorious!

There would never be the Gestapo again, no more police state. From this day on there would be democracy, freedom, sheer happiness.

It was a day worth waiting for.

19
DOUBTFUL FREEDOM

Our new apartment was pleasant, full of sunshine, cheerful, and cozy. The four of us quickly settled in. Alex and I made another trip to Lisen for food. I had to borrow a pair of slacks and a blouse to supplement my wardrobe, the clothes I had on the day the Russians came. Alex borrowed a second shirt. The children at least had a few things, thanks to Robert and the rescued suitcase.

Impatiently we awaited the day we could return to Richky. We hoped that our clothes and personal items were still there, but we could not go there yet. The area had not been cleared of unexploded bombs.

Brno became very active with people removing the rubble of the war and trying to get life back to normal as quickly as possible. The city was still full of Russian soldiers, and as we had more time to observe them, we discovered anew how primitive and childlike they could be.

One day when Alex was looking out of a window he saw a Russian soldier bicycling down the street, attired most incongruously in a striped pajama jacket over his battle dress. He had a bulging sack containing, as Alex discovered shortly after, a collection of alarm clocks, one of which began to ring. The Russian jumped off the bicycle, flung the sack on the ground violently, whipped out his revolver, fired a full six rounds into it, climbed back on his bicycle, and cycled off, leaving the vanquished sack behind. A strange people, the Russians.

Many German prisoners of war were marched through the city, heading east. Comparing this forlorn band with the hated Nazi army that had marched so confidently and arrogantly through the streets of Brno in 1939, we realized how total was the destruction of Hitler's troops.

Disarmed, they looked tired, dirty, and hungry. Thousands and thousands of them shuffled along in torn uniforms, being taken to concentration camps in Russia to work as free labor and possibly die of exhaustion, starvation, and the Siberian cold.

The quality of our life improved substantially when our water supply was finally reestablished. Then came the restoration of electricity, the resumption of streetcar service, and last of all, the resurrection of the telephone. Things once taken for granted were as exciting as new inventions.

Alex went to look at the Biochema offices in the city. The building had not been badly damaged. The employees were returning one by one, clearing up the mess of broken glass, smashed furniture, and the rest of the debris of war.

Then followed a trip to the factory in Modrice. There the damage was far more severe; the Russian soldiers had camped all over the grounds. Many things were missing. Every vehicle the company had owned, including Alex's car, was gone. The offices had been thoroughly looted. As in Brno, many employees were, at their own volition, already at work cleaning up.

Finding another car was not easy. Finally Alex heard of a man living on the outskirts of Brno who had one he was willing to sell. He had managed to hold onto it throughout the war by keeping it in his barn covered with hay. We were fortunate that we were able to buy a car legitimately from its rightful owner.

A friend bought one from a Russian soldier. The first day he drove it, he pulled up in front of a shop. A shopkeeper came running up yelling, "You are driving my car! It was stolen from me. I'll show you all the papers!" Our friend returned home on foot, having lost both his money and the car. This was the danger of buying something from the Russians; one never knew who the rightful owner might be.

A similar incident happened to us. In the street one day Alex saw a baker's cart pulled by a small, skinny, humble little horse. As the cart approached he realized that it was Evie's pony, Regent. Alex asked the baker where he had gotten the horse. The baker answered he had bought him from a Russian soldier for a bottle of vodka. When Alex told him it was our horse, the baker immediately said we could have him back.

A few weeks later Regent returned to Richky, the only one of our horses that was left. When he entered the gate, he stopped, raised his head, and uttered a loud, piercing whinny, a happy homecoming cry of recognition.

Finally we heard that the road to Richky was open. It had taken a long time to clear it of any unexploded bombs. The narrow highway which led from Brno to Obce was in passable condition. With trepidation we entered the winding forest road that led down to our valley. When we came to the spot at the top of the valley where our property began and from which we could view all of Richky, Alex stopped the car. We got out and stared down.

What had been a lovely, gracious cluster of buildings set in rolling fields and meadows, encircled by the twin rivulets and surrounded by deep green forests, was now utter desolation. The central part of the complex, containing Ivan and Jana's apartment as well as that of our gardener, was completely in ruins. The chimney on the main building was down, the roof was nearly destroyed, and there were huge gaping holes in the walls. The garage had partly collapsed and its roof had fallen in. The place looked deserted and forlorn.

Without speaking we got back into the car and continued on down the hill to the main entrance. The solid stone wall was almost demolished. The gate hung on broken hinges. We drove up the drive, stopped in front of the house, and got out of the car.

The first thing that hit us was the stillness. Then we were engulfed by a dreadful smell. The valley, which had in times past overflowed with the fragrance of wildflowers, mown grass, roses, and pine trees, was redolent with putrefaction, the sickening stench of death. I retched, my stomach heaving.

The sweeping front lawn, our gardener's pride and joy, had disappeared. In its place there was an uneven wasteland covered with heaps of soil, piled up hurriedly and surrounded by an indescribable carpet of rubbish, scraps of torn uniforms, jagged pieces of metal and bits of shrapnel, bricks, pieces of wood, and broken glass.

The garden was trampled under by countless hooves and feet, the spring flowers torn and crushed. Among them was one of my shoes. The orchard was full of mounds. Alex and I learned later that 250 Russian soldiers had been buried there.

The walls of the house were splashed with blood and mud. The battered front door was half open, swaying slowly in the slight breeze. Its creaking and the buzzing of thousands of flies were the only sounds. Every window in the entire house was shattered, with jagged ends of glass glittering in the sun and my beautiful draperies hanging in tatters on the smashed casements. The furniture was broken and ripped apart, spotted with blood and stained with un-nameable filth. As I looked toward where the radio used to be and saw the blood covering the wall and ceiling, I remembered the young Russian boy who had bled to death there.

The floor was completely covered with dirt, debris, and horse manure. The Russians had brought their horses in the house with them. Peter later told us that he had asked one of the soldiers why they did not put their horses in our stables. The Russian had looked at him with surprise and replied, "What? And have another comrade steal him? Much safer this way!"

They had in fact slept on the floor with their horses tethered by the reins to the riders' wrists. I wondered if the carpets were still there, down under the mess.

There was mud, blood, and refuse all over the kitchen. And the smell! The odor outside had been bad enough, but the stench in the house was worse. It clung to everything, an almost physically tangible odor, making both of us gasp for breath.

In the pantry no cans or bottles were left. Everything had been emptied out on the floor where the home-preserved fruits and vegetables lay ankle-deep, rotting. I thought I was going to vomit and went quickly to the door of the bathroom.

A most surprising sight met my eyes. Apart from the filth there, it was the toilet bowl that caught my immediate attention. In it were two of Alex's shoes, firmly jammed into the drain opening so that the water could not be flushed down.

We walked up the staircase to the second floor. On the landing in the curve of the stairs was our large, antique grandfather clock. Its stately ticking and sonorous, melodic bells used to measure out to us the happy passage of the hours. We found its glass front smashed, with the splinters littering the stairs. Alex had had a beautiful pair of expensive, handsome riding boots that he had hidden at the last minute behind the clock in the hope of saving them. The space was empty, the boots gone.

All the closets were also empty, even the ones we had so carefully locked. The doors had been forced. I looked in the drawers of the various chests, but nothing was inside. Everything had been removed from the children's rooms, including all toys and clothes. I noticed Janie's favorite doll on the floor and bent down to pick it up. It had not escaped the destruction either. Its stomach had been slit open and its head cut in half by a knife. I laid the doll gently on Janie's bed.

"Let's see what happened in the laboratory," I said to Alex. "We forgot all about my jewelry."

We picked our way through the chaos and went downstairs. The laboratory looked as if it had been caught in an earthquake. The microscope, instruments, jars, beakers, and test tubes had all been smashed and lay scattered around the floor, which was also strewn with the chemical salts. The jewelry was gone. Alex said in a strangled voice, "Let's go and see the safe." The safe was in Janie's bedroom behind a picture. It had not been disturbed.

The upstairs toilets also had shoes stuffed into them. Later someone told us that this had been done to bowls all over the country where Marshal Malinovsky's troops had fought. Apparently his soldiers did not know what these strange porcelain objects were for and deduced that they were for washing. They stuffed things in them to keep the water from running out.

Malinovsky's division that fought at Richky was probably the most primitive and savage in the Soviet army. Though the officers were European Russians, the troops were Mongolians and other Asiatic people from the Siberian steppes. This army contained many prisoners who had been pardoned and then thrown into the areas of the heaviest fighting. The way Malinovsky's men destroyed our house was sheer barbarism.

As we stood there looking at the mess, Peter and Anna arrived. Anna began crying when she saw us.

"Thank God you're all right!" she said, wiping her eyes. "We were sure you were killed. It was so terrible here! We had no idea what happened to you."

"Where are you staying? Is everybody all right?" Alex wanted to know.

"We don't know about the others. We've been staying in Obce, but we came back to see if we could move back here. We've been cleaning our apartment up a bit. All the windows are broken out and it's a mess, but the walls are standing, so we'll soon get it straightened up," Peter said, relieved that life could once again get back to normal.

I remembered the foals and asked him, "What about the foals? Have you seen them?"

"Yes, they were in the meadow, trying to eat the grass, poor little things. They're almost starved. I brought them in and put them in the barn, but I don't know if they'll make it. They look awfully weak."

"Do you know," Anna said, "surprisingly enough the cows are still here! They're in the barn, and I've been milking them and giving the foals some of the milk. Maybe that'll help them a little."

It did help, but it was not enough. One of the little babies died the following week and the other lingered on for a while and then died, too. So much for the Russian idea of sacred motherhood.

Our photograph albums and home movies made of the children from infancy were also gone. Very sad, the four of us returned to the front hall, where I noticed a photograph underfoot. Then I saw several pictures lying among the debris on the floor, crumpled, dirtied, bloodied, and torn. They were so filthy that I did not notice them when we first entered the house. Out in the orchard, photographs and film lay scattered all over. Much of the film had been torn into pieces; the photographs were also ripped up, as if the soldiers had been playing some silly game in the midst of battle. Two small rolls of film apparently intact were lying under a bush. I picked them up and for some reason the sight of these, the only two items from our past life that we found in one piece, brought tears into my eyes. This is all that was left to us, I thought, looking at the two rolls of film. I realized that I did not really mind so much the material possessions being gone, but I did mind this senseless destruction of our treasured photographs, my beloved record of our early years and my little ones' babyhood. I began picking them up, turning them over in my hands, looking at them—pictures of our wedding and of my school years. Here was a photograph of Janie in her crib; here was one of Alex on his favorite horse Jura, now probably dead; here was another of Evie on Regent, her pony—all gone, everything vanished, everything lost in this cruel hurricane that had swept across the land and had taken and ruined so many lives, leaving misery and destruction in its wake.

We gathered up whatever we could and Anna promised she would search for some more later. Back in Anna's apartment for ersatz coffee, I asked about her sister, who had delivered a child during the battle.

"Just fine," Anna beamed, "just fine. It's a miracle. My sister wasn't even sick, and the baby's just wonderful. A beautiful baby, and so healthy."

Then I remembered that we had not looked into Madi's room. Alex and I rushed back to the house to find her room as bare and empty as the rest of the house. When she had left for Austria she told me that she was leaving her best things at Richky where they would be safer. Poor Madi. For the second time she had lost everything, this time even her collection of Parisian shoes.

"What on earth are we going to do with the place?" I asked Alex despairingly as we stood outside surveying the caved-in roof, the collapsed walls, the shattered windows, and the mounds on the lawn.

"Clean it up, of course!" said Alex, "and rebuild. What else? We'll get some people in from the village to help, and surely the authorities will take all these dead bodies away. The smell's terrible and it's a health hazard. They're barely underground!"

In the barn we found another friend, our Great Dane, Gondola, who had hidden there throughout the fighting. She was ecstatic when she saw us, her tail swishing happily. Emaciated as she was, she looked adoringly at us. We patted her great golden head and promised her we would soon be back.

Before leaving we went to the orchard and to the shelter where we had spent so many terrifying moments. I shuddered as we walked in. All the fear and hopelessness, the claustrophobia, the unmitigated horror of those three days came flooding back. In a flash of pain, I relived the endless sitting in the dark listening to the unleashed fury raging outside. I turned to Alex and said, "We were *so* lucky to get out alive, *so* lucky to have lived through this hell and come out of it with the children, and the four of us without a scratch! I can never thank God enough for keeping us safe throughout all that!"

We picked up Janie's broken doll, took from Anna the few photographs she had found, said good-bye to them both and left. We drove up the forest road, and as our car reached the top of the hill we saw ahead a group of policemen and some Russian soldiers. One of the policemen came forward, urgently holding up his hand.

"Just a minute," he called out. "Stop!"

"Why, what happened?" Alex asked.

"We found another unexploded bomb in the middle of the road."

We skirted the area gingerly, realizing that on our way down to the valley we had driven right over the bomb. We returned home safely.

Life gradually improved for us in Brno. Stores finally reopened and we were able to buy some food. Again we were issued ration cards, and the children were allotted extra, small portions of milk.

Alex was concerned about Biochema. No raw materials or vehicles were left. The Russians had cleaned the place out.

Convoy after convoy of loaded trucks with the red-star emblem traveled eastward, just as in 1939 similar convoys with the swastika insignia had headed westward to Germany. Once more Czechoslovakia was being systematically plundered by a foreign power. One day I happened to be in a streetcar when a couple of Russian trucks passed. One was loaded with furniture and the other with carpets.

A lady sitting next to me remarked bitterly, "Well, there go my oriental rugs!"

"Maybe mine, too," I said.

"Yes, I guess everybody's been hit hard by this liberation," she said.

Alex decided to go to Prague to talk to Tony Srba and the chairman of Chemical and Metallurgical, Dr. Martinek, about the future of Biochema. He was informed that the company had been nationalized the moment the new Czech government had taken office. Dr. Benes had flown from London to Moscow, and with his new cabinet he entered Czechoslovakia with the Red Army. All companies with more than a hundred employees had become the property of the state.

How would this new system work? Alex wondered if it was his responsibility to obtain raw materials. He wanted to get answers to this and many more complex questions.

Three days later, he returned from the capital with two large suitcases. I opened the first one and gasped. Our wonderful friends in Prague had sent us many things that we so desperately needed: men's underwear and shirts, two business suits for Alex, dresses, pajamas, and underwear for me. They had sent me the best of their own carefully preserved, treasured wardrobes: two pure silk dresses, a jacket, two sweaters, and some skirts and blouses. I could not have been better outfitted had I shopped for them myself before the war. This was touching. I was moved to tears.

Alex spent the evening telling me all about Prague. He described the damage done in the uprising. Prague, too, was full of Russian soldiers, but of a different kind. They were from the army of Marshal Koniev. One evening, when Alex was at the Martineks' home for dinner, their lovely daughter Sylva went to the theater with a Russian officer.

After they left, Alex, worried, asked if they were not afraid to let her go out alone with a Russian.

"Oh no," Dr. Martinek said, smiling, "they're educated people, correct and gentlemanly. We're not at all afraid for her." Alex told him of our experiences with Malinovsky's army. The Martineks were horrified.

The cleaning up of the country continued. This included ridding the country of those Nazis who had not managed to escape. Levicek, the man who had arrested Alex in 1942 and tortured me with threats of Alex's decapitation, was captured and hanged, as were many others.

Another sinister element returned from our past. One day, to his surprise, Alex received an invitation to attend a meeting of the representatives of the Workers' Union of Biochema in the company's boardroom in Brno. When he walked into the room, he found, among those present, eight men whom he did not know. On the table in front of each of these unknown men lay a revolver. They were Russian ex-partisans who had been accepted into the union and were going to work in Biochema.

The presiding officer of the union Alex knew all too well. He was Novotny, the man who had denounced him to the Gestapo and who was later sentenced to death. I remembered seeing him shuffling along the corridor in the Breslau courthouse, having been brought to testify against Alex. I had felt pity for him and had given him food. Afterward, with the help of our attorney and Dr. Benecke, Alex and I had managed to get his sentence commuted to life imprisonment. He became a free man and was ready for action as head of the union in Biochema.

Novotny announced that the main business of the meeting was to choose new officers of the company and new personnel for all other managerial positions. To Alex's utter astonishment, every one of his key people—the proven executives, accountants, chemists, and production managers, as well as all the others who had been vital to the success of the company—were denounced one by one and proclaimed incompetent by the union. Each and every one was summarily discharged. To fill their place the union had a list of new executives. Most had no education beyond grade school, and Alex, knowing they would have no idea whatever how to run a large corporation, was struck almost speechless.

When Alex recovered from the shock and had marshaled his thoughts, he stood up and said, "I value the advice of the members of the union, but I have to stress that we need people who are skilled and who have had some experience and some job training. We need accountants who can draw up a balance sheet and prepare budgets. We need production men who understand machinery. We need research and development scientists because we have to have new products all the time. We need trained chemists. We need experienced advertising men. In short, we need people who know what they're doing. So as much as I respect the union's proposal, I have to advise you that the people on your list cannot rebuild the company. Of course, some of these people may, with training, in time develop into good company executives, but at the moment it would be irresponsible to place them in such important positions, and I cannot do it."

Novotny looked up from his papers and said, "All that doesn't make any difference. The people for those jobs are the people on this list here. That's how it's going to be!"

"Well, in that case, I thank you for having invited me here, but I have to tell you that you leave me no choice but to resign my position in the company," Alex stated.

"Resignation is accepted!" Novotny said roughly. And Alex left the meeting.

He came home and said, "You'll never guess what happened. I'm out of a job."

He decided to talk to Tony Srba in Prague, but before he could leave he received a phone call from a Mr. Sling who asked Alex to come to his office the next day. Otto Sling was one of the highest-ranking officials in the Communist party of Czechoslovakia. He was in charge of all of southern Moravia. He greeted Alex courteously and offered him a seat.

"I heard that you've had some problems with the union at Biochema! They told me what happened. I know all about it."

"Yes," Alex said, "they want to nominate new, unskilled, and inexperienced management, and it would be irresponsible for me to accept them, so I resigned."

"Well," Sling said soothingly, "don't be upset about it. I can fix it in no time, and I'll tell you what: if you stay in Biochema, you'll have a singularly important position. You'll be very powerful, as we have big plans for this company. It will become the spearhead of the chemical industry in the country. As its president you'll be the head, a great and powerful position. You will have many other companies under your supervision, a wonderful opportunity for research and development, a chance of a lifetime."

Alex listened, and then said, "Yes, that sounds great. I would certainly accept, if I may name my own people."

"Yes, yes, of course, that's only natural and entirely proper!" Sling said effusively. "I had a little chat with those union fellows and everything will be arranged in no time, no time at all. But there's one condition."

Alex braced himself.

"You'll have to join the Communist party," Sling went on.

After a tense silence Alex said, "Well, that would be a problem, because, you know, I'm not a Communist."

"I know you're not at the moment, but you can become one easily enough. We'll welcome your application," Sling countered.

"I don't think I want to join," Alex replied. "I'm not convinced it's a good system of government. I still believe democracy is the best way. It's my deep conviction, so you see I can't become a Communist."

"Well, if I were you," said Sling, "I would think about it seriously. I'll tell you what. Why don't you sleep on it? Come back here anytime tomorrow and tell me you accept. It's a wonderful position."

He stood up, extended his hand, and added, "You'll have real power. You could accomplish much in your field. Think it over."

Alex came home ashen with worry.

"Zdena," he said, "we'll have to leave the country."

"What!" I exclaimed. "Whatever do you mean? After all we've been through, when things are just beginning to get back to normal . . ."

"That's just it, they're not getting back to normal."

He then recounted the interview with Sling.

"Oh, Alex," I said, relieved. "You're exaggerating. Czechoslovakia is a democratic republic. Why should we leave just because some power-hungry official makes ridiculous statements? The Communists have no jurisdiction in Czechoslovakia. Why don't you go to Prague and talk to Tony? It may be just some misunderstanding. After all, Biochema is part of Chemical and Metallurgical, so what's Sling got to say about it?"

But Alex did not take it so lightly.

"Don't you know," he said, "that the Communists have grabbed all the important positions in the country except that of the Foreign Minister? And that's only because they haven't figured out how to get rid of Masaryk, who is tremendously popular, in addition to being the son of our first president. They have everything else. The chief of police in Brno has been fired; the new chief is a Communist. The same thing has happened in Prague. The Ministry of the Interior is in Communist hands as well as the Ministry of Defense. The police in all the big cities are Communists. That's enough to make anyone worry! We won't be safe here if the country turns Communist altogether."

"Alex, you're seeing specters that aren't there," I insisted. "The Communists won't do well in the national elections. The majority of people are for democracy in Czechoslovakia. You'll see. After the new government is elected, everything will turn around."

"I hope you're right. But I don't want to be stuck into another concentration camp," Alex said emphatically.

Once again I felt a sting of fear.

The next day Alex told Sling that he could not accept his offer and formally resigned from Biochema. He then went to Prague to tell Tony Srba and Dr. Martinek what had happened. They, too, were concerned about events and the future of the country. They agreed with him that he had no choice but to resign, and they made him a proposition. Chemical and Metallurgical was looking for a technical representative in Brno, and they offered him the position. It was not a salaried job. Alex would be self-employed, purchasing the raw material from their company and reselling it to individual customers. He accepted, and we started a new life.

First we had to find a warehouse and some office space. We looked around for suitable premises and found a building on Udolni Street, centrally located and well laid out, the ideal property for such a venture. The original owners were Germans who had lived there for fifty years and left for Austria before the Russians came to Brno. The building was managed by the National Council, established for the purpose of administering all the properties abandoned by Germans, though it also had some other functions. The building that we had rented was filthy and dirty, and not a single window was left unbroken. In spite of all that, we saw its potential and rented it. We managed to replace the windows and then started the cleaning. It was a frustrating job, but Peter and Anna from Richky came to help us. When we finished we realized that we had rented a little jewel.

Big glass doors at the street level opened into a marble-tiled foyer from which a wide staircase led up to offices and storage rooms. The second floor consisted of a spacious apartment. Three formal reception rooms opened off the entrance hall. The dining room with a large conservatory and aviary, which immediately enchanted the girls, was next to the middle room. From there a corridor led to the kitchen and two bedrooms, as well as to a small, private sitting room. All these back rooms had large picture windows. The garden located behind the house was adjacent to the hill on which Spielberg

Castle sat. The view from the rear windows was of unlimited greenery, giving one the impression of being in the country. The front windows of the formal rooms had a pleasant view of a wide boulevard at the head of which, almost facing our house, was the church where Alex and I were married. To the left of the house a short distance away on the same street was the maternity hospital where both the children had been born. Moving in was a kind of homecoming.

The formal garden, with a roofed colonnade at its entrance, was bursting with flowering shrubs, charming gazebos and much more. It was surrounded by a high brick wall with a small, locked door leading into Spielberg Park. Our family could go for walks in those magnificent gardens without even going out into the street. It was like having Spielberg for a backyard. The four of us loved our new home and quickly settled in.

Alex immediately set to work. He hired a secretary and a salesman. Tony sent him various supplies, and in no time Alex was in business. This was a busy time in Czechoslovakia. Everyone was in a hurry to get back to normal. A number of small, private industries had just managed to dig themselves out of the rubble and were anxious to start manufacturing. None had raw materials. Everyone was clamoring for chemicals and other supplies. Sales were brisk.

Spielberg Castle opened once again as a museum, and one afternoon Alex and I decided to take the children to look at it. We received a sad surprise.

The castle chapel was full of flowers. In the nave was a large memorial to the people who had died there during the Nazi occupation when Spielberg was a Gestapo prison. The list of names seemed to run into the hundreds.

We went through the entire castle and looked into the old cells which had seen so much suffering in the Middle Ages and again in the progressive twentieth century. The cells stank with old and recent misery.

The castle is immense. There are corridors upon corridors with hundreds of cells opening off them. The four of us wandered around until we came to what appeared to be a new wing. It is actually an old part of the castle that the Gestapo refurbished for their own evil use. Several large rooms have fully tiled walls and floors, like those in a hospital or in a large kitchen. In this new wing a strange kind of gutter runs along the edge of the slightly sloped floors, as if for collecting and carrying away wash water. The guide told us that the Gestapo had prepared these rooms for mass executions. The gutters were for carrying blood. We were glad to get out into the fresh air.

The next day I received an unexpected visit from Fanny. I was happy to see her. We had spent so many years together and shared so many sorrows and tense moments. I hugged her and asked what her plans were. We would have loved to have her back, but we were not going to be so fortunate. She had become friendly with Herr Müller, our neighbor at Richky, whose wife had died during the war. He had proposed to her. She was well into her fifties, and it seemed to her it would be nice to have a husband, a home, and a ready-made family, so she accepted. I understood, told her how happy I was for her, and wished her all the best in the future.

Annitta was our new maid. She was also in her late fifties, a pleasant lady and an excellent cook, and we soon settled down to routine family life. Every morning Alex went downstairs to his offices, Evie went off to a nearby school, and I was left alone to enjoy Janie, who was still too young for school and needed much reassurance and love after her frightful experiences during our last days in the valley.

The cleaning up at Richky continued slowly. We did not mind too much, as living in Brno was beautiful because of our lovely garden and Spielberg Park beyond it. Stores reopened and finally I could buy some textiles to make dresses for the children. To my joy I managed to purchase even some badly needed shoes for the girls. Gradually our wardrobes and our life returned to normal.

The cinemas reopened, too, and Alex and I went to see a movie one night in June, our first evening out in years. Before the main feature a newsreel was shown of the meeting at Yalta between Churchill, Roosevelt, and Stalin. The cinema was full of people getting their first glimpse of the outside world. When Stalin approached Churchill with extended hand, and Churchill likewise put out his own hand, somebody in the audience shouted, "*Davai casy suda!*"—the famous "Give me your watch, quick!" of our Russian liberators. The whole theater burst into laughter. Suddenly the screen went black and the auditorium lights went on. The doors flew open and the Russian military police marched in. They began questioning, trying to find out who had shouted out this insult to the magnificent Red Army.

Of course, no one informed and the Russians never found out who had punctured their pomposity with Czech irony. Yet it had been made painfully clear to us that Czechoslovakia did not have its freedom yet. We were as muzzled and oppressed as we had been under Hitler. The incident left a burning and bitter taste in our mouths. The Gestapo was still with us. Were we ever going to regain our liberty? Were the Russians ever going to go back to the Soviet Union and leave our country to us? We kept on hoping they would. All of us Czechs knew after the last months of so-called "liberation" that there could be no real freedom until the day the last Russian soldier crossed our border headed east.

We had a very good friend, Dr. Kral, a professor at Masaryk University, who was positive the Russians would not willingly leave Czechoslovakia or any other country in eastern Europe. He was convinced, however, that the United States would not countenance Communism in central Europe and would force the Russians to go home. One day Czechoslovakia would be rid of them, and we Czechs awaited that day with impatience and ever-increasing frustration.

20
BITTER DECISION

I had often wondered what had become of Madi, and then one day I received a card from her. I wrote her a long letter telling what had happened at Richky and that everything had been lost including her Parisian shoes. I promised her that when things improved in Czechoslovakia I would send her whatever she needed. She answered promptly, saying that the same plundering had gone on in eastern Austria. Although she had a good job, she never had enough food because of shortages in Vienna. The food situation in Czechoslovakia was improving daily, so I made up a good-sized parcel, sent it off to her, and followed it up with others every couple of weeks or so. Although our food was rationed, there was enough of it—far more than during the war.

When ration cards for shoes were issued I bought two pairs, one for me and one for Madi. She was very happy, as shoes were her passion.

August came and with it the news of the atomic bombing of Hiroshima and Nagasaki, and then peace came to the Pacific and to the whole world, a peace we all fervently hoped would last a long, long time.

Toward the end of that summer Sling called Alex and invited him to his office for a chat. He asked Alex again if he would reconsider returning to Biochema and taking over its management.

"Of course," Alex said, "I'd be more than happy to do that, but are the conditions the same?"

Predictably, Sling answered, "Absolutely. It would be necessary for you to join the Communist party. But just think what it would do for you! You would be president not only of Biochema, but in essence you'd be head of the entire chemical industry in the country. What an opportunity! A position of importance, with foreign travel, fame . . ."

Alex shook his head. "I do appreciate being given such an opportunity, and I'd like to take it because, as you know, I started Biochema and built it up from nothing, but I cannot join the party. I'm not a Communist. I believe in democracy, and I can't live a lie."

"That's most unfortunate, indeed most unfortunate. Membership in the party is the main condition for such an important position."

"In that case, I must regretfully decline. Thank you again, but the answer is still no," Alex said with finality and stood up to leave.

He came home very depressed.

"I don't understand it," he said to me. "Are we a democracy or not? Are we free or aren't we? Do you *have* to be a Communist to hold any position of importance? Apparently you do. You know, I really feel we should think about leaving the country. They are, in fact, trying to force people to join. It's almost blackmail! That's ridiculous. That's no way to live! And I don't want to hear any more about Sling."

———□———

We did though, several years later. A Sydney newspaper article said that Sling, among many other prominent Communists, was executed on Stalin's orders.

———□———

A while later we went to Richky to see how the cleaning up was progressing. Our Great Dane, Gondola, far too large for our Brno apartment, stayed out at Richky and greeted us, as always, with a swishing tail. We found that Franta, our gardener who was married to Herr Müller's younger daughter, had returned. He told us that he was leaving our employment because he had received a wonderful offer to become an owner of a nursery without having to pay a penny.

Many properties had been confiscated by the Nazis and given to German citizens. As the rightful owners had in many cases perished during the war, these properties, as well as the properties formerly owned by Nazis, belonged to the state. The Communist party used this real estate to increase their sphere of influence. All Franta had to do was join the Communist party and he would get his nursery free. He shuffled his feet and looked down.

"But you're not a Communist, are you?" Alex asked.

"Well, not really, but if the Communist party wants to give me such a big property and such a wonderful opportunity just for joining, I'll join. What the hell! Why not?"

Chilled, Alex asked, "And you'll vote for them, then?"

"Of course. If they're so good to me, I'll be good to them. Why not vote for somebody who's given you a free business!"

"Franta, don't do it. You're not a Communist by conviction. You're doing it just to get some free property. If everybody does the same thing, what will happen to us all? What will happen to the republic? Please, don't do it."

But his words had no effect. Franta left, joined the party, and received his free nursery. We went to visit him there one day. It really was a nice little business, and for a time he was happy. But the dream did not last long. When the Communist takeover was complete, all businesses both large and small were nationalized. Franta's nursery was taken away from him, and once again he was an employee, but this time he was an employee of the state. The same charade was acted out all over Czechoslovakia.

Alex and I took the children one day to visit my parents in Vrbatky. One of the neighbors, who had two sons, was told by the local Communist office that if the whole family joined the Communist party the younger son would receive a farm in the Sudetenland absolutely free. Later they lost not only the second farm but also the first one, which had been in their family for generations.

Another time we went to visit some friends in Lisen and saw the same thing there. Our friends, the Fosters, had only one son, but they, too, had been contacted and told that if they would join the party their son would get a farm for free, and so they also joined. As a result, the Communist party in Czechoslovakia grew by leaps and bounds. None of these newly converted people were really Communists by conviction.

The summer brought me another problem. When the first thunderstorm arrived Janie ran up to me, terrified and pale. Her eyes were full of the same shocked, tortured expression that had been there during the battle at Richky. Sobbing convulsively, she clutched at me wildly when I took her into my arms. No amount of comforting would console her. The hysteria was worse when the storm came at night. It did not matter how soundly asleep she was, at the first sound of thunder she would scream and scream in spite of all my efforts to calm her. "It's only a storm, darling, don't be afraid, the war's over!"

Those heartbreaking nights made me feel totally helpless in the face of this deeply rooted fear. I had no idea how to get her over it. The two of us spent hours huddled together as long as the storm lasted.

Alex's business was profitable, but I could see that he missed the stimulation of Biochema. He loved the excitement of big business, of production and competition. Above all, he liked research. Lacking this, he was not entirely content.

In time Brno was mostly cleaned up and rebuilding had started. Most businesses had reopened their doors and goods were in better supply. Theater, symphony, and opera came alive with new and exciting productions. Many concerts and recitals were being held.

Had it not been for the ever-present Russians and the threat of Communism, life would have had almost the same pleasant texture as before the war. We assumed that when the upcoming spring elections disposed of the tiresome problem of the Communists, everything would be as perfect as we had dreamed it would be, during the war.

One day in July our friend Emil Lecian called Alex with some disquieting information. He said that the newly established National Tribunal, which investigated Czechs who had collaborated with the Germans during the war, had some photos that were damaging to Alex. There was talk around Brno that Alex had been a collaborator.

Alex laughed at this. "What? Me? A collaborator? How could

anyone dream that one up? I was in a concentration camp and I lost my job because of it. I kept an illegal radio transmitter in the factory. We had parachutists from England in our house and supplied them with food for years. Is that collaboration? How disgusting." We forgot about it.

The cultural life of Brno was back to normal with many singers and other performers coming over from England, Italy, and the United States. Alex and I attended most of those concerts and recitals. We also enjoyed going to the Brno Opera and to philharmonic concerts. Everyone was hungry for music. Beethoven, Mozart, Chopin, Smetana, Dvorak, and all the modern composers like Stravinsky were played everywhere. Music again filled the air after the deadly silence of the Nazi years.

We went out frequently during those days, and we often ran into Zdenek Ripa. After the war had ended we had not seen him for quite a while, but suddenly, wherever we went, there was Ripa, always greeting us with enthusiasm. We often chatted with him during intermissions. One day Alex asked him about his friend Pokorny with whom he had visited Richky and was told that Pokorny had become an important person in the Communist party, the first secretary of the Ministry of the Interior.

One evening Alex and I went to a recital by an American soprano who sang Negro spirituals. It was the first time we had heard this kind of music and we found it utterly spellbinding. During the intermission we went to the foyer for some refreshments and there was Zdenek Ripa.

"Ah, my friends," he said smoothly. "How have you been? Isn't this music beautiful? Quite unusual, so dramatic, isn't it? You know, we haven't had a chance to have a chat for such a long time. Why don't we go to a nightclub for a drink after the performance? What do you say?"

Alex glanced at me and then said, "I'm a little tired. I'm not really in the mood for a nightclub. Come to our place and we'll have a glass of wine together."

When we arrived home and were settled comfortably in the living room with some wine, Ripa turned the conversation to Pokorny.

"Of course, he's very prominent. He holds one of the most important positions in the government and has a lot of clout, no doubt about it. But I'll tell you something about myself that I'll bet you didn't know."

By this time he had had several glasses of wine and his tone was growing more and more confiding as he helped himself to another glass.

"I am actually far more powerful than Pokorny!" he said. "Yes, far more. You know, I am in fact one of the most powerful men in Czechoslovakia! I'm the contact between the Russian secret police and the Czech Communist party, and, actually, I sort of supervise them, you might say—you know, keeping an eye on their activities. Oh yes, I have a lot of power. If I decide somebody just won't cut the mustard, out he goes. I can topple the highest officials. Now that's power, don't you think?"

Alex and I looked at each other, truly astonished. We had no idea he was a Communist. His father was a prominent and well-off Brno lawyer and it seemed surprising that a man of such background would embrace Communism.

"Yes," he went on, "nobody knows I'm a Communist. It's far better that way, but actually I am one of the few men who make the party decisions in Czechoslovakia. I know about everything that goes on."

He began predicting future political events in the country.

"This government is only temporary," he said. "After the spring elections everything will change."

"Yes, of course," Alex countered, "we'll elect a new democratic government, a president . . ."

Ripa chuckled. "Don't you believe it. We Communists will never let Czechoslovakia go! Russia will never turn it loose. Benes is a figurehead. He has to do what he's told."

"Don't be absurd," I bristled. "We have four political parties. We'll have free elections."

"Oh, that's just for the time being, those four parties. They don't mean anything either. They'll be disbanded soon. The results of the elections are not at all important. Whatever happens, in a short time, maybe one year, maybe two, maybe even three, but in any case very soon, we'll take control of the country. We'll take it over. And I can also tell you what's going to happen in the *near* future."

Alex and I both put it down to too much wine. Surely all this was a product of his being jealous of Pokorny. Ripa was obviously envious of Pokorny's meteoric rise. We listened skeptically.

In spite of his befuddled state he seemed to sense our skepticism and began telling us what the government's short-term actions were going to be. Parliament was debating a law called the Small Decree that would virtually end most of the private enterprise in Czechoslovakia.

"You know this Small Decree everybody's talking about?" Ripa asked. "It's up before Benes now. I suppose you think he will veto it?" We both nodded.

"Well, you're in for a surprise then, because he'll sign it. Bet on it; he'll sign it. And do you know why he'll sign it? Because he's nothing but a figurehead. He has to do what he's told, that's why. He's a nothing, a zero, a zilch!" He snapped his fingers contemptuously.

To our dismay, Ripa's predictions started coming true. Most of them were minor incidents reported in brief, unimportant news items. But one by one they built a wall of credibility under his story.

Maybe, we thought, he is a member of the KGB. Too many of his predictions were coming true. We felt increasingly uneasy.

Shortly before this disturbing evening with Ripa, we had met Mr. Tomas Janda, a native Czechoslovak. As a young man he joined the Bata Shoe Manufacturing Company and was sent to India, where Bata had started a new factory, an expansion that became successful. Mr. Janda was one of its executives for many years. Just before the war, however, he decided to start his own company. At the end of the war he was a millionaire and wanted to modernize his factories and also enter the field of plastics. He came to Brno to talk to Alex and after several meetings offered him a job. Such offers were not unusual at that time. After the war many foreign industrial scouts went looking for young, technically talented people.

Although neither of us had taken Ripa seriously at first, as more and more of his predictions came true, Alex started to worry in earnest.

"Don't you think," he said one day after a long session of sitting and drumming his fingers on the armchair, a sure sign of preoccupation with him, "that maybe I should accept that job in India? If the Communists do take over, as Ripa keeps insisting they will, I wouldn't want to stay here. I wouldn't want to live in a country without freedom. I've had enough of that in the last six years."

Alarmed, I said, "But Alex, that won't happen. Maybe it is just a coincidence that some of Ripa's predictions came true. We're about to have the elections, and you know the Czech people. They don't want Communism! The elections will rid us of this Communist idea once and for all and everything will get back to normal."

Though not quite convinced myself, I was trying hard to sound optimistic. I really did not want to leave my country.

But I did not succeed in calming Alex. He fretted and fussed about it for several days. Finally one morning he said to me, "Would you like to make a deal?"

"What kind of a deal?"

"Look, if Benes signs the Small Decree, it would mean that what Ripa said was true. It would mean that he really does know what he's talking about, and all his other predictions might also happen. If they do happen, I certainly don't want to remain here. So, in that case, let's go to India. If, on the other hand, Benes vetoes it, then it means that Ripa was full of hot air, and we'll stay. Is it a deal?"

"Alex, don't be such a skeptic. Of course, he won't sign it. Then we'll have the elections and everything will settle down to normal. I don't know why you insist on worrying yourself like this."

I desperately wanted to believe that Communism did not have any future in Czechoslovakia, and with all my willpower I was trying to chase away any doubts that Alex was slowly planting into my mind.

I loved living in Czechoslovakia. It was my country and had been my family's country. The last six years had tired me out mentally and physically and all I wanted was to relax and be among my friends and in my own homeland. I was exhausted and afraid of the unknown.

"Fine," Alex said, "but what if everything isn't all right? What if the Communists win, what'll happen to me? I spoke to Sling freely, you know. I made it quite plain that I wouldn't become a Communist out of opportunism, and by doing that I, in fact, implied that he—and a lot of others—had done just that. Such people forget nothing. Would you come and look for me in Russia, in some Siberian labor camp?"

In my last effort to strengthen my disappearing resistance I answered, "Alex, you really are overdramatic. Why do you torture yourself thinking about misfortunes that will never happen?"

"If you're so sure, make the deal! Give me a promise that if he signs, we'll leave. It'll give me some peace of mind at least."

I gave in.

Finally the day came when President Benes was due to make the decision. All day I could not concentrate on a thing. It was another one of the days I would never forget.

I sat in the living room, staring at the ceiling, then I would go to the window and look out at the busy street below, wondering how many of the people passing by were aware that this was really a momentous day in their lives, one that would decide their future and probably their children's future as well.

At noon I turned on the midday news and heard the announcer say, "This morning President Benes signed the Small Decree. . . ."

Heavily, I sat down.

21
FAREWELL

When Alex came home for lunch I ran out to meet him in the hall.

"He signed it!"

"I know."

We stared at each other in silence for a few moments and I felt my eyes fill with tears. I did not want to leave my country. I did not want to go.

"If you feel so strongly about it," Alex said, putting an arm around my shoulders, "we'll stay. We'll do whatever you want."

We talked all afternoon. Eventually I agreed to leave, remembering those long and lonesome evenings at Richky in 1942 when I thought Alex was going to be executed. I could never face that again. Anything would be better than that.

I could see the relief in Alex's face. He had been far more worried than he had let on. He smiled at me encouragingly. "This won't last a long time," he said. "Even if the Communists do take over, I doubt they'll manage to hold on to it for more than three years. It's a temporary madness. The four of us will be back sooner than you think. America will never let us down."

Before we could get ready to leave, Alex received a summons to appear before the National Tribunal on a charge of collaboration with the Nazis. I thought it was some sort of mistake.

"It will just be a matter of attending the hearing and everything will be cleared up," I said.

He was not so sure and pointed out that several of our acquaintances had been similarly accused and imprisoned, among them my own Uncle Josef, a medical doctor in Olomouc, who had hardly spoken a word to the Germans throughout the war. Our dentist had also been arrested. He was born in the eastern part of Czechoslovakia, which was annexed by Russia in 1945. When he was asked by the Russians to explain why he had left Russia and moved here, he answered that when he left his home town it *was* part of Czechoslovakia. He was nevertheless kept in prison for several months.

Alex was beginning to worry about his conversations with Sling. He felt that perhaps Sling was taking revenge on him for having refused his "opportunity of a lifetime" and for having said many things that appeared to him to have been potentially damaging.

We had applied for passports about two weeks earlier, but the application was denied pending the National Tribunal hearing. We were caught. I regretted my indecision deeply.

While waiting for the court hearing we received the news that Uncle Josef had become ill in the prison and had died there. Of my two uncles, one had died in the Nazi Mauthausen concentration camp and the other in a Communist prison. Was there any real difference between the two? I thought back to the days of my childhood when my uncles came to visit us, joking and smiling, bringing us little gifts. I wept for them both and their cruel fate. And I wept for my country and for us all.

After the court hearing was postponed several times, the crucial day finally arrived. Alex had been in touch with his two surviving cellmates from Kounicovy Koleje, Olda the butcher, who had helped us so much with our food supplies, and one-legged Janko, the accountant from Moravska Ostrava. Both volunteered to testify on Alex's behalf. The hearing began. The judge was a lawyer and a Communist. The evidence produced was a newspaper photograph taken sometime in 1939 when the Nazis first occupied the country. In it Alex was shown flanked by several Nazi dignitaries visiting Biochema, all with arms upraised in the Nazi salute. Alex, however, had both his arms down by his sides.

Alex told the judge that he had been in a concentration camp for high treason and that he had lost his job because of it. Then he proceeded to tell the court about his imprisonment in Kounicovy Koleje, his transfer to Breslau, and his near deportation to Auschwitz.

Following his statement, the ex-parachutists were called to the stand and told the court how Alex had, at risk to our lives, provided them with food throughout their sojourn in our woods and how they had sheltered under our roof.

Then Janko took the stand.

"I was near death from starvation and cold," he said somberly, "when the accused was placed in our cell. His wife managed to smuggle in packets of food from time to time, not much, about enough for one man. But Alex shared all his food with us; in fact, he gave us the best part of it. And when our cellmate, the teacher, was sent to Auschwitz, he had no winter clothes at all, and he would have frozen to death if Alex had not given him his only warm winter coat and some warm underwear. Without his help we wouldn't have survived, Your Honor, and we were all grateful to him for what he had done for us. There's no way anyone could accuse him of collaboration. He suffered as much as we did!"

The judge picked up the photograph submitted as evidence.

"The accused is the only one in the photograph who has his hand down. Everyone else has his hand up in the Nazi salute," he said, almost as if to himself. "That took a lot of courage. To accuse this man of collaboration is ridiculous. Case dismissed." Nodding at Alex, he banged his gavel briskly and picked up the papers relating to the next case.

Once again Alex was freed by a court, but this time we were not as elated as that other time in Breslau. This was not the end of it. The fact that the trial could have happened at all, that after surviving the Nazi atrocities and the war, Alex could be accused by his own people, blackened our future. Alex was right. We had to go. Once more we applied for passports and began waiting, and once more the weeks crept by without the passports being issued. Alex became more nervous with each passing day.

I still warmed myself at the tiny ember of hope that perhaps the long-awaited spring elections would make everything right after all. The day came and proved Ripa entirely correct: the Communist party had managed to corner thirty-eight percent of the votes. While they did not have a majority, they did have the largest number of votes of any party. Their leader, Communist Klement Gottwald, became our prime minister.

We both grew equally afraid. We could see the writing on the wall more plainly each day, and I regretted even more my earlier procrastination. The days lengthened into weeks and still the passports were not forthcoming. Then Alex had a brilliant idea. Pokorny was the first secretary of the Ministry of the Interior, and it was this ministry that was in charge of passports. Alex decided to go and see Pokorny and ask him for help.

When he arrived in Prague at the Ministry of the Interior building and told the porter that he was a friend of Pokorny's, he was treated with the utmost respect. After going through several officials, he reached Pokorny's private secretary, who announced him to Bedrich Pokorny.

To Alex's amazement, his office was a huge, sumptuously furnished suite of rooms, with a main office and an adjacent conference room, magnificent antique furniture, and enormous windows that looked out over Prague. At the far end of the room, which, according to Alex, looked as long as a ballroom, was a huge ornate desk, behind which Pokorny sat in state.

As soon as he saw Alex he jumped up and came to meet him.

"How are you, how are you, my friend? How very nice to see you! Please, please, sit down and make yourself comfortable!"

"Thank you," Alex said, sinking into the plush upholstery. "What a magnificent office you have here!"

Pokorny looked at him and after an infinitesimal pause uttered words Alex would never forget: "A golden cage, my friend! Just a golden cage!"

He was inordinately proud of his meteoric rise and told Alex about his important job and his influence with the minister and the party. Eventually, he asked Alex if there was something he could do for him.

Alex told him about the passports. Pokorny listened and when Alex finished he picked up the phone and made a call. He explained the situation briefly, nodded again, hung up, and, returning to Alex, said, "Let's have a cup of coffee and wait a few minutes, and we'll see."

They chatted about old times. Pokorny recalled with nostalgia his visits to Richky. He talked of the mill and of Peter, our miller. Then he started talking about one Sunday afternoon when he arrived at Richky terrified by an imaginary feeling of being strangled on the trail leading down to the valley.

"I still feel that rope around my neck and the great fear and terror that took possession of all my being," he said, after years still brooding over this inexplicable and terrifying experience.

Ten minutes passed in pleasant reminiscence. Then the secretary entered with our passports. Alex was flabbergasted. He certainly had not expected our problem to be resolved so quickly. He thanked Pokorny and left, not suspecting that years later this man, presently so dazzled by his own power and success, was going to meet his death by strangulation on that lonely trail in the deep forest, exactly as his horrifying premonition had indicated.

My feelings were totally ambiguous. Never in my life had I felt such ambivalence about anything. I was happy that we would be able to leave, that we would finally be safe. And yet, a little voice whispered that maybe, just maybe, things would not be so bad here. But I knew better; we had to go.

During the previous months of talking about leaving, applying for passports, waiting for them to be issued, taking English lessons, doing all the things necessary for our departure, I had not really believed we were going. I had managed to banish the stark fact to some back region of my mind, where it had remained, a vaguely possible unpleasant event, but nothing tangible, not real. But inevitably it came back, a concrete, cold reality. I felt we would not be back in three years, that we would never return.

We decided to spend our last summer in Czechoslovakia at Richky. Our home was finished; the last workman had gone. Everything was rebuilt. All rooms were clean and bright. The Russians had dug out their dead for reburial elsewhere. The rose garden had been replanted and the lawn had been rolled and reseeded. The only reminder of the war was a circular mound in its velvety green center where fifty horses were buried. Loving horses as we did, we found that spot unbearably sad. There lay the poor innocent animals, paying with their lives and pain for man's folly. Alex had previously asked the gardener to plant the spot with red, yellow, and orange flowers, and they were vibrantly in bloom and at the height of their beauty.

It was a sad summer. Each fading blossom and falling leaf was a reminder that it was our last summer at home, that we would not see that particular plant in bloom again the next year, that we would then be on foreign soil in a distant land.

The children enjoyed the idea of traveling and seeing exotic countries, especially Evie, who had become somewhat of a heroine at school. India was a place only heard of, barely dreamt about. Alex and I did not discuss our departure. I knew that I could hardly bear thinking about it, much less talking about it, and I was certain he felt the same. Richky had been for so long our home, our refuge, our whole world. It was ours. Together we had watched it take shape, change, and grow in beauty and harmony. We had planned it and worked hard on perfecting it. We had seen it threatened, destroyed, and reborn. Yes, it was a sad summer.

I continued with my English lessons. Because I spoke French and German fluently I found English not too difficult, although the pronunciation seemed to defy all reason. Soon I began to read simple books.

We visited our parents and relatives often that summer. My mother and father came to Richky for two weeks, and then we all went to Vrbatky so I could spend a few final days in that solid old house in which so many generations of my family had been born, had lived, and died.

Alex's parents also came. It was agreed that while we were in India they would look after Richky for us and move into our apartment in Brno as it was more convenient and pleasant than theirs.

We did not have much clothing to pack; the Russians had taken care of that. Alex had many technical books. I wanted to take our paintings, an idea that upset Alex. He wanted to believe that our leaving was not permanent, that we would come back one day. We packed the books, clothing, and a few personal items and left behind everything else.

We were not allowed to take much money with us out of the

country. Our allowance was just enough for tickets to London, with a little left over for brief stops in Paris and Brussels.

We were particularly looking forward to seeing Olga. She had written us in 1945 about Paul's tragic wartime death. They left London for a short vacation in Scotland, she wrote, and while there, Paul had read in the paper that a department store in London was going to have some real coffee for sale. Coffee was almost impossible to get during the war, and Paul was fond of it. He returned to London. While he was in the store, it was hit by a V-2 rocket and many people, including Paul, were killed. It seemed to Olga that her whole life was at an end. Just before the war she and Paul had started in London their own fur salon, which was well established and prospering with a substantial number of employees. Olga understood sales but knew nothing about design and manufacture. She had no idea how to go about cutting fur.

Shortly before Paul's death the store had received an order for a sable coat. The precious furs were there, rolled up and stored away and ready for Paul to begin work on them on their return from Scotland. She did not want to tell the client that she could not fill the order, but at the same time she was afraid to do anything. Sable was expensive. Much of their capital was tied up in that fur.

"Zdena," she wrote, "I was terrified, yes, terrified. 'Mon Dieu,' I said to myself, 'how can I possibly do this?' And then I felt Paul's presence! I actually felt that he was in the room with me. I picked up the scalpel and began to cut, as sure of myself as if I had done it all my life. He was guiding my hand. The coat turned out beautifully and the customer was pleased. She told others about my talent and the orders poured in. It wasn't me that cut out that sable coat. It was Paul! He always took good care of me."

In September we returned to Brno and began the prolonged leave-taking and final packing. This was a difficult time for me. I loved Brno very much; over the years this city had become my home. I loved walking along its tree-lined avenues and strolling through its rolling, wooded parks and I liked visiting our friends. I loved our way of life there.

I knew nothing of India, but one thing I could be sure of: it would be a totally different culture, a completely alien way of life, with strange people speaking a difficult language, and, worst of all, no friends. I was never a person to make new friends easily. Old friends were always, for me, the best friends, and apart from Mr. and Mrs. Janda we did not know a soul in India. Also, I was still so very tired from the war. But there was nothing we could do. Circumstances beyond our control had shaped our lives, and we would have to accept it. Gradually the time came to say farewell to our friends and family.

We said good-bye to my cousin Zdenek and went to pay our last visit to Ivan and Jana. In the summer of 1945 their second child was born, also a boy. They called him Ilya, and he was a little more than a year old. Ivan had lost his job in Biochema at the same time as Alex, and having a wife and two children he decided not to return to his study of law when Masaryk University reopened. He moved his family to a little town in northern Moravia where, together with two friends, he started a small chemical company. Because they employed only fifteen people, their company had not been nationalized, and they were doing very well. The factory was confiscated later, however, when the further wave of nationalization of small industry hit the country.

We spent a whole day with them. They showed us around the plant, which was neat and efficient, and we admired their large, sunny apartment. Ivan, like Alex, was always optimistic. He, too, believed that in three years he would see us again.

Saying good-bye to my parents was the hardest task of all. We stayed with them for two days, and I do not think I ever spent a sadder time. My mother tried very hard to be cheerful, and the conversation centered around "when you come back" and "three years will pass like a flash." I did not believe it, and I knew she did not believe it either. Finally the moment came when we had to say good-bye.

We embraced and promised to write often. I hugged my father, sister, and brother. My mask crumbled when I saw my mother saying good-bye to my two little girls, her only grandchildren. With tears in my eyes, I hugged her once more and climbed into the car.

We started moving away from the place where I had been born and where I had spent so many happy years. Mother, Father, my sister, and my brother remained standing in front of the heavy gate, waving good-bye. We looked back at them out of the car windows and waved, trying to smile. I saw my mother, standing with difficulty and leaning on her cane so that she could get a last glimpse of us, smiling bravely, while huge tears rolled unnoticed down her face. It was a sight I have never forgotten.

Alex was driving very slowly, and the four of them back there became smaller and smaller until we could see them only as a blur outlined against the darker bulk of the house, and then it, too, merged into the blue distance and finally disappeared and we were gone.

"Don't be sad," Alex said. "Three years will pass quickly and before you know it, we'll be back."

It was kind of him, and he believed it, but I felt that I would never be coming back, that I would never again see my mother or my father or my native land.

We returned to Brno and finished packing. Two days later we boarded the train for Prague.

It was a replay of my farewell to my parents. Grandma and Grandpa stood on the platform, looking up at us with smiles on their faces and tears in their eyes, waving and blowing kisses as the train began to move. That was the last time we saw them.

Janie had never been to Prague. She begged to be taken around to see it. As it was such an important, historic city that was deeply embedded in the heart of every Czech, we decided to take the time to show her around. Prague had never looked lovelier. It was October 27, the eve of our national holiday when, in 1918, our republic was founded and we regained our freedom after three hundred years of Habsburg rule. The entire city was lit up with myriads of lights and gaily decorated with thousands of flags and streamers. It looked like a medieval fairy tale.

The four of us walked past Hradcany Castle, so rich in myth and history, where so many of our ancient kings and queens had reigned. We wandered through the Old Town Square past the famous Old Town Hall to Mala Strana with its crooked, quaint houses, and then on past the National Theater. We crossed the old Charles Bridge that was lined with medieval statues of the saints; it was built by Emperor Charles IV in the fourteenth century, the same emperor who also founded Charles University, which, after the Sorbonne in Paris, is the second oldest university in Europe. We saw the river

Moldau, celebrated by Bedrich Smetana in his symphonic poem, *Ma vlast (My Country)*, and from the statue of Saint Wenceslaus, the patron saint of Bohemia, we looked down on beautiful St. Wenceslaus Square. We wanted the girls to see it all, to impress on them that they should be proud to be Czechs and should never forget their heritage and their native land wherever they went.

Early the next morning came the unforgettable moments—the last moments in Czechoslovakia. We boarded the train, the whistle blew, the train jerked forward with the customary creaking and banging and began to inch ahead. The station fell behind. The train huffed through the suburbs of Prague, festive with flags to celebrate the birth of freedom in a country that was now losing it. Then came the Bohemian countryside, as warm and golden in the autumn light as a quiet movement from a Dvorak quartet. Rolling fields with carefully tended meadows alternated with majestic forests and little towns where smiling children raised their bright, sweet Czech faces at the command of the train whistle and waved good-bye to the heartbroken traveler. Under my breath I murmured, "Good-bye, dear ones; good-bye, my homeland; good-bye, my Czechoslovakia."

BOOK FIVE

THE BREAKING OF DAY

22

WEST AGAIN

We crossed the border into quite a different Germany from that through which I had traveled on my way to Breslau! The customs officers were full of courtesy; all arrogance was gone. Many American soldiers were on the station platforms. How I wished they had not stopped there but had advanced into Czechoslovakia.

The countryside was not changed much by war. The cities were another story. Nuremberg, where we arrived late in the afternoon, was a picture of total devastation. It was nothing but rubble, so much rubble that the roads had not been cleared but relaid over the top of it.

The traffic crawled over countless undulating mounds of rubbish under which the original city of Nuremberg was buried. There was one obvious survivor of the mass destruction. In the middle of the rubble stood one large building, the High Court, blazing with floodlights. Here in the midst of the ruins of their dreams of a thousand-year Reich, the Nazis who had not managed to escape were on trial. The highest-ranking official there was Hermann Goering. He later managed to commit suicide by taking poison in order to avoid execution.

France, hardly touched by the war, looked as beautiful as ever. Paris, the charming Paris, was unchanged. Nothing had been destroyed. Paris looked as enchanting as always.

Alex and I showed the girls as much of the city as we could: Les Invalides, the Louvre, Sacre Coeur, Montmartre, and the Eiffel Tower. Versailles looked sad on the rainy day that we visited it. The large halls were gloomy as they awaited restoration to their former splendor. The cold corridors, which had seen so much of France's glory, stretched into the distance, empty, abandoned, and decidedly inglorious.

When we returned to our hotel from the forlorn palace we were exhausted and I thought a light meal in our room was called for. Janie would have none of it. She was hungry but insisted we eat downstairs in the dining room, and I knew why: the waiters, with their Gallic charm, called her Mademoiselle and treated her as a grown-up. Janie just could not get enough of it. For her a Mademoiselle was a lady like Madi. That this exalted title was applied to her own little person delighted her. So Alex and I gave in and off we went to the dining room where she climbed into her special red chair, beaming with happiness. After all the child had gone through, she deserved every little bit of glamour and excitement she could get.

November came and with it my birthday and our wedding anniversary. It was not a year for much celebration, but I had picked out a gift for myself that I hoped Alex would buy for me. It was a good-looking sweater I had seen in a small boutique close to the hotel. I dropped heavy hints when we went by. Alex dutifully agreed with me: yes, it was beautiful; and yes, it would suit me. I felt confident that the sweater would be forthcoming. However, on my birthday, he handed me a small, oblong package. I opened it and saw a tiny, exquisite, and delicate antique book, bound in red leather, a classic of French literature, *Paul et Virginie*, by Bernardine de St. Pierre. I loved it. The famous love story gave it a special sentimental meaning.

I asked Alex later, "Didn't you realize that I wanted that sweater?"

"Oh yes," he said, "but that wouldn't have been a surprise, would it? I wanted to surprise you."

And he succeeded. It was a most successful gift and one that I always cherished. A little the worse for wear, it has since survived the hands of my two children and my granddaughter Carrie, who were as fascinated by its miniature beauty as I had been when I first saw it. Whenever I looked at it I was reminded of the year we left Europe, of our stay in Paris, and of my dear and always surprising husband.

After a few days in France we took the train for Brussels. Madeleine and her sister Mariette were waiting for us at the Gare du Nord station and we had a truly wonderful reunion. We revisited all the places we had loved when we lived there as newlyweds some twelve years before. We had found the food in Paris more plentiful and of a better quality than the food at home, but Belgium was almost back to prewar conditions. For Janie, many items were exciting new discoveries. And when I showed her how to peel a banana and she tasted it, she became an instant banana addict.

In Brussels one could buy real nylon stockings—not on ration cards, and as many pairs as one wanted. With deep pleasure and no regrets, I bade good-bye to the years of saving ration coupons, of scrimping, remaking old clothes, and babying each garment so as to make it last longer.

We went to visit our old friends, the Koutnys. They had all weathered the war successfully. The boys were grown and so tall that I hardly recognized them.

Before leaving, Madeleine, who loved our two girls as her own, bought them farewell gifts. For Evie, she bought some games and books, as Evie, an avid reader, spoke and read French quite well. To Janie she gave a truly magnificent doll with blue eyes that opened and closed, blond curls, and a voice that said, "Mama." This was the ultimate doll. But Janie hated it the moment she saw it. She was already traveling with her favorite doll, the one I had found at Richky, with its head bashed in and its stomach ripped open, now repaired. It was still dreadfully ugly, ungainly, and ungraceful, but Janie loved it with unstinting devotion.

We had quite a scene over it. I resolutely packed the old doll in my traveling bag and made Janie carry the new doll. Madeleine accompanied us all the way to Ostende where after many hugs and kisses and mutual good wishes we boarded a ferry for Dover. As soon as we were on the open sea, out came the old doll and the new beauty was tenderly placed into a suitcase.

In London, Olga greeted us at the railway station. We were so happy to see her, although it seemed strange that she was alone. We were so used to Paul being with her. It was only then, as she was standing there, that the realization of Paul's death came to us fully.

The city looked terrible. Whole blocks, lying in rubble, had no buildings left and were enclosed by tall wooden fences. At our hotel, windows still lacked glass and were boarded over with wooden planks. The rooms were cold and dark. But none of this bothered us since we spent most of our time at Olga's apartment. Its windows had been replaced.

That night Janie again scorned the new doll and snuggled down to sleep with her old Raggedy Ann. After all, that doll was the only tangible link she had with her old life, its security and happiness. Poor little girl, how many upheavals she had gone through in her short life. She was then just six years old.

The next day Alex and I were to see Mr. Mitchell, the British representative of the company for which Alex was to work in India. Mr. Mitchell had been in touch with the Cunard shipping line and was trying to book our passage to Bombay. By now I was slowly getting used to the English accent and every day understood a little more of what was said to me. Before long I found myself speaking more easily. I was surprised to find that I was beginning to look forward to this new adventure, the Indian chapter in our varied and complex life.

It was difficult to book space. The Cunard office told us that we would have to go on two ships, the girls and I on the SS *Britannic*, and Alex on another ship, which would leave about a week later. Alex asked if some way could be found for the whole family to travel together.

"There is one possibility," the booking clerk told us after poring over the passenger list. "There is one berth available, but it's the worst on the ship. It's in the very last cabin aft, just over the ship's propellers, and it would be noisy and most uncomfortable."

Alex accepted immediately. The clerk made the reservation and then asked for our passports.

"But your passports expire on the second of February!" he said with surprise as he looked over them.

"Yes, I know," Alex answered. "They issued them only for a few months. We asked for two years but this is all they would give us."

"Well, that's most unfortunate because, you see, the ship will arrive in Bombay on the tenth of February and by then your passports will have expired, so I'm afraid they won't let you off the ship. You'll have to go to the Czech embassy and get these renewed before I can issue your tickets."

We returned to Olga's apartment very upset indeed. Alex worried that if he went to the Czech embassy he might find himself detained since the embassy was theoretically Czech territory and therefore outside British jurisdiction, and he had the distinct impression that his departure from Czechoslovakia had not gone unnoticed. We mulled this over and decided that I would go to the embassy alone. With some trepidation I entered the embassy building and found my way to the appropriate office. I explained the situation to the officer behind the counter and showed him the passports. He looked them over carefully.

"You must leave them here. We'll have to send them to Prague as we don't have the authority to renew them."

"Couldn't the ambassador do it?" I asked him. "Our ship leaves on January 7, and we are already in the middle of December, so what with Christmas and all, I'm afraid they won't be returned here in time. May I see the ambassador?"

"No," said the clerk with customary bureaucratic insensitivity. "The ambassador is busy. He doesn't have the time to see anyone, and, in any case, the passports have to be returned to Prague. That's the rule."

Apparently there was no getting around this, so I gave him the passports and left the embassy. But I had barely gone a block before I was beset by doubts. Supposing they did not return them at all? Then what? We would be in a foreign country without any papers. I turned and went back. Fortunately the same clerk was still at the counter.

"Excuse me," I said. "I left those passports with you, but I realized that I need them to obtain our ration cards, so could I have them back, please? I'll return them after our ration cards have been issued."

"All right," the clerk said carelessly and shoved them back across the counter at me.

When I told Alex what had happened he was glad I had not left the passports at the embassy. The problem remained. We went to see Mr. Mitchell, who listened gravely, thought a while, and then said, "I think the best thing would be to go and see the Indian commissioner." At that time India was still part of the British Empire as a British colony, and the Indian commissioner held a powerful position.

He turned out to be a very pleasant and charming gentleman. As soon as Mr. Mitchell explained our difficulties, the commissioner dictated a letter to the Czech ambassador saying that Alex was needed in India and that he would deem it a favor if the ambassador would renew our passports for at least six months. He signed the letter with a flourish and gave it to me to take to the Czech embassy, promising to telephone the ambassador as well.

Accompanied by Mr. Mitchell, I again confronted the clerk at the Czech embassy. To my amazement, when we asked to see the ambassador, the instant response was, "Yes, of course, Madam, the ambassador will be delighted to see you and Mr. Mitchell."

I showed the ambassador our passports, explained the situation, and gave him the letter from the Indian commissioner. On the spot he extended the passports for another six months.

"Isn't it sad," said Mr. Mitchell once we were out on the street again, "that an Englishman has to come with you so that you can get what is rightfully yours?"

With our passports in order, we went back and reserved our passage on the SS *Britannic*, which was to sail from Southampton on January 7.

Life in London continued to be very pleasant. We had met some of Olga's French-speaking friends and were invited to many parties and afternoon teas. It was at one of these that we met Mr. Kerwin, who was then the editor-in-chief of a magazine called *British Plastics*. Naturally Alex and he found a lot in common, and we began seeing quite a lot of him and his charming French wife. One day we were having afternoon tea at their home when Mr. Kerwin returned from his office, apologizing for his lateness.

"I had to attend a press conference given by ICI," he explained. ICI, Imperial Chemical Industries, was at that time the largest chemical company in the British Empire.

"Look," he said to Alex, "this will interest you," and he handed him a sheet of something pinkish and translucent. "They developed this material during the war and don't know yet what to do with it. They're trying to find a use for it."

Alex took it in his hand. It was quite soft and pliable, and had a strange feel to it, a different kind of texture and no taste.

"What is it?" he asked.

"It's . . . it's . . . I can't remember what they call it. It's such a queer name. Wait a minute," and Mr. Kerwin dug into his breast pocket and pulled out a piece of paper. "They call it po-ly-ethylene."

"What on earth can it be used for?" I wondered.

Mrs. Kerwin came up with the idea that perhaps one could make lamp shades out of it.

"Yes," said her husband, "it might find some small domestic application like that. They spent a lot of research time and money on it. They'll come up with something. Here," he turned to Alex, "you can have this if you like."

And that is how Alex came into possession of one of the first pieces of polyethylene ever produced. We never dreamed then, of course, that polyethylene would eventually have thousands of uses, become a household word, and be produced in millions of tons all over the world.

Christmas and homesickness arrived together, though Olga did her best to cheer us up. We decorated a beautiful Christmas tree, put our modest presents under it, and Olga made a superb dinner, accompanied by a 1927 vintage bottle of French champagne that she had been saving for a special occasion. It was delicious and we drank to the new year shortly to begin and to our collective good luck and good health. It turned out to be a lovely Christmas after all.

Our last days in London passed quickly. On the morning of January 7, Olga took us to the railway station, where we were to take the train to Southampton. Sadly we said a last farewell in Europe and boarded the train.

Olga stood outside on the platform, waving, and calling out, "Good luck! Take care of yourselves and come back soon!"

The train began to move and we were on our way toward our new life in India.

23

ON THE HIGH SEA

Soon we arrived at the Southampton pier, where our ship, the SS *Britannic*, was moored. The *Queen Mary*, at the next dock, had just returned from the United States after an extremely rough crossing. Several sick and injured people were being carried ashore on stretchers. Alex and I did not worry though. The *Britannic* was heading south toward Gibraltar, toward calm and sunlit tropic seas.

The girls and I were to share a cabin with two other passengers, an Englishwoman joining her husband in India in government service, and a young Dutch girl who was going to do missionary work in the slums of Calcutta. Both were very pleasant and liked children.

Alex's cabin was even worse than the booking clerk had said. Large enough to accommodate seven other men, it was located at the stern, just above the propeller. While the ship was rocking just slightly, the stern moved up and down so much that one had the illusion of a storm at sea without ever having left the harbor. The noise was gargantuan. At least, I thought, there was one consolation: it could not get much worse on the open sea.

Later we all went to look around the ship and found the dining room and a playroom for the children. Otherwise all lounges and other public rooms were changed into soldiers' quarters. The ship was overcrowded. In peacetime, before it was converted to a troop carrier, the *Britannic* must have been a handsome liner, making glamorous crossings from Southampton to New York, to Bombay, and to other exotic and exciting places. A string quartet would have been playing while swift and silent stewards provided champagne to lovely people in evening clothes, strolling down the deck under the stars. On this voyage, the *Britannic* was stuffed with uncomfortable civilian passengers, soldiers, Gurkha troops returning home, rich and prosperous-looking Indians, and a couple of maharajahs with their wives. It was a comparatively large ship, weighing about forty thousand tons, but seeing this teeming human cargo, we fervently hoped it would survive the passage and not sink under the weight.

After dinner the four of us went on deck to look at the wild and stormy English Channel. With a deep, churning sound from below decks, white water boiled around the ship's stern and the *Britannic* inched away from the dock. Alex and I, hand in hand, watched the tugs maneuver this giant vessel into open water, thankful that the voyage had begun at last.

Our moment of reflection was brief. We had hardly cleared the harbor when the *Queen Mary*'s difficult passage became our reality. The sea was stormy, with gray water and gray sky. Waves rolling toward the ship seemed large enough to bury it.

Clutching the rail we felt the huge vessel being lifted up like a toy, then, sickeningly, the bow would drop down, the foaming sea horizon sweeping upward as the *Britannic* slid into the waves' valley. It was a frightening, repetitive dance to the accompaniment of the screeching wind.

The passengers were ordered to leave the deck; no one was permitted to stay outside. After we kissed Alex good-night, the girls and I stumbled along to our cabin, thrown from wall to wall along the narrow passageway. Our two fellow travelers were already there and we settled in for the night.

The ship's wild motion made us seasick. Janie turned green and I felt quite miserable. The only one in the cabin who suffered no ill effects was Evie. Sprightly as ever, she was full of life and bounced around the cabin, investigating its every nook and cranny. The storm intensified. In my agony, half awake, I was haunted by the fear that we might capsize.

The girls finally fell asleep, but I could not keep my eyes closed. I lay on the narrow bunk, being tossed from side to side and certain that I would never feel well again. The long night inched by. At dawn the motion of the ship was even worse. But Evie jumped out of bed "terribly hungry," ready for breakfast. Since I could barely stand, I sent her by herself. She was away for some time and returned full of enthusiasm for the breakfast menu. She had been alone in the dining room.

The stewards had been somewhat surprised to see her, but, recognizing a kindred spirit, served her a "wonderful, scrumptious breakfast," as Evie called it, the details of which she insisted on recounting to us, though her cabin mates begged her to keep quiet. The storm lasted three days, and Janie and I and the two ladies suffered through every minute of it. But Evie did not miss a single meal.

In between bouts of nausea, whenever I was able to focus my thoughts beyond my misery, I thought of Alex. Our cabin was situated amidships, where the motion was certainly bad enough, but what it must have been like at the very stern of the ship defied imagination.

On the third day the movement of the vessel was less violent and I was able to get up. Janie, while still refusing any food, also felt better, was more cheerful and played a little with her Raggedy Ann doll.

I went to see how Alex was doing. There was no answer to my knock on his door, so I pushed it open and peered in. The cabin was empty except for Alex. He was lying on his bunk with a sheet over his head like a corpse.

"How are you?" I asked.

"Oh, don't talk to me," he groaned. "I feel so sick. It's terrible. I've never been so sick."

I could well believe it. Being in the stern of that ship was like being in an insane elevator, zipping up three stories and then falling three stories—up and down, up and down. The pitching of the liner escalated dimensions of discomfort. Idly I looked around the cabin and saw a very funny sight.

The passengers had their suitcases stored under their bunks. As the ship moved, the suitcases slid from their hiding places and in unison, like some crazy corps de ballet, skated toward the center of the cabin. As they reached the middle of the floor the suitcases paused and, as accurately as a chorus line, slid back again, each one obediently to its own little spot where it had started from. The ballet of the suitcases added considerably to the noise coming from below the water line, where the huge propellers churned and thrashed their way through the sea.

I was suddenly overcome by the humor of it all and I began to laugh. "Just look at those crazy suitcases!" I said to Alex. "They look as if they've come alive, and watch how each one always returns exactly to its rightful spot! Isn't that funny?"

Alex did not think it was funny. Opening one red eye he glared at me and opened his mouth to speak. Just then the ship gave another sickening lurch, and he quickly closed it again. Contritely, I smoothed down his bed and kissed him.

"I'll check on you again in the evening," I promised, and I staggered back to my cabin.

By evening Alex had recovered sufficiently to have dinner with us, his first meal in three days. People began emerging from their cabins. As soon as we passed the Rock of Gibraltar and entered the Mediterranean Sea, the water calmed as if by magic, and the sun, unseen for days, took possession of a clear, rain-washed sky.

Our holiday mood was dampened by an unexpected order to man the lifeboats. Since many unexploded mines were still in the Mediterranean Sea, the ship sailed close to the African coast, and until the vessel cleared the danger zone, the passengers, wearing life jackets, had to remain by their boats. Standing there for hours, we had little to do but stare at the houses, palm trees, and people on shore. We could see them quite clearly as we steamed very slowly at only a short distance from the land.

At Port Said, the entrance to the Suez Canal, the ship stopped for several hours and we were able to observe the life in this ancient city. I found it fascinating and quite biblical. The Arabs in their billowing, ageless garb riding their camels through the streets, the merchants scrambling over themselves trying to sell us various trinkets and leather goods, the children begging, all the confusion and fascination of the Middle East, which we had known only in books, came alive for us.

In the afternoon the ship entered the Suez Canal. I was surprised to see how narrow it was. On the western bank the famous sand dunes of the Sahara whispered their secrets as they shifted with the wind. The *Britannic* steamed past a few small oases and settlements that were scattered along the canal shore, then slowly entered a large lake that served as a waiting lane for vessels too large to pass in the narrow channel. Several ships had been sunk there during the war and were still visible. The fighting over the Suez had been fierce. We continued on through the second half of the canal, passed another lake, and headed toward the Red Sea.

Suddenly the climate changed completely. In the canal the weather had been cool by day and downright cold in the evenings. In the Red Sea the heat set in. The cabins had no air conditioning and the temperature soon grew unbearable, particularly to people from the temperate climates of central and northern Europe. We spent most of our time on the deck. Not only was it cooler and more pleasant, but the four of us could be together. We encountered two Czech families that were returning to the Bata factories in Batanagar after vacationing in Czechoslovakia. They told us interesting stories about India and the way of life there. They were familiar with Lahore, our destination.

Alex and I also made the acquaintance of a young Czech woman named Helen, who was traveling to Bombay. She had left Czechoslovakia before the war and had studied at the University of Edinburgh. There she had met her husband-to-be, an Indian, who was a professor of chemistry at the university. They married, and shortly afterward he was offered a teaching position at the University of Bombay. After much thought he accepted, and Helen was on her way to join him. She was somewhat nervous about her new life in India, having been warned by many of her friends that a successful marriage to an Indian in England was possible, but it was hard to achieve in India because of the alien values and customs the wife was expected to adopt.

The children had many playmates on board. Evie, who spoke French, had several friends, and even Janie could make herself understood in the universal language of children and played happily all day long. The center of their activities was the playroom where they were supervised by a stewardess, an arrangement greatly appreciated by all parents. To my surprise old Raggedy Ann became a big hit with all the little girls. As her proud owner, Janie shared her glory.

One day, Janie said, "Mommy, I want to show you something," and she fetched one of her nursery-rhyme books, opened it, and proceeded to read. I was amazed. I had no idea she had been even trying to learn. She had asked Evie here and there to identify this letter or that, but Janie had, in fact, taught herself to read. She was a marvel. I showed her how to write, and by the time we arrived in Bombay she could both read and write Czech fluently.

Once the ship entered the Arabian Sea, shipboard life became more social. As the weather was pleasantly warm, we were able to stay on the deck most of the day. We began to notice the Indian passengers more and more. The women particularly blossomed out in their beautiful, exotic saris, embroidered with gold and silver thread. I admired their many gold bracelets and the diamonds that were set in their nostrils. It was fascinating to observe a life so alien to ours. The two maharajahs held court in the ship's entrance hall where the purser's office was. They were evidently of some importance because all the other Indians and many of the English people on board were deferential to them.

As we approached Bombay, my early hesitations about our move to India had become completely dispelled. During the voyage I became curious about that immense subcontinent. Each person on the ship I spoke to who had been there told me different things about this mysterious land, and no two reports agreed. I was confused until it dawned on me that there was no *one* India, that this vast and fascinating land had many facets, each as captivating as the next. We had been on the ship for more than four weeks and became increasingly impatient to see the land that was to be our new home. On the final day, we leaned on the ship's rail for hours, straining our eyes for the first glimpse of its shore.

Finally on the thirty-fourth day we arrived. The absence of the rocking movement woke us up early that morning. Through the salty portholes we saw a silhouette of the big city of Bombay. Alex was already on deck and together we walked around the ship to look at the other side of the harbor. Islands of various sizes are in the bay, the best known of them being the Elephanta, famous for its countless Hindu temples and statues of gods and goddesses carved out of solid rock inside the island's many caves.

We had our last breakfast on the *Britannic* and then the good-byes began. We had made many friends on the voyage. We felt as if we had known them for years and it was difficult to bid farewell to them all. These people were about to scatter all over the vastness of India, some to Calcutta, some to New Delhi, to Madras, Hyderabad, Darjeeling, or other places. The immensity of this subcontinent was beginning to impress itself upon me more and more. We all promised to write, hoping to see each other again somewhere, sometime.

The pilot arrived on board just as the sun came up, and the ship began to move slowly toward the pier. As the morning wore on, the heat and humidity increased, and when we finally docked, it was so hot I thought survival unlikely. The air was almost liquid. Clothes were already soaked with perspiration and bodies limp with exhaustion. Helen arrived with a good-looking, tall Hindu, her husband. They made a handsome though strangely contrasting pair. The professor was dark; Helen was blond and blue-eyed. They were obviously very much in love.

Our guide from Alex's employer had not come yet. We leaned against the rail and inquisitively observed life in the port. Countless Indian coolies, dressed only in white loincloths, scurried all over the place, balancing heavy luggage on their heads. In some cases it looked as if the suitcase weighed more than the little man underneath.

Prosperous-looking Hindu merchants bustled around seeing to their cargo. Graceful, dark-skinned women, dressed in their beautifully embroidered saris and adorned with many jewels, walked by in pairs. Many English ladies and gentlemen had obviously come to meet their friends and relatives on the ship.

Apart from the unusual dockside smells, the air was also permeated with a special, pungent odor. I had never smelt anything like it before, and nowhere else in India was I to come across it, so that it came to signify Bombay to me, and I always remembered it as a part of our arrival in India.

After a few minutes a man rushed up to us and introduced himself as Karel Vanek, the representative of Mr. Janda's company and our guide. He was a pleasant Czech, cheerful, optimistic, and full of

fun. He had come to India only about a year before, right at the end
of the war. He helped us with customs and with our luggage and
took us to our hotel, which, after the heat of the outdoors, seemed
like a cool oasis. It was pleasantly air-conditioned, and we were able
to wash and change our clothes.

When we felt a little better, we all went outside on the balcony to
see the sights. On the sidewalk across from the hotel a man sat
playing a flute. Three cobra snakes were dancing to his tune, hyp-
notically weaving and swaying in time to the music. A little farther
off was a man selling bananas. The street was very noisy, full of people, filled with life and excitement: the Indian women in saris, the
Hindu and Moslem men in apparel according to their various customs, and the British men in tropical suits and pith helmets.

We saw our luggage arrive in front of the hotel. Several coolies
came running to unload it. Then one slight, thin little man bent over
and took our heavy cabin trunk on his back. It had taken four burly
men to carry it in London. In Bombay one thin coolie with skinny,
rickety legs carried it all by himself up the steps of the hotel and all
the way up to our floor, using not the elevator but the staircase! I
could not believe my eyes. How could such strength possibly be
contained in such a small, undernourished body? But I did not know
India yet.

In the afternoon the heat was even more fierce. The four of us lay
down and rested until evening, when the air cooled a little. Then
our spirit of adventure revived. Not far from our hotel was the
famous and glamorous Taj Mahal Hotel, the most elegant establish-
ment in India. We admired its fanciful architecture and opulent
entrance. Also close by was the beautiful, decorative arch of the
Gateway of India, erected to commemorate the arrival of King
George V and Queen Mary when, as emperor and empress of India,
they came on a state visit in 1911. We strolled along the beautiful
seashore, and the fresh breeze made me feel a little more optimistic
about our future life.

The day ended with dinner at Karel's apartment, and we spent a
pleasant evening with him and his family.

Back in our hotel rooms the girls and I fell asleep immediately,
but poor Alex just could not relax. He fidgeted, tossed, and turned
until he managed to wake me up as well.

"What's the matter with you?" I asked, fighting to keep my eyes open. "Why can't you sleep? Aren't you tired? I'm just exhausted!"

"I am tired," he said, "but I can't sleep. You know, I think I miss the up-and-down movement of the ship."

The next morning Karel Vanek took Alex to see the local branch of the company, and his wife Annie offered to take me and the girls to see the Bombay bazaar. To me it was complete confusion with countless stalls and shops selling everything imaginable. There were textiles, leather goods, one whole street of shoe shops, and everywhere a seething mass of people, pushing, rushing here and there, reaching out to us from their shops and booths, imploring us to "Buy, buy, Memsahib, buy! Come into my shop, I give you good price, excellent price!" Roaring all around us everywhere was the cacophonic explosion of color that is India itself.

Coming from Europe I was not used to beggars of any kind, but we encountered many particularly sad and pathetic beggars in Bombay. There were children without limbs, cripples of all kinds, men with horribly disfigured faces, all with outstretched hands and imploring, hopeless eyes. I gave out money right and left, but the more I gave, the more there were, an endless stream of beggars, arriving in greater and greater numbers, clamoring for a coin or two with outstretched hands, jostling, touching me, pulling at me from all sides, until Annie said, "It's no use, Zdena, you can't give to all of them. There isn't that much money in your purse. You'll have to get used to it. I know it's dreadful, but there's nothing we can do about it. It's just India."

I could not find an answer. I was staring at a man who had no arms or legs, only tiny withered stumps where his limbs should have been, and who was getting around the filthy streets by wriggling along on his belly like a snake. He held a hat in his mouth and people were throwing rupees into it. Poor, poor man, I thought, poor man. My heart ached for him.

"How is it possible that anyone is born like this!" I said. "What a cruel life!"

"Oh, but he wasn't born like that!" Annie replied. "This was done to him. There are poor people who deliberately maim their children in order to make good beggars out of them, and the more crippled the child, the better the alms, and then the whole family can live on what the child makes. Oh no, this was done to him. They do it by putting a tourniquet around a baby's limbs when it is still very tiny, then the limbs atrophy."

I followed her down the street, unable to forget that poor man. A little farther on I noticed several people with terribly mutilated faces, and one man in particular who had a gaping hole where his nose should have been.

"They're lepers," Annie said, anticipating my question. "There's a big leper colony just outside Bombay and they're supposed to stay in there, but they don't. I guess they miss normal life. One's always meeting them on the street. And, of course, they beg, too."

Now I recalled the disfigured beggars I had seen; they were all lepers. I shuddered.

"It's not really very catching, you know," Annie added comfortingly. "You would have to be in very direct and constant contact to catch it. I guess that's why the authorities aren't all that strict with them."

She turned into a store to buy some dress material and we followed her in. To my amazement, after selecting her purchase, she began energetically haggling with the merchant over the price. With growing astonishment I listened to her spirited exchange. Several times Annie put down the material and began to march out of the store, and each time the merchant rushed after her, imploring her to come back, each time giving in a little on the price. She came back each time and in her turn increased her offer a little, and after several such exchanges they came to a mutually acceptable figure. They beamed happily at each other. She handed over the money, he gave her the little package, and we left the store.

"How ever can you do that?" I exclaimed. "I could never haggle like that. I wouldn't have the nerve."

"You will in time," she answered, "and before very long, I promise you. And they expect it, you know. If I had just given him the first amount he asked for, he would have been most disappointed. I would have quite ruined his day. Haggling is a way of life here, and the better you can do it, the more they respect you."

Annie was right. Before long I could haggle along with the best of them. On the odd occasion when I gave in too soon, I thought I could detect in my opponent a faint disappointment mixed with contempt.

From the textile market we went to the produce hall. It was enormous and completely filled with hundreds of stalls full of all kinds of vegetables and fruit, and other stalls with many exotic items I had never heard of. Annie explained what they were and showed me the best way to buy things.

Then we went to the meat market and again I was overwhelmed by the amount of food. This huge conglomeration of meat, fish, and poultry was all the more striking in view of the many starving beggars outside. Would I ever get used to India? I wondered. Would I ever get accustomed to her contrasts, her cruelty, her paradoxes? In the meat market Annie explained that one had to be careful not to ask for pork at a Moslem market or beef at a Hindu market since to do so would offend the religious beliefs of the owner. Bewildered, I nodded, wondering how long it would take me to master it all in this strange, exotic land.

That evening we were invited to visit some people who lived on Marine Drive, where we saw yet another aspect of Indian life. Marine Drive, one of the most prestigious parts of Bombay, was a long, curving boulevard along the seashore, lined with large houses and apartment buildings. In the evening, when all the buildings were lit up with their myriads of lights reflecting in the still, dark water, Marine Drive looked like a fairyland. I could see how it had gained its other name, the Queen's Necklace.

An evening sea breeze blew in through the windows and cooled the party we attended. To my surprise, several of the ladies wore light sweaters or jackets. I was in my lightest summer dress and yet sweltered. They were amused at my astonishment. "Your blood will thin out. You'll see. And you'll feel the cold more," they said.

They were right; a year later I needed that light jacket, too.

The next day Karel showed us more of Bombay. First we went to the famous Hanging Gardens on Malabar Hill, said to be one of the wonders of the world. The carefully laid-out trees and bushes had all been clipped into the most fantastic shapes of all kinds of animals. There were elephants, giraffes, horses—a complete zoo fashioned of meticulously sculptured hedges, overlooking a beautiful panoramic view of Bombay. The girls were especially enchanted with this verdant statuary, and we found it difficult to drag them away.

We drove farther up Malabar Hill. The houses lining the road gave way to a high wall that enclosed huge gardens full of ancient towering trees. I looked at the wall and at the greenery inside, all of which seemed somewhat oppressive and strangely menacing. I looked closer and found out why. Nearly every branch of those tall, majestic trees was covered with large, black, well-fed vultures.

Karel explained that in the center of the garden was the Tower of Silence, the holy place and funeral grounds of the Parsee population of Bombay. Parsees are a comparatively small, western-oriented religious group, consisting mainly of well-to-do members of the business community. They believe that earth, water, and fire are sacred, and for this reason they cannot commit to them the bodies of their dead. Therefore, when a Parsee dies, after the funeral the body is brought to the Tower of Silence. Soon the tower is surrounded by hundreds of huge, flapping, quarreling vultures, and before long, all that is left of the body is a pile of bones, which are then thrown into a pit in the middle of the tower.

Karel explained to us that India has four main religions. The largest religious sect comprises the Hindus, and most Indians belong to this faith. The next are the Moslems, followed by the Buddhists and then the Christians. The Hindus are divided into four castes, the highest of which are the Brahmins. They are usually of lighter complexion and generally follow the professions and become teachers, administrators, priests, doctors, and so on, forming the top layer of society. Next come the soldiers, and then the merchants and traders. These are the top three castes. Those in the fourth caste are servants to the other three groups.

Outside the four divisions of the Hindu caste system are several sects known collectively as Untouchables. To the orthodox Hindus, the Untouchables are just that: untouchable, unclean. In ancient times even their shadow was not allowed to fall on a member of another caste, and they were relegated to only the meanest and dirtiest jobs. From the Untouchable caste there was no escape, as the caste system had a religious significance.

Soon the car swung out into the wide streets of Bombay's exclusive residential district, mostly occupied by the town palaces of rajahs and maharajahs. Each palace was surrounded by acres of parkland and gardens, but since they were also enclosed by tall walls, we could not see more than the tree tops.

The next morning we decided to go to the Czech consulate. "Who knows," Alex said to me, "maybe we can get those passports renewed. Let's try."

The Czech consul was a pleasant gentleman who, we were pleased to learn, was unenthusiastic about the current developments in Czechoslovakia. We told him about our troubles in London.

"Oh, I don't know what's happening over there!" he said. "Everything is changing so fast. I don't even know how long I'll be here. Let's do it right now so you'll have no problems," and on the spot he renewed our passports for all of seven years.

We returned to our hotel tired but relaxed, and I began once again the tiresome business of packing. We were due to leave for Lahore the next day and, although I liked Bombay, I was anxious to see the city where we were to spend the next three years.

As we boarded the train and presented our tickets to the conductor, he asked Alex if we had our servant with us. When Alex told him that we did not, he strongly recommended we hire a man for the journey.

"You will need a bearer, Sahib," he said emphatically. "The dining car is a long way from your car, and you cannot go through the train. It is much better if you have a bearer to bring your meals to your compartment. I can find you one. There are many here quite willing to make the trip, Sahib."

He pointed to a row of turbaned men squatting in the timeless Indian fashion along the wall of the station buildings.

"Also," he continued, "he will clean your room, make the beds, and bring your drinks. He will travel in a special servants' car." Alex nodded agreement, and the conductor brought us a servant.

We settled ourselves in, said good-bye to the Vaneks, who had come to see us off, and soon the train began to move.

Our compartment occupied a good part of a railway car and was arranged like a sitting room, with four daybeds, a table, and comfortable chairs. Adjoining it was a spacious bathroom. We could walk around and move freely, without the cramped feeling usually engendered by train travel. Even the temperature was quite pleasant, as the car was cooled by a huge block of ice placed over the top of the ceiling.

As we traveled, I gazed out the window fascinated. The railway stations we passed were full of people, mostly squatting on the ground, waiting for trains. Many were eating from small bowls, and although they were using only their fingers, they managed to do it as delicately as any duchess using a silver spoon. Even curry and rice they ate in this fashion.

I saw for the first time how the poor Indians traveled. While we were stopped at one station, we saw a passing train that was not only full but was actually festooned with people. Passengers were clinging to the roof, hanging out of the windows, and standing on the steps leading into the carriages. It was a mystery why hundreds of them were not killed.

In one station, monkeys were mingling freely with the Indians on the platform. Amused, I watched their antics. They were not afraid of the people and cheekily stole from them as much as they could—a banana here or a bowl of rice there—and nobody seemed to mind. Monkeys are considered sacred in India and for this reason are allowed all sorts of license.

One of them even jumped into the carriage with us when Alex opened the door. It was a job to chase it out again. Fortunately we managed to get rid of the unwelcomed visitor just when the train started moving out of the station.

24

LAHORE

The train chugged through the arid jungle drenched by hot, tropical sun. The land was overgrown with underbrush, tangled vegetation, and some occasional trees. Exotic birds of luminous colors whirled up at the approach of the noisy train and flapped squawking from tree to tree.

On the third day we reached New Delhi, the capital of India. The city seemed to be huge and the railway station even more ornate than the one in Bombay and just as overcrowded and noisy. Half a day later we finally arrived in Lahore, a city of one million people, where the company representatives met us at the station.

Lahore is an ancient town with innumerable mosques and minarets that are beautifully decorated. The tree-lined streets were overflowing with traffic, and people on foot were hurrying here and there amidst a confusion of taxicabs, automobiles, cyclists, and hackney cabs called tongas, pulled by thin, dispirited, trotting horses. In February 1947, Lahore was largely a Moslem city with a significant population of Hindus and Sikhs.

The Sikhs, unlike the Hindus, believe in only one god. Men are forbidden to shave or cut their hair and therefore sport wild-looking beards and big turbans, inside of which they coil their braided hair. They are a warlike race and always wear at their belt a kukri, a large, curved, scimitar-like knife. The combination of tall stature and bellicose attitude makes them look terrifying.

Alex and I liked Lahore immediately. It seemed friendly and well laid out. On the first carriage ride around the city I thought the bazaar looked much cleaner and neater than the one in Bombay, with fewer beggars and more better-dressed people. The famous Shalimar gardens, built a few centuries ago by a Moslem ruler, were beautiful.

Returning to the hotel, our carriage was stopped by a political demonstration of people shouting, "Pakistan Zindabar! Pakistan Zindabar!" Long live Pakistan! At that time India was still a British colony, but the Indians were demanding independence. The Moslems also wanted their own state, which they were going to call Pakistan.

When we were in Europe, Alex and I had had only the vaguest awareness of these developments; in Lahore they exploded in our faces. The people in the procession mistook us for British and began throwing stones at us. Alex shouted at the driver to turn into a side street. We drove back to the hotel trying to minimize the moderately disturbing impression the violence had made on us and the girls.

That evening we were invited to dinner at the home of Mr. and Mrs. Janda. They lived in a large, elegantly furnished bungalow that was set in a walled, well-tended garden and insulated from the bustle of the city and its noise. Several other couples were present, and after dinner a general discussion ensued with the conclusion that Alex and I should look for a house.

Alex's job was to build a chemical factory about six miles from Lahore, in the middle of a large banana-and-orange plantation that the Jandas recently bought. "Don't worry about looking for a house, my dear," Mrs. Janda said to me. "I have already found one that I think you will like. It's on the outskirts of Lahore, on the way to the plantation. You can look at it tomorrow."

We were told several servants would have to be hired. The most important was the cook. Then there had to be a bearer to serve at the table and bring the morning and afternoon tea, and a gardener, a chauffeur, and a chamadar.

"What's a chamadar?" I asked.

"The chamadar does the cleaning," Mrs. Janda answered. "He

washes the bathrooms, scrubs the floors, and empties the garbage. He belongs to the lowest caste of all, the Untouchables, the only Indians who do such work. None of the other servants would even consider doing work like that. He is really very important."

Early the next morning Mr. Janda picked us up at the hotel. The first stop was at the house his wife had found for us. A graceful, white tropical bungalow with deep, cool verandas in both the front and back, it was set in a large, walled garden with tall trees, lush bushes with shining leaves, and bright flower beds. The air was redolent with the smells of blossoming jasmine.

From the wrought-iron gate a curving drive led to the entrance portico, supported by fluted white columns. Steps led up to the front veranda and the main entrance, opening into a broad, marble-floored hallway that ran down the entire length of the house. It provided a dim, soothing breezeway in the afternoon heat and ended in another wide doorway to the back veranda and garden.

A door on the left led to a large sitting room, a library, the dining room, and the kitchen beyond. On the other side of the hallway were two large bedrooms, each with its own dressing room and bathroom with a door opening directly to the outside of the house so servants could clean the bathrooms and run the bath water without disturbing their masters. The servants' quarters were in the rear of the garden.

In the kitchen I discovered a stove constructed of compact dry mud with five round holes chiseled out in the surface.

"How can one cook on this?" I wondered aloud.

Mr. Janda explained that this was a chula, a centuries-old device used in Indian homes.

"Don't you worry," he said, "the Indians know how to cook on this. You'll be surprised!"

He was right. For cooking or baking, our cook filled the holes with burning charcoal, the heat from which he controlled masterfully. He never burnt anything, baked even the most delicate cakes on it, and prepared the best caramel flan I ever ate.

Mr. Janda continued, "I think my wife has found a cook for you, too. He speaks good English and has cooked for years for a European family."

Mrs. Janda was indeed kind. She had also found us a used

refrigerator, which, as she said, was like finding gold. Since the beginning of the war no new goods had been shipped to India, and consumer goods of any kind were hard to come by.

We left the house and continued on down the road. After two miles of hot, arid countryside we arrived in the small village of Mahmabuti, which consisted of a multitude of one-room mud huts. At the edge of the village, next to an enormous tree, was the community well. Women dressed in white cotton saris were gathered around it, some drawing water into large earthenware jars, others carrying away the heavy containers gracefully balanced on their heads. Children, with brown eyes as deep and mysterious as the well, played among freely wandering cows and chickens. The whole area was full of noise and confusion, life, dust, flies, cow dung, and laughter. I thought that it must have been just this way around the hamlet's well every day for thousands of years.

The site of the new chemical factory was surrounded by a high wall with a large ornate gate. The watchman on duty recognized the car, saluted Mr. Janda, and opened the gate. We drove into modernity as if by magic. The dusty dirt road became paved and swept. It curved elegantly through a double line of tall, stately palm trees holding back groves of banana and orange trees like quiet, well-mannered servants. Everything was manicured, lusciously green and fresh, sanitary, and orderly.

Such perfection continued for half a mile and culminated at a large, modern building, the staff clubhouse. It had been built even before the factory because the company thought their employees would appreciate it. We were led to the back of the building and shown an enormous swimming pool complete with an ornamental waterfall and a huge, shaded patio. Inside the clubhouse were several large meeting rooms, a kitchen, a dining room, and off to one side a number of small dressing rooms.

Next, Mr. Janda showed us the laboratory. Like everything else on the plantation, it was huge. The construction was finished and all Alex had to do was to order the furnishings and equipment. The adjoining production building was only partially complete. It was going to be very large.

We were impressed. Such an oasis of beauty and civilization in the middle of the Indian plain was truly miraculous. Masses of flowering shrubs, carefully manicured lawns, citrus trees laden with lemons and oranges, and tall stately banana bushes loaded with their ripening fruit displayed the lush abundance and charm of the plantation. Swimming in the scent of orange blossoms was so unexpected and so unbelievable that I felt we had wandered into the Garden of Eden.

Over the next several days we bought the necessary furniture for our house, and I carpeted the marble floors with the most sumptuous Persian carpets, haggled for in the carpet bazaar for comparatively little money. With our personal mementos unlocked and photographs of our family and friends placed here and there, the house looked beautiful and began to feel like home.

Our cook and main employee, Mohammed, was a small, dark-skinned Moslem with very shifty eyes. He spoke English fairly well, which was a relief, and lost no time in informing us that actually he was a man of substance in his village three hundred miles away.

"Yes, Memsahib," he told me, "and there I have my wife and my children, and I also have three camels! I don't really need to work!"

He nodded vigorously to lend emphasis to these words, confident that I was suitably impressed with his importance.

When I repeated this to Mrs. Janda, she laughed.

"Three camels! Anyone who has three camels in India is a rich man, and he would never consent to be a servant! He's a liar, that's what he is. Three camels, indeed!"

Before long a tall, dark Hindu man, who looked remarkably like the young Joseph Stalin, turned up and said he was the chamadar. I began talking to him, but he looked blank.

"He does not understand me!" I exclaimed to Mohammed, who had brought him. "How can I talk to him if he can't understand English?"

The cook turned to the chamadar and jabbered something at him, to which the chamadar gave an answer.

"He speaks French," the cook told me.

"French! How nice! I am so glad," I said to him in that language but was met with the same blank look. Disappointed, I turned to the cook again.

"He doesn't understand French either!"

The cook loosed another torrent of Hindustani at the chamadar, to which the chamadar gave a reply.

"He made a mistake. He doesn't speak French. He speaks Italian!" he informed me victoriously.

Of course, he did not speak Italian either. He spoke only Hindustani, but I employed him anyway, and instead of him learning to speak English, I began to learn Hindustani.

On the third day the cook brought another man, the gardener, who did not speak English or French either, but with Mohammed to translate we got on well.

All the gardens of Lahore, including ours, were lush, verdant, and rich with green lawns and profusely blooming flowers. The British had constructed a number of irrigation canals throughout the region of Punjab, and every Tuesday and Friday the gardens of our section of Lahore were flood irrigated. This regular, deep soaking, combined with the warmth and the bright sunshine, produced a plant life the likes of which I had never seen before.

Alex bought a British car, a used Rover, and soon our life settled into a pleasant pattern. In the morning we all had breakfast together, and then Alex left in the car for the plant, while the girls and I went shopping. We still needed many little household items, and in the beginning I also shopped for food. However, before long I discovered that if I sent Mohammed, the cook, he was able to buy all we needed for a much lower price than I would have had to pay, and even though I knew he made a nice little profit on the deal, it still worked out cheaper to send him than to go myself. He was definitely a master of the art of haggling.

On the weekends we usually drove over to the plantation club and spent the day in the pleasant company of our new friends, playing volleyball, table tennis, and, to the horror of the old-time residents, even went swimming.

"You'll catch your death of cold!" they warned us, huddling in their sweaters, but to us this was like the best of summer weather at home and we could not get enough of it.

Alex generally returned from work at five in the evening, when it had started to cool off. By the time we had eaten our dinner it was chilly enough to make a fire in the fireplace and sit around it, talking and reading. It was a quiet, happy life after the years of agony in Czechoslovakia. The four of us had, it seemed, escaped the storm of the twentieth century.

School was going to start soon. Where should I send Janie and Evie? We asked our acquaintances, but most of Alex's co-workers were childless. I was told that there were no English schools for girls in the city because Lahore in summer was a very unhealthy place. There were mosquitoes and therefore a lot of malaria, and the gardens were infested with poisonous cobras. And the heat was unbearable. It was much safer and healthier to send the children to a boarding school in the Himalayas. All the European families did it, and there were several excellent schools in Simla or in Rawalpindi in Kashmir.

I managed to get some addresses and wrote to a few boarding schools for additional information, when one day a car came into our drive and a lady accompanied by a little girl about Evie's age stepped out.

She introduced herself as Mrs. McDonald, the wife of an English director of a mint situated close by. "Dawn has been so impatient to meet your two girls," she said with a smile, nodding at her daughter.

Mrs. McDonald was slim and beautiful, with masses of dark hair, large, blue eyes, and a flawless, very white complexion. She had been born in northern Italy, and, although she liked India, she missed her homeland and welcomed being able to chat with another European. We drank tea and talked for a while, and then it suddenly occurred to me that little Dawn must go to school somewhere.

"Oh yes," Jenny McDonald exclaimed when I asked her, "Dawnie goes to school in Simla, up in the Himalayas. There's a wonderful boarding school for girls there called Tara Hall. It's a Loretto Convent, and the nuns are just sweethearts. The school is affiliated with Cambridge University and it is really excellent. Dawn is very happy there."

She offered to write to the Mother Superior and ask her to send application papers to me. The school year began, she said, on March 15, which was very soon, so we had no time to lose.

Jenny McDonald was as good as her word. The return mail contained a letter from the Mother Superior of Loretto Convent, telling me that on Mrs. McDonald's recommendation she was accepting the children into Tara Hall. She enclosed the application form and a long list of items for me to buy, such as uniforms, blankets, and so on. "I doubt that you will be able to have all this ready by the fifteenth," she wrote, "so we shall expect you and the girls around the twentieth of March."

Jenny and I scoured the bazaar, bought material, found a tailor to sew uniforms, and exacted from him a promise that they would be ready in two weeks. Back at the house, I settled down on the front veranda to embroider monograms on the endless supply of socks, underwear, towels, and blankets, with Jenny helping me whenever she had time.

Meanwhile, the animal population of our compound began to grow. First we acquired a small, stray mongrel dog. He began appearing at the house at intervals, wagging his tail and wearing an expectant expression, and in spite of being chased away he returned again and again, so finally we let him stay. We called him Jackie and were all happy to have a dog around the house again. Animals had always been a part of our lives, and we had missed having them.

Soon afterwards the chamadar brought a baby goat, which he tied up outside his quarters. The girls, of course, promptly claimed it as another addition to their menagerie. They played with it constantly and loved it dearly. Then one day the kid disappeared. Evie, who by now knew quite a few words of Hindustani, asked the chamadar if he had seen it.

"Oh yes," the chamadar told her with a straight face, "the poor baby goat got sick in the night, so I took it to Lahore to the hospital."

The girls believed him. Daily they asked him about the goat's progress, and daily he improvised ongoing health bulletins until the girls finally lost interest and the matter was quietly dropped. I knew what had happened: the chamadar butchered the kid and had it for dinner. I thought the story enterprising of him and was grateful for his tact.

Then, almost involuntarily, we added two horses to our animal kingdom. One day Alex was driving home in his Rover on a rough road when suddenly the car door fell off. Since spare parts were difficult to find, Alex, remembering his daily rides from Richky to Brno, decided to commute to work on horseback. He found two well-trained ex-polo ponies that were responsive and pleasant to ride, and soon the forty-minute ride to the factory in the cool of the day became a routine.

Our second horse was idle during the day as I did not enjoy riding alone, so we bought a victoria to provide transportation for me and the girls. This in turn necessitated hiring a coachman, something of a problem.

The man we hired was pleasant enough and seemed to know a lot about horses and their management, but he did not speak English, and what was even worse, he did not speak any Hindustani either. India has some forty-five different dialects and languages, and for many Indians English was the common tongue. However, Mohammed, who could never admit to a lack of knowledge about anything at all, assured me he could understand him, and so we hired him. I soon found out the coachman's limitations.

On our first horse-drawn trip to the city we stopped at a shoe store. While shopping, I heard a commotion outside and ran to the door to see what happened. A short distance down the street a group of Sikhs, brandishing their long kukris, had attacked some Moslems who, armed with long knives, fought back. Several dead and wounded were already lying on the pavement. A horde of onlookers had gathered instantly, screaming and shouting encouragement and condemnation for this faction or that. More and more people were running to join the melee.

Grabbing the girls, I ran to our carriage. I opened my mouth and realized I had no way of telling the coachman what I wanted. Fortunately, he was as frightened as we were and needed no instructions. He turned the horse and whipped him into a fast trot. We careened back toward our bungalow and safety.

The incident made me glad the girls were leaving for Simla soon. The tension in Lahore was growing rapidly, and the newspapers carried stories daily of street fighting and deliberately set fires. The Sikhs and Hindus, a quarter of Lahore's population, wanted Lahore in India, but the Moslems, the other three quarters, wanted it to belong to Pakistan. The shopkeepers in the bazaar began slashing their prices in an effort to liquidate their inventories, and people began stockpiling food.

The atmosphere grew oppressive. Because of these disturbances, and as Alex and I wanted to accompany the girls to Simla, we hired a night watchman. The Gurkha turned out to be a good man, and he spoke English. Equipped with a sizable club and the inevitable wicked-looking kukri, he reported for work every evening after sunset and spent the night alternately patrolling the property and dozing on our front veranda.

As the girls' departure day neared, they gathered their special belongings, which I began to pack. I was touched to see Janie had diligently included her Raggedy Ann doll.

As part of their farewell, Mrs. Janda invited the children and me to afternoon tea. I planned to hire a cab but decided instead to take our victoria. By now the coachman had mastered a few basic words of Hindustani, such as stop, go, left, and right, and I felt confident that the communications gap had been sufficiently bridged for us to undertake the trip. We got dressed in our best, climbed into the victoria, and settled back to enjoy the trip.

The way to Janda's home led alongside the main irrigation canal, the real heart of Lahore. Never deserted, the canal throbbed with life: children splashing in the water, boys bathing elephants, pigs wallowing in the cold mud, women doing their washing. It was the place to gossip, cool off, meet your friends, and to a newly arrived Westerner it was a place of infinite fascination.

With a shiver, I noticed our speed increasing. The horse moved to a canter and went faster and faster. Alarmed, I nudged the driver in the back and shouted at him, "*Aste, aste!* Slow, slow." He either did not want to understand me or his few words of Hindustani deserted him. Instead of slowing he urged the horse to yet greater speed.

"*Aste!*" I yelled, but with no result. The more I yelled the faster he went.

Chickens scattered alongside the road, children screamed, dogs barked, and we careered along, the carriage swaying perilously from side to side. Small pebbles flung up by the horse's hooves whizzed by my face. I was sure we would plunge headlong into the canal among the elephants, horses, and pigs. Grimly the girls and I held on as we raced along, huge clouds of dust billowing up behind us.

An intersection loomed ahead. I became anxious because the traffic was quite heavy. To my immense relief, however, our speed slowed until the horse was actually just walking again. With a shaking hand I wiped the dust off my face and tried to straighten the girls' dresses so that by the time we arrived at Mrs. Janda's we would not look as if we had crossed the Great Indian Desert on foot.

We had a pleasant visit with her. On our departure I took the precaution of asking her servants to explain to our coachman that he should go s-l-o-w-l-y . . . aste . . . s-l-o-w-l-y back. He apparently understood this time, as our return trip was accomplished at a far more sober speed.

Finally, on March 20, we set out for Simla. The train went east from Lahore across what later became the border between Pakistan and India, to Kalka, a small town at the foot of the Himalayas, where the main railroad ended. From there one could take either a narrow-gauge train or a cab. Everyone we spoke to recommended the cab. The trip from Kalka to Simla, we were told, would take about eight hours. For safety reasons the cabs were not allowed to complete the trip any faster. A checkpoint took each driver's departure time and telephoned it up to Simla. If the cab arrived at the other end sooner than the allotted eight hours, the driver lost his license. Until the rule was instituted, many cabs tried to hurry the trip in order to make more money and several of them were lost forever in some precipice.

The road began to climb and twist through magnificent, breath-taking country—scenery so dazzling that, as Alex remarked, were it painted, one could accuse the artist of exaggeration. Towering mountains of burning white loomed above forests so deep and primeval that one had the feeling of seeing the earth as it had been millions of years before. Dim gorges and chasms opened before us as the road shoulders dropped thousands of feet and travelers looked straight down onto tiny, green, match-stick trees growing in a world as remote from us, and as indifferent to us and our fate, as the moon. The sheer beauty and the awesome majesty of the Himalayas, mountain range upon mountain range higher and yet higher above us, remote and impersonal in their vast, glittering magnificence, was something I had never expected. A thousand books, photographs, or films could never capture even a hint of their stupendous beauty.

We were all gazing spellbound out of the window when I turned to find Janie looking unwell. Her face was pale and green, and even as I noticed her she wailed, "Mommy, I feel so sick. Stop the car, quick."

From then on the trip was nothing but misery for her. Every twist of the road seemed to bring on a new spasm of car sickness. Finally the last bend brought us to the entry gate to Simla. The official on duty checked our time in, waved us through, and soon we were in the hotel.

Our balcony afforded a view of the town clinging to the pine-covered mountains below us. Enchanted, we gazed at the endless, green evening scenery, translucent as jade. Silhouetted on the horizon were high mountains decked out in white and decorated with several diamond stars shimmering slightly in the thin Himalayan air.

Simla at that time was a town of forty thousand inhabitants, mainly a resort for people escaping the hot weather of the plains. As it was also the summer seat of the viceroys of India, it was unusually tidy and pretty, a picturesque little settlement. The only more or less straight street in the whole town was the Mall, the main street, where most of the shops were situated. The other streets meandered up and down hills, twisting and turning, becoming flights of stone steps or narrow lanes balancing along rocky ledges, passable only on foot or by rickshaw manned by four coolies, two pushing and two pulling.

The next morning we took the girls to school. The road leading to Tara Hall zigzagged up a hill until finally the rickshaws stopped on a level clearing in front of a large gate. The school was built on the edge of a cliff along a series of terraces, with the main buildings and classrooms on one level, the dormitories on the next level down, and the recreation areas and playing fields on the lowest terrace bordering a sheer drop. From there one could see, several hundred feet below, a large boys' boarding school and the rest of the town, scattered among the tall pines down the mountainside. The view from everywhere was spectacular.

The watchman at the front gate directed us across the meticulously landscaped main quadrangle to the office of the Mother Superior, an efficient, kind-looking nun in her late fifties, with a charming Irish lilt to her voice. She welcomed the girls to the school, explained a little about visiting hours and privileges, and then dropped her bombshell.

"I don't think it would be good for the girls to spend too much time together," she explained. "There is quite an age difference between them, and it will be best for the little one to sleep with children of her own age, and for Evie to sleep in the dormitory with the older girls."

Poor little Janie could not speak English yet. It would be hard on her to be so completely separated from her sister. Evie could probably cope, since she was able to make herself understood. I tried to explain all this to Mother Superior, but she waved my fear aside.

"We often get girls from European countries who cannot speak a word of English," she assured me, "and we find this is much the best way. You see, children are very adaptable. She will be speaking English in no time. She may be a little miserable for the first couple of days, but believe me, this is the best way in the long run."

Reluctantly I gave in, and to my surprise the girls seemed to take our parting in good spirits. Cheerfully they kissed us good-bye, and Alex and I, feeling a little happier, returned to our hotel.

The next morning we went again to the school and were received graciously by the Mother Superior. She told us that the girls were settled in quite well, and I felt reassured.

Evie came in first and did not look at all happy. Her eyes were sad, but before I could say anything to her, a nun entered, leading Janie. She was crying and her little chubby face was smudged and swollen. When she saw me she hurled herself in my arms, sobbing, "Oh, Mommy, take me home. I don't like it here, please take me home, I'll be good, I'll do anything you like, but don't leave me here."

Helplessly I looked at Mother Superior. She opened her mouth to speak, but Evie forestalled her.

"I am not going to stay here without Janie, Mommy. You know that, don't you? If she goes home, I do, too. I'm not staying here without her."

"I'll come back to see you, sweethearts," I told them. "Just be a little patient. The time will pass like a flash and I'll be back in Simla in no time. And then I'll come and see you every day. Maybe on weekends you'll be able to spend some time with me in the hotel."

I found it difficult to meet their accusing, betrayed eyes.

"Don't feel so bad," Mother said gently after a while. "Children are very resilient, you know. This is the hardest time, but in a couple of days they'll be quite settled in, I promise you. Write to them as often as you can, and when you return you'll be surprised at how well they've adapted."

Alex and I hugged and kissed both girls and tore ourselves away. My parting with Janie was one of the most difficult things I had ever done. She was crying so much that she was almost hysterical, and finally the kind nun took her from my arms, hugging and comforting her, so that Janie, crying in her arms instead of mine, was carried away from the room and from my sight.

We returned to Lahore and I wrote each girl a long letter immediately, telling them all about Jackie, the dog, and the horses, trying to be as cheerful as I could and hoping that by the time they received it they would be feeling a little better.

Later, I received letters from both of them. Evie sounded cheerful. To her surprise she found that a British girl who had been her best friend on the ship was also a student at Tara Hall. Dawn was also there, and Evie could make herself understood. She was settling down quite nicely. But Janie's letter broke my heart.

"Dear Mommy and Daddy," she wrote. "I'm sitting here by the fence looking out toward Lahore, and I'm crying, and I wish I were a little bird so I could fly away from here to Lahore and to you."

I could see evidence of her tears on the page. The ink was smudged and the paper was crumpled and wet looking. Holding it in my hand, gazing out over the hot, dusty plains of Lahore in the direction of the distant Himalayas, I began to cry, too, thinking about us all, exiled in this alien land, so vast, so cruel, so indifferent.

The sporadic fighting in Lahore continued and the oppressive atmosphere only added to my loneliness for the children. I missed them very much. The house seemed to be empty without them, and the memory of poor Janie's unhappiness haunted me night and day.

Just as we were settling into our new lives, Lord Mountbatten was appointed the last viceroy to India. His special duty was to transfer the reins of government to India on Independence Day, no easy job. Mahatma Gandhi and Jawaharlal Nehru, the leaders of the Hindus, wanted to keep India as one country, but the Moslem minority under Mohammed Ali Jinnah demanded an independent state to be called Pakistan.

Simla was in India; Lahore was in Pakistan-to-be. The British

shared the view of Gandhi and Nehru. Lord Mountbatten's difficult
task was to convince the Moslems of its wisdom.

He had been chosen because he was respected and liked in India
because of his service as the Allied supreme commander in southeast
Asia during the war. He and Lady Mountbatten were received in
New Delhi with great pomp and ceremony. Alex and I hoped he
would succeed, and succeed soon.

I began horseback riding regularly with Alex. Every night after
dinner we would saddle up and ride out beyond the outskirts of
Lahore to the edge of the jungle. The air was a little cooler at that
time of day because of a slight breeze, and the outing was not only
enjoyable but also as refreshing as anything could be in the Punjab
heat. We never ventured too far because we knew that the jungle
around Lahore was well populated with cheetahs, jackals, and other
wild animals. One could hear them snarling and growling at each
other in the night.

Gradually our circle of friends in Lahore increased. We were
invited to teas, dinners, and parties, and a dance was held at the
hotel every Saturday. Also I saw Jenny McDonald quite often. Life
in colonial India began to seem more interesting.

At last, Janie's letters began to be more and more cheerful, and
finally one started with "Mommy, I have a best friend here, her
name is Susie. . . ." A great burden fell from my heart. "And I go
roller-skating," the letter continued with childlike enthusiasm. "She
has a pair of roller skates and she lets me use them, but Mommy, it
would be nice if I had a pair of my own, so I wanted to ask you,
when you come to visit us, could you please buy me a pair of roller
skates?"

Mother Superior had been right. Left alone, both girls settled in
faster than I would have believed possible. So with a lighter heart
now, I began to enjoy myself in Lahore. After all the years of
anguish, my life brightened.

One evening when Alex arrived home from work, on horseback as
usual, he proclaimed dramatically as soon as he entered the house,
"You will never believe what happened to me today."

On his trip to work he came across a herd of water buffalo grazing
by the side of the road. Although huge animals, they were peaceful.
Alex had passed that particular herd often, so on that day he barely

noticed them as they munched away at their grass breakfast. A calf, however, decided that Alex's horse looked like its mother and it trotted after him.

Alex did not think this was a healthy behavior on the calf's part, so he spurred his horse into a canter. But the calf stuck to him doggedly. Its mother, grazing some distance off, lifted her massive head to check on her offspring and saw it running off after the flying Alex. She gave a throaty bellow, ordering the baby back. When it paid no attention, she took off after it in a mixture of anger and maternal concern.

Alex was cantering fast, but the baby buffalo was keeping up with ease. The cow, in order to catch up with them, had to break into a gallop. At the sight of this, the rest of the herd became startled and took off after her. The chase was on.

Galloping Alex led the procession, frantically spurring his horse, the calf happily following. Mamma and the rest of her associates thundered behind, racing across the landscape. Alex knew that if they ever caught him and knocked his horse down, he was as good as dead, so he went faster and faster, the miles vanishing in sweat and dust behind, until at last, to his relief, he saw ahead the gates to the plantation, a vision of salvation.

The watchman saw him coming, swung the gate open, and Alex streaked through. The gatekeeper slammed it shut just ahead of the buffalo herd, leaving the bereft calf to the care of its real mother. Alex recounted the story with suitable drama. I was appropriately and genuinely horrified. After all, what if his horse had stumbled and thrown him, or fallen with him?

The heat was increasing and soon the midday temperatures soared to 130 degrees. I could never have imagined such discomfort. Whenever we drove in our old Rover we had to keep the windows tightly closed even though the car was not air-conditioned, because the outside air blowing in burnt us. The house had no air conditioning either, only fans. The chamadar's frequent sluicing of the marble floors put some humidity into the dry desert air, but the heat indoors remained unbearable.

In an effort to cool off a little, I took to riding in the morning to the plantation with Alex and spending the days at the swimming pool. I was thirsty from morning to night, and no matter how much water I drank I never seemed to get enough, so finally I adopted the British habit of drinking warm tea with lemon, which surprisingly turned out to be the best thirst-quencher of all.

As the spring progressed, so did the growth of the malaria-carrying mosquito population. We had to sleep under mosquito nets, which stifled the movement of the air provided by the large, lazy fan overhead. Our bed sheets were as hot to the touch as if they had just been ironed. I found that spraying sheets lightly with water just before lying down provided at least temporary relief.

Even in the bathroom one could not escape the heat. The water tank was on the roof and the shower produced unbearably hot water. The only source of refreshment was water from the well, which was pleasingly cool and provided a relaxing bath.

I returned to Simla in the second half of May, carrying two pairs of roller skates. After the furnace of Lahore, Simla was a paradise. The forests of tall pine trees and the moist, resinous mountain air reminded me so much of Czechoslovakia and our beloved Richky that they opened wounds of memory I had thought were scabbing over.

Both girls had grown, even in that short time. Janie flew into my arms, and both of them started talking nineteen to the dozen, telling me all their adventures. It was as if I had never left them. Mother Superior told me that they had both made good progress in learning English, even though, as she smilingly related, the little one had initially had some problems.

In the dining room Janie had been assigned to a table with five other little girls her own age. The vegetable one day was mashed pumpkin, a delicacy heartily detested by all the children. The school rule was that each child had to eat everything on her plate. Some genius at the table, realizing that Janie without knowledge of English could not defend herself, devised a way of getting rid of her pumpkin. She plopped it onto Janie's plate.

The example was quickly followed by the other four girls and Janie was faced with a huge plate of pumpkin. She ate it valiantly; but the following days brought fresh disasters—endless piles of carrots, cabbage, mountains of beans, all gleefully heaped onto her plate by the giggling children.

Pumpkin day came around again, but Janie had had enough. She took the burdened plate with both hands, stood up, and bravely made her way across the silent refectory to the reading nun who was supervising the children. When she reached her, with a gesture worthy of David Copperfield, she mutely held out her plate to the sister. The nun needed only a glance at the tottering mass of pumpkin to guess what had happened. Retribution and redress followed quickly. Every little girl at Janie's table was given the same quantity of pumpkin and could not leave the table until she ate it all. The incident brought Janie much respect among the other children and many new friends. As her English improved she found that she was happy in school.

I stayed in Simla for two weeks and the girls were allowed to spend the weekends with me at the hotel. We enjoyed our time together immensely. We went for walks, had a lot of silly girl talk that was three quarters laughter, and went to movies and for ice cream. What made me happiest was that they appeared content to return to the school on Sunday nights.

After two wonderful weeks I returned to Lahore. I was happy to see Alex again, but the climate of Punjab, after the balmy air of Simla, was hellish. Then the sandstorms began.

One morning we woke up exhausted and sweating. The light in the bedroom was dim and gloomy when it should have been sharp and bright. The heaviness was not moisture—that would have been a miraculous blessing—but sand, microscopic particles of grit floating in the air and filling our mouths, plugging our ears and nostrils, packing our eyelids, and lacerating our eyeballs. It was not merely uncomfortable but actually painful. The still air, which did not have even a hint of a breeze, was viscous and shimmering dully under its load of abrasive sand. Even with the doors and windows tightly closed, sand soon covered the furniture, floor, dishes, and everything else in the house, as the world turned more and more opaquely dim. It lasted four days. Everyone was irritable and depressed. It went as swiftly as it had come. Then the life-sapping heat continued.

One hot evening Alex returned from work especially tired. As soon as the servants left for their quarters, we went to the bedroom to spend the evening reading.

Before settling in I went to the kitchen, filled two glasses with orange juice, and walked back to the bedroom. Suddenly I heard a

peculiar noise behind me. I turned around and almost fainted. Five
feet away from my bare ankles in the shadow of the doorway was an
enormous cobra, with hood spread, watching me. It was coiled and
poised to strike, the first quarter of its body topped by its evil head
weaving from side to side, hissing fiercely directly at me.

I was terrified and at the same time possessed by the compulsion
to gain some height, to get off the floor. A table stood nearby, and
still clutching two glasses of orange juice I very slowly climbed up
onto it.

With my eyes glued to the vicious snake I whispered wildly to
Alex, "There's a cobra in the room."

Alex did not look up.

"Stop the silly jokes and give me the orange juice, Zdena. I'm
thirsty and tired and I want to go to sleep."

I did not want to excite the intruder. It was clear to me that the
cobra did not like the sound of Alex's voice. Almost choking with
fear, I barely murmured, "No, really, there is a snake in here.
Please don't talk so much. Do something."

"Whoever heard of a cobra coming into the house?" Alex began
good-naturedly. The snake hissed loudly. Alex sat up as if pulled
erect by a divine force. The cobra undulated and swayed with increasing agitation.

"My God," I thought, "where do I jump if it starts to come this
way?" The bed was the only place, but it seemed so far. It was vain
speculation; I was paralyzed with terror.

Alex came to life. Quietly and carefully he slid off the bed on the
side away from the door and went out through the bathroom to the
garden. I watched the cobra intensely, trying not to move but well
prepared to leap onto the bed the moment the snake started wiggling
toward me. Time stopped. Each second seemed to be an eternity. I
was terrified.

Finally Alex returned with the night watchman, who was armed
with a four-yard-long bamboo pole. Carefully the man maneuvered
himself behind the cobra and then, taking a precise aim, struck a
vicious blow. He killed it immediately. Not trusting his luck he
continued to beat the dead snake, mashing its body into a pulp until
I was sickened by the sight of flesh and blood smeared all over the
floor in a large circle.

I climbed down off the table, horrified by the event. Had the cobra struck, death would have arrived in a short time. The nearest doctor was ten miles away.

The door was a double one, exceptionally wide, kept open for better air circulation. Luckily I had chosen to walk on the vacant side of the doorway.

Once again, in my innocence, I had escaped fate. The next day we had guests for dinner and I learned only then how close to doom I had been. Cobras can leap great distances, up to ten feet. The table had not been the safe refuge I had imagined.

"And did you find the other one?" one of the ladies inquired with a gracious smile.

"What other one?"

"Cobras always live in pairs, my dear. There must be another one somewhere in the house," was the cheering reply.

After the guests left, we called in all the servants and all of us hunted snakes until the early morning hours. The other cobra did not materialize. We did, however, find how the first had entered the house. The floors in each room were slightly sloped toward a small drainage hole in the corner, where the water ran out into the garden when the floors were sluiced down. These holes were all protected with screening, but we found one where the screen had been torn off and where undoubtedly the snake had entered the house in search of coolness.

Civil unrest in the country accelerated. The outbreaks of fighting throughout Punjab became more and more violent. Lord Mountbatten settled on August 15 as the day on which India would formally gain its independence. It was also decided that the country would be divided into India and Pakistan, with the two capitals being Karachi in Pakistan and New Delhi in India. In our area the border was to run between Amritsar in India and Lahore in Pakistan, about three miles south of Alex's new factory.

The Hindus and Sikhs were convinced that continued rioting would keep Lahore in India. The Moslems fought back. Every day in the city more fires were set, more fights were started, and more people were killed. All goods were now being sold at far below their value. The merchants tried to get back whatever they could of their initial investments. One by one the stores closed, as did the banks. Factories also shut down. Life in Lahore was slowly coming to a halt.

Alex and I were strangers. We understood the conflict only super-ficially and our thoughts turned to the safety of the two little girls, roller-skating in the Himalayas without any sense of danger. After discussion, we decided I would go to the children. On the first day of July I found myself once more in a taxi winding its way up the mountainside into that enchanting city that seemed completely un-aware of the tearing apart of the subcontinent.

Simla looked as beautiful as ever, and after the Punjab heat I truly enjoyed the refreshing mountain air. I went to see the children nearly every day.

One afternoon when the girls and I were sitting again on a bench in the school quadrangle, unpacking the goodies I had brought them, we heard a loud rattling noise next to us. Jumping up, we saw a large baboon sliding down the drain pipe behind our bench. We backed off nervously to a safe distance and tried to scare him away by shouting and waving our arms, but the baboon unhurriedly settled down on the bench, and opening one food packet after another he calmly ate the fruit I brought, surveying us all the while with a most irritating, superior air. The girls almost had hysterics—all their wonderful tidbits gone! But there was nothing to be done. Finally satisfied, the baboon selected a final apple to munch on the way and calmly strolled off.

When I had been in Simla for two weeks, I received a phone call from Alex suggesting I return home because the situation in Lahore was starting to get dangerous and we would have to close the house. Lahore was the last place I wanted to go, but there was no alterna-tive.

For a change, this time I took the narrow-gauge mountain train from Simla to Kalka, a shattering experience. The track was ex-tremely narrow. The two-car train jerked unsteadily, spiraling down the mountains, winding through deep gorges and valleys, over bridges so insubstantial that I was certain the wheels would slip off the rails altogether and plunge us all to our death thousands of feet below. As the train rails curved downward along switchback after switchback, from my window I had an excellent view of the under-side of the bridges we had just crossed. They were incredibly skimpy.

Lahore had been seized by civil war. Fires were burning everywhere, looted shops gaped open, and litter from collapsed, burnt-out buildings covered the streets. The roads were choked with Hindu refugees migrating south, trying to reach the safety of New Delhi. Many of them were dying of starvation and exhaustion. The collapse of the city was complete. Our servants departed, leaving a sad, echoing house. Alex and I started packing. Our plan was that he would take our possessions to Karachi, and I would return to Simla and the children. The partition of the subcontinent into India and Pakistan on August 15 and expected peace would come soon, and then we would all meet back in Lahore.

Alex took me back to the railway station where we kissed and said a sad good-bye as we had so many times before. I begged him not to wait until the train left. Railway stations were particularly dangerous places. Fighting erupted constantly. He hugged me again and left. I closed the door and sat down.

A moment later some Moslems threw a Molotov cocktail into the next compartment. A passenger grabbed the sputtering bomb and threw it back out onto the platform. It exploded, killing the man who had thrown it, only a few feet away from the spot where Alex had been standing only a few minutes before. I stared at the crumpled, torn body. It could have been Alex lying there. Was this a prelude to worse things?

To my amazement the resort town of Simla was peaceful and quiet. The shops were open and European residents continued their rounds of afternoon teas and dances. When I spoke of the situation in the Punjab, they were amazed. The unrest would never reach Simla, they all agreed. It was so high and so remote in the mountains.

A letter from Alex told me he had successfully moved everything to Karachi. He gave me the address and telephone number of his hotel. It was a relief to know that he was out of Lahore and safe.

Around this time the monsoons arrived in Simla. The torrential downpour produced, seemingly overnight, beautiful blossoms set in fresh greenery. Even more striking were the days, when we floated above the clouds in sunshine while the black, rolling thunderheads formed below us and heavy rains drenched the mountains beneath. It was all a spectacular sight.

The news from the plains was getting worse daily. August 15

arrived. Many ceremonies were held, first in Karachi and then in New Delhi, with Lord Mountbatten symbolically handing over power to the new prime ministers, Mohammed Ali Jinnah in Pakistan and Jawaharlal Nehru in India. India elected Lord Mountbatten to be its first governor general. The maharajahs, independent rulers of the princely states in what had been British India, joined the new nation. All awaited peace.

But the fighting in Lahore and in the Punjab continued. Leaving their possessions behind, people fled toward the country of their respective religion: the Sikhs and Hindus from northern Punjab toward India, the Moslems toward Lahore in Pakistan. It was a terrible double migration. Human beings without number died on the roads from exhaustion, hunger, and thirst. Disease erupted. Cholera, typhoid fever, and plague were everywhere.

In Simla, however, life continued with unshakable normality. Occasionally there was a shortage of fresh produce and meat from the plains and the standard of living was somewhat restricted. But there was no fighting.

25

INDIA ON FIRE

Mail from Alex stopped. The phone operator informed me that all telephone contact between India and Pakistan had ceased. Worry arrived in earnest. The three of us were stranded in Simla, in India. Alex was in Karachi, in Pakistan. Money was running out, and I had no one to turn to. I could not eat and felt ill. I simply did not know what to do alone with two children in a subcontinent that had fallen into anarchy.

I considered taking the girls by train to New Delhi as the first stage of a trip to Karachi while I still had enough money for fare. Jenny McDonald, who came up from Lahore, told me that no air-planes were flying between New Delhi and Karachi. She advised me that it was better to remain in Simla, where at least I knew a few people and where she could help me if necessary, than to be stranded with the girls in New Delhi. I was glad she was in town. It was nice to have there a good friend I could depend on.

The civil war did, however, reach the beautiful Himalayan resort. Fighting broke out one day on the mall and several people were killed. Many shops were set on fire while others were closed imme-diately. Rioting soon spread throughout Simla and more and more people were killed every day. The situation was getting worse by the hour.

My first thought was to run to the school to see if the girls were all right. A telephone call to Mother Superior confirmed that so far everything was quiet. Its location would protect the school, she thought, as it was built on a cliff, surrounded by a high stone wall, with a watchman at the iron gate twenty-four hours a day. She assured me there was nothing to worry about. The girls were safe.

Hard times came to Simla. The town depended on the outside for food, and only one road led to the source below. The supplies ceased coming altogether. Our meals grew smaller and smaller in an effort to make the food last as long as possible. No one felt hungry anyway since we all were far too worried. The main thing was that we had sufficient supplies of tea, which we drank all day long. The fighting in all parts of Simla continued. More people were killed and new fires were reported every day. Chaos ruled the city.

Then one afternoon when I was trying to call the girls, I found that the telephone line to the school had been cut. Fear gripped me and I felt trapped. I simply did not know what I could do. I was sick with anxiety and terribly worried. The menace was great and impersonal. Even my limited options promised nothing but a further entanglement in despair.

Unable to go to my girls, separated from my husband, unsure of my own power to choose any right course, I went up to my room and lay down on my bed, defeated. I was trying to analyze my situation and decide what to do when I heard a noise at the door.

As I turned my head, Alex walked in—Alex, Alex himself, with his clarity, strength, and perpetually young smile. The fact was simplicity itself: I needed him; my heart pain had called him and he had come. "I finally got here," he said, as if apologizing for being late to lunch. All at once I was in his arms, crying and laughing. I was safe again and sure that with Alex beside me everything would work out, that all would end well. Holding him tightly, I realized more clearly than ever during our strange, happy and sad, turbulent life together, exactly what he meant to me. My heart was well again; my body was strong. Through my tears, I stammered, "I thought you were in Karachi."

"I was, yesterday morning. I'll tell you about it later. I've got a taxi waiting outside. We're going to the school to fetch the girls. The taxi will take us down the mountains to Kalka in the morning. We mustn't miss that train. It's the last train for New Delhi. If we miss it, we're finished. There's fighting all over the place, a full-scale civil war, and we have to get to Karachi. But don't worry, we'll make it."

Mother Superior was happy to see us. Most of the children had left already. Only a few girls were still in her care. We thanked her for everything, promised we would bring the girls back when things had settled down again, and left.

When we returned to the hotel with Janie and Evie, Alex told us his story. Although he had not heard from me, he had continued to write and send money, which I never received. He had tried to phone but could not get through. A newspaper account of the fighting in Simla made him decide to come for us. He went to the American Express office, where he was told no planes were flying from Karachi to New Delhi. The border between the two countries was closed. Some trains were still getting through, and that would be his only chance.

Alex then went to his hotel, picked up some luggage, and went straight to the railway station. He was just in time to get on a train going to New Delhi. He had hardly settled down when he was paged by an American Express messenger. A plane was flying from Karachi to New Delhi to evacuate the American Embassy personnel. The aircraft was going empty and they were willing to take Alex along. He raced to the airport and caught the plane. From the air he saw so many fires that it looked as if all of India was burning.

In New Delhi everything seemed to be calm and normal. He took a taxi and caught the overnight train for Kalka. Many Sikhs with their big sabers were also on the station platform and climbed aboard as the train was pulling out. He wondered at this, but it was late in the evening, and he was tired and soon fell asleep.

At some point the train jerked to a stop. Alex looked out the window and saw that they were in the country, about three hundred yards from a midsize village. He looked at his watch. It was four o'clock in the morning. Compartment doors crashed open. Sikhs jumped down from the train and ran into the village. Reaching the first huts, they set them on fire. The poor villagers ran out shrieking and lamenting. The Sikhs opened fire with the guns. Sabers were glistening with blood in the new morning light. The villagers had nothing but stones and farm implements, but they fought back valiantly. Then they started throwing some bombs made of coconut shells, one of which exploded outside Alex's compartment. When the bomb supply was exhausted, the Sikhs started the killing in earnest. They savored their work. Dead bodies piled in mangled heaps like badly stacked cordwood. All the villagers were slaughtered, every one of them. When there was no one left alive, the Sikhs returned to the train, the locomotive huffed into life, and the train continued on to Kalka.

Alex could not believe his eyes. He had seen many grim sights, but never, he said, had he witnessed anything so inhuman, so terrible. The killing was so matter of fact, so mechanical. Leaning out the window, he looked back at the vanishing ruins, seeing for a long time across the empty plain the still silhouette of the dead village, animated only by the devouring flames leaping into the dawn sky. And suddenly he was back in Czechoslovakia remembering the tragic destiny of Lidice.

At Kalka the station master told Alex that if he planned to return to New Delhi, he had to do it on the next day's train, which would be the last one. There was so much fighting and killing along the route, the man said, that the railway officials had decided to discontinue the train service until peace came.

"So you see, it's important we don't miss the train," Alex concluded. I sat still, paralyzed by the picture he had drawn. Those poor people, the children, the women, I thought in anguish. Even after our own experiences during the war, I could not comprehend the brutality of this civil war.

The next morning we were ready very early. When the taxi arrived, we said good-bye to Jenny and to all my friends and left Simla for the last time.

We arrived in Kalka and boarded the train. I noticed that among the many passengers going to New Delhi were several British army officers and that the carriage behind the locomotive was full of Indian soldiers. We thought they were being transferred from Kalka to New Delhi, but we learned later that they were there for our protection.

We had no sooner settled ourselves in our compartment when the train started moving. It must have rained during the night because the countryside was full of mud and puddles of dirty water, and even though it was late afternoon, there was sufficient light left for us to see the tragic results of the fighting. Burnt-out villages and dead bodies flung about in the grotesque attitudes of violent death lined the railroad track. The body of one man in particular caught my attention. He was lying half submerged in a ditch of dirty rain water, his head turned to one side, and his arm, with clenched fist outstretched, reaching up as if in mute protest to heaven, while three vultures circled lazily above him.

Time passed slowly. I was tired but unable to close my eyes because I was incapable of turning away from the sights sliding by the windows. Phrases that I had always thought were clichés came true. I was sick with dread and stunned with fear. Sustained experiences of extreme horror do unexpected things to human consciousness when it is forced to contain more than it can absorb and see more than can be taken in by the mind and eye.

The train was not air-conditioned, and after the cool days of Simla the heat was oppressive. We did not dare open the unscreened windows because of the myriads of disease-spreading flies.

Suddenly, in the middle of nowhere, the train stopped. Alex called out to the conductor to ask what happened.

"We've been advised that the track is mined, Sahib. The locomotive and the soldiers are going on to check it. It is safer that way, Sahib. Just a little delay."

It was more than a little delay. We waited for hours before the locomotive returned and the train started up. Soon it stopped again and the procedure was repeated. This went on throughout the journey. The trip to New Delhi, which was normally an overnight ride, took three days and three nights. No meals were provided, and although we stopped at a few stations, no food was available anywhere and we did not dare drink the water. We grew unbearably thirsty. The only relief was afforded by the juicy apples and oranges thrust into my hands by Jenny together with some bananas and cookies when we were leaving Simla. I was immensely grateful to her. We had no other food for seventy-two hours.

Indian soldiers were everywhere, trying to get the situation under control, but it was too late for so many people. Most of the country we passed through looked like a battlefield, with burnt-out villages and dead bodies everywhere. To make matters worse, it started to rain again and the heat grew oppressively humid.

We sat immobilized in our faded plush seats, prickly with salt and nearing suffocation. The girls were tortured by the hunger and thirst. Little Janie, reliving the traumas of the battle that had engulfed Richky, whimpered by the hour. I held her burning body in my arms, trying to give her some feeling of security.

Ever courageous and bright-spirited, Alex told us about his plans to get us to safety. I can still hear him soothing the three of us, as much with the soft melody of his voice as by what he said. He was sure that New Delhi would be peaceful and that we could reach Bombay quickly and go on to Karachi by ship, although we both knew it would not be that easy. Still, I was comforted and the girls quieted as we drew from his heart the unspoken reassurance that he would stand between us and despair as he had always done.

The heat in the car mounted. The British officers estimated that the temperature was approaching 130 degrees. I gave the girls the last of the hoarded cookies. They gobbled them down, crying at the pain the dry mouthfuls were causing their seared throats. New Delhi seemed to be receding as we drew closer. The thought of the city was nearly hallucinatory: New Delhi, the clean, shining, civilized oasis of coolness, refreshment, and sanity.

Finally, on the third morning we arrived on the outskirts of the capital. The train slowed down entering the station, but at the beginning of the long platform we could already see that a full-scale battle was in progress. However, battle was hardly the word for it. The Moslems, greatly outnumbered and quite defenseless, were being slaughtered in great numbers by the Sikhs. Countless dead bodies were strewn all over the platform. As we stared horrified out of our window, we saw another train pull in at the opposite platform. It was filled with Moslem refugees trying to reach Pakistan.

When the train came to a stop, the Sikhs boarded it and began pulling out the wretched passengers, massacring them on the spot. Men, women, and children, screaming and terrified, tried to save themselves by running back into the train, jumping from carriage to carriage, but the Sikhs pursued them mercilessly, catching them one by one and killing them most barbarously with their long knives.

Unbelieving, I stared at the carnage, and then, sickened and full of useless pity, I turned away. How can any people do this, and do it in the name of their god?

The situation in Delhi was obviously even worse than in other parts of the country, and Alex could not believe it was the same quiet city he had passed through only five days before. It was unlikely that we would be able to catch another train for Bombay.

Debating our course of action, we suddenly remembered the British army officers in the next compartment, and Alex went to ask their advice. They told him they were also traveling to Bombay.

"There's nothing we can do about all this killing," one of them said sadly. "India is an independent country now, and we can't intervene. The best thing would be for us to go and get some information about trains to Bombay."

Two of them went with Alex to see the stationmaster while the third one waited with the girls and me in our compartment. They were gone quite a while and returned with bad news. The fighting was getting much worse, they said. Furthermore, the stationmaster had told them that New Delhi was virtually a city under siege. No trains and no planes were coming in or going out, nor were there any other means of leaving the city. The capital had become one huge battlefield. People were fighting in all parts of town, and as if in confirmation of this, heavy shooting suddenly erupted near us.

We decided to take the advice of the stationmaster and go to the first-class waiting room, which he said was protected by a military guard. He had sent two soldiers back with Alex, and they offered to carry our luggage. With each of us taking one girl by the hand, we started our long trip along the platform to the waiting room.

It was a gruesome, frightening walk. Dead bodies were all around us. We turned a corner and encountered several coolies sitting on the ground, leaning against a row of sacks. All of them were dead. Their throats had been cut, their heads resting in grotesque positions, their emaciated bodies covered by a profusion of blood still flowing from their ghastly wounds.

I tried to get Janie to look the other way, but it was even worse on the other side, where torn and mutilated bodies were piled on top of one another. And so much blood everywhere! It was like a nightmare. Some people were shot, but most were killed by a powerful swing of a kukri and their bodies were ripped open; it was horrible.

Holding Janie tightly by the hand, I was sad to see the same shocked, frozen expression on her face as when we were fleeing

Richky in 1945. I looked at Evie. She was clutching Alex's hand, and her face was deathly pale.

We hurried along the platform, walking as fast as we could. The soldiers with the luggage went ahead of us. Perhaps their uniforms cleared the way because we reached the waiting room safely. It was on the second floor behind a heavy door guarded by four soldiers. Thankful to be safely inside, we settled ourselves in one corner. Alex and one of the officers went to the stationmaster to see if we could get some food.

"There's nothing to eat," they reported, "but he said he will send a couple of servants with some tea."

Soon two bearers appeared with a pot of strong, fragrant tea. I was never to forget how good it tasted. It was our first hot drink in three days.

Gradually more and more people came into the waiting room, Europeans as well as Indians. I particularly remember a maharajah with an entourage of about fifteen wives and numerous children, who, as soon as they were settled in their corner, began ministering to his comfort. They brought him a chair and fluttered around him, bringing him cups of tea, while he lay back on the chair fanning his face with a small, pudgy hand, his family seated on the floor around him, watching him anxiously with adoring eyes.

We were also sitting on the floor. Fortunately, we had our bedrolls with us. No one in India in those days traveled without his bedroll, which consisted of a very thin mattress, pillow, blanket, and sheets all rolled up in a canvas. It was on these that we sat now, drinking our tea and watching the maharajah.

He presided over a large and varied family. The oldest wife appeared to be around fifty, while the youngest was a girl who looked about sixteen, and there were many children. It was fascinating for us to watch this vignette of Indian life, and it helped us to forget our predicament.

Soon the room was packed with refugees. So many people were sheltering in the waiting room that we all sat shoulder to shoulder.

Suddenly loud shooting began, not from the direction of the platforms, but from the pedestrian square in front of the station. Almost at the same time the heavy monsoon started up again, drumming on the roof and splashing loudly on the pavement below. The sky turned a dark, gloomy gray, and everything took on a glum and hopeless appearance, contributing to our feeling of being trapped.

Late in the evening Alex saw a familiar sight, the cap of an American Express messenger. Calling the man, Alex gave him ten rupees and said, "Listen, I need some advice. We have to get to Bombay. Can you tell us how to go about it?"

"Sahib, that's impossible. You can't do anything right now, Sahib. There is heavy fighting in the square in front of the station. If you give me a hundred and fifty rupees, Sahib, I'll come back in the morning with a taxi and take you to the New Maidens Hotel. It's not too far from here, and you'll be safe there, Sahib."

Alex reached into his pocket. I said to him in Czech, with more than a touch of doubt, "Do you really trust him? We'll probably never see him again."

"What else can we do?" Alex said. "It's our only chance." He handed over the hundred and fifty rupees and the man left.

We spent a long, uncomfortable night. I unrolled the beddings for the children, and tired as they were, they fell asleep immediately. I dozed only fitfully, waking from time to time as the shooting grew louder. When I opened my eyes once and saw mice scampering on our bedrolls, I became fully awake and from then on could not sleep at all, trying to keep the rodents away from us.

When daylight came at last, we got ready to leave, but time passed and the American Express man did not return. Seven o'clock came, then eight o'clock, and still nobody showed up, and we began to think I had been right and that we had lost our hundred and fifty rupees. At about nine o'clock, the messenger appeared.

"Good morning, Sahib, Memsahib," he said. "I have a taxi outside, and the situation is a little quieter. We can make it, Sahib."

He had brought another man with him to help with the luggage. We said good bye to the British officers, picked up our gear, and followed him downstairs. The heavy station gates were open, and through the pouring rain I could see a waiting taxi.

The American Express man said, "Let us get the luggage first, Sahib, and then you can come." We stood in the doorway of the railway station and watched the men load our belongings. Just as they put in the last piece the shooting started up again, more fiercely than before. Without a second of hesitation, the two men jumped into the car, and shouting that they would come back later they drove away. With our luggage the taxi had taken away our hope of ever getting out of this horrible place. We had no expectation that it would return.

Standing in the doorway of the railway station in despair, I gazed out across at the square in front of the building. The monsoon rain was flooding the area where there had been so much killing that the ground was saturated with blood. The whole square was transformed into a vast, bloody lake into which new bodies were continually falling as the fighting continued.

To blot out the scene I turned the other way. There, however, lined in neat order up against the wall, were twelve luggage carts piled with bodies, some well dressed, others with only loincloths. All were jumbled together in the uncaring equality of death. Thick, dark puddles spread on the dirty floor beneath.

I was staring at them, half uncomprehending, when I saw a leg move. It belonged to a man well over halfway down the heap. I blinked to clear my vision. The leg moved again. "My God," I thought, "that man's still alive!" And pushing the children into the corridor so that they could not see it, I tried to get someone to help. No one was interested. Amid so much confusion and horror no one cared about the fate of one man. I looked again. The leg did not move anymore.

We stood in that dreadful place for more than two hours. There was nowhere else to go. The fighting quieted down around eleven o'clock, and to my surprise the American Express messenger came running toward us from the far side of the square shouting, "Sahib, you'll have to cross the square on foot. The taxi doesn't want to drive in front of the station. Come quickly, Sahib, he is waiting on the other side of the square."

"Dear God," I prayed, "just don't let them start fighting again while we're out in the open."

But everything remained quiet while we were crossing the bloody lake. The taxi had its engine running. All of us, including the American Express messenger, piled inside and the taxi quickly drove away.

We arrived at a large, ornate gate set in a high brick wall, guarded by two Indian soldiers. They waved us through, and we entered an incredible paradise. Manicured green lawns, colorful flowerbeds, and stately palm trees surrounded a gracious building with deep verandas furnished with tables and comfortable chairs. People in white tropical suits, lovely dresses, and beautifully embroidered saris lounged in the clean, green shade with glasses and tea cups in their hands.

At the front entrance the hotel manager came out to greet us. He already knew our story from the American Express messenger and was full of sympathy. He had reserved rooms for us, and making civilized small talk he escorted us there himself. He suggested that we rest a little and, when we were ready, come down to the dining room for lunch.

"You must be so tired, so hungry," he said with a polite smile. "This is indeed a dreadful time for all of us, a terrible time."

His compassion was generous but unobtrusive; his tact, faultless. The four of us were filthy dirty. We had not even been able to wash our hands for four days. It was heavenly to take a hot bath and put on clean clothes. Soon we were all ready for lunch.

The enormous dining room was magnificent. Its floor was covered with a thick, royal blue carpet. Flowers and greenery were everywhere. Large crystal chandeliers hung from the ceiling, summing up the elegance and luxury of the room. The tables were covered with white, starched linen and impeccably set with silver, fine china, and shining glassware. Waiters, dressed in white uniforms with gold-and-feather-decorated turbans, were standing attentively around the room waiting to serve us.

On a podium at the far end a small orchestra was playing Strauss's *Blue Danube* waltz. The soft, happy music swelled and filled the room. But I still saw the burnt-out villages, those poor people dying in the bloody lake by the railway station, the mutilated bodies piled up in luggage carts dripping blood. When the waiter placed a plate of food in front of me, my throat closed up. I did not bother to pick up my fork. It was useless. I sat and silently wept.

The fighting in New Delhi continued for many days. Only our hotel remained an island of security and peace, but even from the safety of our rooms we could hear continuous sounds of the battle. We heard that three Moslem servants of Lord and Lady Mountbatten were murdered inside Viceroy Palace.

Before long even the hotel was affected by the food shortages. The menus became shorter, the portions smaller. The hotel was crowded not only with refugees but also with newsmen from all over the world. Many children were also there, and the girls soon found playmates to help them forget what they had seen.

The heavy monsoon continued. The air conditioning broke down and windows had to be opened. The night was filled with shooting and screaming.

Every day we hoped that the fighting would stop, but each day brought fresh outbreaks. At the end of our second week at the hotel the shooting gradually diminished. Apparently the Indian army was managing to restore some order at last.

Finally one day we heard of a plane leaving for Karachi and luckily managed to buy tickets.

On the evening before departure Janie came down with a high fever. I was thrown into panic, fearing cholera or typhoid fever. I wanted to call a doctor, but Alex was against it.

"Are you crazy?" he said. "Do you know what they'll do? They'll put her in the hospital, where she's most likely to catch something like that. We'll take her along like this and in Karachi we'll take her to a doctor. But we're leaving tomorrow and that's that."

I knew there might not be another plane for a month, but yet, I did not want to undertake the journey with a sick child. Finally, after a heated argument Alex decided to go and consult with a friend we had met at the hotel. To my amazement he returned shortly with our own doctor from Lahore, whom he encountered on the hotel grounds. We had no idea he was in New Delhi.

The doctor checked Janie over and assured us she did not have cholera or typhoid fever, only a touch of the flu. He gave me a prescription to be filled at the hotel dispensary. He added that we were wise to get out of that plague-ridden atmosphere as soon as possible.

Early the next morning we were at the airport. Our plane was the only aircraft leaving New Delhi, and the airport was crowded with anxious people. Before boarding, we had to pass a checkpoint where soldiers searched our belongings, and I became fully aware for the first time of the partition of India, realizing that we were actually leaving one country for another.

Ahead of us in the line was a shabby man carrying no luggage, only a lunch box. He answered the soldier's query as to its contents by saying, "Nothing, just food. I had no time for breakfast." Unfortunately for him they insisted on opening it, and inside under a few sandwiches they found about four pounds of gold. Taking gold out of India was strictly forbidden, and the man was arrested and taken away.

We walked across the tarmac toward the plane, a battered DC3. As always, I reached for Janie's hand. To my surprise she resolutely grabbed hold of Alex, and in response to my puzzled look she said, "I'm going with Daddy today because he knows better how to fly."

As soon as we boarded the plane, the rain began again, this time accompanied by strong gusty winds, and the trip to Karachi remains in my memory as the most horrifying air journey of my life. The monsoon threw us around the sky like a toy. Time after time we zoomed up hundreds of feet only to fall earthward, buffeted by winds so strong that I was certain the aircraft would break up at any moment. Many of the passengers in the crowded cabin became airsick, adding to everyone's misery. When at last we reached Karachi, the crosswind on the runway was so strong that the pilot had to make several approaches before being able to land. Finally, the plane rolled to a stop.

We staggered out, happy to be on the ground again, thankful we were safely out of the living hell of New Delhi.

──[26]──
GANDHI-JI

As we had been hoping, Karachi was quiet, and our life, on the surface, at least, returned to a semblance of normality. Below the surface, however, the four of us remained agonized by the recent events.

We went straight to the hotel where Alex had been staying. It was a pleasant building in the middle of a large tropical garden located opposite the government house where Mohammed Ali Jinnah, the founder and first prime minister of Pakistan, was in residence.

We were inexpressibly relieved to have reached the temporary safety of Karachi; the massacre in Lahore was still going on and it seemed the killing would continue indefinitely. But our problems were by no means over.

Alex's company, worried that the new factory was only three miles from the India-Pakistan border, decided to suspend operations and further building. They offered Alex a settlement for the termination of his contract. He accepted. There was no other choice. As a result the four of us found ourselves stranded in a foreign country with a moderate amount of ready cash but with Alex unemployed and without a solid prospect for steady income again soon.

Alex and I discussed our next move. Karachi was a dead end, so we decided to try Bombay. Once more we packed our possessions, and in order to avoid violence on land we boarded a coastal steamer.

For some reason, Bombay, a huge Hindu city with a Moslem minority, was at peace. The Moslems were not bothered and went about their daily affairs without hindrance. I could not understand nor could anyone explain to me why Lahore and New Delhi could be convulsed by civil war and Bombay remain calm.

The move proved to be the right choice. Within two weeks Alex got a well-paying position in research at a large chemical company and we were able to leave our hotel rooms. We took a modest apartment close to our friends, the Vaneks, and hired some servants.

I found a school for the girls, the Loretto Convent, like the one in Simla. Evie and Janie commuted daily on a school bus. When Janie's classes finished early I would walk across the park to meet her and walk back with her, hand in hand. The regularity of these days under the blazing, blue Indian sky contributed much to a growing sense of peace that was slowly cleaning away the fear and anguish left over from our encounter with horror and death. Yet, the dread was never fully dissolved, for we knew that death might return for us at any time.

One day Alex came home from work perturbed. Close to his laboratory was a refugee camp overflowing with singularly miserable Hindus who had escaped the fighting in Punjab and other parts of India. The camp was full beyond capacity and every day more and more people drifted in to add the weight of their suffering to an already overcrowded situation. The conditions were deteriorating as the population increased.

This particular day Alex had noticed a large black flag fluttering overhead. He asked what it meant and was told it signified an outbreak in the camp of the Black Death, or bubonic plague. Daily the deaths multiplied, and the situation rocketed out of control. Such a plague is usually a fatal disease, one which progresses with such rapidity that a victim begins to feel ill in the morning and after a day of horrible torture is dead that evening. It was the same disease that had wiped out half the population of Europe in the fourteenth century. It was spreading rapidly in the suburbs of Bombay.

Alex went to a doctor in search of immunization only to be told that no inoculation was available and that prevention was the only protection. The plague was transmitted by fleas, plentiful in that part of Bombay. The doctor advised him to dust his feet and legs heavily with DDT powder, the advice being based on a theory that any flea that might jump on him would die before it had a chance to bite him.

I was horrified. Even the thought that he might catch this cruel disease filled me with panic. It would be a total catastrophe for all of us. I wanted Alex to quit his job. To me it seemed the only sensible thing to do, but Alex argued that although we had some money, it was not much and he had to work.

He continued going to the lab dusted diligently with DDT powder, applied so heavily that he looked as if he had stepped out of a flour barrel. I was living under extreme tension, not knowing what was happening to him during the day, just hoping that in the evening he would return to us in good health. Those were terrible days, terrible weeks.

Fortunately DDT was effective and Alex remained well. In time the authorities closed the refugee camp and moved the inmates out of the city into less-populated areas. The black flags disappeared from the suburbs of Bombay.

Soon it was Christmas. We bought a small artificial tree, decorated it beautifully, and put a few gifts underneath it. It was our first Christmas in the tropics. I missed the snow, the cool fresh air, the fire cracking in the fireplace. I felt quite homesick.

The girls, however, were full of high spirits, joy, and laughter, especially Evie. How little they needed in order to be happy. They received their modest presents with great enthusiasm, and afterward, with shining eyes and smiling faces, they started singing Czech and English carols. Soon they made me forget my nostalgic mood. I realized how lucky we were to be all together, to be healthy, and to be able to enjoy one another's company. In spite of everything we had a beautiful Christmas.

The local British swimming-pool club became more and more the social center of our lives. It was called Breach Candy, and its main feature was an immense pool created by walling off a natural cove in the Arabian Sea. The wall was high enough to keep out unwelcome visitors, like sharks, but low enough to allow the breakers rolling from the ocean to spill over its top. The result was a continuous exchange of water and consequently a natural, sparkling cleanliness.

The land side of the pool was an immaculately kept garden with an emerald green lawn and rank on rank of palm trees as stately and sinuous as traditional Indian dancers. Between them were numerous chaise longues and many tables with large shady umbrellas and comfortable chairs.

There was an excellent restaurant where the specialty for afternoon tea consisted of delicious club sandwiches, served in the garden by Indian bearers impeccably dressed in white uniforms with richly ornamented white turbans. Especially after we had had a long swim, the sandwiches were delicious: bread toasted to a rich, golden color, tasty tomatoes, and fresh, crisp bacon. Breach Candy always offered a feeling of elegance, luxury, coolness, and comfort. We spent every weekend there and all school vacations and holidays.

When Alex had a free day he came with us. Otherwise we usually went with our neighbor, Margaret Porter, who soon became a very good friend. She and her husband were British. They did not have any children, and before long Margaret grew quite attached to our two girls and spent a lot of time with us. She also taught Janie how to swim. As Evie already was a good swimmer, often all four of us ventured across the huge pool. When little Janie got tired, Margaret put her on her back and carried her to the shore.

I renewed my friendship with Helen, the Czech woman with an Indian husband we had met on the *Britannic*. The two of us had maintained a correspondence and I had written to her that we were in Bombay. When she came to visit us I hardly recognized her. She was not the cheerful, laughing young bride I remembered, looking forward to a reunion with her handsome young bridegroom. Her luxuriant blond hair had turned nearly completely white. She looked haggard and ten years older and was desperately unhappy.

She said that the British had ostracized her because she had married an Indian, even though he was a Brahmin, while the Indians, including her husband's family, shunned them both because he had married a white woman. They refused to see her good qualities, her sweet personality, excellent education, and great intelligence, and focused their attention only on her fair skin.

She was without friends in Bombay, immobilized in a net of silent racial hostility. Her husband, absorbed in his work, was content enough, but Helen was trembling on the edge of a nervous breakdown, not knowing what to do. She still loved him and did not want to leave him. Yet her pain was all but intolerable, forcing her to the sad realization that her British friends had been right: moving to India had been a mistake.

Helen was ecstatic that we had settled in Bombay. She often came to visit us and we grew even closer than we had been on the ship. Sometimes she came with her husband to have dinner with us and we became quite fond of him. Alex found he was an excellent chemist with an open mind, aware of all new developments.

When we went to visit them, I could see where Helen had made a mistake. They lived in a completely Indian section of Bombay. She could not make any British friends because no British or other Europeans were living there. I advised her to move into a European neighborhood, but she thought that was impossible. Her husband was a great patriot and wanted to stay only in an Indian part of the city. It was a very difficult situation for Helen. Our family rapidly became a haven for her, a moment of parole from her imprisonment in racial jealousies.

Alex, the girls, and I developed a strong attachment to the movies. Cinemas and restaurants were the only air-conditioned buildings in Bombay. It was like heaven to be able to sink into blessed coolness for a few hours after a day of searing, humid heat.

On one occasion the four of us went to see Gary Cooper. The movie was exciting, a rough-and-tumble classic western, and we had become absorbed in the action. A burst of shooting erupted on the screen as the hero pursued the villains. Like a blow, a high, sobbing scream, not from the screen but from beside me, shocked me out of the innocent fantasy into stark reality. It was Janie.

Scream followed scream and then she began to shout, "Don't let them fight! Stop them from fighting! I don't want them to fight!"

Her voice had the same hysterical tone as years before during the battle at Richky. Her screams instantly transformed me back to 1945 and suddenly I was holding my baby daughter again, kneeling beside the body of our dead horse, and seeing over the top of her head the walls of my home crumble while I was promising her that nothing would hurt her, nothing. And here we were again, reliving the same suffering, the same uprooting, the same sense of being lost amid the world's turmoil. We gathered up the child, now choking on her sobs, and left the theater.

We grew used to our new life in Bombay. We made many British, Czech, and Indian friends. The most interesting of them was Jan Meyer, a Czech who lived in the apartment building opposite us. He was Jewish. He and his sister had managed to escape from Czechoslovakia just before the Nazi invasion. Their parents, who were wealthy textile industrialists, kept postponing their departure until it was too late and had perished in a concentration camp.

The sister had married and moved to Venezuela, but Jan settled in Bombay, where he lived a life of gentlemanly idleness. Whenever people asked him his profession, he said with a charming, self-deprecating smile that he was a millionaire in retirement. He had a wonderful, outgoing personality, and a grand talent for telling jokes.

Jan had many friends. He was a character out of the typical novel about Europeans in the Orient. He had no profession, did no work, had no visible means of support, yet he belonged to the cream of both Indian and British societies. He was on the best of terms with scores of maharajahs and was invited to their sumptuous parties where he played poker till dawn. Since he was an excellent player he frequently won. One day Alex and I realized, in a flash of mutual enlightenment, that it was poker that supported him.

He had a devoted servant, a young Indian man who performed the duties of cook, houseboy, valet, and butler. Far more important, he periodically rescued Jan from financial disaster when the cards were bad and lady luck smiled on someone else. At those times the servant would provide money for them both, buying food to cook and serve to his master, never losing his faith in him, never doubting that their luck would turn.

And sure enough Jan would rally his forces. Refreshed and rested after a vacation from the game, he would venture out once more to some palace festivity, where he would win significant amounts of money. As the sky turned rosy with the fingers of dawn, the charming gambler would return home to reimburse his faithful servant. The good times were back once again.

Jan was about Alex's age, and the three of us soon became fast friends. In his normal, excellent spirits he would arrive at our apartment in the late afternoons just as Alex returned from work. We would offer him a cocktail, then another, and the three of us would spend the early evening in entertaining and amusing conversation, laughing at the jokes Jan could tell so brilliantly. His friendship was a boon during those days.

In January, Karel Vanek, who lived nearby, was invited to join a tiger hunt in Jaipur. He departed for the north with great expectations and a veritable explosion of excitement. When he returned a week later he invited us over to his apartment to hear about the adventure.

"I didn't shoot a tiger; no use asking to see a trophy head," he said the moment we had been seated. "But I didn't come home empty-handed either." And he rose and went to the door, beckoning us to join him. Mystified, we followed Karel to a guest bedroom. In the far corner of the room was a large basket, inside of which were two tiger cubs.

"We came across them in the jungle," our friend explained. "I think their mother had been killed. They were hungry and crying, so I thought I should take them home to show the children. When they get bigger, I'll give them to the zoo. They'd have died if I'd left them in the jungle."

He bent over and picked up one of the cubs. With its tiny, sleepy eyes and a little pink mouth, it looked embarrassingly like a stuffed toy. Karel thrust the warm, little body into my hands. I took it, marveling at its perfection and awed that I was actually holding a real tiger in my arms. Its fur was soft and the little, slanty eyes peered up at me with such trust that I could not believe this was a killer, the universally feared epitome of terror. The two of them looked like a pair of exotic, outsized kittens. The sight of my daughters sitting on the living-room carpet with two tigers was indeed endearing.

The Vaneks kept the cubs for three weeks. At first the cubs were good natured and gentle, but they grew fast and their instincts began to manifest themselves. Before long their play became rougher. When one of them scratched one of the Vaneks' children, Karel's wife announced they had to go. Karel telephoned to ask for my help in taking the tigers to the zoo.

On the appointed morning we put the tigers on leashes and carried them into the car. They did not seem to mind at first, but when the car started to move they grew restless. The idea of a trip across Bombay with two adolescent tigers suddenly presented something of a challenge. I sensed that they felt trapped in the enclosed vehicle. I wound down the window. Delighted, they stuck their heads out into the breeze, which they seemed to enjoy. I kept their leashes tight. The effect was a comic triumph.

Traffic came to a halt as we drove along, and especially when the car paused at intersections. Drivers, passengers, and people on the sidewalk stopped, pointed, and stared with fascination at our two tiger cubs complacently leaning out of a car window, surveying Bombay traffic as calmly as if they were examining a section of their home jungle.

Their interest in the big world outside kept them sufficiently distracted for us to reach the zoo without incident. They were gratefully received, fussed over, and installed in their new home.

One afternoon at the end of January I took the children after school to a tailor to be fitted for new school uniforms. The tailors in India were a marvel. They were extremely skillful and could cut out and sew together a suit or an evening gown in the shortest possible time. Garments they made fitted perfectly and were made with meticulous attention to detail; every seam was bound, every buttonhole was flawless. Their perseverance awed me. They worked for hour after hour sitting cross-legged on the floor, with the sewing machine in front of them, never pausing, never resting, always courteous.

The three of us were getting ready to leave that day when the shop door burst open and an Indian staggered in, face contorted with pain, and crying as if he had suffered a physical blow.

"Gandhi-Ji is dead!" he gasped. "Gandhi-Ji died! Gandhi-Ji was shot! Gandhi-Ji is dead!"

The quiet shop erupted. The tailors rushed up to ask for details, but the man was capable only of a dull, stunned repetition of the bare facts: "Gandhi-Ji is dead! Gandhi-Ji died! Gandhi-Ji was shot! Gandhi-Ji is dead!"

The murmur of questions transformed itself into wailing, a semiconscious keening of a heart-wrenching intensity as the dreadful news spread throughout Bombay. The same wailing flooded the streets. It was as if the populace as one person was weeping over their own parents' death.

No one knew in those first terrible moments who had killed Gandhi. The fear that it was a Moslem froze my heart. If so, a religious war would surely erupt in Bombay that would make all previous killings seem minor. However, it became known quickly that the murderer had been a Hindu, a young male member of the conservative sect opposing the changes Gandhi had made in the country. The day was January 30, 1948.

This great tragedy had a disquieting effect on Alex and me. We had hardly settled down to a normal life after the horrors of our trip from Simla when we were facing a possibility of a new upheaval. On the surface everything seemed calm enough in Bombay, but walking in the streets or going to the market gave me feeling that, deep inside, all those masses were gravely disturbed. It was like sitting on a volcano—would it erupt? No one knew.

Their spiritual leader was dead; they did not know what to expect. Jawaharlal Nehru, trying hard to fill the void, made many speeches to the nation, and finally succeeded. The populace calmed down and all India entered a period of mourning. From the lowest Untouchable to the richest merchant, everyone was subdued and sad. The nation's soul had died.

I remember particularly a film made in India shortly after the murder. I believe it was entitled *The Life of Gandhi*. Gandhi was portrayed not by an actor, but symbolically by the flame of a candle moving on the screen. At the end, the flame went out and one felt the loss of the good and "great little saint" more fully than any realistic treatment would have allowed. It was a very touching movie.

During this extended period of national grief in India we received the saddest possible news from Prague near the end of February. In Czechoslovakia the general election had been scheduled for the spring and the Communist party was expected to lose. Unwilling to surrender power, it organized a coup d'état before the people could speak. Factory workers from all over the country were bused to the capital and a mass demonstration was staged with many pro-Communist speeches. This provoked many counter-demonstrations by students and Czech patriots, who marched through Prague carrying Czechoslovak flags. When I heard of it I was vividly reminded of the events of 1939.

These protests were spontaneous and unorganized. They were too little too late. Some marchers were arrested and some shots were fired. The government proclaimed what amounted to martial law and the election was canceled. A new cabinet was nominated. Half the members were Communists, the others renegades from old democratic parties, and it also included Jan Masaryk.

The entire Czech community around us, including Alex and I, were shocked. Why did Masaryk, of all men, the patriot and son of Czechoslovakia's founder, stay in the new Gottwald cabinet? What sinister force impelled him to accept this degrading position?

On March 10, 1948, Jan Masaryk was found dead in the yard of the Czernin Palace in Prague, where he lived. Communists proclaimed the death a suicide, maintaining that he jumped out of a second-floor window. No one who knew Masaryk believed this story for an instant. He was a sophisticated, fastidious person who would never have chosen such a gruesome and crude way to end his life. Czechs knew that he had been murdered.

How much grief can the human heart hold? Jan Masaryk was the last link to our republic, that great experiment in democracy, the final link to the times when our nation had been happy and prosperous, when liberty had seemed natural and courtesy the only way of conducting government business, and when human rights guaranteed by our constitution had been preserved by action. Maybe that was why he had to die. He still represented all of those fine, sound, and honest qualities to Czech people. He had to be removed before the regime of lesser men could begin.

The deaths of Jan Masaryk and Mahatma Gandhi merged in our hearts, two good men assassinated because they stood for peace and good will, martyrs for truth and freedom. Sadly, Alex and I began to realize that returning to our homeland was becoming more and more unlikely, and that cruel, senseless forces beyond our control and far away were transforming us and our children into landless, homeless wanderers. Before, we had always been bonded to our heritage, bonded with filaments of love no less strong for being invisible. Before, we had a place, a time, a people. With the death of Masaryk and the Communist annihilation of the republic, all this was suddenly no longer present but past, a ray of hope remembered, a well gone dry, a star extinguished. We were alone, all we Czechs everywhere were alone, forsaken, abandoned.

When departing for India, Alex and I had left at Richky many valuable paintings by several noted Czech artists, as well as portraits of myself and the children and a library full of books. We wrote to ask Alex's mother to collect them and take them to her apartment in Brno. She did not answer immediately, but before we could write again we received a letter from her saying that she had been too late.

She had gone out to Richky but found our friendly old door, which had always been open to happiness, locked up and sealed like a tomb. There was something strange about the familiar place. She looked around and suddenly realized that our chestnut tree, whose welcoming presence always greeted us when we were returning home, was not there anymore. It had been cut down; it was destroyed, as was our freedom, as was the way of life we loved so much. Grandma was heartbroken. Tears came into her eyes when she remembered how many times we enjoyed having afternoon tea in the shade of this friendly giant, how the children played underneath its protecting, voluminous crown. Who did this? Why?

On inquiry she was informed that the land, the house, and everything in it were now the property of the state. Richky had been nationalized without any compensation. She was not even allowed to pick up our pictures and the few personal things we had left behind. Everything belonged to the state. My portrait, the children's portraits, the books, and the furniture Alex acquired with such love while I was so ill in the hospital, everything belonged to the state. Even the old chestnut tree. They did not like it, so they destroyed it.

"I was so upset about it," wrote Grandma, "that I took to going out and sitting down on top of the hill, just to be able to look down at the place and think about you and the times we all were there together. They found out about it, and I received a letter telling me that I had no right to go there anymore, that I was trespassing."

Reading these sentences, seeing dear old Grandma slowly descending the hill, only to be expelled, broke our hearts. I thought of Richky, of happy times we had spent there and of the many tribulations that our farm had helped us defeat. Our home was taken from us. Our pain was real. And the question came: "Why?" We had not done anything wrong. Alex had worked hard to build Richky and we loved the beautiful valley so much. It was our rightful property. We lost not only our pictures and books, we lost our home. Nothing was left but memories. They had taken from us not only a house, a mill, farm, furnishings and the like, they had taken from us the songs of brooks and birds, the smell of pine trees. They had taken away no small part of ourselves.

———☐———

Several weeks passed. With the approaching summer the heat and the humidity increased. To cool off a little the girls and I often took a stroll on Marine Drive, a promenade built along the water's edge where there was always a refreshing sea breeze. On one of our walks Evie suddenly said that she did not feel well. She dragged along listlessly and complained that she was cold. The temperature was around ninety degrees. I felt her forehead. To my alarm it was burning hot, and I rushed her home.

The doctor diagnosed it as malaria. Evie was *very* ill. One minute she burned with fever and the next she shivered so violently that the bed shook. She developed wracking headaches, was nauseous, and vomited constantly.

"Mommy," she would whisper, "my head hurts dreadfully. Please give me something to make it stop. The pain's behind my eyes. I can't move my eyes. Help me."

I could only stand by, useless.

The doctor came to see her every day. After two weeks of continuous torture, she began to feel better. The chills and fever abated and her strength gradually returned, although she was too weak to go to school for another three weeks.

Then it was I who developed a shivering spell. Once again the temperature was in the nineties. I put on a sweater but I was still cold. I also had malaria. It took me three weeks to get over the worst of it, but even then I felt limp for a long time. I was faint continually, and the fear of collapsing on the streets of Bombay kept me indoors for weeks.

As the spring months passed, the heat increased and one longed for the monsoons. One Saturday Alex was invited on a consulting visit to a factory belonging to a rich Parsee. It was on a peninsula across the bay from Bombay, and while it was possible to reach it by road, most people took the ferry.

Alex and his Parsee friend chose the ferry. Not long after their departure a fierce wind began to blow, its velocity accelerating by the minute. Worried, I turned on the radio and heard a voice announce that a cyclone was approaching Bombay, that many boats in the harbor had capsized, and the ships in port had already left for open waters to ride out the storm.

I rushed to the window and saw that the cyclone had already reached us. Objects of all kinds were propelled through the air as if fired from guns, and even as I watched, the windows of the apartment building across the street crashed open. Pillows followed by a bedspread and a small mattress came flying out, sucked into the yellow-gray sky by the air pressure.

I wondered anxiously about Alex. Was he returning on the ferry, or had his host decided to drive? How safe would it be in the car? I peered out of our third-story window into the rain and gathering darkness. A huge piece of galvanized iron roofing came sailing down the street. The force of the wind was unbelievable. The roofing was followed by uprooted trees bowling along with the soil still clinging to their roots. Full-grown trees bounced about like toys. Chairs, tables, bedding, a baby's crib, chunks of wood, and a cascade of unidentifiable junk, the general flotsam of a big city, were all flying through the air. Luckily our apartment was in the lee of the wind. The windows and doors held firm. Our belongings were safe.

Alex returned home in the early evening. When the wind began to rise, he and his friend immediately took a company car and drove back around the bay. It would have been impossible to cross by ferry. They barely made it back to the city.

The storm blasted the city for three days and nights and did extensive damage. Thousands of dwellings were torn apart; cars and buses were overturned. Hundreds of people were killed. Many fishermen out on the bay were drowned. We heard that the perpetual howling of the wind had so depressed one man that he committed suicide by jumping from a window of the building opposite us. The wind was reported to have reached a velocity of 150 miles per hour.

When it stopped, we returned to a different world. Streets were full of rubbish, the windows on many houses were broken, and some roofs were stripped away. In our neighborhood park the gnarled, old shade trees were lying on the ground, their passing marked only by gaping craters in the torn earth.

It reminded me of war. I realized clearly the enormous force that nature itself can unleash on us humans, so puny and insignificant. Even a sense of the trustworthiness of physical things themselves had been stripped from us. Nothing and no one is finally safe. We felt very exposed.

At last the long-awaited monsoons arrived. Tempers improved in spite of the increased humidity. The filthy streets of the city were washed clean as if by magic, and Bombay took on a fresher, newer look. I spent hours at the window watching multitudes of poor coolies, clad only in white cotton loincloths, who, walking majestically in the rain, sheltered under the large, black umbrellas of the sort traditionally carried by London businessmen. I discovered later that an umbrella was a symbol of status, as much for the native Indian as for the Britisher.

Summer vacation from school was during July and August, the monsoon months in Bombay. The girls and I spent most of our days at Breach Candy. It was an odd sensation, swimming in the rain. The water in the pool and the water from the skies were the same temperature, and in the heat of the high summer this was most refreshing.

I worried about Alex. He was not looking healthy and had lost weight. One day on a visit to the Vaneks, he interrupted the conversation with, "I don't feel too well. I'm going home to lie down."

Alarmed by the bluntness of the statement I rose from my seat to go with him, but he gestured me back.

"You stay here," he added. "The children are having a good time. I'll be all right."

When we returned home I was shocked by the sick man I found. Alex was in bed, deathly pale. His skin was cold to the touch, yet he was perspiring heavily. He had a pain in his chest. Panicked by the idea of a heart attack, I called our doctor.

The problem was kidney sand. Alex's condition was substantially worsened by the fact that he did not drink enough water. In India all water had to be boiled before drinking. Alex took a thermos flask with him to work every day, but apparently it was not enough. He recovered after several days of torture and was able to return to his job, but he did not feel completely himself for several weeks.

This was the last straw. After a long conversation we decided we had to leave India in search of some place, some community, where we would be free not just of physical illness but of the distress of constantly recurring violence. We needed a home. India was not it.

The reality of our situation broke in on us with numbing force. Czechoslovakia was under Communist rule, and our house at Richky was gone. The simple fact was that we had nowhere to go. We were homeless. Though with some financial resources, our situation was essentially no different than that of millions of refugees, uprooted like cyclone-destroyed trees by the storm of world war.

There was one obvious possibility, a possibility that is never completely out of the minds of tired people forced to wander homeless through foreign lands. Alex went to the United States Consulate and asked for immigration visas. The officials informed him that unfortunately it would take two years for them to be issued. The many homeless Czechs in refugee camps in West Germany and Austria had precedence.

Alex came home limp with dejection. To stay in India for another two years seemed to him utterly impossible. I agreed. He looked almost as washed out as when he returned from the German prison. The problem was where to go.

We had a friend, a Major Kalvoda, who, as an officer in the British army, had lived for some years in Ethiopia. He was most enthusiastic about that country, spinning long tales of its beauty. Emperor Haile Selassie had returned after the war and had great plans for the modernization of his state. Major Kalvoda said that many opportunities were there for technical people. In time, Alex became sanguine about prospects in Ethiopia and asked the major how he should go about getting more information.

"Write to the emperor," Kalvoda advised. "He knows me personally and I'm certain that you won't have any trouble getting visas."

We wrote a carefully worded letter detailing Alex's skills and accomplishments and addressed it to the emperor. To our amazement a reply was received by return mail and was signed by Emperor Haile Selassie himself, advising us to go to Djibuti where we could get our visas. Ethiopia, he added, drastically needed specialists. We would be most welcome.

Alex was overjoyed at the idea of a great new adventure. I was not. I was against the whole thing. We argued heatedly. I pointed out that he had no job there, not even an offer, no friends or even acquaintances. Central Africa to me seemed more dangerous and more inhospitable than India. Evie was entering her teens and Janie was eight years old. Both needed a good education and a stable environment. I felt Ethiopia was not the country for us. Alex presented counter arguments.

The debate went on for some time, but before we could reach a mutually satisfying decision, Alex met Mr. Gould, an Australian who owned a plastics factory in Sydney. He knew of Alex's reputation and when he heard that Alex wanted to leave India, he offered him a job.

Though certainly better than the exotic reaches of Africa, I was not particularly attracted by Australia either. I would have much preferred the United States. I think I knew in my heart that America was the new, true home we longed for. On my own initiative I went to the American consulate and all but pleaded that the visas be issued earlier because of my husband's health. The official, who was kind but firm, assured me that he would do his best, but no one could promise for sure a period shorter than two years. Knowing that we could not remain in India much longer and that I had to get Alex away, I gave in. It was to be Australia.

After the decision was made, the search for passage to Australia began. It proved to be difficult. Few ships sailed to Sydney via Bombay in 1949. Our old friends, the American Express Company, promised to inform us immediately if they found suitable berths.

A week later, when I returned with the children from Breach Candy, Alex greeted us with: "I have a surprise for you. We are leaving this Saturday for Calcutta."

A Norwegian freighter, the *Hoegh Silvermoon*, was leaving Calcutta for Sydney. Although it was a cargo vessel, it had about fourteen first-class passenger cabins, and by luck two cabins were available. Alex's face was more animated than it had been for some time. An invisible tremor of relief shot through me.

On the practical level, I was aghast: three days, a mere seventy-two hours, to pack up everything and make all necessary arrangements. But the opportunity could not be lost. Who knew when the next ship for Australia might come through? I did not want to disappoint Alex's reborn enthusiasm and threw myself into action. Furiously we packed and prepared to leave. People rushed in to say good-bye. It was all done, but I never remembered how.

The train left Bombay Saturday evening. A great many friends came to see us off. The trip was long, taking us all the way across this vast subcontinent. I had much time to sit, watch India pass my window, and think about our situation.

The years in India had hardly been good. Fear, anxiety, and illness had left us only occasionally. We had seen terrible and savage cruelties during the brutal civil war. Evie and I had had malaria; Janie had been traumatized by the violence around her. Alex had those awful kidney troubles. We had lived in constant uncertainty. But in spite of all this, as the train clattered its way toward Calcutta, I was transfixed by a genuine sorrow that I was leaving this country, this magical and fascinating land. I realized that there was something, a spirit, a mystery in the heart of India, persistent in the midst of worry and difficulties and transcending danger. Something in the atmosphere let me relax, blessed me with inner peace, and awakened me with renewed hope in any difficult situation.

I was sorry that we were leaving. If circumstances had been different, I could have become like the British people we met who, having lived in India for many years, discovered that they did not have the desire to leave this strange, captivating land and go back to England. What drew me and made our departure wrenching? I did not know, unless it was, perhaps, life itself, so abundant, so fertile, so sustaining in the midst of so much agony.

After a tiring three-day journey we arrived in Calcutta. It was a large city, not as elegant as Bombay, with much more poverty. By chance Alex had an acquaintance there, a prewar friend who had escaped from Czechoslovakia before the Nazis took over and who was now manager of one of the best hotels. It was at this hotel that we had made reservations. The expense was more than we would have liked, but we expected to stay only three days there.

The first night the girls and I went up to our rooms early. Alex remained downstairs in the lobby, chatting with his friend and exchanging news of mutual acquaintances. They sat together, lost in conversation until the lobby emptied and they were alone. Suddenly Alex realized that a small animal the size of a cat had scurried by. He blinked and saw another.

"What is this?" he said to his friend. "Why have you got so many cats around here?"

His friend smiled wistfully and said, "They're not cats; they're rats."

"Rats?" Alex exclaimed, jumping up. "In such a fashionable hotel? Rats? How can you put up with it? That's disgusting."

His friend shrugged. "India . . . ," he said philosophically. He went on to explain that when he had first taken the position as manager of the hotel he had every intention of eradicating the rats once and for all. However, he was told that the Hindu religion forbids the killing of anything, including rats. No one on his staff was willing to supervise the extermination. He had to resort to catching them in cages and dumping them outside the city limits.

"But," he continued sadly, "the rats beat us home, so I gave up."

When Alex told me about it I sat up in bed as if pulled by a hook. I was sure I would not sleep a moment all night, but search as I did, I found no trace of rats in our rooms. I concluded, thankfully, that the beasts preferred staying near the kitchens and did not venture as far as the fifth floor. I did sleep a little.

The next day we went to the American Express office to find out when we could board our ship. The agent informed us that the *Hoegh Silvermoon* had been delayed by a typhoon in the Pacific and would be two weeks late.

"And this after all that unholy rush in Bombay," I thought resentfully.

I expressed myself not overly gently to Alex on the subject.

"And what's more," I added, "now we have to pay this expensive hotel with its rats for all that extra time. Think what it's going to cost us."

Ten days later, the ship came into port. Alex went down to the dock to look it over. It was not a large vessel, only ten thousand tons. Would it be safe if it ran into a storm like the one the *Britannic* encountered on our trip from England to Bombay?

Alex wanted to see the freighter before committing the welfare of his family to it. The Calcutta harbor is on the Hooghly River. Ships anchor in midstream and passengers have to be ferried out to the moorings. Alex took a taxi-boat to the *Silvermoon*. The gangway was down and he climbed on board.

The ship, while clean and neat, was deserted. After wandering around for a few minutes Alex came face-to-face with a man in uniform. He was tall and impressive, with blond hair and piercing blue eyes. His sleeves and epaulets were festooned with gold braid. It was obviously the captain.

His English was not good, but he was most affable and offered to show Alex around the ship. He also took him to our prospective cabins, which were most satisfactory and quite large, each with its own bathroom. Alex was impressed. He thanked the captain and prepared to leave when he remembered our everlasting argument about the route to Australia.

"Oh, yes, one more thing," he said. "Could you tell me which route we are going to take, Captain? Will it be the northern route or the southern?"

The Norwegian was perplexed. He looked at Alex uncertainly and saying, "Follow me, please," led him to the chart room, where a map of the Pacific was hanging on the wall.

Alex pointed to the map and explained his question. "What I want to know is, will we be going past Burma and Thailand, then Singapore and Indonesia to Sydney, or will we go directly south from Calcutta around the bottom of Australia?" We had been hoping for the former and the possibility of visiting all those exotic ports of call.

The Norwegian looked at the map closely. "Which do you think would be shorter?" he asked. "I have never been to Australia."

Alex looked at him startled. He's asking me? he thought. The ship is small, has a large ocean to cross, and he is asking me which way to go? He smiled wanly at the man and left.

When he arrived home and told me about the encounter, I was uneasy. The trip with an inexperienced captain would be dangerous. Should we cancel the reservation? We had spent nearly all our money on the passage. Alex had given up his job in India.

Neither of us slept that night. Eventually we realized no other course lay open to us. We had to go—and hope for the best.

The next morning we boarded the *Hoegh Silvermoon*.

27
DOWN UNDER

The *Silvermoon* was a fine, well-built ship. Each of our two spacious cabins had two sofa beds, soft armchairs, and lovely furniture. Our stewards were Indians. The arrangements were more than adequate. The only problem was the captain.

A card in our cabin informed us we had been invited to eat at the captain's table for the duration of the voyage. This was a great honor. The comparatively small dining room was handsome. Our table was set for six people. At the appointed hour the four of us arrived and a few minutes later the captain came with his wife. She was celebrating their twenty-fifth wedding anniversary by spending the whole year with him on his ship.

I was immediately impressed by the captain. He was a tall, strong, blond, and blue-eyed Norwegian, his complexion tanned by many years of exposure to the sun and winds. He seemed self-confident. I wondered about Alex's reaction. How could he have mistrusted such a Viking?

I glanced at my husband and caught enormous surprise on his face. Then Alex told his story and the truth came to light. On his visit to the ship the day before, he had not, in fact, met the captain but rather the head steward, who had been a maître d' in a renowned Oslo restaurant before joining the ship. This was his maiden voyage. We learned later he hated it and was homesick.

Genuine laughter buzzed around the table at Alex's confusion of the steward's gold braid decorations with the far more significant stripes of the master of the *Silvermoon*. The captain and his wife were charming, interesting, and hospitable people and we all became good friends. To our chagrin the ship sailed south without putting in at the exotic ports of Thailand, Malaysia, or Indonesia, and also missing the Great Barrier Reef.

We left Calcutta a couple of days before Christmas, and I had been dreading spending it at sea, afraid that the strangeness of the setting, a freighter plowing through a tropical ocean, would underscore our uprootedness and increase our pain at being separated from our homeland. But this did not happen at all. It turned out to be an intensely moving and very beautiful experience.

The Norwegians, also far from their homes and families, decorated the entire ship extensively and with exquisite taste. In the lounge was an enormous, real fir Christmas tree and the dining room was transformed into a festive hall for a sumptuous classic Christmas dinner.

On Christmas Eve, everyone—officers, passengers, cooks, stewards, children, and sailors—feasted together in the crew's messroom. All social and professional distinctions were erased for the whole, joyous evening. We were, in fact, one large family. The messroom had another tall, handsome Christmas tree, and silvery, golden, and green garlands adorned the walls. Evie and Janie were delighted.

Dinner was a traditional Norwegian Christmas menu consisting of appetizing hors d'oeuvres, tasty fish, savory meat, and delicious dessert. It was truly a feast, an old-fashioned Christmas Eve dinner like we used to have back home.

After dessert the captain invited us to sing Christmas carols, and in Norwegian no less. We protested that we did not know the language, but he laughingly refused to have mercy. Printed words were handed out. "Silent Night" sounded especially odd. But it made no difference what particular language we used, for in our hearts we all sang in one voice and were transformed into one people celebrating the birth of Christ—Norwegians, British, Czechs, Italians, and Indians alike. In a quiet, warm, human way it was thrilling and deeply moving how united we felt.

Later on, the four of us celebrated our family's Christmas in the children's cabin with our small Christmas tree and a few presents under it. As we all were avid readers, the presents were mainly books.

When the girls had fallen asleep at last, Alex and I went on the deck, hand in hand, and watched the stars, an avalanche of diamonds over the dark, peaceful Bay of Bengal. I thought about many past Christmases, about our families, about the way our lives had changed. Only ten years before we had a charming happy home of our own. Alex had a guaranteed job he loved. Life had been pleasant and stable—in fact, perfect.

Then through no fault of our own, it had all exploded. A crazy German dictator had a dream of controlling and ruling the world. When his dream ended in the total destruction of his country, another man, equally insane, equally evil, possessed by the desire to be the most powerful man in the world and to make his nation the strongest nation the world had ever known, seized control of our government and we lost everything we cherished: our freedom, our liberty, and finally our home. Yet I was not afraid; not as long as Alex was here with me; not as long as the girls stood beside me. I knew that we would overcome even exile and that we would again find a corner in the world where we would attain peace, security, and happiness. Like the small *Silvermoon* that bright Christmas Eve, all alone on a limitless churning ocean, we four sailed forward with undiminished hope.

New Year's Eve came with another grand celebration and even more Norwegian songs. The ship moved slowly southward. The ocean was azure and the sun floated every day across a cloudless sky.

One day the captain invited Evie to join him on the bridge to see something special. When a proud but puzzled Evie arrived, the captain told her to stand precisely in front of him and look straight ahead over the bow.

"Do you see that long line on the ocean in front of us?"

"No, I don't see anything."

"Look again, you must see it."

"No, I don't."

"Be careful, we are about to cross it and you will feel a big bump. Ah, there, did you feel it?"

"No, I did not feel anything," Evie answered, now completely confused.

"Well, Evie, you should have. We just crossed the equator."

Evie was still laughing when she returned to tell us the great news. She was impressed to be the first to know we were in the southern hemisphere.

Four other girls and a boy were on the ship. They organized themselves into an informal gang and spent the days happily playing together. Janie's Raggedy Ann doll again became a hit with the younger girls.

The children decided to build a sailboat from wooden planks the captain donated. Evie and the boy, named Bryan, who was about a year younger than Evie, supervised the project with the captain giving them valuable advice. He seemed to enjoy it as much as the children did. When the ship had been constructed and the sails pieced together, the captain, as helpful as ever, gave them pots of paint in vivid colors. The shipmates were proud of their masterpiece.

Friendship on board flourished among the adults as well. After dinner the passengers and the officers usually retired to the lounge to chat. It turned out that we were all horse lovers, and horses and animals became a frequent subject of our conversations.

The seas were calm and the sailing was smooth until we approached Western Australia. Then everything changed. West of Freemantle and Perth the *Silvermoon* ran into a heavy storm. Gale-force winds straight from the South Pole attacked. The sky became dark, the seas rough and violent. The freighter was small and was thrown around like a toy boat in a child's bath. Passengers could hardly walk because the freighter did not have stabilizers. We all had to support ourselves by holding on to the bars attached to either side of the corridor. Fortunately, no one was seasick. Apparently we had all gotten used to the motion on a moving vessel. The waves washed over the deck in sheets of green water, making it impossible to venture outside.

One night while we were having dinner, the ocean was so violent that in spite of a low barrier edging on the dining-room table, several plates loaded with food were tossed into my lap. That night the wind increased in force. Alex worried that the ship would turn over and we would drown. I did not believe that was possible and trusted the captain implicitly.

But Alex kept fussing until he decided to join the captain on the bridge. They both stayed there all night. Toward morning the storm became so severe that the captain decided to pump water into empty storage tanks to lower the center of gravity. The *Silvermoon* was going to Sydney to be loaded with wheat for India and the ship was light. But even this step did not help much and the battering went on. Worry increased as the storm continued for nearly three days. Then the winds calmed down and the ocean became more peaceful, which was a great relief to all of us. The sky became blue again and the friendly sun greeted us with its warm brightness. The peaceful life returned to the *Silvermoon*.

Land was constantly in sight as we sailed along the coast of South Australia. In the evening we looked for lights, but none were to be seen. Australia is nearly as large as the United States, but in 1949 it only had nine million people, most of whom lived in the large cities, such as Sydney, Melbourne, Brisbane, Adelaide, Perth, and Freemantle. Very few were living inland.

We passed the coast of Victoria and sailed along the southern part of New South Wales. Our ship was nearing its destination and all the travelers were full of anticipation, anxious to start a new life in this vast land.

Early one morning, the smooth rocking movements of the ship suddenly stopped. We dressed as fast as we could and all four of us hurried onto the deck.

I never forgot my first impression of Sydney that morning. The *Silvermoon* entered an immense harbor, a very deep and wide bay spanned by a magnificent bridge, the famous Sydney Harbor Bridge. On the left side was the center of the city with many tall buildings. Green hills with smaller structures formed a background, while in the foreground were the Sydney Botanical Gardens.

The area at the right end of the bridge was suburban with hundreds of cheerful red roofs that scintillated against the emerald green of trees and lawns. In the clear morning sunlight everything was bathed in clarity. Optimism surged in me. Surely things would be different here. Surely here, in such a radiant setting, we could renew our life.

The pilot came on board and guided the ship to its dock. With gratitude and genuine sadness, we said good-bye to our Norwegian friends. The captain's wife, with whom I had become exceptionally friendly, was worried about us. She gave me her address in Oslo and pleaded with me to let her know how we made out. She could not understand how we dared to move with two children to an unknown country where we did not have a single acquaintance, not realizing that we had no choice in the matter. We were refugees, exiles, caught in the destiny of all those who had been deprived of their native land and who were driven by the cruelty of history to search for a new home. Few people who have not experienced it can understand what such homelessness does to human beings, leaving them with no foundations, no starting point and therefore always subtly adrift on a sea of impermanence. I faced an entire continent without one inhabitant I could recognize on sight. We did not even know where we were going to spend the night.

The custom officials were friendly and cooperative. We found a taxi and asked the driver to take us to a small, good hotel, preferably in the suburbs. While I was unpacking, Alex went to buy a newspaper to find out what had happened in the world during our voyage.

He returned soon with an afternoon edition, exclaiming after he looked at it, "Look, this girl looks exactly like our Evie."

I took the paper from him, looked at the picture, and in shock laughed. "It is Evie, Evie with the sailboat they made."

The picture illustrated an article with the headline: "New Australians coming to Sydney." Evie had graciously given the newsmen an interview. She told them we were coming from Bombay by way of Calcutta and that she with the other children made the sailboat on their trip aboard the *Silvermoon*. The entire first page of the paper was filled up with a story of Evie, her life in India, and the history of our family. I asked her when this happened.

"When you went to the cabin to get your handbag and your coats, these two men with a camera came and asked if they could take my picture with the sailboat. I said, 'Of course, you can.' And then they asked me a few questions which I answered. Was it wrong?"

"No, darling, there was nothing wrong with it," I answered. I never thought that the story of our arrival would be on the front page of the main Australian newspaper. It was as if Sydney itself was saying "Welcome."

Sydney is a beautiful city. It has many beaches and the climate is perfect. Numerous parks are filled with bright flowers, decorative bushes, and shade trees. Everything is a manifestation of order, cleanliness, and enjoyment of life. After living two years in India I found downtown Sydney well organized, spotless, and enormously pleasant in comparison.

Before World War II Australia had been an isolated country, but after the war, and especially after having had Japanese submarines in Sydney harbor, the government decided to strengthen the country by increasing the size of the population. They opened their shores to immigrants, preferably Britishers and other Europeans. We were among the first to arrive.

Alex started work the next day and I set out to find an apartment, an extremely difficult task. At long last I discovered a small place directly on Bondi Beach. The living-room windows had a magnificent view, straight out onto the blue Pacific.

Finding schools for the girls was the next problem. Evie was in high school and Janie was going into the third grade. No schools were nearby, but the girls, accustomed to buses from their Bombay experience, quickly adjusted to new conditions.

Life in Sydney was very restful and pleasant. Every Saturday at noon all the groceries, bakeries, and all other shops and department stores as well as most of the restaurants closed and did not open until Monday morning. Everyone went to the beach or they just stayed at home in their pretty little gardens. Relaxation and recreation were almost secular religions. The Bondi Beach, where we were living, was one of the nicest in the area and was crowded all weekend. When the surf was up, long breakers rolled in with a majestic roar on the white sand. We had never seen such a seascape before.

It was not the ocean we had known in Bombay. Juhu Beach was flat without any surf at all. The Pacific in Sydney was magnificent. Every Saturday and Sunday the four of us went swimming and surfing, as both girls were exceptional swimmers. At the beginning Australia was for us a dreamland from a fable, a bright light after much dimness, a fabulous way of life. We were soon converted into bronzed Australians. Ocean, beaches, palm trees, the sun, and the sky spoke a language of health and relaxation that seemed like a native tongue.

On weekends Alex often drove us to the national park north of the city to see the wallabies and kangaroos hopping happily about, the females with their little ones in their pouches peering inquisitively at the world from the safety of their unusual habitat. We watched them for hours.

Even more bewitching were the koala bears. They were so sweet and looked like big teddy bears as they sat in the branches of eucalyptus trees. We all wanted to cuddle one. Asleep during the day and active at night, they looked dreamy, content, and happy and were therefore a rather fine symbol of the Australian way of life.

We were in Sydney barely four months when one day we received a call from the American consulate. Our immigration visas arrived. At first we were very happy, but then we realized that we would not be able to go. We did not have enough money for the passage. Most of our savings had been spent on the trip to Australia and on some furniture for our home there. Our happiness was short-lived and an air of sadness hung over the household for many days.

Alex was not happy in his job in Sydney. A restless searcher by nature, he lived on the excitement of finding and developing new things, of stretching for the new and unknown. He did not fear the impossible. He did not like the bland regularity of work in the laboratory, doing quality control. He was wasted and knew it.

Alex tolerated the boredom for some time before he gave up in order to do independent consulting. He built a malt-extract plant and brewery for a group of investors and had an interest in it himself. Beer is very popular in Australia, and success seemed assured.

Unfortunately, the venture was destroyed by a powerful syndicate. Alex was immensely bitter about the whole affair, especially when he learned that one of his lawyers, whom he had considered to be a good friend, was secretly working for the syndicate while taking Alex's money.

We moved from Bondi to Harbord, a suburb north of the city. Janie was now within walking distance of her school, but Evie still had to take a bus. Our home was near public tennis courts and both girls started to play tennis. Harbord was thoroughly Australian in population. Our neighbors were friendly, pleasant, and welcoming and the girls soon had a flock of friends. Our house was constantly filled by music and laughter.

At that time, there was another development: the letters from Czechoslovakia stopped. Alex and I continued writing and sending photos regularly, but no answers were received. Several Czech families who had immigrated to Sydney had also lost contact with their relatives at home. Mail was not coming through. Something dire was obviously happening in Czechoslovakia.

In October 1951, after almost a year of silence, I received a long letter from my mother. I had been worried to distraction about her, and the sight of the thick envelope addressed in the familiar handwriting pierced me with happiness.

She wrote that she had been terribly anxious about us, not having had any news from us for more than a year. Not one of our letters had reached her. She went on to tell me with gentle grace and, as was typical of her, without complaint that times were difficult and getting worse every year. It was a touching letter, overflowing with love and tinged with sadness.

I rushed to write back at length and stuffed the envelope with photographs of the four of us and of our present home, wondering what she would make of the strange land so distant from our old farm. Not long afterward, letters came from Grandma and Grandpa and from Jana and Ivan. It seemed that the crisis had passed and that the mail, though censored, was going to be delivered in a normal way.

November 1951 came. In Australia it was a season of springtime flowers. On November 28 a cablegram was delivered to the house. It was from Czechoslovakia. I ripped it open. Mother was dead.

She had been in the hospital with pneumonia. Feeling that she was going to die, she asked my father to take her home to Vrbatky, to take her back to her own house, to their farm, to the sights and sounds, the smells and the memories among which she had lived her life. My father had brought her back. She had died in her own bed in her own room, after having spoken one last time of Alex, Janie, Evie, and me, missing us.

I was devastated. The news was crushing. If only I had been with her to hold her hand. But we were far away. In a corner of my heart I had hoped that a miracle would happen and that the four of us would some day return home, return to where we belonged; that I would be able to present my daughters to their grandmother and that

I would see her dear face and touch her hands again. The expectation was now erased as if it had never been. The distance between us and our homeland was uncrossable. She could not have been there even if our exile had ended. The parting was permanent. I could not take it in, though I knew it was so. Mother was dead. How could that be? She had just written; here was the letter. She had told me she was fine. How could she be gone? But I knew she was.

The following days passed. Like a robot I did what was necessary, keeping up my daily routine. But I thought of nothing but Mother with a daughter on the other side of the earth, dying in her room as the rains of late autumn streaked her window. Around me, spring passed unnoticed with the palm trees stirring in a meaningless breeze and the bright flowers blooming listlessly. I thought of nothing but Mother and the distance.

The only peace I could find was on the beach. I went there every day after getting the girls off to school and sat there for hours, gazing into the unfailing blue. The waves came toward me in an endless sequence. The ocean silently spoke of eternity. Memory, rising once more from the oblivion of daily care, solaced me. I sat and thought of my mother.

I wandered with her through my childhood; and back in the ancient kitchen, looking up from the big basket of potatoes I was peeling, I was filled with the same tender childlike love that had flowed in my six-year-old heart as I had watched her cooking for the farm family at harvest time. I was once more sent off to school by her smile, and saw her seeing her children's happy faces lit by the myriad of candles of our Christmas tree, watching the joy in our eyes. I lived again many, many small moments of happiness near her.

I remembered her unfailing courage as multiple sclerosis twisted her body, and I heard her again tell me to leave her and go to Alex. In how many ways had she given me life! And then I remembered when I saw her last, standing in front of our ancient gate, waving good-bye to us, smiling bravely while tears were running down her face; a picture engraved into my heart forever.

One question returned again and again, wounding my mind as relentlessly as the Pacific surf beat on the Australian shore. Why was it we had to wander? Why was it that after having suffered so long and so deeply during the dismemberment of our homeland, the four of us had been forced to leave people we loved and everything that meant anything to us? Why were we so far away? Why were we compelled to move from one place to another, each interesting, even benevolent in its own way, but none of them what we needed? What were we longing for?

It was for the peaceful and serene life we had before the war, for the enchanting country we lost when the Russians came, for our beautiful green valley we would never see again.

And something more: as I sat day after day before a vast ocean panorama of endless beauty, my heart and soul ached to go home, ached for my sweet, dead mother, for her smile, for a touch of her hand. And the blue ocean, reaching the edge of the sky far away on the horizon, brought a certain peace, and I was able to return to the house and face the rest of the day.

December passed slowly. A sad Christmas came and went. In 1952 I received another tragic letter from my father. He had lost all of his land. He had lost our farm. He had lost the land that had been owned by our family since 1525. The farm had been nationalized. All his land, every acre, had been taken from him without compensation and merged with the other farms into one big *kolkhoz*, or collective farm. No one owned anything anymore. Every farm, every factory, every shop had become nationalized. Even one-chair barber stands were owned by the state.

My sister wrote that this had been a terrible blow for my father. It was not the financial loss that mattered; for him the land itself, the very soil, was alive. It was part of him all his life, as it had been for his father and mother and all his ancestors. He loved it with his whole heart. It was holy, a blessing the good God had given to him and his family to tend forever. The idea that it was not his anymore, that it was gone, could not enter his mind, even after it happened.

My sister told us that she often found him sitting in the garden paralyzed with sadness, a broken man. I cried over her letter. I cried for my father, for Alex and myself and our daughters who would never know again the soil from which they had come, for our beloved, tortured, tormented country, for my homeland.

Letters from Czechoslovakia came more regularly that year though it took up to five weeks before we got them. We could see that they had been heavily censored. Occasionally entire sections had been cut out. The Australian newspapers reported that Stalin had ordered a heavy purge in Czechoslovakia. The Communists had become no less ruthless than the Nazis. Patriots still struggling to save some small appearance of democracy and some semblance of human rights were executed. Some were shot, some hanged. Among them was Dr. Milada Horakova, a brave woman and staunch defender of the freedom of the Czechoslovak people.

The Stalinist government got rid of members of the opposition, and many Communists were executed as well. We never found out why. Dr. Clementis, who became foreign minister after the death of Jan Masaryk, and Rudolf Slansky, the general secretary of the Communist party when we left Czechoslovakia, were exterminated. Closer to home, there was a report that Otto Sling had been executed. He was the head of the Communist party in Brno, the man who tried to make Alex join the party by promising him a bright future and the leadership not only of Biochema but of the entire chemical industry of Czechoslovakia. The promise of a bright future was certainly not fulfilled for him. These people had all helped the Russians destroy democracy, freedom, and liberty in Czechoslovakia, and then they were destroyed themselves.

In 1953 we moved again. This time, instead of renting, we bought a house close to Coogee Beach. Evie was at the University of Sydney and Janie was going to high school. They were happy in Sydney, had many friends, and settled snugly into the Australian way of life.

Both girls liked music and played the piano well. It seemed to flow around and through them. I remembered one day back in Harbord when Janie was ten years old and had returned from school before I came home from shopping downtown. From far down the street I could hear the triumphant majesty of the Toscanini recording of Beethoven's Fifth Symphony flooding the neighborhood from our open windows. In the front garden I found my little Janie sitting on the grass with a most exalted expression on her face. When the music released her for a moment, she saw me, jumped up, embraced me, and said, "This is such beautiful music, Mommy, so beautiful."

A great light was in her eyes, eyes that had been forced to see so much cruelty. That Beethoven symphony remained her favorite record. I thought such passion and sensitivity for the sublime was marvelous in such a young child.

Evie's favorite composers were Bach first, then Smetana, Dvorak, and Janacek. Both girls had beautiful voices, and every evening while doing the dishes they sang together. Sometimes they became so engrossed that it took them two hours to wash and dry the dishes. The sight of them standing next to each other in the warm light of the kitchen—tall, handsome, and rapt in music, singing Czech national songs, popular American hits, anything and everything, now and then interrupting their singing with peals of laughter—remained with me always.

I rejoiced in their gift and companionship. The four of us were a good, warm family. Talk at the dinner table was always lively and full of humor. Alex and I enjoyed our daughters' company, and many times at dinner, without their knowing it, they soothed our pain and eased our worries.

Our new home was not far from downtown Sydney. Alex rented some rooms nearby for a laboratory and office. He was still doing consulting as well as working hard on the development of several patents of his own. I started helping him in the lab and in the office. I kept his books and records, and, because I had always liked chemistry, sometimes I even helped with simple tests. We worked well together and we always enjoyed it.

I was also trying hard to keep his spirits up. The years in Australia had not been good for him and it was at this time that his hopes were at the lowest point since leaving Czechoslovakia. It hurt me seeing him so discouraged and depressed by his stagnant career. Research, Alex's forte and special love, was not much needed in Australia, where the chemical industry was small compared to that in Czechoslovakia. When he had successfully solved some problem, established his patent, and approached a potential customer, he was invariably met with the inquiry: "Is this the way that things are done in the United States?"

Alex would bristle politely and answer that this was a new idea that he himself had discovered. Then the deal would fall through. At first he found the situation frustrating, then irritating, and ultimately infuriating. The Australian spirit was stifling him. He had spent his working life forging ahead, making roads into the unknown, inventing new products as well as new methods of manufacturing. Sorrowfully, he finally had to admit to himself that we had not come to the right country, that we had been correct in wanting to move the family to the United States. He came to realize that only there would his ideas find the audience he needed. In time we both began to sense that this was more than a matter of career. The family itself needed a wider openness, a broader and more nourishing environment. Australia was not after all our new homeland.

Then fortune smiled. Prosana Pharmaceuticals, a company that had employed Alex from time to time, asked him to improve a dermatological product. He worked on the problem for some time and was successful in his research. The resulting patent belonged to the company in Australia, while Alex owned the world rights. The product sold well. That seemed to be the end of the matter.

About one year later Alex was surprised by a telephone call from a representative of a large American pharmaceutical company who asked to meet him. The American firm was more than casually interested in the product, and Alex himself was invited to fly over to the United States for discussions and further negotiations. In October 1956, he flew to Chicago, a grueling trip before the advent of the jet engine.

He stayed there for six weeks and returned home just before Christmas. He was exalted by the experience. He had sold the United States rights without difficulty, but far more important, he had acquired a number of influential contacts who had promised to arrange for our immigration visas to be reissued and forwarded to the consulate in Sydney. Alex was jubilant. The door had opened.

The quality of life in the United States appealed to him strongly. Everything was fresh and new to him, yet somehow seemed familiar and comforting. He liked the Americans, their acuity and their generosity. He admired the fact that professional people were not merely tolerant of new ideas, they expected them.

I was filled with gladness listening to him talk. As he went on, it became clear that a sort of kinship existed between the gigantic country that was beckoning to us and the small central European republic from which we had been driven. Though fed by traditions reaching down into the past of the Western world, both were relatively new countries and charged with the vitality of youth. Both were experiments in democracy, rising from a rejection of ancient monarchial rule. Both were a conglomeration of different ethnic and racial groups held together by the hope that eventually the democratic process would prevail. The tragedy of Czechoslovakia was that it was not allowed the time necessary to complete the experiment.

As I listened to Alex that December day, none of those similarities were as obvious to me as they were later. But I did sense vividly that he and I were being given not just a place of shelter but a real chance at a second homeland. We had been in Australia eight years, but Alex and I had, more often than not, felt that our time there was more of an interlude than anything permanent. There had never been any challenge there for Alex, who had not been satisfied to live without the bustle of the new. As the days passed, we awaited the visas with genuine eagerness and were elated when they finally arrived.

Before leaving Australia, Alex had to go to Melbourne and Canberra on business. He asked me to go with him. We had traveled the world together, but there was a special quality to those few days. Part of it was the result of Alex's feeling that he had a future again, a demand laid on him against which he could again measure his strength. He seemed younger to me than he had been for months, perhaps years. I could sense in him again the slim, young boy with clear blue eyes, so full of tenderness, with whom I had fallen in love.

On our drive to Melbourne we also talked about the future, but mostly sat in stillness, overwhelmed with gratitude that we were together and were getting ready for another step in our lives. The infinite Australian countryside rolled by. On our drive through the farming country, where many great properties were situated, we were delayed at one point by a single, enormous flock of sheep that took two hours to cross the road in front of us, herded along by only one man and a dozen remarkably adroit dogs.

I found Melbourne to be a modern, elegant city with wide boulevards and many parks. After Alex took care of his business, we went out on the town. It had been some time since we had been to a nightclub, and we danced late into the night. Alex had lost none of his charm or high spirits and we both enjoyed every moment of our stay.

For our return trip home we had chosen to go via Canberra and the Blue Mountains. The road between Melbourne and the capital of Australia led through a seemingly endless subtropical forest. It was a quiet drive among groves of ancient trees. Large, bright flowers splashed the blue shadows with color, and when we stopped, exotic birds sang us songs we had never heard before. The day was full of the unexpected and inexplicable poetry that Australia will offer suddenly to the traveler. We did not meet even one other car on the road and did not see a gas station for six hours.

After an unwarranted scare about filling the gas tank, we stayed overnight in a country hotel and continued on to Canberra in the morning. A day of business and sightseeing among the impressive government buildings and a long drive through the beautiful Blue Mountains took us back to Sydney. It was a happy trip.

We finished packing. We had gathered a strange collection of articles, bits and pieces from each of the places we had wandered: a few rugs bought in the bazaar in Lahore; beautiful embroideries from Simla; small, carved ebony tables from Karachi; delicate ivory carvings, silver ornaments, and an intricate, large, color inlaid copper enamel vase bought in Bombay; a beautiful kangaroo skin rug and a little koala bear toy from Sydney; and many other curios.

This collection was precious to us, and more like a group of friends than mere possessions. They were a visible witness to the continuity of our life together, reminding me of some happy moments of the past. One of the things I stored carefully for its trip to America was the miniature love novel that Alex had bought me in Paris when we were leaving Europe after the war.

The crates were to go by ship, but we intended to fly. However, a major overseas airlines strike intervened. We were fortunate in being able to book passage on an American cruise ship sailing from Auckland, New Zealand, for Honolulu.

Once again we went through the painful rite of saying good-bye to all our friends, some of whom had become more than dear to us during the eight Australian years. I fervently hoped that this would be the last of these separations. To be sure, life is full of comings and goings, of faces appearing and disappearing, but I longed for a taste of permanence.

The flight to New Zealand was memorable. The pilot, to impress us with the majestic scenery of his homeland, flew us through, not over, the New Zealand Alps. We entered the country by flying between the mountains. On the right was Mt. Cook, decked out in blue glaciers and ermine-white snowfields. We looked up at the summit and then down at gaping crevasses. Looking from one to the other left us with a slight sense of discomfort. It would not have been a good place to land. Colossal peaks followed as the pilot chanted their names and praised their virtues. Then we soared free of their magnificent presence and flew in wide, smooth air over green meadows reaching from horizon to horizon, dotted with flocks of sheep and an occasional homestead. The colors were fresh and as vibrant as those in an oil painting. In the distance appeared the roofs of the many houses of Christchurch, bordering a turquoise expanse of such intensity that the breath caught in my throat. It was the Pacific. America was beyond.

On the advice of the hotel manager, we stopped in Rotorua, a region of geysers, hot springs, and bubbling mud. It was also the home of the indigenous New Zealanders, the Maoris. Our guide, an old native woman of great dignity, told us much about their history and traditions. She showed us a river that flowed hot along one bank and cold at the opposite bank and told us that her ancestors had caught fish on one side and cooked them on the other.

In the evening we were invited to a performance of Maori dances and songs. Young people danced with grace and women sang sad melodies. I was enchanted by them.

How pleasant it is to travel when you are going toward a desired destination rather than escaping from difficulty or danger. Things shine within the brightness of one's own expectations. Our new life seemed to be coming forward to welcome us in the radiance of the New Zealand landscape and the charm of the Maoris. Though a little afraid of the future, we were happy and relaxed by the time we arrived in Auckland.

28
THE NEW WORLD

Our ship was already in the harbor. Such a lovely name, *Mariposa.* Later I found that "mariposa," Spanish for "butterfly," also is a name of a flower growing freely in the mountains of the American West.

The vessel was painted a sparkling white and was larger by far than the *Silvermoon* that had brought us to Australia. Floating at anchor with a serene majesty, waiting to take us on the last stage of our journey, it symbolized our dream about the future.

We were in the United States the moment we stepped on board. We were swept up by friendliness and eager hospitality. People spoke with a different accent; their English seemed clearer and sharper to us than that of the British people and firmer and more musical than that of the Australians. We were greeted by everyone we met as if they had spent the earlier part of the trip in anticipation of our embarkation at Auckland. Everyone was on a first-name basis. It was quite overwhelming. Alex and I agreed that it did not seem likely we were moving to a country of chilly, distant people.

The trip itself was tranquil and enjoyable. The weather was glorious and the seas calm. The ship was luxurious and our cabins comfortable. Each new port of call held new surprises and pleasures. At Suva in Fiji, the handsome Papuan policemen directed traffic in short pleated skirts. At Pago Pago in Samoa, the offshore breeze as we approached was scented with ginger and cinnamon by the flowers that covered the mountains. None of us felt the bump of the equator, though we thought with affection of the captain of the *Silvermoon*. The Americans made a grand occasion of the crossing. King Neptune in crown and long black beard held court; music played; and girls, dressed in short grass skirts, danced.

Days in the northern hemisphere continued much like those before. All passengers were amiable companions, and the staff did everything imaginable to guarantee that no one was left unamused.

Alex and I often slipped away from the merriment to be alone together, to sit in some isolated corner of an upper deck in silence, thinking long thoughts about the past and the future. The *Mariposa* seemed to be traveling in a timeless moment between two worlds, a moment that both allowed and urged remembrance and reflection.

As I had done during the other times of transition in my life, I found myself reliving my past, opening the book and rereading the chapters one by one. I was a child again back in Vrbatky. I saw Mother and Father and felt the sorrow of our separation. I fell in love with Alex again and walked with him in the park on the afternoon he had all but stolen me from my boarding school. I saw Brussels and Paris, walked through apartments and houses that had been home. I remembered my girls: babies, children, young people all at once. I was riven by Munich and underwent again the sadness of the crucifixion of my country.

I remembered Alex's face as he stood before me in prison clothes expecting to be guillotined in the German factory of death. I talked to Frau Thomas and Mr. Horky. Richky was found, rebuilt, destroyed, rebuilt, and lost forever. We traveled across India, faint with heat and fear. It was all there. The long list of our dead rolled itself before my eyes: my mother, uncles, aunts, friends, our country—all gone. Why had I survived?

I finally had an answer to the question I had been asking for so many years. It was sitting next to me in the Pacific sun. Dear, dear Alex. When I looked into his face, I was suffused with deep tenderness. It had been that tenderness that had given me the power to break out of danger and death into new life.

He was my courage. With him, I had lived and would continue to live. I survived.

But my survival was not pointless. The fact that I had not succumbed to a German bullet, the blows of a drunken Red Army soldier, or sickness was for a reason. The others had not died because of implicit malice or weakness; I was not being rewarded for something they were being punished for. My survival had to mean something. Certainly part of it was so that Alex and I could go on living, not only for ourselves, but for our daughters and for the others, too.

In the years ahead of us in the United States I was confident that Alex and I would accomplish many good things. Together we would build new homes full of color, comfort, and warmth. There were going to be successors to Richky, and new business ventures to bring prosperity to ourselves and others. We would enjoy new friendships, and our lives would be a tribute to our departed country.

But was there not something more? A more concise answer was needed if grief was not to overwhelm me, an answer to the question of survival that would work for us. Alex and I knew, of course, that we were not the only survivors. We belonged to a whole nation, a new race scattered throughout the world. The twentieth century had created a world of survivors, of uprooted people, who in terror and amazement discovered that they had been left standing as the sword scythes its way across the years.

As the sun made the ocean flash like a perfect piece of jewelry that morning, I was very much with my sisters and brothers who had been rejected by death, with the survivors of the Nazi extermination camps, with the pitifully small remnant of Jews who had fallen out of the grip of Hitler, Heydrich, and Himmler, and with the few Russians and Poles who had returned from Stalin's Siberia mumbling about cold, slavery, and starvation to ears that could not hear them. In my heart I would always be very close to all the Czechs living in exile, and I felt a sense of almost physical solidarity with the bereft everywhere. We were one people, one family in affliction. If I could but answer the why of my life, I would also be answering it for them, too.

———□———

Only later, much later, already in the United States, did I begin to understand that we survivors had survived so that we might raise our voices.

The reason I was not dead was so that I might tell our story, that

I might take my place among those who bear witness, so that Alex and I might throw words into the face of destruction to confuse it and hasten its own annihilation.

We two, full of love for our daughters, our adopted country, and life itself, were left among those who do not know the tale to tell it, to attest in our own small, unsophisticated way to what did indeed happen, as best we can, as people who were actually there, who saw and who knew the pain and terror in our own bodies and souls.

Through our statement and the way we have lived with hope in spite of sorrow, we want to remind the others of the pitiful fate and suffering of all the captive people, whether Christian, Jew, Hindu, or Moslem, of the endless and avoidable misery of all the victims of the twentieth century. That is our duty. We survivors earn our living and pay our debts by combating the greatest enemy, *forgetfulness*.

We remember, and remembering helps the others turn away from the drowsiness of spirit that makes violence possible.

We survived and are not dead in order to speak. Over the years, Alex and I have come to cherish this about the United States: that there is freedom of speech, freedom to express an opinion, freedom to tell a story. It is not always easy to do that, especially for a person like me, to whom sometimes words come hesitantly. But the effort to remember and relate the facts is always worth it. It gives life and ends by making one glad.

In spite of the struggles that Alex and I endured, our life has been one of genuine beauty. The two of us have lived through moments that have endeared us to one another, and these I have always treasured. I bless life for the years past and the years to come, for what went before and what will follow.

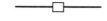

The time on the *Mariposa* passed slowly as we were coming closer to Honolulu, our entrance port to America, our future homeland. We were not destined to enter the United States through New York. No Statue of Liberty would be there to greet us; but, then, our lives had never followed customary paths. Yet, there was a certain poetic justice in the fact that we came out of the darkness of Europe's most tragic years to America through the sunlit splendor of Hawaii.

Again we were standing on the deck looking at the shore that was getting closer and closer. Finally we reached the pier, and what a welcome it was! On the wharf a band was playing while pretty Polynesian girls in grass skirts with leis around their necks were dancing and at the same time singing those hauntingly beautiful Hawaiian songs. After *Mariposa* docked they came on board to deck us out with exquisite necklaces of sweet-smelling flowers. Alex and I were delighted and felt as if the celebration had been organized specifically to greet us.

The immigration officials came on board to examine documents. We were the only immigrants on the ship. There was a swift inspection, our passports were dutifully stamped, and all formalities executed.

Then, to my surprise, the officer in charge rose to his feet, smiled with an honest friendliness, and took my hand.

"Welcome to the United States," he said. "We hope you will be very happy here."

Something inside me moved. I was profoundly touched by the simple grace and sincerity of the man. The gesture was so unexpected. We had crossed many borders, had been to many countries, but this was the first time we had heard the words we had been listening for without knowing it.

It was May 2, 1957. We had reached the land of our dreams, the land of our hopes. Our arrival was filled with charm and beauty, with gratitude and happiness.

EPILOGUE

A great many waters have run down the hills and into the rivulets of Richky Valley since we left our native land. After nearly forty-two years of Communist dictatorship, bright rays of hope are breaking through the heavy clouds of despair as freedom and democracy begin to return to Czechoslovakia.

But for Alex and me it is too late. Our home now is in America. Sitting in front of the fireplace, I remember our departure from Prague, our many travels, and our arrival in Hawaii on the *Mariposa* as clearly as if it had happened only yesterday.

After we settled in Chicago, we were nearly penniless. To increase the family income I got a job in the accounting department of a fashionable store on Michigan Avenue. Janie entered Marquette University and Evie continued her studies at the University of Sydney.

Alex decided to pursue an independent career as an industrial chemist. In Chicago he met Josef Bursik, a friend and fellow immigrant from Brno, who had just purchased an old warehouse for his new company that manufactured chemical compounds for the building industry. Josef offered Alex use of part of the factory in exchange for the commitment to develop several new products for him. Alex accepted and installed a small laboratory there with the financial help of some of his clients from the paper industry.

Life was not easy for us. We lived through many difficult times and had to overcome many obstacles. However, our financial situation slowly improved, and the moment finally came when I was able to join Alex in his venture by taking care of the office and the accounting.

At that time, Edgewater Paper Company in Wisconsin asked Alex to find some use for their gumming machine that was standing idle. Alex suggested silicone-release coating. Unfortunately, the curing time on the rollers of the gummer was only eighteen seconds, while the silicone coating commercially available demanded three full minutes of heat. Alex realized that reducing the curing time to eighteen seconds or less would be an important improvement in the silicone-release application, and he started working on the problem.

After six years of tests, disappointments, and more tests, he developed a coating that worked in just a few seconds. The Edgewater paper mill started producing silicone paper and film unseen on the market at that time. The old gummer and the newly acquired coater worked day and night. Alex had his coating patented, and a few months later a large chemical company offered him a substantial amount of money for his technology. He accepted and we started to prepare for retirement.

Then an unexpected event halted our plans. The president of a Wisconsin bank told Alex that the Edgewater Paper Corporation, which had been in trust, was in a difficult financial situation and, as a trustee, offered Alex the opportunity to purchase the majority of the stock providing he would invest in the company, personally run it, and pay off its outstanding bank notes. Alex was enthusiastic, but I was skeptical and opposed the purchase. To me it was a gamble. Why risk what we had achieved with so much hardship for such an insecure venture? Jack Cullinane, our accountant and a good friend, examined the company books and agreed with me fully. Alex, however, closed the transaction anyway, and we moved to Wisconsin, where we settled in a lovely home on the shore of Lake Winnebago.

Alex became the chairman of the board, and I joined as a vice-president and treasurer. Although originally I was against the project, once the decision was made, I supported my husband wholeheartedly, knowing well that only with closest cooperation could we manage the desperate financial situation.

Once again, life became difficult, especially for me, the treasurer, as we were constantly short of funds. We struggled for several years and slowly got out of danger. Soon after Alex introduced new lines of silicone-coated film and paper onto the market, our sales started to grow rapidly, and before long, several coating machines were producing new products under a new company name, Akrosil Corporation. Our net profits increased dramatically. Akrosil's offices and the plant itself were completely rebuilt, enlarged, and modernized to become a model of high efficiency in an aesthetic surrounding: the entire operation was transformed from an old, nearly extinct mill into a modern technological miracle. Many jobs were saved and more jobs were created, and in the months to come, many employees profited from Akrosil's stock options.

Overtures started to arrive from larger companies wanting to take over the operation. We favored Hammermill Paper Company, an established and well-respected corporation. In 1975, they acquired Akrosil through an exchange of stock.

Following a later merger of Hammermill with International Paper Company, Akrosil became a part of this industrial giant. Akrosil's modern plants are successfully operating not only in Wisconsin and Ohio but also in Europe, at de Beitel in the Netherlands. Present capacity and volume of export make Akrosil the largest silicone-coating operation in the world.

———□———

After several years in Australia, Evie joined us in the United States and, true to her love for horses and nature, settled with her husband in the American West. Janie graduated from Marquette University with a teaching degree in English, French, and history. She is married and has been living with her family in New York City.

As soon as all business transactions were concluded, Alex and I retired. Realizing our dream, we took a three-month cruise around the world on the *Queen Elizabeth 2*. One of our many ports of call was Bombay. India still held for me the same mystical fascination I had felt so deeply many years ago. We went to all the places we used to frequent, remembering many happy moments and many sad ones.

It was a very nostalgic and sentimental visit. Bombay had lost much of its glamour of the 1940s, but the children looked healthier, and there were not as many beggars on the streets.

We returned home by way of New York, and this time we were greeted by the Statue of Liberty. It was an unforgettable moment when, coming from faraway lands, we saw her standing there majestically tall and graceful, surrounded by water, welcoming us home.

We love our new homeland. It has been good to us. But in the evening, when the sun is disappearing below the horizon, I often think about Richky valley and its enchanting charm and beauty. I can hear again the singing of the birds and the rustle of the trees; I can smell the delicious aroma of flowers and pines in the forest. And the cool, crystal-clear water in the stream is dancing joyfully around the little pebbles, telling them how happy and pleasant the world would be without war, without hate. . . .

January 1990

PRODUCTION NOTES

This book was set in Fairfield, a typeface from the hand
of the distinguished American artist, engraver and book
designer of Czech descent, Rudolph Ruzicka, who was
born in Bohemia in 1883 and came to the United States
in 1894.

The text was designed by Karen Scott of Great Scott
Design and composed by Andresen Typographics in
Tucson, Arizona. It was printed on 60 lb. acid-free offset
book paper and bound in starch-filled cotton cloth by
Ringier America at their Olathe, Kansas, plant.